D1571318

Possessed

Christine D. Worobec

Possessed

WOMEN, WITCHES, AND DEMONS IN IMPERIAL RUSSIA

Northern Illinois University Press / DeKalb

© 2001 by Northern Illinois University Press
Published by the Northern Illinois University Press,
DeKalb, Illinois 60115
Manufactured in the United States using
acid-free paper
All Rights Reserved
Design by Julia Fauci

Library of Congress Cataloging-in-Publication Data
Worobec, Christine.
Possessed : women, witches, and demons in
Imperial Russia / Christine D. Worobec.
p. cm.
Includes bibliographical references and index.
ISBN 0-87580-273-7 (alk. paper)
1. Demoniac possession—Russia. 2. Witchcraft—
Russia. 3. Women peasants—Russia—Social
conditions. 4. Mentally ill women—Russia.
5. Russia—Rural conditions. I. Title.
BF1555.W795 2001
133.4'26'0820947—dc2100-062519

To David

CONTENTS

T A B L E S

PREFACE

✦ Through the ages and around the globe societies have structured themselves upon an elemental principle that subordinates one half of the population to the other half. For almost all of human history women have been denied equality with men. In most cultures, women are viewed as inferior and weak, on the one hand, and potentially disruptive, deviant, and threatening, on the other. These negative traits, in turn, justify the cultural perception that women are inferior.

Similarly, in peasant states government officials categorize the ruling class and rural peoples as gendered mirror images of each other, identifying the ruling class with masculinity and the peasantry with femininity in an effort to maintain authority. By imposing the binary opposition of masculine/feminine upon the ruling minority and exploited majority, governments assign positive characteristics to the upper class and pejorative ones to peasants. Thus landowners and government officials are deemed superior, strong, normal, and orderly in comparison to villagers who are viewed as inferior, weak, abnormal, and volatile. Such distinctions preserve hierarchical power relationships and serve as a brake upon fundamental reforms.

The parallels between the subordination of women to men and peasants to the ruling class and the existence, if you will, of a disadvantaged or subaltern group within a disadvantaged class drew me to the study of Russian peasants in the postemancipation period. Accounting for more than four out of five Russians, peasants lived in a world obsessed with concerns of survival and regulated by a patriarchal system and notions of a moral economy or a rough-and-ready egalitarianism. Having previously examined women's economic and social roles in postemancipation Russian peasant society within the patriarchal household and family as both agents and victims, I felt the need to go a step further. Only by penetrating the cultural world of the Russian peasant, a sphere that by definition had a fundamental religious component to it, could I grapple with notions about women.

From this quest emerged the figure of the *klikusha,* a woman who believed herself and was perceived by others to be demon possessed. She symbolized the out-of-control woman within a peasant society that, according to governmental authorities and educated upper classes, could at any moment explode with elemental force, shattering the stability of modern Imperial Russia. She also invoked a culture of misfortune in which human beings, specifically witches and sorcerers, could be held responsible for various natural phenomena and maladies, including possession.

Historians of witchcraft in Western Europe, the American colonies, and non-Christian societies will recognize some of the elements of Russian witchcraft and possession. They will find themselves familiar with the descriptions of demoniac convulsing, shrieking, and writhing. They will also see similarities in the depictions of witches and sorcerers. At the same time, however, they will be struck by the intimate relationship between possession and the Russian Orthodox Church, the Russian peasants' appropriation of orthodox tenets, the existence of male witches, the feminization of possession victims over the course of the eighteenth and nineteenth centuries, and the underdeveloped nature of the witches' sabbath in the Russian context. Russian peasants' compassion toward women demoniacs, who tended to be married and in their childbearing years, will illuminate the complexity and flexibility of peasant societies. Furthermore, the timing of Russian *klikushestvo* will remind scholars of witchcraft that possession phenomena continued to exist after the great witchcraft trials in Western Europe and the American colonies during the sixteenth and seventeenth centuries and after the supposed triumph of rationalism over superstition.

As in Western Europe, the culture of misfortune in Russia eventually became relegated to the countryside. In the Russian case that development came later, somewhere in the early nineteenth century when courts refused to prosecute witches and assumed, on the basis of laws already introduced in the early eighteenth century, that demoniacs might, in fact, be frauds. Witchcraft, bewitchment, and possession, however, did not disappear from a peasant culture in the midst of changes associated with industrialization and urbanization or from the larger religious culture. As in the case of Western Europe, possession and witchcraft in Russia did not become anachronisms despite fundamental social and economic changes. By the end of the nineteenth century, the democratization of pilgrimages through mass transportation ensured that the miraculous exerted a profound hold on the popular mind. Monasteries specializing in the treatment of demoniacs beckoned these sufferers and their families and friends to them. And as in Western Europe, the established church found itself under attack from psychiatrists. However, because the possessed in Russia remained distinct from the witches and sorcerers believed to have bewitched them, Russian psychiatrists looked to wrest control over the demoniacs rather than the witches. The female peasant demoniac accordingly became the focus of this book, which explores various representations of her over the course of the eighteenth and nineteenth centuries and explains the elements that produced possession.

Researching and writing about possession in Imperial Russia has been a wonderful experience from start to finish. Not only has the topic richly rewarded me with insights into various aspects of Imperial Russia, it has also put me in contact with numerous people and institutions who have contributed to the final product. While I alone bear responsibility for what appears on the following pages, I am deeply indebted to those who took time away from their own endeavors to aid me. The generosity of spirit among academics in the Russian field is to be cherished.

This book benefited from valuable institutional support. Two summer grants as well as a yearlong fellowship from the National Endowment for the Humanities permitted me to conduct research in Helsinki and Moscow, to attend a stimulating Moscow seminar on Orthodoxy in Russian and Soviet History led by Gregory Freeze, and to devote a year's time to writing. I would also like to thank the Research Council of Kent State University for supporting both academic year and summer research appointments. Kent State University generously provided me with a Faculty Improvement Leave as well.

I value the assistance of numerous staff members in libraries in Russia, Finland, and the United States. I would like to extend my warmest thanks to the staffs of the former State Lenin Library, the Historical Library, the Russian State Historical Archive, the Russian State Archive for Ancient Acts, and the Russian State Historical Archive of the City of Moscow. I also profited from the superb holdings of and helpful staffs at the Helsinki University Library's Slavic Collection, the Hilandar Library at Ohio State University, and the library of the University of Illinois at Urbana-Champaign. Special thanks must be given to the staff of the interlibrary loan department at Kent State University who tracked down rare items for this project.

So many individuals sent me references, gave me documentary

records, and critiqued all or portions of the manuscript that I fear that I may have left someone out. I am indebted to Laura Phillips for ordering microfilms for me at the Russian State Historical Archive in St. Petersburg and to Jeffrey Burds for sharing with me notes that he took on two files from the Tenishev Ethnographic Archive in St. Petersburg. Elena Borisovna Smilianskaia helped me to decipher early-eighteenth-century Russian from poor microfilm copies and generously shared with me the contents of an eighteenth-century file from the State Archive of Iaroslavl' Oblast. John Bushnell, Bob Nichols, and Christine Ruane gave me references to religious hysteria, serfowner complaints against demoniacs, and miraculous cures in Russia.

The Midwest Russian History Workshop provided invaluable assistance by allowing me to present my preliminary and later findings. It was at one of the early meetings of the workshop that the late Allan Wildman, David Ransel, and Bill Rosenberg encouraged me to extend my approach from that of social history to the broader methodology of cultural history for which poststructuralist analysis was essential. I am particularly grateful to them for pushing me in that direction and hope that my use of the approach fulfills their aspiration.

Other people have given me other types of support. Greg Freeze, Bill Husband, and Roy Robson all encouraged my work during and after our time together in Moscow. Valerie Kivelson engaged me in fruitful discussions of magic and Orthodoxy in medieval and modern Russia, sharing her unpublished materials with me. Isolde Thyrêt taught me a great deal about medieval Russian Orthodoxy and iconography. Ellen Dwyer, Stephen Frank, David Ransel, Christine Ruane, and Elise Wirtschafter read portions of the manuscript, while Barbara Clements, Mark Steinberg, Elena Smilianskaia, Maureen Tighe-Brown, and anonymous readers read the entire manuscript. All the advice I received helped make the book much better. Thanks also go to Mary Lincoln, who saw merit in the project when it was in an early stage and who has been supportive ever since. The book's title grew out of stimulating conversations with the late Bruce Lincoln, whose generosity and friendship touched my heart and spirit.

Finally, I owe a great deal to my colleague and spouse, David E. Kyvig, to whom this book is dedicated. David has lived with this book as long as I have. His constant encouragement, unflagging optimism, companionship, and love have enriched my life immeasurably.

An earlier version of a portion of chapter 2 appeared as "Witchcraft Beliefs and Practices in Prerevolutionary Russian and Ukrainian Villages," in *Russian Review* 54, no. 2 (April 1995): 165–87. I would like to thank the editors for permission to reproduce some of the materials here.

Russian terms used in this book have been transliterated following the Library of Congress system, with the exception of the names of monarchs and such commonly accepted spellings as Leo Tolstoy (rather than Lev Tolstoi). For the sake of consistency, all Ukrainian geographical locations have been rendered in their Russian imperial forms. Pre-1917 spelling has been retained.

Possessed

CONFRONTING *KLIKUSHESTVO*

An Introduction

✦ In Russian peasant villages, a stranger usually meant trouble. During the summer of 1895, a peasant by the name of Zakhar wandered aimlessly from village to village in Central Russia, wondering where he might spend the night and eat. Not far from the Moscow and Kaluga provincial borders and seven versts (4.6 miles) from the nearest railway station, he came upon the Smolensk village of Ashchepkovo. Walking along the settlement's only street, he stopped by the hut of Vasilisa Alekseeva and, through her open window, asked her for a match. When Vasilisa handed him a box, Zakhar settled his weary haunches down on her stoop and lit a cigarette. Worried that the stranger might set the hut on fire, Vasilisa ordered him to go away and leave her in peace. At the sound of her raised voice, other villagers came running and escorted Zakhar out of the village. That was not, however, the last time that either Vasilisa or the other Ashchepkovo peasants would see him.[1]

In a pasture on the evening of the same day, the village shepherd caught a suspicious-looking man holding a bridle. The shepherd's shouts for help summoned villagers who, beset by a rash of horse thefts in the area, undoubtedly suspected the stranger of trying to steal a horse.[2] They dragged him back to the village where they could keep an eye on him while they decided whether to punish him on the spot or to turn him over to the authorities. Upon seeing the suspect, Vasilisa recognized him as the same Zakhar to whom she had earlier given a box of matches. Frightened that he would take revenge on her and the village by starting a fire, for which she would be indirectly responsible, Vasilisa yelled out "thief!" and confirmed her neighbors' suspicions about the stranger.[3] Hearing her cry, the crowd attacked and beat the unlucky stranger to death. Zakhar's murder came to the attention of the Smolensk circuit court, which sentenced several Ashchepkovo inhabitants, including Vasilisa's neighbor, Nikolai Babaev, to three months in jail for participating in an illegal act of collective violence.[4]

This set of events stirred up animosity between Vasilisa and her next-door neighbor, Siklitin'ia Nikiforova. Having witnessed Vasilisa handing over matches to the stranger Zakhar, Siklitin'ia held the woman responsible for Zakhar's murder and for the arrest of her husband, Nikolai Babaev. When Vasilisa denied under oath giving Zakhar matches and thus tried to absolve herself of any culpability in the crime, she incurred Siklitin'ia's wrath: Siklitin'ia accused her of lying. From that point onward the neighbors were openly hostile to one another.

In the meantime Vasilisa's upstanding position within the village began to decline. Others began to question her role in the incident with Zakhar. Not having the immediate support of her husband, who worked in Moscow; hounded by her in-laws for being lazy; and subject to pangs of remorse, Vasilisa became more and more depressed. She found solace in prayer and pilgrimages to local monasteries.

On one of these pilgrimages during the drought-stricken summer of 1897,[5] two years after Zakhar's murder, Vasilisa walked 20 versts (just over 13 miles) to the Kalochskii Monastery. There she witnessed the seizures of *klikushi* (shriekers)—women who believed themselves to be demon possessed. In the presence of holy objects and in response to the monks' prayers and ministrations with the communion cup, holy oil, and holy water, the devils inhabiting the women's bodies reacted furiously, growling and barking like animals. The demons uttered blasphemous and abusive statements through the mouths of the possessed, while their antics caused the women to have seizures. The faces and eyes of the shriekers twitched; they tore at their hair and clothing, thrashed about on the floor, and eventually lost consciousness. In the midst of the commotion of these highly distraught women, Vasilisa experienced her first convulsions of demon possession.

Vasilisa's second seizure occurred in the fall of that year in Ashchepkovo. A special religious service was being held in honor of a miracle-working icon that had been brought to the village from the Kalochskii Monastery, the same monastery where Vasilisa had witnessed the *klikushi*'s behavior. When a woman asked Vasilisa what was wrong with her, she replied, "Your sister, Siklitin'ia, has cast a spell over me."[6] Word that Vasilisa had accused Siklitin'ia of sorcery quickly spread through the community.

At first the villagers dismissed Vasilisa's accusation against her neighbor. They respected Siklitin'ia and her family as honest and hardworking and could not imagine Siklitin'ia dabbling in witchcraft or harming anyone. The matter appeared to be over after Siklitin'ia, in response to Vasilisa's calumnious charge, took up the issue with the Mokrin cantonal court. There, before peasant judges, Vasilisa denied being angry with her neighbor and swore that she did not remember making the accusation. Laughing at the quarrel between the two women, the judges advised Siklitin'ia to drop the case.

The matter was not over, however. Vasilisa experienced a third seizure during the religious celebration of the Epiphany in January 1898 in the neighboring parish of Moker. During that episode, a man approached Vasilisa and demanded that she tell him who had bewitched her. The nature of the question suggested that parishioners were beginning to accept the possibility that Vasilisa was possessed. Vasilisa replied, screaming, "Siklitin'ia bewitched me! She planted many [devils] in me; she planted another seven in me, and they are still screaming! Don't you believe me? Wait, you'll see, we'll dance together!"[7] Vasilisa's threat that others would succumb to Siklitin'ia's malevolent powers made an impression on some of the residents of Ashchepkovo. Rumors began to fly that other villagers were in danger of becoming possessed.

Meanwhile, Vasilisa's fits occurred more frequently and with greater intensity. During religious services or when icons were brought to her, she fell down, cried, shook, screamed, and claimed to ache all over, but later remembered nothing about her seizures. Her family decided that she needed spiritual help and took her to several holy sites where monks confirmed that she was possessed. The holy men chanted special prayers and masses and administered communion and extreme unction to Vasilisa and other *klikushi,* all in an attempt to exorcise their demons.

With Vasilisa and her kin away on pilgrimage, the inhabitants of Ashchepkovo and Moker became convinced that Vasilisa was possessed. In the shrieker's absence an epidemic of *klikushestvo* began to sweep Ashchepkovo. At the beginning of Lent, Neonila Titova, who had just returned to the village after a visit to Moscow, suddenly shrieked in her home that Siklitin'ia had bewitched her. When incense and holy water were brought, Neonila began to shout and shake all over. A week later two other women showed signs of possession. Shortly thereafter, a fourth woman declared in the midst of a seizure that Siklitin'ia's daughter, Marina, had bewitched her.

The rest of the women in Ashchepkovo became anxious about their health. They began to jog their memories about past encounters with Siklitin'ia and her daughter. Those who had eaten something at Siklitin'ia's home became extremely apprehensive as they subscribed to the belief that a hex could be transmitted through food. A simple stomach pain was all that was necessary to make a woman believe that she too was possessed by the devil.

The number of possessed women who blamed their affliction on Siklitin'ia increased dramatically during Easter services and the customary Easter icon procession from hut to hut.[8] In the end, 15 residents of Ashchepkovo and neighboring Ivanika, 13 women and 2 men, became victims of demon possession. Convinced that Siklitin'ia was the source of their troubles, they sought retribution.

During the icon procession one of the *klikushi* suddenly attacked Siklitin'ia's daughter Marina and began to bite her. The shrieker's father-in-law and husband stood by and encouraged her, shouting, "Hit her . . . ! Poke her hard, and since she is full of devils, poke her eyes out!"[9] Another *klikusha* joined in the attack. After the priest admonished the crowd for not coming to Marina's aid, he and Siklitin'ia finally rescued the helpless Marina from the *klikushi*'s hands. Later that day one of the possessed women attacked Siklitin'ia's son Ivan. In an attempt to restore order, the village elder advised Siklitin'ia's family to stay away from the icon procession.

Siklitin'ia was unwilling to stand by while her reputation and that of her family was compromised. She again sought the help of the cantonal court. When the judges were unable to reach a decision because of the disruption caused by the seizures of the shriekers who were called in as witnesses, she appealed to the higher authority of the land captain. A relatively new government representative in the countryside, the land captain was charged with overseeing peasant affairs. While Siklitin'ia's appeal to his authority expressed her frustration with the peasant cantonal court's mishandling of the serious accusation against her, it also represented a direct challenge to her community. Turning to a government official who was not one of them, in the eyes of peasants, was akin to supplicating the enemy who could only harm the community in some way.[10] This act confirmed villagers' suspicions of Siklitin'ia's being a witch.

On 5 May 1898 Land Captain N. O. Iziumskii arrived in Ashchepkovo to interview the individuals who claimed that they were possessed. According to his written account, all the *klikushi* acted normally when they responded to his questions, that is, until he mentioned Siklitin'ia Nikiforova's name. Nine women subsequently had seizures. In the words of Land Captain Iziumskii,

> Initially their faces and eyes twitched. They jumped up and down on the bench. Then came a frightening shriek which caused them to go into a frenzy, tear at their clothing and hair and throw themselves from the bench onto the floor or under the table in the hut. They struck their heads against the boards so hard that I was afraid that several of them would smash their skulls. During their fits their strength was so great that six strong peasants could not restrain one ill woman who

> tore herself from their grips and stuck her head under the table. Thanks to the presence of forty peasants we prevented them from mutilating themselves. After the fits the ill women were like corpses. All of them were almost without a trace of life: their faces were ghastly white, they were lying down with their eyes closed, their breathing was almost imperceptible, [and] their stomachs were all frighteningly distended. . . . Several of the women stayed in that position more than an hour, and one was like that for more than two and a half hours.

The land captain concluded that the seizures he witnessed were genuine as "it is impossible to distend the stomach voluntarily."[11] Judging the illness to be an infectious form of hysterical epilepsy, medical experts agreed that the afflicted women of Ashchepkovo were not malingerers.

Upon the land captain's recommendation, the governor of Smolensk ordered the police chief to convince Siklitin'ia and her daughter Marina to leave the village for their own safety and for the restoration of order in the community. Siklitin'ia agreed to move to Moscow temporarily, noting with astonishment that God had saved her many times from the wrath of her neighbors, who were now convinced that she was a sorceress. According to her, every time she crossed paths with villagers, they uttered, "an enemy is passing by, an enemy is passing by" or "Christ has Risen."[12] People walking past her home covered their mouths with a kerchief as a precautionary measure.

After Siklitin'ia's departure, only one other woman, sixty-four-year-old Mavra Mikhailova, became ill. The other possessed women and men did not recover, however. They continued to have seizures during church services or when they came in contact with holy objects. This state of affairs continued through the beginning of the summer of 1899 when the Novgorod psychiatrist Nikolai Vasilevich Krainskii, upon orders from the Medical Department of the Ministry of the Interior, arrived in the village to examine the victims of and to control the outbreak of what appeared to be an epidemic of demon possession.

At first glance, the Ashchepkovo epidemic of *klikushestvo* might seem to have been a bizarre, unique episode in the turn-of-the-century Russian village. Indeed, if Nikolai Krainskii had not published his copious notes regarding his investigation of the epidemic and examination of the individuals who claimed to be the victims of demon possession through the malevolence of a community member, the incident would have passed unnoticed among the larger educated Russian public. Although other Russian psychiatrists wrote about similar epidemics of possession and outbreaks of what they deemed religious hysteria, most saved their analyses for specialized psychiatric journals. Krainskii's publishing a book on the subject of *klikushestvo* and its relationship to witchcraft and sorcery suggests that interest in the phenomenon extended beyond physicians to educated Russian society as a whole.

The Ashchepkovo story of possession exhibits all the components of a lurid melodrama—murder, personal conflicts, and revenge—to which are added witchcraft and the supernatural. Krainskii captured the Gothic atmosphere in his description of the *klikushi*'s behavior during a church service:

> It is difficult to imagine this unusual picture, worthy of the brush of a medieval artist, when under the open sky, in the presence of a hundred worshipers, [and] during a service, several demon-possessed women, in terrifying body contortions and apparent convulsions, are rolling around on the ground, blaspheming and shouting in various voices in the name of the demons implanted in them. It is difficult to describe the expression that superstition stamps on the faces of the affected crowd—at the very moment when the priest goes up to her with a cross or sprinkles her with holy water, a woman who had until then been able to control herself, falls to the ground unconscious, while in front of her under the icons are standing ten wide-eyed village girls, with fearful and inquisitive faces, who solidly imprint that picture on their souls.[13]

Readers of such prose became spectators of a highly orchestrated ritual drama involving savage and deviant behavior that was not safely ensconced in the Middle Ages, but was occurring right at their doorstep in the countryside. The Ashchepkovo example was all the more troubling because the Smolensk village was not in a remote corner of Russia. Located near a railway station and in fairly close proximity to Moscow, it represented an area upon which modernity had made an impact. Yet, in spite of comparatively high literacy and an absence of alcoholism among its inhabitants, medieval beliefs in witchcraft and demon possession still held sway.

Reflecting late-nineteenth-century anxieties of the Russian middle and upper classes about the nature and future of their civilization, Krainskii's book joined a score of others in proposing ways in which the Russian village was caught in a time warp. An amateur historian and professional psychiatrist, Krainskii was not satisfied with describing the Ashchepkovo affair and similar possession-like behavior in Novgorod province, where he practiced psychiatry. He traced *klikushestvo* back to the medieval Muscovite period and chronicled individual incidents and epidemics of demon possession from the seventeenth through the nineteenth centuries. Adding to a burgeoning ethnographic literature about the violence inherent in Russian peasant culture and about peasant superstitions involving possession and witchcraft, Krainskii provided educated society with further proof of the countryside's backwardness in spite of the advances of industrialization, urbanization, and increasing literacy. Ashchepkovo's proximity to the railway, the nineteenth century's symbol of progress, suggested that modernization itself might not vanquish what intellectuals perceived to be the barbarity of the village. The fact that the railroad transported elements of uncivilized culture to the cities was not lost on Krainskii's readers as they grappled with the dread of hooliganism on their urban streets, a dread fulfilled in the 1905 Revolution.[14] But whereas petty criminals, who attacked their social betters, were by definition men, *klikushi* were women whose feminine characteristics of backwardness, atavism, and unbridled passions could be tamed only by masculine scientific rationalism.

Krainskii's study of the Ashchepkovo epidemic and its historical precedents served as my first introduction to the fascinating topic of demon possession in the Russian countryside. As a historian of the Russian peasantry, I was particularly intrigued by the possibility that the events in that Smolensk village could provide insights about village dynamics, popular religious beliefs, women's religiosity, the interaction between the village and the monastery, and the degree to which the Russian village had been affected by modernity by the close of the imperial period. At the same time, influenced by poststructuralism's emphasis on critical textual analysis and Michel Foucault's insistence that knowledge translates into power, I questioned Krainskii's reading of what had transpired in Ashchepkovo.[15]

The psychiatrist's account constituted a cultural and medical construction of *klikushestvo* for specific ends. By studying demon possession in the distant and recent past, he joined the debate among a growing Russian educated public about Russia's relative backwardness in comparison to Western Europe and about the peasantry's, especially peasant women's, role in that backwardness. The study pointed to Russian psychiatrists' desire to wrest authority away from spiritual and lay healers to whom the possessed turned for aid. In this battle a majority of these trained specialists classified *klikushestvo* as deviant and therefore unacceptable female behavior. Placing it under the rubric of hysteria, they engaged in larger discussions of woman's character that preoccupied the attention of Western European medical specialists.

Like Krainskii and other Russian psychiatrists, I found myself interested in the roots of *klikushestvo*. But I was not preoccupied, as they were, with either the backwardness of the Russian peasantry or the pathological roots of demon possession. Instead, I was intrigued with the cultural construction of the phenomenon and the different meanings of the construct for various groups in Russian society over time.

A historical investigation of *klikushestvo* suggests that demon possession did not represent a fleeting moment in Russian history. It made its appearance as early as the eleventh century but did not become commonplace until the sixteenth and seventeenth centuries. Throughout the medieval and modern periods, it exhibited consistent features. Individuals who believed themselves to be possessed acted out a highly ritualized drama, the very one the Ashchepkovo peasants enacted. During mass, in the midst of an icon procession, or in the presence of holy objects, *klikushi* convulsed uncontrollably, tore at their hair and clothing, made animal sounds, swore, and blasphemed. These actions were all believed to be products of the demons who inhabited these individuals' bodies and who could not tolerate holy symbols. The victims of possession accordingly did not bear responsibility for their actions. With the encouragement of witnesses who became players in the ritual drama of possession, they sometimes shrieked out the name of the individual they thought had bewitched them and had planted the demons inside their bodies, hence the origin of the designation *klikusha,* or shrieker. Possession could result directly from God's wrath for a sinful soul or from his momentary concession to Satan.[16] More often, Russians believed that possession stemmed from the malefic powers of a sorcerer or witch who consorted with the devil.

Convinced that other individuals could harm them by way of magical powers, demoniacs, as well as those suffering from a variety of illnesses, thought they were the victims of a hex or bewitchment. According to their understanding, a sorcerer could cast a spell or bewitch them in various ways: by tainting their food or drink, by sending a spell through the air, or by cutting out an imprint of their feet in the dirt and casting a spell over that as the representation of the individual. Bewitchment, what the Russians call *porcha* (spoiling), could result in demon possession or other horrifying illnesses. Possession could be cured only by lifting the spell or hex, by religious exorcisms performed by monks and clerics, or by the intercession of saints.

Belief in the causal relationship between witchcraft and possession, shared by all classes of Russian society until well into the eighteenth century, came under attack at the beginning of Peter I's reign. Peter's questioning of individuals who believed themselves to be possessed—suggesting that they had ulterior motives in denouncing others as sorcerers—began a process whereby church and state struggled over definitions of possession and over the role that magic played in the cosmic order. The substitution of the gender-laden term *klikushi* (female shriekers) for gender-neutral terminology suggested that the loss of control over the body constituted a feminine trait. By demoting the importance of possession and casting doubt on its reality, Peter and his religious advisers consequently ensured that the experience of demon possession would become confined almost exclusively to women. The eventual triumph of the Enlightenment and skepticism among the Russian nobility meant that by the mid-nineteenth century, demoniacs hailed overwhelmingly from the peasant class or from recent peasant migrants to the cities.

In the nineteenth century interest in *klikushestvo* remained fairly widespread, but that interest reflected two worldviews. The peasantry, between 80 and 90 percent of the population, had long believed in *klikushestvo* and a causal relationship between witchcraft and possession; that is, that demon possession could occur as a result of bewitchment. But in the nineteenth century the miraculous healings of the possessed at religious shrines had just as much and perhaps more importance than the routing out of witches. Some of the common stressors—reasons for succumbing to possession—had changed to reflect alterations in the economic and social order. Among the elite, the phenomenon of *klikushestvo* held an abiding fascination as well.

Psychiatrists, ethnographers, and literati were drawn to the subjects of possession and witchcraft, at times emphasizing one over the other. As men of rationalism and science, nineteenth-century intellectuals did not subscribe to the belief that possession was related to witchcraft. They could accordingly separate the two phenomena. In the main, they were also "unwilling to concede that witchcraft [and possession] had a reality for those who believed" in them.[17] At the beginning of the nineteenth century and again at the turn of the twentieth century, interest in witchcraft took precedence over demon possession in literature and ethnography, while *klikushestvo* elicited greater attention in the middle of the nineteenth century. Although possession did not constitute a dominant theme in Russian literature, from the 1840s onward, major Russian writers, including Aleksei Pisemskii, Nikolai Leskov, Feodor Dostoevsky, and Leo Tolstoy, tried their hand at depicting victims of possession. They were extremely sympathetic to female shriekers, seeing them as victims of the brutal environment of serfdom or, in Tolstoy's interpretation, of the insatiable sexual desires of men. By the fin de siècle, psychiatrists tried to shift the focus away from witchcraft back to *klikushestvo*. Representations of demon possession in nineteenth-century Russia accordingly reflect an arena within which two worlds—one of popular Orthodoxy and the other of secular rationalism—collided and at times converged, as intellectuals tried to make sense of a peasant culture that seemed impervious to the advances of modern civilization.

By exploring these two worlds, this book is as much a study of perceptions of possession as it is an attempt to understand the culture of possession. This study engages broader issues in Imperial Russian history by examining *klikushestvo* in relation to Orthodox Christian ideas about the demonic and possession, the changing official notions of bewitchment and modern rationalism in the eighteenth and nineteenth centuries, popular religious culture, attitudes among writers and ethnographers about popular culture and modernity, and the development of psychiatric explanations of deviance. The stories and experiences of possessed peasant women in Ashchepkovo and elsewhere might appear on the surface to be "trivial and irrelevant."[18] But it is only through a careful reading of their individual biographies and their representations in the hands of others that historians can penetrate larger cultural and social issues.

Findings of a study of *klikushestvo* and witchcraft from the beginning of the eighteenth century, when both phenomena came under the scrutiny of the state and reforming church, suggest that peasant culture remained vibrant throughout the imperial period. Profoundly shaped by Orthodoxy and traditions of older centuries, peasants were not immune to the impact of modernity. New forces that impinged upon women's lives as a result of industrialization and male outmigration as well as a growth in monastic institutions in the second half of the nineteenth century found expression in women's suffering and redemption through spiritual healing.

The role of the Russian Orthodox Church in providing spiritual aid to demoniacs demonstrates the continuing relevance of that institution in the late imperial period to a significant portion of the population. Unlike traditional portrayals of the church as stuck in the morass of a medieval era, this study looks at the ways in which the church engaged secular ideas. At no time was the impact of secularization greater than at the turn of the twentieth century when the Holy Synod turned to physicians for expert examination of individuals who claimed to have been miraculously healed of possession or other illnesses. Only if investigators could rule out any positive impact of medical care and treatment on specific individuals' illnesses did the church entertain the possibility of a miraculous cure. The fin de siècle church thus was prepared to adapt to certain notions of scientific rationalism without, however, giving up its prerogatives regarding the miraculous. Miracles took on even greater significance "at precisely the moment when science attained an apparently unquestionable authority."[19]

As a result, the Russian Orthodox Church was not prepared to relinquish to physicians and psychiatrists its thaumaturgical function. Monasteries continued to serve important functions as spiritual centers where individual monks and nuns might administer healings through what they believed to be the grace of God. Saints' shrines and reliquaries in these institutions were also believed to have curative powers, with monks interceding with saints on behalf of the faithful. By way of prayer; confession and communion; and administration of holy oil, holy water, and blessed herbs, monks effectively treated pilgrims who had a variety of ailments. Such afflictions, including those connected to demon possession, were understood to be both physical and spiritual in nature.

An investigation of *klikushestvo* also reveals that Orthodoxy and popular beliefs were remarkably accepting of a variety of behaviors that in the age of scientific rationalism and the advent of psychiatry would be labeled psychological in nature. The medieval veneration of *iurodivye* (holy fools in Christ), individuals imbued with God's grace who through unconventional behavior criticized the political and social status quo, provides a compelling example of this benevolence. Popular reverence of these holy fools continued into the modern period in spite of their association with the Old Belief fundamentalist opposition to major church reforms in the mid-seventeenth century, an association that prompted secular and religious authorities to cast doubt upon their authenticity. Members of Russian society, ranging from the upper classes to peasants, continued to find spiritual and thaumaturgical solace in these religious types who by the nineteenth century were increasingly incarcerated in insane asylums. Shriekers, similarly tolerated by the population at large, came under the scrutiny of psychiatrists at the end of the nineteenth century.

The similarities and differences between *klikushi* and holy fools underscore not only a compassionate religious culture, but other aspects of religious belief as well. Unlike holy fools, shriekers were not believed to enjoy spiritual powers. However, neither bore responsibility for their actions: demons guided the behavior of *klikushi,* while God instructed holy fools to do his bidding. Like holy fools, the possessed blasphemed and created public disorders within religious settings, although holy fools were just as likely to act in the nonreligious domain. The source of the demoniacs' ailment, however, was rooted in difficulties that women encountered in their everyday lives and in a perceived vulnerability to evil spirits. Like holy fools, the possessed enjoyed a place within the popular belief system and folk idioms. Released from their burdens and responsibilities during the course of their possession, they could seek the help of popular and spiritual healers. But by forsaking their responsibilities, if only for a time, *klikushi* were also unconsciously saying that they were no longer able, at least temporarily, to cope with the adversity that life placed before them. Peasant and Orthodox culture allowed such frustrations to play themselves out in the ritual drama of possession.

In the nineteenth and early twentieth centuries, clergy as well as Russian peasant society subscribed to a common myth of possession. Their cosmic worldview had a place for spirits and malevolence that needed to be rooted out so that the victims of possession could be cured and reincorporated into their societies. While peasants and their spiritual advisers shared similar beliefs and understood idioms of possession, not everyone experienced *klikushestvo*. Indeed, it was the rare individual who became possessed. Nevertheless, according to anthropologist Gananath Obeyesekere in his study of spirit possession among contemporary Sri Lankan Buddhists, "spirit attack is both a personal experience and a cultural performance" in a public setting in which the witnesses understand the symbols of possession and act swiftly to neutralize the spirits before they cause greater harm.[20] Community participation remained critical to the integrity of the possession drama.

Contradictory and incomplete sources prevent confident speculation on whether *klikushestvo* was increasing or declining in incidence by the end of the nineteenth century. In the early 1860s an educated writer noted, "It is the rare person among us, especially having visited places, known for miraculous cures from relics and icons, who hasn't had the opportunity to see and hear so-called *klikushi* or the demon possessed."[21] Yet a mere decade later the novelist Feodor Dostoevsky suggested that incidents of *klikushestvo* had been more common when he was a child. In 1901 the ethnographer A. V. Balov echoed Dostoevsky's words, but this time in reference to Iaroslavl' province.[22] Dostoevsky's and Balov's observations could say more about the two individuals' regular attendance at village churches (where they were likely to observe shriekers) when they were youngsters, however, than an actual decline in incidents of possession. Ironically, Balov's assertion of waning *klikushestvo* coincided with the nascent Russian psychiatric profession's fascination with possession and with the first systematic attempts to count demoniacs. In 1903 the radical psychiatrist P. Iakobii declared in the influential liberal journal *Vestnik Evropy* that the prevalence of *klikushestvo* had been significantly underestimated. Indeed, his 1893 figures for Orel province suggest that 13 out of every 10,000 women were *klikushi*.[23] Establishing the frequency of *klikushestvo* is further complicated by the fact that peasants did not consider possessed individuals to be suffering from a mental illness. Accordingly, they neither incarcerated shriekers in asylums nor cooperated with zemstvo statisticians intent upon enumerating the mentally incompetent. While the issue of frequency cannot be resolved definitively, it is evident that the symptoms of demon possession were still widely recognized in Russian rural and educated society at the turn of the twentieth century. A victim of Soviet repression, *klikushestvo* went underground in the 1930s, only to resurface with the collapse of communism and resurrection of religious freedoms in 1991.[24] Its presence in Russian culture continues.

The multifaceted governmental, religious, literary, ethnographic, and psychiatric sources are far better in recording perceptions of *klikushestvo* and the phenomenon's place within the larger issues confronting Imperial Russia. Initially, I despaired of finding sufficient documentary sources to place in perspective the turn-of-the-century published psychiatric analyses. The hitherto unexamined nineteenth- and early-twentieth-century archival records of Moscow's Preobrazhenskaia Hospital for the Insane, including admittance forms and files on individual patients, revealed few examples of individuals suffering from possession. However, once I understood the importance of the religious and political components of possession, I realized that the archive of the eighteenth-century Preobrazhenskii Prikaz and Secret Chancery, the Spiritual Regulation of 1721, other eighteenth-century imperial decrees and Senate decisions, as well as nineteenth-century religious journals and newspapers were a veritable treasure trove of references to and examples of *klikushestvo*. The Holy Synod's published series of eighteenth-century documents and the post-1861 eparchial newspapers are replete with listings of faith healings or miraculous cures, including successful exorcisms of demons. The publications of lists generally coincided with the canonizations of Russian Orthodox saints, 11 of which occurred between 1757 and 1916, although miraculous cures at the site of miracle-working icons were less time specific. Early-twentieth-century documents pertaining to the posthumous miracles of Bishop Pitirim of Tambov (1685–1698) and late-nineteenth- and early-twentieth-century records of cures in the popular religious journals for pilgrims, *Russkii palomnik* and *Strannik,* in conjunction with these lists, permitted a comparison of modern miracle stories of the possessed with similar tales of medieval Muscovy.

Individual cases of *klikushestvo* in the nineteenth and early twentieth centuries, culled from the religious sources, supplemented data from psychiatric, legal, and ethnographic materials. The database constructed for this study consists of 260 women and men who between 1820 and 1926 identified themselves or were identified by others as shriekers or whose symptoms corresponded to those associated with *klikushestvo*. The few examples from the early Soviet period are included in the database because they follow the profile of demoniacs in the prerevolutionary era and suggest some continuity over time. Unfortunately, but unavoidably, missing from the source base are the rich, if flawed, late-nineteenth-century records on *klikushi* in the ethnographic files of the Tenishev archive. That archive has recently closed off its collection to foreigners, unless they are willing to pay exorbitant user fees.[25] Also absent from the sample are individuals suffering from ailments that they attributed to "unclean spirits" or demons, but whose afflictions did not take on the cultural attributes of possession. While the database cannot be viewed as exhaustive, it gives some sense of the estate, gender, and age profiles of the victims of possession as well as instances when possession assumed epidemic proportions. The cases that make up the database also allow the study to treat the demoniacs as individuals rather than simply as "the objects of hegemonic discourses."[26]

Psychiatric, legal, and ethnographic sources made possible the creation of a second database containing 80 published cases of witchcraft and sorcery in the Russian and Ukrainian countryside between 1861 and 1917. The record on such cases is even more limited than that on demoniacs. When popular beliefs in witchcraft and *klikushestvo* are discussed, materials pertaining to the database on shriekers are confined to the postemancipation period, unless otherwise noted. Unfortunately, the sources did not permit me to extend the period of witchcraft and sorcery cases back to the late decades of serfdom or to expand upon the postemancipation and prerevolutionary base. The Moscow City Archive allowed access to only three cases involving witchcraft that came before the Moscow *sovestnyi sud* (a court dealing with matters of conscience and morality) in the late eighteenth and early nineteenth centuries, claiming that other files were either so badly damaged as to require binding or were unreadable. Inquiries and examination of other archival materials revealed that individual files pertaining to cases brought before *volost'* or cantonal courts after emancipation had generally been destroyed after World War II.[27] The purging of those regional materials can only be bemoaned by historians.

While dependent on primary sources, a multidisciplinary study of a previously unexamined topic must also rely upon a substantial secondary literature. The significant work of historians on the witchcraft trials of early modern Europe and the American colonies, the development of psychiatry in modern Europe and the United States, the hystericization of women, as well as the work of specialists on Russian literature and culture help establish the methodological and interpretative framework of this book. Such research provides a comparative context for the analysis of possession in rural Russia in the nineteenth and early twentieth centuries. Special mention must be made of the influence that anthropology, especially medical anthropology, has had upon my work.

In studying possession cults in various parts of the world, anthropologists are as sensitive to victims of possession as they are to those individuals identified as witches. Even though they have charted behaviors that are more exotic than those found among Russian demoniacs, the ways in which they contextualize the possessed within their various religious cultures are refreshing. With a few exceptions, much of the literature on Western European witchcraft focuses on the ways in which elite culture elaborated upon popular beliefs regarding witches so as to create the infamous witchcraft trials of the sixteenth and seventeenth centuries.[28] Such studies also examine the waning of beliefs in witches among educated members of European society. However, they pay little attention to individuals who believed themselves to have been bewitched. The fact that demoniacs in medieval Europe became merged into the ranks of those identified as witches in the fifteenth century helps explain that lack of attention.[29] The reluctance of historians to recognize that witchcraft had real meaning for the average person in various periods (or to put it another way, the assumption that it "would not have meant anything at all if people had known better") further explains the limitations of most studies of Western European witchcraft.[30] Recent anthropological studies are far less judgmental of the peoples they chronicle.

By far the most significant finding in medical anthropology is that illness and suffering are cultural and social constructs—a discovery that has had tremendous impact on the writing of medical history. The latter "has moved from a positivist to a cultural phase, which means that it has begun to shift from the scientific history of disease to the cultural history of diseases and the study of illness as metaphor."[31] There is now a recognition among medical practitioners as well that "culture, groups, and individuals respond in different ways to life's pains and pressures" and that the ways in which suffering and sickness are expressed varies considerably from culture to culture.[32]

As the following discussion should make clear, *klikushestvo* represents a socially understood illness as opposed to a medical disease. Sophisticated anthropological and cross-cultural psychiatric studies have demonstrated convincingly the unfeasibility of universalizing psychiatric diagnostic categories derived mainly from clinical studies of upper-middle-class European-Americans. In fact, their authors' arguments have resulted in a modification of the fourth edition of the American Psychiatric Association's *Diagnostic and Statistical Manual* (1994). Incorporating cultural assessments of behaviors in the developing world that psychiatrists in the West would consider mental illnesses, the DSM-IV accordingly advises medical specialists to respect non-Western societies' evaluations of illnesses as nonpsychological in origin.[33] For the study of demon possession in Imperial Russia this sensitivity to cultural differences means that such psychiatric categories as paranoia, multiple personality disorder, Tourette's syndrome, and hysteria cannot be applied indiscriminately to demoniacs. Clinically, some of the *klikushi* may have displayed symptoms that correspond to these illnesses. Use of those classifications, however, ends up being reductionist and ignores the social meaning or religious understandings of demon possession.[34]

Ultimately, premodern communities possess a wider range of acceptable behaviors than highly urbanized and industrial Western societies. What might appear aberrant and therefore pathological to the latter can be a recognizable behavior to the former. That behavior is part of the public, rather than private, domain; the victim of an affliction such as possession communicates to a wider audience her problems in order to receive aid. In the case of possession, "the aim of healing . . . is to demonstrate that evil does indeed exist, that it can be objectified in the external world, understood, and at times controlled, by magical means."[35] The physical and spiritual anguish of the possessed is no less genuine within this cultural context.

A key to the cultural construction of *klikushestvo* may be found in the phenomenon's relative absence from Orthodox Ukrainian areas of the Russian Empire. Underreporting in the nineteenth century may provide a partial explanation for the lack of examples of *klikushestvo* in Ukrainian provinces. Ethnographers and other observers seized on its almost complete absence as a given without verifying the validity of their assertion. Low rates of Ukrainian rural-urban-rural migration for nonagricultural pursuits may also have been a factor. On the other hand, the drama or myth model of possession relied on a sympathetic relationship between representatives of the Orthodox Church and their parishioners, that is, on their subscribing to a cosmology in language comprehensible to both. The Russified character of the Orthodox Church in Ukraine may have sundered that relationship as clerics and monks did not speak the same language as their congregation, preferring Russian over the so-called Little Russian dialect. Thus, Ukrainian peasants confronted religious matters in two nonvernacular languages, Old Church Slavonic as well as Russian. That they shared with their Russian counterparts beliefs in maleficence and sorcery without the corollary of *klikushestvo* suggests that they had a less pronounced Orthodox conceptualization of bewitchment. The comparative dimension of witchcraft among Russian and Ukrainian peasants in the late imperial period will be examined as this inquiry elaborates further the cultural components of *klikushestvo* and bewitchment.

For the study of demon possession and perceptions of the phenomenon in Russia from the eighteenth through the early twentieth centuries, the drama metaphor, as implied earlier, is particularly apt. In each of the following chapters, the *klikushi* or shriekers appear as protagonists who capture the attention of those around them. While they play a major role in each segment, the groups and individuals reacting to them change. Defined and vilified by eighteenth-century government officials, yet shown to be protected by church hierarchs in chapter 1, the shriekers become part of a much larger ritual drama in chapter 2. That ritual play involves peasants and clerics in a script encompassing detection, countermagic, pilgrimage, exorcism, and sometimes violence against witches, all of which can result in redemption and deliverance not only for the possessed, but for the rural community as well. Chapter 3 revisits the tensions of church and state perceptions, this time with mainstream nineteenth-century Russian writers constructing positive images of the possessed and giving voice to them in new ways in contrast to the pejorative stereotypes of the Russian village favored by late nineteenth-century ethnographers. Turn-of-the-century psychiatrists move to center stage in chapter 4, providing diagnoses of *klikushestvo* and casting aspersions on the Russian Orthodox Church. The final chapter takes the analysis of the phenomenon of *klikushestvo* within a sociocultural context a step further. By examining the age, gender, and marital profiles as well as individual experiences of the victims of demon possession, it underscores the fact that *klikushi* were cultural actors within their society.

Chapter One

STATE AND CHURCH PERCEPTIONS

✦ On 17 August 1720 authorities arrested "three *klikushi,* namely Avdot'ia, Iakovlev's daughter, wife of the eatery worker Ul'ian Denisov, the blind girl Arina, Ivanov's daughter, of the Tikhvinskaia workhouse which is in Sushchevo, Avdot'ia, Iakimov's daughter, the wife of the merchant of the Meshchanskaia suburb, Nikifor Ivanov," for shrieking in several Moscow churches. After questioning them at the provincial office, Vice-Governor Voeikov dispatched them to St. Petersburg, whereupon His Majesty Peter I ordered the Secret Chancery, his chief organ of political repression, to interrogate the women.[1] According to the depositions sent from Moscow, the merchant's wife Avdot'ia Iakimova testified that on 12 July 1720 she had been attending the divine liturgy in the Moscow Kremlin's Uspenskii Cathedral when she shrieked "in an absurd voice [and] barked like a dog." "This grief," as she called it, had struck her 40 years before when she was a child and had continued to occur once, twice, and even three times a month when she was in church or at home. Insisting upon the truth of her statement by noting that "if she, Avdot'ia, has said something false, then the great autocrat can punish her, Avdot'ia, with death," Avdot'ia Iakimova named her spiritual father, the parish priest Mikhail Kostiantinov, as being well acquainted with "this sorrow of hers." Father Kostiantinov corroborated Avdot'ia's statement that she had lived in his home for three years, attested to her fulfilling her duty of going to confession, and noted that her shrieking had been confined to the home. Avdot'ia Iakovleva also admitted to having shrieked on occasion, but mainly at home. Her affliction began in February 1720 during a service in the Church of Kozma and Damian in

Nizhnie Sadovniki when she began to shout in an "unnatural voice." The only other time she shrieked in a sanctuary occurred a few months later on 6 May when she attended the liturgy at the Church of the Adorning of the Mother of God, the resting place of Ioann the Blessed's relics. But she did not remember what she had shouted at that time. The workhouse inmate Arina Ivanova also acknowledged shrieking, asserting that on 17 May 1720 she "shouted in an unnatural voice" in the Nikitskii Monastery's church during the reading of the Gospels, "but what she shouted, she does not know." Arina went on to say that earlier she had often shrieked during the liturgy at the Church of the Tikhvin Mother of God and in the workhouse had "frequently shouted day and night." As in the case of Avdot'ia Iakimova, Arina claimed that she had been stricken thus since birth, "because my mother and her other relatives did not guard against this above-mentioned affliction."[2]

In the hands of the investigators of the Secret Chancery, the three *klikushi* were tortured on the rack and lashed with the knout. Despite the torments inflicted on their bodies on 18 August, all three maintained their earlier testimony. This time Avdot'ia Iakimova added that when she shrieked in the church she had sounded not only like a dog but also like a frog. In response to specific questions, she vowed that she had not faked her affliction and that "no one taught her to shout." Avdot'ia Iakovleva and Arina Ivanova also swore that they had not been pretending when they shrieked, with Arina attributing her illness to the falling sickness and claiming as well that "no one taught her to shout."[3] Subjected to the rack a second time on 22 August, the shriekers upheld their previous testimony. Hoping to substantiate her claims by naming a witness, Avdot'ia Iakovleva added that she had experienced an attack of possession in the prison the previous evening in the presence of a guard. Under questioning, Ivan Nelidov, the named prison sentry and member of the Imperial Preobrazhenskii regiment, confirmed Iakovleva's description of her seizure the previous evening: On "this 21 August the woman, under guard, prayed during the holy liturgy . . . and at three o'clock suddenly fell and shook, and she started to cringe and, as a result of this, lay on the floor an hour and a half as if she were dead, and, as a result of this, he, Nelidov, became frightened." Two weeks later on 7 September, the investigators decided to free Avdot'ia Iakovleva "because her illness had been full strength before witnesses," but ordered her not to shriek in church and sentenced the other two shriekers to work in a *manufaktura* (textile mill).[4]

Almost a century and a half later, in 1866, a miraculous healing of a possessed woman occurred in the Voskresenskii Monastery at the grave of Nikon, patriarch of the Russian Orthodox Church from 1652 until 1666. Claiming to be the recipient of divine grace through the prayers of the deceased Nikon, the soldier's wife Pelagiia Flavionova Sukhareva described her experience with demon possession. She maintained that she had been afflicted for 15 years, shrieking in "an unnatural voice" and denouncing people around her. On 17 May 1866, she attended a morning funeral service at Patriarch Nikon's grave during which she experienced a seizure and asked, "why have you brought me here?" Shortly thereafter, in the presence of her husband Prokof'ii Anisimov Sukharev, his sister Natal'ia Anisimova, and a retired noncommissioned officer, Fedor Volkov, Pelagiia was "relieved of her affliction." According to the monk Makarii's verification of this miraculous healing, Pelagiia's spouse and relatives described her fits as having been so severe that she was prone to falling on the ground, beating herself, and uttering blasphemies. After unsuccessful visitations to several religious shrines, they found themselves at Nikon's tomb. There, according to the eyewitnesses, the possessed woman said, "Why have you brought me to New Jerusalem? You said that we were going to the Trinity–Sergii Monastery, but I cannot be here." The woman then fell to the ground, shrieking and again asking her relatives why they had brought her there. Struck unconscious, "as if dead," the woman was placed on a stool. When she came to, she said the prayer "Glory be to God," quietly thanked Patriarch Nikon for interceding with God on her behalf and healing her of her affliction, and asked the officiating monk to hold a memorial service for the patriarch as a further expression of her gratitude. In the evening the monk Makarii acquiesced to the healed woman's request that she be confessed and the following day gave her communion.[5]

Almost five decades later in September 1911, the priest P. Skubachevskii reported to clerical and lay readers of the conservative religious journal *Vera i razum* his participation in an exorcism at the relics of St. Ioasaf of Belgorod (a former bishop of Kursk) in the immediate aftermath of Ioasaf's canonization. Father Skubachevskii described the Belgorod cathedral on the evening of 4 September as being full of those worshipers fortunate enough to have tickets of admission.[6] "Near the northern wall of the church a barrier had been erected, along which an unending chain, two deep, of pilgrims, wishing to kiss the holy relics, ran." Father Skubachevskii described the pilgrims as "mainly simple peasants," many of whom had waited in line for days and nights and among whom were "many sick and those dispirited by grief." Wishing to extend words of solace to the afflicted and to pray for them, the priest worked his way through the crowd and approached the monks on duty at the reliquary, asking them for permission to participate in the services. With their authorization, Father Skubachevskii donned his robes and began a prayer service. "When they carried or led the sick [up to me], I asked their name and tried to say a few words of comfort and encouragement to each one." After another parish priest replaced him in the service, Father Skubachevskii stood at the head of the reliquary, covering "the heads of the sick with a paten [*vosdukh*]." He estimated that at least 500 seriously ill and many more healthy pilgrims had filed past the relics within five hours. Nothing unusual occurred until, he noted, "five strong peasant men led a demon possessed woman" into the church. "'I will not go, I will not go!' . . . that poor woman shouted in a wild voice." According to Father Skubachevskii, several policemen rushed over to help the peasants bring the struggling woman before St. Ioasaf's relics. Father Skubachevskii noted,

> [I] covered her head, laid [it] upon the holy relics and covered it with the paten. "I am coming out, I am coming out," the unfortunate woman began to cry in a wild voice. It went on like this for ten minutes. The shouts became quieter and quieter, and finally she was overcome by silence. I bowed my head to her and asked: "What is your name?" [directing the question to the demon possessing the woman]. The sick woman was silent.
>
> "Pray with me," said I. "St. Ioasaf, pray to God for me!"
>
> The woman was silent.

In response to the demon's refusal to speak through the woman's mouth, Father Skubachevskii and the other priests began to pray for the demoniac as a monk began to intone the prayer for the sick. In response the *klikusha* began to shout loudly and repeatedly, "I am coming out," but soon her wail became quieter and quieter until she fell silent from exhaustion. When Father Skubachevskii bent over her and again asked her her name, the woman replied "Elena"; the response signified the demon's departure. As the priest directed her to pray with him to Saint Ioasaf, the woman "began quietly to repeat the words of the prayer after me and began to cry." As she kissed the holy relics, Father Skubachevskii ordered her to lift her head up so that he could bless her with the life-giving cross and then asked her to give thanks to "God's holy saint." The woman prostrated herself before the holy relics, and "all those present could not keep back the tears." Describing the pious crowds outside the church, Father Skubachevskii ended his impassioned report with the rhetorical flourish, "O Holy Russia, your faith is still strong."[7]

These incidents—the 1720 trial of three women, the 1866 miraculous cure of a woman at Patriarch Nikon's gravesite, and the 1911 exorcism of a woman at the relics of St. Ioasaf—all involved *klikushi,* women who believed themselves to be demon possessed. These unfortunate individuals are similarly described as reacting negatively to holy objects or the holy liturgy by shouting or shrieking in the unnatural voices of the demons that inhabited them. Yet their treatment differed dramatically. The earliest episode entailed investigation and torture by secular government officials in an attempt to elicit the truth about the state of being of the possessed, whether they were feigning their possession, and whether they were the victims of others' schemes. Criminal investigations of the possessed, exorcisms of demons, and miraculous cures of possessed individuals occurred repeatedly between the early eighteenth and early twentieth century. While criminal courts in the reign of Catherine II (1762–1796) eventually dropped torture as a way of determining the veracity of defendants' statements, they periodically investigated the activities of the demon possessed, punishing those who falsely accused individuals of having harmed them. The later stories involved the other extreme: a public display of divine beneficence through intercession and the miraculous cure of possession.

How does the historian reconcile these two extremes? Was the secular state at loggerheads with the church over the meaning of and authority over possession? Or were the interests of church and state intertwined in the case of the *klikushi*? Did attitudes toward possession change over time?

Given the tsar's roles as defender of the faith and as orthodox emperor (after the fall of Constantinople in 1453 to the Turks), the interests of church and state were necessarily linked. In the sixteenth and seventeenth centuries, Muscovy defined itself in religious terms as a community of Orthodox believers. The early Romanovs held differing notions about the authority of the patriarch, the ecclesiastical head of the church from 1589 onward, climaxing in the 1721 abolition of that position by Peter I (1682–1725). At the same time, however, the tsars participated fully in the drafting of reform legislation vis-à-vis the church. Beginning in the mid-sixteenth century, the civil government increasingly cooperated in punishing offenses against religion. Peter I's attempts to modernize the Orthodox Church by making it a full department of state and ridding popular religious practices of superstition continued traditions already established in the late Muscovite period.

Using Muscovite laws against sorcery and witchcraft as precedent, Peter I and his advisers campaigned against individuals who falsely charged others with sorcery by claiming to be victims of witchcraft and hence possession. As feigning possession became a punishable crime in Imperial Russia, doubt was cast for the first time in Russian history upon the possibility of demons invading a human body. Rooted in Enlightenment thinking and skepticism regarding the powers of the supernatural, civil and ecclesiastical laws required the Orthodox Church, the authority in issues of good and evil, to identify malingerers. Legislation, which introduced the concepts of the deserving and undeserving poor, similarly distinguished between legitimate and fraudulent religious behavior. It identified *klikushi,* women or men who believed themselves to be possessed, as charlatans who had ulterior motives that had nothing to do with evil spirits. This modern definition did not sit easily with all church representatives, nor, for that matter, did it sit well with government officials obliged to carry out the letter of the law.[8] For while Peter I and his immediate successors as well as their European-educated Ukrainian bishops attempted to enforce rationalist and critical thinking, the attack on demon possession struck at the heart of Orthodox Church teaching and the continuing belief in sorcery at all levels of society, at least until the nineteenth century.

Orthodox canons, the teachings of the church fathers, prayers and hymns, hagiographical literature, and miracle stories were replete with references to human struggles with demons and the ability of the Christian faith and symbols to triumph over the devil. Indeed, the devil's existence as a genuine creature, who as God's instrument continually tested humans and at times possessed them, with or without human agency, constituted a critical ingredient in the Orthodox worldview. In the Muscovite past the combating of evil had been highlighted by miraculous cures of demoniacs through the intercession of saints.

While cures of the demon possessed at saints' shrines and before miracle-working icons continued to be reported throughout the eighteenth and nineteenth centuries, cures of all types of ailments had to be subjected to intense questioning and verification. Enlightened eighteenth-century rulers and ecclesiastical hierarchs had become skeptical about the possibility of miracles in the modern age, particularly those reportedly experienced by common believers. "Such skepticism was all the more intense if there were grounds to believe that the clergy were exploiting . . . relics for personal gain."[9] False miracles could also be damaging to the church's reputation and a victory for the schismatic Old Belief, sectarianism, and other competing faiths. Although miracles recorded and sanctioned by the ancient Rus' and Muscovite churches retained their accepted validity, miracles since that time did not automatically receive official approval from a church bent on centralization and control of popular practices. When scrutiny of the latter had the undesirable effect by the early nineteenth century of turning the faithful away from the Orthodox Church into the hands of Old Believers and sectarians, the church relaxed its skepticism toward miracles. Indeed, it even began to publish regular accounts of miracles, including exorcisms at the grave sites of saints or before miracle-working icons, in the religious press, a pattern that continued into the twentieth century. Church and state actions against superstitions, nevertheless, had had a noticeable impact on *klikushestvo*. Demoniacs by the end of the eighteenth century were predominantly women, reflecting a reversal of the medieval pattern whereby men outnumbered women among the possessed. The feminization of demoniacs continued into the nineteenth and early twentieth centuries, when medical expertise regarding the nature of the illnesses cured and doctors' validation of the miraculous became increasingly important.

By the end of the nineteenth century, the Orthodox Church found itself on the defensive. It sometimes used biblical exegesis to defend the possibility of the miraculous in an increasingly secular world and at other times accepted various tenets of scientific rationalism. These were not so much contradictory trends as attempts by the Orthodox Church to remain relevant and credible in a rapidly changing world where scientific knowledge of the universe had developed sufficiently to limit the scope but not necessarily the possibility of preternatural intervention.[10]

In a discussion of such matters, it is difficult at times to avoid treating the eighteenth- and nineteenth-century Russian Orthodox Church as a monolithic institution, which it surely was not. Representatives of the church, ranging from bishops to parish priests and sacristans, did not always follow legal prescriptions, and the Holy Synod did not have an adequate bureaucracy to ensure that its decrees were carried out. Consequently, the church did not follow a single path.

At the same time, the Russian Orthodox Church presented itself as a monolithic structure that defined acceptable beliefs and practices in contrast to those it considered pernicious and harmful to human salvation. From the Orthodox Church's point of view, as in the case of the Roman Catholic Church, proper religious ritual and the invocation of pious words in the form of prayers could affect the preternatural and bestow divine mercy upon humans.[11] What the ecclesiastical hierarchy in its various pronouncements and decrees branded superstitious had to do with competing sources of power vis-à-vis the supernatural. Purposely using the less weighted term "superstition" rather than "magic" to identify "relations with the supernatural that were outside the regular channels of the church," churchmen attempted to deny sorcerers, fortune-tellers, and witches, to whom Orthodox believers might turn for help, their magical powers.[12]

From the mid-seventeenth century onward, the Orthodox Church particularly guarded against the incantations intoned by healers and sorcerers over the sick as well as those intended to make a person ill. Even variations of Christian prayers that healers and the laity might use on a daily basis were suspect as far as the church authorities were concerned because such incantations had not received the sanction of trained theological authorities.[13] Far better for a priest or monk to chant officially sanctioned prayers over the ill or perform a religious service at an agricultural field to elicit rain than to risk abetting the devil through a layperson's performance of such rituals.

The church, after all, had a responsibility to guard against apostasy. While Orthodoxy viewed the devil as a divine creation less powerful than God, the church could not take risks against this evil being who continually manipulated humans' will in favor of sin. Even the church's representatives were not immune to the devil's wiles. Thus the church believed that it had to be vigilant within and without its own ranks, punishing deviation from proscribed beliefs, especially in the eighteenth century as Old Belief and sectarianism proliferated, or turning, as it did increasingly by the late eighteenth century, to more rigorous training for parish priests and education in the catechism for the laity.

THE LEGAL CASE

In the early eighteenth century, Peter I and his spiritual adviser, Feofan Prokopovich, the Ukrainian bishop of Pskov (1718–1725; promoted to archbishop in 1720), issued legal provisions designed to wipe out the Orthodox believers' practices deemed contrary to Orthodoxy and potentially seditious in nature. They prosecuted blasphemers and individuals who falsely claimed religious experiences, charging them with adversely affecting the faithful and threatening the social order, the person of the tsar, or the tsar's family. *Klikushi* or shriekers, accordingly, came under scrutiny as potential impostors.

As an orthodox prince, Peter I followed an ancient tradition whereby Russian rulers had responsibility for upholding and preserving church dogma. Throughout the Muscovite period the Russian Orthodox Church had denounced various practices of the laity that it considered remnants of paganism. Since torture and corporal punishment of laypersons did not fall under the jurisdiction of ecclesiastical courts, the church hierarchy at times turned to the tsar to take civil action against practitioners of superstition. Thus, for example, the 1551 Stoglav (Hundred Chapters) Church Council specifically referred to the evils of fortune-tellers, astrologers, and magicians and recommended that the tsar execute these practitioners after the church had excommunicated them. A year later in 1552, Ivan IV (1547–1584) endorsed part of the recommendation by stipulating in a decree that people were not to seek the services of sorcerers, magicians, and astrologers, or they would feel the brunt of civil and ecclesiastical laws. By the mid-seventeenth century Alexis Mikhailovich (1645–1676) issued two types of decrees, one set defining sorcery and witchcraft as violations of secular law and order and the other series focusing on them as moral-religious offenses. Finally, in 1652, responding to civil disorders, he added the death sentence for sorcery to the legal code.[14]

The imposition of the death penalty for the secular crime of sorcery reflected the seventeenth-century Muscovite government's increased wariness of political sorcery, a concern that had originated in the mid-fifteenth century. Individuals who were believed to employ magic, sorcery, necromancy, and apostasy against their political enemies had to answer to the Muscovite legal system and the interrogators in the torture chambers of the Razriadnyi Prikaz. In the seventeenth century the state's vigilance extended to royal advisers whom it suspected of using black magic to deprive the tsar of mind and reason.[15] In "an intrusive and authoritarian political system that demanded submission above all . . ., any act or utterance [could be construed] as a symbol of disobedience."[16]

Peter's decrees against shriekers, who believed themselves to be victims of sorcerers' magic, can only be understood in the Muscovite political context. While these edicts represented the first of their kind specifically against *klikushestvo,* they constituted a logical follow-up to previous attempts to rout out individuals and groups who were suspected of using the pretext of witchcraft as a weapon against others, especially members of the royal family.[17] The rulings also stemmed from a fear of widespread intrigues that manifested political and, from the mid-seventeenth century onward, religious dissent.[18] The notion of malingering had already made its appearance in 1636 when Patriarch Ioasaf issued a decree against false holy fools—those who pretended to be simpleminded beneficiaries of God's grace and who earned a living out of claiming to be fools for Christ. Allowing church and state to distinguish between counterfeit and authentic holy fools, the decree took on greater significance with the schism of the mid-seventeenth century. Holy fools did not publicly support Patriarch Nikon's religious reforms, which modified Orthodox ritual to accord better with ancient Byzantine practices, but tended to gravitate toward the oppositional Old Belief. As a result, Nikon, and eventually Tsar Alexis, turned against them.[19] The political instability of late-seventeenth-century Muscovy left its impression on Peter I, who stepped up the prosecution of political-religious crimes that now included false *klikushestvo*. In the "cosmic order" of the Russian realm, as was the case elsewhere in Europe, "social and even private acts acquired political and ideological content, and nonconformist acts were implicitly seen . . . as political disloyalty and as religious heresy."[20]

Peter issued his initial decree against *klikushi* on 7 May 1715, demanding that all shriekers be seized and questioned by government officials. He used the example of Varvara Loginova, who under interrogation by his Secret Chancery had admitted to feigning her shrieking in order to take vengeance on a carpenter named Grigorii. By pointing to a concrete case, Peter was able to justify his abhorrence of individuals who, he believed, fraudulently used possession as a means of slandering others. His investigators reported:

> On the 7th and 8th of last November 1714, in the Cathedral of St. Isaak Dalmatskii in St. Petersburg, during the holy liturgy, the carpenter's wife Varvara Loginova screamed as if she were hexed [*isporchena*] . . . and under interrogation said that . . . she screamed pretending that she had been hexed, only for the reason that today was close to a year since . . . the carpenter Grigorii came to blows with her brother-in-law . . . and af-

> ter that Varvara began to think how she might take revenge on the carpenter Grigorii for beating her brother-in-law, and that if she screamed that she was hexed and identified Grigorii as having hexed her, that would ruin him; and a week after the above-mentioned fight she began to shriek at home twice and three times a week, and as if demented screamed out that Grigorii had hexed her; and on the above-mentioned 7th and 8th of November, being in the Cathedral of St. Isaak Dalmatskii, during the liturgy, also shrieked on purpose as though she were hexed and said that Grigorii had hexed her; and she did this only so as to take revenge on Grigorii for her brother-in-law and to ruin him; but no one hexed her, Varvara, and she shrieked fraudulently, and in this lies her guilt.[21]

The crux of Peter's concern regarding shriekers involved individuals appropriating a concrete religious phenomenon—demon possession—to cast aspersions on the character of others by falsely claiming that they were dabbling in magic or sorcery and had planted demons inside them.

Peter's 1715 censure of shriekers reappeared in subsequent legislation. In January 1716 the Senate ordered bishops to send individuals faking possession to secular authorities.[22] The Spiritual Regulation of 1721, which turned the Orthodox Church into a bureaucratic arm of the state by creating the Holy Synod as a substitute for the patriarchate, constituted the next major assault on *klikushestvo*.

Feofan Prokopovich, the regulation's author, continued the attack in Peter I's name. Influenced by the rationalist thinking of Protestantism and the Catholic Counter-Reformation, he defined superstition broadly as "that which is superfluous, not essential to salvation, devised by hypocrites only for their own interest, beguiling the simple people, and like snowdrifts, hindering passage along the right path of truth."[23] He ordered Orthodox bishops to be vigilant against aimlessly wandering monks, the building of unnecessary churches, false miracles before holy icons, "squallers [i.e., *klikushi*], noncertified corpses,[24] and all other suchlike"(in that order). Since bishops could not be everywhere at once, Prokopovich demanded that their "stewards, or ecclesiastical superintendents, especially appointed for that purpose" report any problems to them. On their visits to diocesan churches, bishops were furthermore obliged to consult with parish priests and others about superstitious practices. Once again, Prokopovich drew attention to the *klikushi* as perpetrators of superstition, but this time he listed them first, before "false miracles connected with icons, wells, springs, etc." He ended with a stern command that bishops obey these provisions, "And he [the bishop] shall forbid such nonsense, with the threat of malediction against recalcitrants who resist."[25] In practice, bishops were obliged to hand offenders over to civil authorities for sentencing and to impose penances upon those who had sincerely recanted. The Spiritual Regulation did not spell out the penalties the civil authorities were to mete out to shriekers and others who indulged in fraudulent activity. In fact, Peter I was not specific about this until the spring of 1722, when he commented on memoranda the Holy Synod sent him that such persons deserved "eternal banishment to the galleys with [their] nostrils slit."[26]

While the Spiritual Regulation remained the basis for church actions throughout the imperial period, within a decade Empress Anna (1730–1740) found it necessary to reinforce the provisions of that edict and Peter's earlier decrees. Influenced by the German Enlightenment, the empress had no tolerance for beliefs in sorcery, witchcraft, and *klikushestvo,* against which the laws had been ineffective. On 20 May 1731, the Governing Senate, in response to the empress's outrage that sorcery had not been eradicated, announced in Her Imperial Majesty's name that

> if henceforth, someone does not fear the wrath of God and . . . summons sorcerers to his home, or goes to their houses for some kind of magical assistance, or has conversations about magic with them . . . or follows their teaching, or if any sorcerers carry out evil [deeds] for themselves or on behalf of someone else, then these deceivers will be punished by death at the stake; and for those who request their [services] for soul-destroying profit, there will be severe punishment; they will be beaten with the knout, while others, by the seriousness of their guilt, will be sentenced to death.

Christian mercy was evident, however, as the decree concluded, "If the aforesaid swindlers . . . acknowledge their guilt, not having been reported by others, their guilt will be absolved without [their undergoing] any kind of torture."[27]

Responding to Empress Anna's ire that Peter the Great's laws were being ignored and to Prokopovich's continuing insistence upon vigilance against superstition, the Holy Synod in 1733 examined the case of a *klikusha* from Novgorod province who had been apprehended by civil authorities a few times for begging and traveling without a passport. While the archbishop of Novgorod, none other than Prokopovich himself, charged Mar'ia Semenova with fraudulently claiming to be possessed by 27 demons, his lengthy deposition focused on what he perceived to be the woman's immoral lifestyle for which she, not imaginary demons, was responsible. Semenova had given birth to an illegitimate child in the archbishop's home. Under interrogation, the unmarried woman admitted to having previously given birth to twins. After rejecting Semenova's claims that the illegitimate births had been the result of rapes, Prokopovich blamed her for having "the French disease" (i.e., syphilis). The authors of the Holy Synod's final report suspected Semenova of having committed infanticide. They furthermore found her guilty not only of deceiving others into believing that she was possessed but also of using salt in a love potion, saying an improper incantation over her cross, and threatening and using inappropriate language in addressing high-ranking individuals.[28]

Semenova's was an example par excellence of a woman who had defied all state and religious attempts to control a woman's body. Her transgressions of secular laws on mobility and of religious laws regarding morality were far more offensive to religious authorities than fraudulent possession. However, Prokopovich certainly had planted the seeds for equating shrieking with immorality.

Prosecution of this case did not mollify Empress Anna's concerns that laws against superstition were being violated. In November 1737 she again noted her displeasure, this time by pointing out that the number of shriekers had actually increased. She accused clerics and monks of openly defying these laws and encouraging *klikushestvo* by saying prayers of exorcism over demoniacs. Since the problem was particularly acute in Moscow, Anna ordered that the bishop of Moscow's spiritual administration be reprimanded for failing to uphold the provisions of the Spiritual Regulation pertaining to shriekers, whom she defined as "practitioners of superstition." The empress further proposed to Count Semen Andreevich Saltykov, the commander-in-chief of Moscow, that in order "to eradicate superstitions, not only should the bishop but also you [Saltykov] not hold back from the necessary eradication [of] and nipping [them] in the bud, because we have trust in you that you will have there both control over all such matters and adventures and will not . . . allow anything contrary to happen and will not abandon [your] earnest zeal, because you will have to answer for such matters and carelessness." All *klikushi* in Moscow were henceforth to be arrested and interrogated.[29]

In fulfilling the empress's command, Count Saltykov immediately seized two shriekers, Nenila Rzhavchikova and Anis'ia Bocharnikova. Rzhavchikova (née Eremeeva) had suffered from demon possession since 1701 when she was a sixteen-year-old peasant girl about to marry the soldier Sidor Rzhavchikov. She was currently living in Moscow. Anis'ia Fedorova also lived in Moscow and had turned for help to the miracle-working icon of the Mother of God in the Church of Varlaam the Miracle-Worker as well as the spiritual care of nuns at the Novodevichii Monastery. Under interrogation, no doubt accompanied by torture, both women upheld the stories of their possession, claiming that their illness was genuine and that they had not dabbled in magic or employed incantations. At the risk of angering the empress further, but with no evidence to the contrary, Saltykov had to release the women on bail on the provision that they not depart Moscow and that they immediately report to the appropriate judge upon request.[30]

Meanwhile, the Holy Synod had little choice but to respond to Her Majesty's indignation over the continuing existence of *klikushi.* A decree of 15 November reminded "not only the court but also other ecclesiastical and secular ranks" of their duty to uphold the Orthodox faith. In years past, the decree remarked, there "appeared among the people several who do not know the laws and rules and the true path to salvation completely, among whom one sometimes finds *klikushi* who create various superstitions that drive the simple people to doubt." Labeling the shriekers "ill-intentioned creators of superstition," the decree likened them to magicians and sorcerers. The Holy Synod reiterated the need for every bishop to be on the watch for these *klikushi* and to appoint special officers who would report the shriekers' identity and antics so that the civil authorities could take action against them. Repeating the Spiritual Regulation's stipulations regarding shriekers, the decree reminded bishops that they must send reports twice a year to the Holy Synod with information about the persistence of shriekers and other superstitious activities.[31]

While incensed at monks and parish clergy for accepting *klikushi* as genuinely possessed and not turning them over to the civil authorities, Empress Anna may have also been reacting to Senate reports from the summer and fall of 1737 when she issued her 1737 decree. Information from Russia's highest juridical body prompted the crown to consider the dangers of lax attitudes toward popular beliefs in bewitchment and accompanying ailments, including possession, on the part of secular government officials. An epidemic of *ikota* or severe and persistent hiccuping that had gotten out of hand among peasants in Mezensk district in Archangel province, striking more than 200 men and women, had come to the Senate's attention.[32] The symptoms of the ailment were akin to those of *klikushestvo,* with the exception that instead of the victims shrieking in the voices of wild animals, their speech patterns during a seizure were punctuated with continuous and painful hiccups. Like the *klikushi,* those who had *ikota* believed themselves to be bewitched; some also thought that they were possessed by demons that sorcerers had planted in their bodies.[33] In this epidemic, which had begun more than ten years earlier and spread over several villages, the victims had identified eight individuals they believed to have hexed them. As evidence mounted against the sacristan Emel'ian Popov and the villagers Nikifor and Osip Salmin, Onufii Titov, Ipat Klokotov, Ivan Sibiriakov, Aleksei Ul'ianov, and Dmitrii Suvorov, the sick, their relatives, and their neighbors brought the accused one at a time between 1730 and 1737 to the Mezensk governor's office, demanding justice. If irate peasants hoped the authorities would take swift action, they were sorely disappointed. The case dragged on for several years.

In 1737 the governor's office turned the matter over to higher authorities. Investigators had thus far determined the extent of the *ikota* epidemic and had gathered testimonies from numerous eyewitnesses. While co-villagers of the eight accused men testified that they could not be sure that the accused were actually dabbling in magic, they were convinced that the men were evil and consequently responsible for the epidemic. All the defendants denied any wrongdoing. Not knowing how to deal with the problem, the governor of Mezensk directed the case to the Archangel provincial office which, in turn, sent the matter on to the Senate. In late July 1737 the Senate issued a statement supporting the Mezensk governor's opinion that the interests of public order dictated exiling the defendants to remote ironworks in Siberia where they would be unable to harm the local population. Even though the accused had not confessed to causing the epidemic, local peasants were convinced of their guilt. The matter did not end there, however.[34]

Vice-Chancellor Count Mikhail Gavrilovich Golovin, having heard the decision, immediately overturned it on the grounds that the Senate had not conducted a rigorous investigation of its own to determine whether the epidemic involved a genuine illness. On 2 August 1737 he ordered the Senate to send a trustworthy detective to the villages infected by the epidemic of *ikota* so that he could view the sick firsthand and in the presence of a doctor. The detective and examining doctor could then determine conclusively whether the illness was a matter of God's will or had been caused by an evil delusion. Golovin also wanted the detective to gather character references regarding the accused persons from individuals not directly affected by the epidemic.[35]

In compliance with Golovin's demands, the Senate reopened the case. Under questioning, the victims of the epidemic pledged that they were not feigning their illness but could not prove that the accused had actually bewitched them. After almost 300 witnesses attested to the good characters of the accused men, the Senate ordered the Archangel provincial authorities to torture a few of the persons suffering from possession to find out if their affliction was genuine. Seven persons were suspended from gallows and beaten with whips and rods, but the punishments did not break their will. Finally on 11 January 1740, for lack of evidence, the Senate chose not to prosecute either the accused or the 207 individuals with the mysterious ailment.[36] Undoubtedly, the Mezensk incident remained a powerful reminder to the imperial government of the social disorder that an epidemic of *ikota* or *klikushestvo* could cause as well as the likelihood that similar disturbances were underreported.

In spite of continuing royal insistence that legal sanctions be taken against *klikushestvo,* shriekers were rarely detained for questioning. Of the 36 cases involving superstition that came before the Preobrazhenskii Prikaz and Secret Chancery from the time of Peter through 1760 (see Table 1.1), only 2 involved shriekers, the 1720 case involving 3 Moscow women and another case against a household serf who believed that she was hexed or demon possessed.[37] The government agencies were far more interested in slander against important personages, particularly against the ruler. Five cases concerned individuals who had cast aspersions on Empress Elizabeth's (1741–1762) character or on the reputation of her family members. Of these, four are particularly significant because of their connection to beliefs in possession and sorcery. Investigations were directed at the peasant Evdokim Tomilin (in 1746) and the townsman Petr Volkov (in 1750) for falsely claiming that Empress Elizabeth was bewitched. Given the tight association between possession and bewitchment, that accusation implied that Elizabeth was demon possessed. Such a charge questioned the ruler's legitimacy, which in itself was a sensitive issue because a palace coup had placed Elizabeth on the Russian throne. Subsequently, in 1752 the merchant Ivan Pichiuchin and the soldier Grigor Vorob'ev were tried separately for spreading the false rumor that the mother of Count Aleksei Razumovskii was a sorceress. This accusation struck at the heart of Empress Elizabeth's family since Count Razumovskii was Elizabeth's morganatic husband. Furthermore, the merchant Pichiuchin used his characterization of Razumovskii's mother to explain why Grand Duke Petr Fedorovich, the future Peter III, had no children by his wife Catherine.[38]

By far the greatest number of cases examined by the Preobrazhenskii Prikaz and Secret Chancery concerned individuals who through the use of magic could harm others. Many of the accused had in their posses-

Table 1.1 Religious Offenses Investigated by the Preobrazhenskii Prikaz and Tainaia Kantseliariia, 1700s–1760

Type	*Number*
Sorcery	17
Accused others of sorcery or of consulting sorcerers and fortunetellers	5
Apostasy	3
Superstition	2
Klikushestvo	2
Spreading false rumors that an important person is a witch	2
Veneration of false miracle-working icons or unsanctioned relics	2
Crimes against the sovereign	3
TOTAL	**36**

Source: RGADA, f. 7, op. 1, dela 75, 128, 328, 349, 393, 411, 440, 442, 546, 550, 553, 567, 635, 720, 964, 982, 1045, 1063, 1081, 1082, 1144, 1260, 1298, 1323, 1359, 1548, 1572, 1714, 1730, 1788, 1880, 1897, 1917, 1923, 1965, 1970.

sion talismans, papers or small booklets full of incantations for the purpose of either white or black magic, as well as roots and herbs that could be used to bewitch others. Others were guilty of consulting sorcerers. By focusing on individuals perceived to be capable of turning persons into *klikushi* or afflicting individuals in other ways rather than on the *klikushi* themselves, as dictated by law, the investigations illuminate the widespread belief, even among eighteenth-century government officials, in the possibility of bewitchment and accompanying possession. They were part of what John LeDonne calls "a frenzy of denunciations" in the first half of the eighteenth century that resulted from the anxiety and instability caused by two decades of war under Peter I, palace coups, and the fiscal crisis of the 1730s.[39]

The findings of Elena Borisovna Smilianskaia confirm the pattern exhibited by the cases heard before the Preobrazhenskii Prikaz and Secret Chancery: investigators were far more interested in apprehending magicians, sorcerers, and blasphemers than shriekers. Smilianskaia has studied 198 legal cases involving magic and superstition in the first half of the eighteenth century, extending her examination beyond the Preobrazhenskii Prikaz and Secret Chancery to include the Chancery of Searches (Sysknoi Prikaz); the regimental, voevoda, and provincial offices; the Chancery of Land Affairs; the Chief Magistrate's Office; and the Chancery of the Police. Just over 50 percent of these cases concerned individuals who used incantations and charms, with approximately a third of them involving instances of bewitchment or prevention against bewitchment.[40] The preponderance of men over women among the accused (in a ratio of almost 5:1) can be explained by the greater public roles of men and the greater likelihood that the activities of soldiers, clerics, scribes, and merchants attracted the authorities' attention.

With governmental offices not systematically apprehending shriekers, the Holy Synod, dependent upon denunciations of superstitious activity and blasphemy from diocesan sources, was no more vigilant against *klikushestvo*. Despite the 1737 reminder that bishops were required to send reports with this type of information to the Synod twice a year and the 1746 plea to clerical elders to report *klikushi* to their bishop, the bishops' communiqués were irregularly dispatched and the responses usually formalized.[41] In 1751, for example, only the bishops of Rostov, Suzdal', Archangel, and Pereiaslavl' mentioned incidents of superstition in a cryptic fashion, the latter two noting the presence of shriekers in their dioceses. Archbishop Varsonofii of Archangel reported that his diocese had a total of one *klikun* (the masculine form of *klikusha*) and seven *klikushi* in Kevrol'sk and Mezensk districts, all of whom were being investigated. The notoriety of the *ikota* epidemic in Mezensk district in the 1720s and 1730s, resulting in a Senate investigation, undoubtedly pressured the Archangel bishop to identify shriekers. Reporting the existence of one demon-possessed woman in its diocese, the Pereiaslavl' Consistory assured the Synod that she as well as those she had accused of bewitching her had been summoned. The remaining 21 bishops notified the Synod that "thanks be to God, everything is good [*slava Bogu vse dobre*]" in their dioceses.[42]

A major departure from the bishops' relative silence about superstitions, including beliefs in demon possession and bewitchment, appeared in the 1754 memorandum from Bishop Porfirii of Suzdal'. The bishop noted that while monasteries, clerical elders, and the spiritual administration had not supplied information about superstitious activity in the diocese between June 1751 and January 1752, magic, fortune-telling, and sorcery were so ubiquitous "that there is hardly a home in the city or surrounding villages without instances of satanic activity." After reassuring his superiors that he had battled false beliefs in sorcery and bewitchment as well as apostasy for half a dozen years, he had to admit that genuine cases of sorcerers releasing demons onto individuals had occurred in his diocese. "Hardly a wedding or birth" took place, Porfirii pointed out, without demonic interference, which in turn resulted in a decline in people's health and occasional deaths. He went on to explain that ecclesiastical courts were reluctant to investigate the perpetrators of such satanic activity because "everyone is gripped with fear" that they might die as a result and that he too was afraid of *porcha* or bewitchment. In fact, so afraid for his life was the bishop that he asked the Synod to relieve him of his post.[43]

The Suzdal' bishop's refreshing honesty regarding the pervasive belief in malefic magic bears comment. While legislation and a church campaign from 1740 onward had decried superstitious beliefs, Orthodox practices continued to make a connection between sorcery or witchcraft and demon possession. Priests asked their Orthodox communicants in the confessional not only if they had consulted magicians and sorcerers but also if they had used their services to bewitch individuals and make them ill.[44] Orthodox pronouncements in the confessional and religious texts confirmed in the minds of the faithful that evildoers could cause both illness and demon possession. As late as 1803 Archbishop Veniamin (1739–1811), in his manual explaining Orthodox rites, symbols, sacraments, and various prayers, pointed out, "Some people repudiate that the power and evil of demons bring illness upon people; but pious people do not doubt this truth." He cited Luke 13 to support this belief, noting on another page that prayer services for the possessed were necessary because of sorcerers' evil actions. The sixteenth edition of the manual, published in 1899, retained the section on the intimate relationship between bewitchment and possession.[45]

A case that came to the attention of the Holy Synod in 1770 underlines continuing beliefs in sorcery in Russian society and the continuing lax attitude toward *klikushi* among the ecclesiastical hierarchy. Pelageia Nikitina, a serf on the estate of Count Matvei Fedorovich Bukholov in Kostroma province, had been handed over to church authorities by the governor's office for causing demon possession and *klikota* (a merger of the terms *klikat'* [to shriek] and *ikota* [severe hiccuping as a result of bewitchment and sometimes possession]) among peasant women. Bishop Simon of Kostroma later reported to the Holy Synod that his investigation of the matter had revealed that Nikitina had been falsely charged with dabbling in sorcery by Bukholov's bailiff, Afanasii. The latter had extracted a confession out of the woman after severely beating her. A proponent of Enlightenment ideas that censured torture, Bishop Simon ordered that the bailiff be punished for his cruel behavior. Curiously, however, he said nothing about the women identified as shriekers, who, according to the law, should have been investigated and punished.[46]

A case before the Rostov Consistory in the mid-1760s sheds some light on ecclesiastical procedures regarding *klikushi* by suggesting that churchmen took seriously the question of a shrieker's authenticity when she was brought to their attention. The case concerned a 1764 incident in the village of Tishino, Iaroslavl' district, in which two peasant women accused their neighbor, Katerina Ivanova, of turning them into *klikushi*. That accusation led to Ivanova's incarceration in a provincial jail. When the matter came to the Rostov Consistory's attention, an investigation was ordered. After hearing various testimonies, the churchmen decided in April 1766 to send Ivanova to the women's monastery in Rostov. They instructed the abbess to use the Holy Scriptures to instill the fear of God in Ivanova to determine whether the peasant woman had in fact communicated with demons and bewitched her neighbors. They also summoned a physician to examine the possessed women. Upon learning from the abbess that Ivanova's earlier confession of dabbling in witchcraft and consorting with demons to civil authorities had been extracted under torture, the ecclesiastics absolved Ivanova of sorcery, setting a precedent for Bishop Simon's 1770 decision. At the same time, they also refrained from punishing the *klikushi* because the medical examiner pronounced the women to be suffering from a genuine ailment. In other words, because the shriekers were not feigning their possession, they were not punishable by law.[47]

In 1771 the Holy Synod did prosecute shriekers who appeared to have falsely accused others of bewitching them.[48] The church had a particular interest in a case involving members of the lower clergy, including a parish priest who had previously committed other infractions of ecclesiastical law. In such instances the Synod did not have to defer to civil authorities, but could directly punish the clerical offenders. The initial report to Bishop Feodosii of Kolomna came from the priest Iakov Timofeev of the Bogoslovskaia Church in January 1770. Father Iakov noted that the Kolomna merchant Makar Shchurov's twelve-year-old nephew Pamfil had been acting like a shrieker by speaking in the manner of a bird and dog and claiming that someone had hexed him. Responding to the communiqué, the Kolomna Consistory dispatched a magistrate to query the boy who explained that two years earlier he had been in priest Iakov Timofeev's home learning how to write "when he was suddenly struck to the ground." Since that time, the boy had been ill almost every day but did not know either the cause of the illness or the nature of his fits.

When Pamfil was taken to the consistory for further questioning, he had a seizure during which he fell to the floor, thrashed his legs and arms about, and again shrieked like a *klikusha;* this time he identified the sacristan Stepan Prokopiev and the priest's son Vasilii Evseev as those who had bewitched and caused him to be possessed. To ascertain whether he was telling the truth, the investigators stuck a needle in the boy's foot while he was having the seizure. They incredulously reported that his response was to get up immediately as if there were nothing wrong with him. The bishop of Kolomna continued the interrogation of Pamfil. Faced with repeated admonitions to speak the truth or face the consequences of God's wrath and no doubt afraid of yet another assault with the needle, the boy succumbed to pressure and abandoned his previous story. He now confessed that Father Iakov's wife, Praskov'ia Petrova, and son Tikhon had promised him a shirt and money, in return for which he was to act as though he were possessed and cast aspersions on the sacristan and another priest's son. Noting that he had received money from Iakov as well, Pamfil implicated the priest in the scam.

With Pamfil's confessions in hand, the Kolomna Consistory summoned the Timofeev family for questioning. They immediately denied Pamfil's charges against them. Praskov'ia Petrova claimed that she herself had been struck by the same affliction as Pamfil and that the source of that illness was nothing other than the sacristan Prokopiev who was angry at her for refusing to buy cloth from him. After supporting his wife's testimony, the priest Timofeev added that a sorcerer from the village Nadeevo, now deceased, had treated his wife and that he had confessed this action to his spiritual confessor, also deceased, for which he had received a penance. Further investigation disclosed that Timofeev possessed questionable booklets containing prescriptions for the treatment of bewitched individuals. It also revealed that both the priest and his wife had slandered the sacristan Prokopiev in order to force him to vacate his position in favor of their son Tikhon.

Timofeev's previous misdemeanors did not bode well for him in this case. In 1752 he had been fined and barred from conducting religious services for giving holy relics to the Simeonovskii sacristan Petr Kozmin without requisite permission. Twelve years later, the consistory ordered Father Iakov to do four months' penance in the Predtechevo Monastery in Tula because he had slandered a priest by calling him a demon. Subsequently, he served two months' penance in another monastery for quarreling with a priest in church and uttering abusive words in the consistory. In the meantime, the consistory began investigating Timofeev's participation in the conversion of 83 peasants to Old Belief.

Given Timofeev's latest attempt at slander, the Holy Synod upheld the consistory's decisions. It ordered that Timofeev be defrocked and exiled with his wife, and their son Tikhon dispatched into the army. Commanding that the questionable booklets be burned, the Synod left the Kolomna magistrate responsible for dealing with the merchant's son Pamfil. Lastly, it lessened the sentence of Timofeev's father-in-law, the priest Petr Sergeev, requiring him to sing in a monastery choir for half a year instead of a year as penance for having given Timofeev one of the suspect notebooks.

The tendency of both the Holy Synod and civil authorities in the eighteenth century to be concerned more with individuals they believed dabbled in magic than with *klikushi* who thought themselves the victims of such magic provoked the Senate into action in 1770. Members of the Senate were reacting negatively to a case from the previous year in which the Holy Synod, in the aftermath of civil and ecclesiastical investigations, had instructed the bishop of Ustiug (in Archangel province) to admonish the peasants Egor Pystin, Zakhar Martiushev, the maiden Avdot'ia Bozhukova, and the soldier's wife Avdot'ia Pystina of Iarensk district for having engaged in sorcery and abjured the Christian faith. Since the bishop's report noted that the culprits wished to repent voluntarily, the Synod had also ordered that the deviants undergo a penance once they had served their criminal sentence. The penance involved a five-year incarceration in appropriate monasteries where the penitents were to perform heavy labor for the first year, routinely attend church services, and go to confession and take communion four times a year during the fast periods. In accordance with the law, the Synod turned the peasants over to the Ustiug Provincial Office for sentencing at the secular level. Having been asked by the provincial office for advice on the case and having reviewed all of the documentation, the Senate berated the judges at the Iarensk governor's office for their "ignorance and unforgivable carelessness," resulting in what it termed a preposterous investigation. It went on to accuse local officials of acting above the law in whipping the alleged sorcerers and judges for accepting contradictory and incredible confessions from the accused.[49]

The real culprits who had started the above affair, as far as the senators were concerned, were *klikushi*. The Senate described the shriekers as "several dissolute girls and women [who], pretending to be bewitched, out of spite and in a drunken state shrieked out the names of the abovementioned" peasants. The women had accordingly falsely charged the named persons as having caused their possession.[50] The senators' focus on the shriekers as women is pivotal here. While previous legislation and cases favored the gender-laden term *klikushi* (female shriekers), they mentioned the possibility of men being shriekers and sometimes identified men among victims of possession. However, there is no doubt here of the gendered distinction of *klikushestvo* as specifically female deviant behavior. The senators' characterization of the *klikushi* as drunken evoked a similar characterization by the church father John Chrysostom in his censure of women who had unwittingly served demons.[51] By using the adjective "dissolute," the senators also echoed the sentiments expressed by the Holy Synod in a 1733 case concerning a false shrieker. Adding lewd sexual behavior to the list of shriekers' characteristics made these women rather than demons responsible for their actions.

The Senate believed that Ustiug authorities had been remiss in not apprehending and investigating the demoniacs and instead forcing false confessions out of innocent victims through torture. It consequently ordered the delinquent local police and elders to be cudgeled publicly and "without mercy" and the shriekers to be whipped in their neighbors' presence. The Senate announced that the details and outcome of this unfortunate matter as well as the obligation to uphold the decrees of Peter I and Anna against shriekers needed to be brought to officials' attention not only in Archangel province but also in all other provinces and towns. Furthermore, the senators pronounced that "every sensible person [knows] . . . it is impossible to bewitch people by any supernatural means."[52] The 1770 Senate ruling thus underscored the failure of both government officials and the Orthodox Church to prosecute *klikushi* and the continuing beliefs in sorcery and witchcraft at all levels of Russian society.

The church's continuing reluctance to punish shriekers according to the law is exemplified by the 1785 plea of Veniamin, bishop of Archangel and Kholmogory. While bringing a case involving 19 *klikushi* to the Archangel governor's attention, he nonetheless asked that the shriekers not be punished as criminals. Veniamin stressed that because the individuals were suffering from natural illnesses, they required "the means to cure those illnesses."[53]

It was only during the nineteenth century that criminal courts began to reject the premise that individuals could actually control the supernatural by magical means. In the first half of the century, judges convicted alleged sorcerers and witches, but more willingly followed the precepts of the law by charging them with sedition and deception. By the middle of the century, however, as the belief in malefic magic became mainly that of peasants and the poor urban folk, judges voiced their reluctance to hear such cases. Criminal courts in the nineteenth century were far more likely to convict shriekers on the charge of fraud.[54] Judges accordingly consulted doctors on a more regular basis to provide medical evaluations of *klikushi*.[55] Trained to find specific ailments, doctors rejected demon possession or bewitchment as legitimate causes of *klikushestvo,* preferring to use the increasingly popular term "hysteria" to identify these women's illnesses.

The Russian Orthodox Church, however, retained its reluctance to follow the Spiritual Regulation and state law to the letter and to turn *klikushi* over to civil authorities. And it resisted the temptation to hold the possessed responsible for their actions. Explanations for the church's continuing reluctance to punish *klikushi* may be found in its attitude toward the devil and demons and in the role that verified miraculous cures of possession played in identifying holy individuals as saints in the Orthodox Church. As long as miraculous exorcisms continued to provide a key to religious truth, the church was not prepared to relegate demon possession to the status of mere superstition.

ORTHODOXY'S TRIUMPH OVER THE DEVIL

The Orthodox understanding of the devil and the miraculous are intertwined because both are predicated upon the notion of a sinful world ushered in by Adam and Eve's obedience to the devil.[56] According to Orthodoxy, the devil is a divine creature subordinate to God. Early Orthodox theologians believed that "though he [the devil] was 'the enemy of God,' he was also the 'vindicator' and the 'servant' of God" who needed God's permission to act against humans, who, despite the Fall, exercised free will.[57] The catechism of the Russian Orthodox Church describes evil angels as "devils, that is, slanderers or deceivers," "because they are ever laying snares for men, seeking to deceive them, and inspire them with false notions and evil wishes." However, the Orthodox Church maintains, demonic power is temporary and inferior to that of goodness, which ultimately triumphs. Through Christ, prayer, confession, and contrition, Orthodox theologians contend, the sins of humanity can be absolved. By receiving Holy Communion the faithful seek spiritual and physical well-being. According to the communion prayer of John Chrysostom, the Blood and Body of Christ not only relieve believers of the gravity of their sins, but also protect them against the devil's actions by conquering their evil instincts.[58] The Lord's Prayer also asks God to save believers from the devil.[59] Those who thus embrace the Son of God, according to Orthodox dogma, can attain God's infinite mercy through the intercession of saints and the Mother of God, all of whom "partake of the Divine Spirit."[60] Miracles involving saints' exorcisms and the healing of other bodily afflictions brought on by demons constitute a further sign of God's grace and love of humankind. Even the most holy person's faith, according to Orthodoxy, is repeatedly tested on earth by assaults by the devil or his demonic minions. Because not all humans are capable of achieving the state of holiness, the Orthodox argument continues, their travails against the devil are not always successful. Demons can inhabit and torment a Christian's body. But there is always hope of victory over darkness.

That triumph is best represented in the Russian Orthodox preparation for Easter, the most important festival in the Orthodox calendar, which relives not only Christ's Resurrection but also the victory over hell, the devil, evil spirits, and sin.[61] During Matins on the Sunday of Forgiveness on the eve of Lent, the Orthodox faithful are reminded: "the time is now at hand for us to start upon the spiritual contest and to gain the victory over the demonic powers." On the first Sunday in Lent, the text of Matins invokes the power of Christ in his iconographic images: "Depicting Thy divine form in ikons, O Christ, we openly proclaim Thy Nativity, Thine ineffable miracles and Thy voluntary Crucifixion. So the devils are driven out in fear." "Great is the power of the Cross!" the faithful are told on the Third Sunday in Lent, for "when devils look upon it, they are burnt; by the sign of the Cross they are consumed with fire." Finally, in the fifth week of Lent, the faithful beseech God to snatch them from the devil's snares, "for it is Thy will that all men should be saved and come to knowledge of the truth."[62]

Victory over the devil is also a theme in the Orthodox baptismal liturgy. The exorcism rites in the baptismal service, as in the Latin Church, were holdovers from ancient times when baptism of adults in conversions from paganism to Christianity liberated them from demonic influences and emphasized the authority of the apostles and, later, bishops. Expelling demons from infants through baptism served to "mitigat[e] demonic influences with each new addition to the human race."[63]

Liturgical texts and prayers were not the only sources that taught the Orthodox faithful in the eighteenth and nineteenth centuries to believe in the triumphant powers of Christ, the Holy Cross, and the saints over the powers of the devil and his servant demons. For the mass of illiterate believers, iconography served an important didactic function. Given the strict rules governing the images that could be depicted on icons and in frescoes, the limited number of Byzantine prototypes for such images, and the late onset of apocalyptic thinking in Russian religious culture, representations of the devil and demons were relatively few in Russian Orthodox art.

Iconographic Images

It was not until 1405 that iconographic representations of the Apocalypse first appeared in Muscovy in the frescoes by Theophanes the Greek in the Kremlin's Annunciation Cathedral. Over the next two centuries, depictions of the Apocalypse became commonplace in Russian Orthodox churches and part of parishioners' overall spiritual understanding. With the emphasis on the resurrection of the righteous and the ultimate triumph of the angels over their demonic adversaries, however, these portrayals conveyed a more positive message than apocalyptic images in Western European art.[64]

Apocalyptic images influenced portrayals of the Last Judgment, but once again they emphasized the Resurrection. Scenes depicting hell and the torments awaiting unrepentant sinners did not constitute the focus of the frescoes and icons. In a representative example of the Russian genre, a mid-fifteenth-century Novgorodian icon of the Last Judgment, the images of evil occupy about a third of the icon, relegated to the lower right-hand corner.[65] A small, human-figured Satan with raised hair, shaggy beard, and wings but no other discernible features is seated in a fiery red hell holding the soul of Judas. Out of hell a long serpent with rings along its body extends upward toward Adam's heel. The souls of the dead have to pass through all 20 or so rings, or tollgates, which signify various vices. The tollgates are manned by tiny winged demons ready to deliver rejected souls to hell. As an angel weighs the good and evil acts of each soul making its way through the tollgate to heaven, a small winged demon attempts to hook and weigh down the cup containing evil to increase the devil's bounty. Two larger cloaked demons with wings and raised hair are poised on the serpent to deliver the eternally damned to the underworld, but even these demons are smaller in size than the angels and archangels. Also insignificant in size, bound in a circle of red to the left of the archangel Michael, are the four beasts cited in the seventh chapter of Daniel.[66]

The icon painter of the 1680s' Last Judgment in the Church of the Savior in Rostov added a ferocious-looking beast upon which Satan sits with Judas on his lap. Out of the jaws of Hades comes the reptilian tail of the serpent.[67] Even here, however, the emphasis of the Last Judgment is on salvation, resurrection, and a defeated Antichrist.

The mouth of hell image is far more ominous than depictions of hell in portrayals of the "Heavenly Ladder," that is, the ladder to salvation, a common theme in sixteenth- and seventeenth-century icons.[68] As monks ascend the ladder toward heaven and the safe arms of angels, others are flung off the rungs by demons into the gaping mouth of hell, personified by the Devil. "In an inversion of spirit possession, torment after death involves being inside the Devil's body, rather than having demons inside . . . [the] body. . . . This iconographic teaching emphasizes that the body is the locus of punishment and damnation as well as of sin."[69]

The triumph of good over evil prevails in other images of the devil in popular icons such as those of the archangel Michael, St. George, and St. Nikita. Depicted either as a serpent or a human with bestial and sometimes reptilian features, the devil imparts to his viewers "a lack of moral discernment."[70] Nowhere is the immorality of the devil clearer than in the nineteenth-century icon of the trumpeter archangel Michael (Moscow school).[71] Astride a magnificent winged horse, the archangel is spearing a naked devil who is depicted with a human male face in his groin. Tumbled buildings signifying the archangel's destruction of Sodom and Gomorrah in the Old Testament and "the visionary destruction of Sodom in the Apocalypse" line the top of the devil's prostrate body.[72] In all icons depicting the vanquished devil, the archangel or saint looms above him. The holy figure is always portrayed as several times larger and more powerful than his foe.

Images of demon possession in Russian iconography are rare. When they do appear, they tend to be part of icons that contain multiple scenes bordering the figure of either a saint or the Mother of God. Such scenes illustrate events in the saint's life as well as examples of his miracles. Icons of St. Nicholas the Wonderworker, one of the most popular of this genre, sometimes include one or both of his miracles involving demons. One depicts the healing of a possessed man, the other the exorcism of a devil from a monastery.[73] In the representation of the exorcism on an early-sixteenth-century icon, the black winged demon is tiny so as not to detract viewers' attention from the overwhelming light and power of goodness.[74] By far the most striking image of demons possessing a man appears in the 1697 icon "Miracles from the Icon *Znamenie* [Sign] Mother of God," found in the Church of Il'ia Prorok (the Prophet) in Iaroslavl'.[75] The *Znamenie* Mother of God is distinguished by the portrayal of Mary with her hands raised and with the infant Christ centered on her chest. In a border miniature, three demons, one of whom wields an axe, attack the Kievan monk Gavriil. The evil spirits are composites of humans and beasts: they have the bodies of men, but also tails, horns, wings, taloned feet, and clawed paws. Their faces vary, with one of the demons having an animal-like head and bird's beak and the other two caricatures of human visages. The main demon, painted completely in black, appears clean-shaven, while the other human-faced (and lighter colored) unclean spirit sports a pointed beard and bulbous nose. In the presence of male onlookers, including among them a saint (depicted in the lower right-hand corner), an archangel rescues the monk from his tormentors.

Much darker in tone, but nonetheless positive in its message, is a sixteenth-century icon miniature attributed to the theologian and philologist Maxim the Greek (1480–1556). It portrays the demons' victory over a commoner who neglected to make the sign of the cross. A demon literally possesses the man by sitting on his head, while the demon to the man's left holds the man's right hand and the demon on his right carries a pen and a piece of parchment on which a contract with the devil is written.[76] The miniature's purpose is to impress upon its viewers the importance of making the sign of the cross upon all occasions as protection against the devil. As Archbishop Veniamin explained at the beginning of the nineteenth century,

> And if you make the sign of the cross . . . on your face not one of the unclean spirits can come close to you because he sees the sword that will fatally wound him. For, if we, seeing the location where the damned are punished, are horrified, then think about how the devils and demons will suffer when they see the instrument with which Christ will destroy all their strength, and chop off the serpent's head.[77]

Strikingly absent from the possession icons is the image of the disheveled and writhing woman, so common in Western European, particularly Italian, medieval iconography.[78] In medieval Russia diabolic possession was constructed in religious art as a male phenomenon. That emphasis on men is mirrored in the early medieval lives of the saints, only to be modified from the fifteenth century onward as individual experiences of laymen and laywomen with the miraculous became more commonplace.

Miraculous Exorcisms

Hagiographies or biographies of the saints supplemented iconographic and liturgical sources of information for the laity. Composed by monks and clerics, they taught Christians how to live exemplary lives, to maintain their faith during times of adversity, and to depend upon the saints for exorcism and healing. Such stories were widely available to and popular among the laity in the eighteenth and particularly the nineteenth centuries in printed form. Thus the lives of the earliest saints and their experiences with demons were just as relevant to laypersons as those of later saints. Depictions of demon possession changed subtly over the centuries as the focus shifted in the fifteenth century from saints' experiences to those of laymen and laywomen, and then in the late eighteenth century to those of predominantly women.

Because the Kievan and early Muscovite vitae were an integral part of the process of Christianization and the Russian Orthodox Church's goal of supplementing Byzantine saints with native sources of holy men, these hagiographies focused on hermit monks who imitated the earliest saints in rejecting the civilized world; their retreat into the wilderness meant that they had to contend continuously with attacks by demons. They highlighted monks' personal physical struggles with demons who appeared before them in various guises, such as "shameless" women, beasts of all types, and reptiles. In most cases, the ascetics' bodies suffered horrifying physical assaults from demons but rarely actual penetration. Rather than emphasizing individual miracle cures and exorcisms, the pre-fifteenth-century vitae showcased public miracles (for example, the divine provisioning of aid in battle, the multiplying of loaves of bread, and the eradication of a plague) that affected an entire community, a monastery, or the state. Descriptions of commoners being miraculously cured of ailments were infrequent, although the author of the combined vitae of the popular saints Boris and Gleb, Kievan Rus's (880–1237) first holy martyrs, in quoting John the Theologian, pointed to the saints' powers of exorcism: "'Those who believe in God and in the hope of the resurrection we call not dead, for dead flesh, O Lord, can work miracles': For demons are exorcised by them, diseases are driven out, infirmities expelled, the blind given sight, lepers cleansed, and injury and sorrow ended."[79]

The compendium of vitae from Kievan Rus's first and most important monastic institution, the Monastery of the Caves, written in the late eleventh and early twelfth centuries, however, does include a description of a demon-possessed commoner that served as a model for later descriptions of demoniacs as having incredible strength and requiring restraints to prevent them from injuring themselves and others. According to the story about "Lavrentii the Solitary," "A certain man was brought to him [Lavrentii] from Kiev, who was possessed by a demon which the solitary was unable to cast out. It was a ferocious demon, like wood, which ten men could scarcely carry, and yet this monk singlehandedly took hold of him and bound him." Lavrentii eventually set off with the demoniac for the Monastery of the Caves; the miraculous exorcism at the hands of 30 deceased holy men, previously monks at that monastery, occurred on the road.[80]

Miracle tales relating similar testimonies of laypersons became standard additions to saints' vitae from the late fifteenth century onward. Paul Bushkovitch describes the shift from public miracles to those on a personal level as mirroring a change that had occurred earlier in Western Europe in the twelfth and thirteenth centuries. The focus on the individual's recovery through the intercession of a holy person, according to Bushkovitch, reflected "a more private and inward Orthodoxy."[81]

As the church became interested in recognizing locally venerated saints, it held inquests into the miraculous workings reported to have occurred at particular holy persons' graves or before individual icons. Monks and parish priests recorded oral testimonies of individuals who had experienced and witnessed the miraculous. Although the recorders standardized the testimonies' language to conform to previous models of hagiographical literature, the miracle stories constitute an invaluable source for the study of possession.[82] They reveal different experiences of possession, the ways in which the gendering of possession changed with time, and ways in which the church sought to teach believers aspects of good Christian living.

Examples from the miracle cycle in the life of St. Kirill of Beloozero (founder of the Uspenskii Monastery, also known as the Kirillo-Belozerskii Monastery, in 1397), composed in the mid-fifteenth century, provide a sense of the variety of experiences of those suffering from demon possession. The first example contains the typical components of a miracle story: the individual about to be healed, the length of time he was afflicted, and the exorcism at the saint's grave. Details of the exorcism are somewhat truncated:

> They brought a certain man named Feodor, cruelly tortured by a demon, to Blessed Kirill's monastery. That Feodor was a person of a certain master named Vasilii, who, as a result of many torments, constantly seeing at home how the demon distressed that Feodor, sent him away. And he suffered, tortured by the demon, for eleven years. And when they brought him to the blessed Kirill's grave, he received a healing and became healthy with the help of Our Lady, the Mother of God, through St. Kirill's prayers.

The story's focus—and this is where it departs from most miracle stories—is on Feodor's bringing a demon back upon himself through an action of self-will:

> And that Feodor received from the prior a commandment never to eat meat. But that Feodor happened to be mowing hay with other people and when they all began to eat meat, so that Feodor began to eat meat, having forgotten the commandment never to eat meat. And when this happened, [i.e.,] when he ate the meat, the demon once again attacked him and began to torment him more than before. But later he regained consciousness and, recognizing his sin, understood that he would endure this, having violated the commandment. And he once again rushed to the blessed Kirill's monastery and to his miracle-working grave and with tears asked forgiveness, which he received as a result of Christ's grace and the blessed Kirill's prayers. And after that he served in that cloister in various works of penance for many years, and I saw him there as well.[83]

The first part of the miracle story maintains silence on the causation of Feodor's possession, while the second lays responsibility for Feodor's possession directly on him. Although Feodor might not have been able to ward off the demons' initial attack, he could have prevented their invasion of his person the second time by obeying the prior and not defiling his mouth and body. Here the unclean spirits are clearly identified as not only entering a human through the mouth, but also inhabiting the realm of the body's impurities, the digestive tract. Although believers receive the Eucharist through the mouth, they first have to cleanse their bodies by fasting. The Body and Blood of Christ bypass the stomach as it heads straight for the soul.[84] The binary oppositions of purity/impurity and good/evil are thus starkly presented.

Another tale in the miracle cycle of St. Kirill describes in far greater detail than the first story the characteristics of demon possession. The victim this time is Ivan, a priest's son, who, "cruelly tortured by an evil demon, was tied by the arms and legs. And that Ivan raged so strongly and suffered cruelly that they even blindfolded him" in order to lead him forcibly to the Kirillo-Belozerskii Monastery. "His eyes," continues the tale, "were bloody and frightened everyone, and he made indecent sounds: he growled like an animal, and sang in a horribly squeaky and frightening [voice]. And as a result, his appearance was absurd [i.e., unnatural] and frightening. He struck everyone [and] barked at everyone. And he spoke a lot: he even abused God,—he himself did not speak, but the demon living inside him spoke through his mouth."[85] The demon's violent incursion into and total occupation of its victim's body strips the demoniac of control over his limbs and voice. The possessed is but a shell of his former self as his body is subjected to the torments of hell. Such descriptions became standard in tales of the demon possessed.

In the pre-Petrine miracle cycles of northern saints, such as St. Kirill, miraculous cures of demoniacs figure prominently. According to Isolde Thyrêt, the percentage of miracles involving possession ranges from about a third (in the miracle cycles of Nil Stolbenskii and Ioann and Loggin of Iarenga) to more than half (59% in the miracle cycle of St. Sergii of Obnora and 62% in that of Aleksandr Kushtskii). Harking back to the ancient Christian tradition, saints' cures of pagan demoniacs were part of the Christianization process and establishment of powerful local saints' cults by new communities of believers. Women appear far less frequently than men as recipients of miraculous cures of all types of illnesses, including possession: only 25 percent of those cured are women.[86]

Thyrêt explains the gender discrepancies in the northern miracle cycles as resulting from the monastic control of saints' cults in the sixteenth and seventeenth centuries. Most of the saints celebrated in the Muscovite period were monks or hermits. Since monasteries often barred or at least discouraged women from entering their grounds, for fear of their defiling holy space and threatening the monks' salvation, women were more often than not denied personal access to sacred relics and monastic shrines. It is little wonder that their participation in the veneration of saints was more limited. Women's access to saints tended to come more commonly through apparitions and dreams, and their spiritual experience thus tended to take place in domestic rather than public settings.[87]

A comparison of the vitae and supplemental miracle cycles of Kirill and Martinian of Beloozero (the latter was canonized at the church councils of 1547 and 1549 and buried in the Ferapontov Monastery) illustrates the differences encountered by male and female demoniacs.[88] Only one of eight possession cures attributed to the holy intercession of St. Kirill involved a woman, in this case a member of the Muscovite aristocracy (a *boiarynia*). While the narrative acknowledges the woman's visit to the Kirillo-Belozerskii Monastery, it makes no mention of the monks allowing Feodosiia to venerate and pray before St. Kirill's relics.[89] By contrast, three of the tales involving possessed men specifically refer to the men being cured at the saint's grave.

The miracle stories connected to Martinian of Beloozero have a higher representation of women among the possessed (three women to two men). The fact that monks permitted all three women to pray before St. Martinian's grave suggests that the abbot was more lenient about allowing women inside the monastery. Interestingly, two of the stories note that the possessed women had previously been unsuccessful in their supplications to St. Kirill, who clearly had little sympathy for women. In contrast to the men's cure narratives, each of the three women's stories emphasizes the direct intercession of God or the saint, rather than the supplication of monks, on their behalf.[90]

According to one tale, relatives who brought a possessed woman named Ekaterina from a nearby village to Martinian's grave "were not in a position to have a service sung, hampered [as they were] by poverty and did not find help among any of those present." However, the narrator reminds his readers, "God cares for everyone equally. From that time onward that woman became healthy, healed from her ailment by the grace of God."[91] Ekaterina's faith and the sincere tears she shed as she prayed, not the monks' prayers, were at the root of her healing.

In another miracle tale a priest began to perform a service to the Immaculate Mother of God when suddenly a possessed woman at the monastery gates had a vision of St. Martinian attacking her demon. None of the possessed men in the cycle had the benefit of an apparition of Martinian. In other words, Martinian had already begun exorcising the demon before the female demoniac had reached his relics and the service had commenced.[92]

A third possessed woman claimed to have seen St. Martinian as well: "That Miracle worker, having raised himself from the grave, blessed me with the cross and left." This story also does not credit the priest performing the liturgy with any part in the successful exorcism. The afflicted woman's direct access to the saint was key in invoking God's grace.[93] Thus, as a result of strict monastic codes, medieval Russian women experienced sympathetic saints more personally than did men.

Another striking contrast between female and male demoniacs appears in a few sixteenth- and seventeenth-century Muscovite miracle stories in which women are sexually assaulted by demons. While demons are generally portrayed in the genre as successfully penetrating the bodies of both laymen and laywomen, sexual relations between unclean spirits and men are not part of the miracle narratives, in spite of the fact that demons sometimes appear before men in the guise of women and awaken their lust. Ultimately, the demons of the miracle tales are male, having the same physical desires as men. In the Sol'vychegodskii cycle of miracles attributed to St. Prokopii of Ustiug, for example, a demon deceives a married woman into thinking that he is her husband. He lives with her a long time and "sleeps with her at night." Similarly, in the life of Sergei of Nurom, the maiden Antonida is duped by a demon in human form; he "entered her and lived with her for a year and a half."[94] The most famous of the miracle stories about sexually active devils involved the married woman Solomoniia, whom the demons impregnated (to be discussed below). While sexual relations between demons and women occur in some miracle tales, the theme is not pervasive; in fact, it is the exception rather than the rule, mirroring the dominant medieval Orthodox images of women as good wives and mothers.[95]

Miracles involving exorcisms of demons continued to play an important role in defining sainthood in the post-Petrine period, but possession itself became increasingly the experience of women. While far more skeptical about the possibility of miracles in an age of rationalism, the Holy Synod occasionally sanctioned a canonization, but only if the saint's miracles were thoroughly verified. The Holy Synod's published list of miracles ascribed to the relics of Dmitrii, metropolitan of Rostov from 1702 to 1709,[96] for example, provides fascinating testimony about the gender and social identity of mid-eighteenth-century demoniacs. The 232 miracles (affecting 243 persons) attributed to Dmitrii, occurred between 1753 and 1762, that is, both before and after his 1757 canonization.[97] Because two of the cases do not involve healings but other issues (one concerned a "heathen's" conversion to Orthodoxy, the other a soldier saved in battle), they are not considered here. Of the 241 individuals cured of ailments at Dmitrii's grave, just under 20 percent are identified as suffering from possession by demons or unclean spirits or having characteristics associated with demon possession (hiccuping and shaking; a wind-borne illness; illness as a result of a hex or bewitchment; and shouting, fits, and beating oneself). Nearly 45 percent of the demoniacs are either peasants or serfs, and almost 28 percent stem from the urban and merchant estates. Women outnumber men by a striking ratio of 3.3:1, thus reversing the predominance of men over women as recipients of cures in Muscovite miracle tales. Even in the late-seventeenth-century miracle stories attributed to Patriarch Nikon, only 4 of 18 individuals (or 22%) cured of evil spirits are women.[98] Similarly, men continued significantly to outnumber women (five to two) among demoniacs exorcised miraculously by the Icon of the Tolg Theotokos in the early eighteenth century.[99] Already by the mid-eighteenth century, however, the gender ratio began to change as women accounted for 41 percent of those cured of possession in the officially recognized miracles that occurred before the Akhtyrka icon of the Most Holy Mother of God.[100] Together with the Dmitrii miracle stories, the Akhtyrka miracle tales suggest a growing number of women among the demon possessed in the eighteenth century.

The preponderance of women as victims of demon possession in the Dmitrii miracle stories suggests that by the mid-eighteenth century, women were more likely than men to identify themselves as being possessed. The influence of the 1670s miracle story involving the demoniac Solomoniia may account in part for the rise in the number of female demoniacs. Popularized in the eighteenth century, the tale focuses upon a recently married woman being seduced by demons who appear before her in different forms, sometimes as handsome youths and sometimes as hairy, shaggy animals. A pregnant and tormented Solomoniia is miraculously divested of her demons and devilish offspring through a cesarean section performed by Saints Prokopii and Ioann of Ustiug and the intercession of the Mother of God. What is most interesting about the story is its emphasis on Solomoniia's involuntary seduction and possession. The tale's author lays blame for the woman's possession squarely on the shoulders of the parish priest who baptized her. Disobeying church regulations, the priest had been inebriated during the baptism and had conducted only half the service. Given the integral role that exorcism plays in the baptismal service, the priest's sloppiness guaranteed that at some point Solomoniia would be assaulted by the devil or his minions. Some readers and editors of the miracle story, according to A. V. Pigin, considered Solomoniia to be a holy woman. Absolved of responsibility for her actions and acting in the passive manner believed appropriate for a woman, Solomoniia represented for eighteenth-century Russian women a role model of a saved religious woman. Her experience with demons was far more plausible for laywomen than that of the Byzantine saint Theodora of Aleksandria who, constantly hounded by demons to commit adultery, left her husband, dressed as a man, and entered a monastery to live among men, only to have the demons follow her there. At the same time, "The Tale of Solomoniia" emphasized women's vulnerability to demons. The demons' torments brought together in one place for the first time the tortures described in other miracle stories: "The demons carry Solomoniia into the forest and water, leave her in a field naked, throw her from one corner of a church to another, hang her up to the ceiling, throw her from up there onto the ground, force her to bear their children, cut her with knives, throw lances at her, spit and blow their noses at her, suck her breasts, tear her womb to pieces, gnaw her left side, yell in various voices, throw her down on the church floor during a service, etc."[101] The impact of "The Tale of Solomoniia" on a lay audience, and especially on women, must have been powerful.

The predominance of female demoniacs in the Dmitrii miracle tales also reflects the cultural demotion of possession by state and church from acceptable to fraudulent behavior in the Petrine period and the preference for the gender-laden term *"klikushi"* (i.e., female shriekers) over the gender-neutral term *"besnovatye"* (demon possessed) to identify that behavior. The notion that the loss of control over the body constituted a feminine rather than a masculine trait played a role in the change of nomenclature. If a man became possessed, he was assumed to betray feminine characteristics. Given the cultural and legal reconfiguration of possession in the eighteenth century, men were less likely to identify themselves and to be identified as demoniacs.

Despite their following the structural pattern that Muscovite writers had devised, the Dmitrii miracle stories depart from the medieval representation of women's private spiritual encounters with saints. All of them involve a visitation to Dmitrii's grave at the Iakovlevskii Monastery in Rostov and an exorcism by a monk, suggesting a relaxation in rules concerning women's access to saints' relics within monastery walls. Women's experience with the miraculous, as recounted in the hagiography, now commonly occurred in public and depended upon the intercession of a monk or cleric to mediate between the believer and saint. The tale of the possessed peasant woman, Evfimiia Petrova, is representative of the new genre. According to the narrator, this widow of the village Ugodich' in Rostov district had been tormented by an unclean spirit since 1743. Fourteen years later, she traveled to the Iakovlevskii Monastery to seek the help of the miracle worker Dmitrii. "As she began to enter the church, the unclean spirit began to shake her; the closer she got to the tomb the more the devil tormented her. And when the people escorted her to the tomb of the miracle worker Dmitrii, she began to shout in various voices, besides [which] she spat on the cross when the monk held it in his hands and sprinkled holy water on her, [and] fell on the ground from the torment, . . . lying there one and a half hours." The tale concludes with the claim that Evfimiia awoke from her unconscious state completely healed as a result of St. Dmitrii's prayers.[102] The role that the monk played in helping to bring the demon forth from the woman's body by confronting it with the cross and holy water is also underscored in the narrative.

The Dmitrii miracle stories contain another innovation. Two of the miracle stories indicate that women still believed in the powers of sorcerers and needed male guidance to seek out spiritual aid at monasteries. In the case of the demon-possessed serf Dar'ia Afanas'eva, for example, her husband had to trick her into going to St. Dmitrii's grave by saying that he would take her to a soothsayer. In the other story a nun from the Uspenskii Monastery in Vladimir had already sought the ministrations of both sorcerers and doctors during a five-week illness that had caused her mouth to shift to one side and her eyes to cross. Subsequently, the nun had an apparition of an old man who disabused her of her unquestioning faith in sorcerers and commanded her to rely solely on faith in God by visiting St. Dmitrii's relics, which already had a reputation for wondrous miracles.[103] Men in the miracle tales might on occasion have sought the help of doctors, but not sorcerers, before seeking the spiritual aid of Dmitrii of Rostov. By implication, the authors of the Dmitrii miracle stories were suggesting that women were more prone to retain traditional superstitious ideas about magic than men and that they were more likely than men to be ensnared by the devil.

The feminization of possession victims in officially verified miracles continued apace so that, by the middle of the nineteenth century, demoniacs were exclusively women; at the same time the medical diagnosis of hysteria as an alternative descriptor of women's loss of control appeared in the miracle stories. For example, of 51 miracles ascribed to the intercession of St. Tikhon—former bishop of Voronezh and Tambov—both before his canonization and during the translation of his relics in 1861, almost 18 percent involved demon possession among only women, including five peasants, two petty townswomen, a merchant woman and a captain's daughter. Two other women, the merchant's daughter, Aleksandra Iakovleva Eliseeva, and the noblewoman Ol'ga Petrovna Dendeberi, were described as suffering from "hysteria."[104] In earlier decades they would have been identified as demoniacs. The medicalization of possession and hystericization of women's bodies by medical professionals was beginning to take effect.

By the end of the nineteenth century, possession retained its exclusive female base and represented a significant percentage of the verified miracles ascribed to Feodosii of Chernigov. Feodosii had served as archbishop of Chernigov at the end of the seventeenth century and was canonized in September 1896.[105] After ascertaining on 5 July 1895 that "the body of St. Feodosii, praise be to God, was preserved uncorrupted," a precondition for glorification, the Holy Synod set up a commission to solicit testimonies from individuals who had experienced miraculous cures themselves or who had relatives who had been healed miraculously as a result of Feodosii's intercession with God.[106] Demon possession occupied pride of place in the list of ailments; as Antonii, bishop of Chernigov and Nezhinsk, explained, "It became necessary to investigate cases of the exorcism of demons from the demon possessed, healings of dumbness, deafness, blindness, various incurable diseases before which the doctors were completely powerless."[107] Just over a quarter (27%) of the miracle stories reported by the Chernigov diocesan newspaper to celebrate Feodosii's canonization involved demon possession, and all those cured of possession were women (among whom 70% were peasants, the rest urban).[108] As in the case of miracles ascribed to St. Tikhon, men had completely disappeared from official church pronouncements as victims of demon possession.

After the 1896 celebration of Feodosii's sainthood, another major shift, connected to four canonizations between 1903 and the beginning of World War I, occurred in the officially recognized miracle stories. This time *klikushi* rarely figured among the recipients of cures, although they did not disappear from general descriptions of pilgrims visiting the saints' graves. The officially sanctioned tales reveal the Russian Orthodox Church's reliance upon the medical profession to provide scientific explanations for cures and to confirm the miraculous nature of those cures for which such explanations did not exist. Medicine's reluctance to view possession as a spiritual illness had a powerful influence on the church.

SCIENTIFIC RATIONALISM AND THE MIRACULOUS

Already in 1894, two years prior to the canonization of Feodosii of Chernigov, a three-part article appeared in the Holy Synod's journal targeted specifically for parish priests that, in the name of science, attacked Russian peasants' belief in witchcraft and the closely linked phenomenon of *klikushestvo*. Lifting examples from the secular press of peasants' violent actions against witches and sorcerers in the 1870s and 1880s, the anonymous clergyman particularly decried the superstitions of peasant women: "An eternal laborer, even less enlightened than her peasant husband, she [a peasant woman] cruelly and frequently bears the cost for her superstition. Either she herself is a sorceress—and for that she frequently pays with her life—or suffers as a result of sorcerers. Women, as a result of sorcerers' magic, very frequently become *klikushi*." So numerous were shriekers, the author pointed out, that "no attention is paid to them." Echoing the sentiments of educated observers of the peasantry, he argued that enlightenment of the masses was necessary to eradicate the problem. In order to convince the parish clergy to take on the responsibility of combating possession, the clergyman provided a scientific explanation for *klikushestvo*. Interestingly, he did not refer to church injunctions against superstition, including the Spiritual Regulation of 1721, which was still in effect at the turn of the twentieth century. Rather, he noted the importance of hypnotism in demonstrating "that many abnormal phenomena in a human organism, which superstitious people have explained as the result of the interference of an unclean and evil spirit, should be ascribed to natural processes, although the essence of those processes, as in the case with many laws of nature in general, at the present time are either completely inexplicable or insufficiently illuminated by science." The author enjoined the clergy to inform doctors of the whereabouts of *klikushi* so that medical experts could isolate the demoniacs before their behavior infected others. He also cautioned priests against belittling the beliefs of those seeking cures in church when they made an effort "to eliminate the extremely undesirable, nationwide shrieking in church[es]."[109] A few months later a similar article, also by a cleric (in this case a former parish priest), appeared in the same journal. It praised the first author's advice to parish priests to encourage peasants to seek professional medical treatment for their ailments.[110]

The clergymen's publications had the imprimatur of the Holy Synod's censors and consequently of the Holy Synod itself. How does one reconcile the explanation in 1894 of attacks on *klikushestvo* as a dangerous superstition and the recognition in 1896 of demoniacs being miraculously cured by the relics of St. Feodosii? Given subsequent contradictory evidence, it is apparent that by the end of the nineteenth century, tensions existed among ecclesiastics over the meaning of the miraculous and the possibility of their occurring in a world dominated by science. By embracing the authority of medicine, the Russian Orthodox Church was part of a broader trend among educated society to modernize peasants' worldview by promoting secularization. *Klikushestvo,* as a consequence, was demoted from the ranks of spiritual afflictions that saints cured. At the same time, however, the church did not refrain from mentioning demoniacs in public descriptions of canonization celebrations. Nor did the Holy Synod prohibit monks from treating *klikushi* or ban exorcisms. Parish priests, monks, and the laity were receiving mixed messages from a church that was not so monolithic and rigid as its critics viewed it to be.

The demotion of miraculous exorcisms from the list of officially recognized miracles began with the Holy Synod's late-nineteenth-century inquiries into the miracles attributed to Serafim of Sarov (1759–1833). Serafim had been a simple monk who participated in "the mystical and contemplative revival" in Russian monasteries during the reign of Alexander I (1801–1825).[111] The archives of the Sarovskaia Uspenskaia Hermitage (located on Tambov province's northern border with Nizhnii Novgorod province) contained testimonies of persons from whom the monk had posthumously exorcised demons. However, the Holy Synod dismissed the validity of those accounts as well as archival reports of other cures on the grounds that they could not be verified.[112] After repeatedly delaying Serafim's canonization, the Holy Synod finally bowed to Nicholas II's appeal on the anniversary of Serafim's birth in July 1902 that Serafim be glorified the following year.[113] The miracles published in the religious press to attest to Serafim's sanctity, with one exception, were bereft of miracle stories involving demon possession.[114] Yet a report in the secular press noted several miraculous healings of possessed women at Serafim's reliquary just after the glorification.[115] Four years later a publication sanctioned by the Holy Synod listed three more such cures.[116] Demoniacs were also absent from the officially verified miracles for Pitirim, a seventeenth-century bishop of Tambov (1685–1698), who was canonized in 1913.[117]

The influence of doctors, who were part of the investigations of miraculous healings, helps explain the sudden decline in *klikushi*. The medicalization of various ailments appears in the descriptions of miracles ascribed to Serafim and Pitirim. References were made to shingles, internal hemorrhaging, rheumatism, and nervous disorders. Furthermore, instances of hysteria were far more common by the turn of the century than they had been previously. That physicians, on whom the Holy Synod relied for medical prognoses of individuals who were cured of various ailments, did not consider demon possession a legitimate diagnosis meant that some women who might have identified themselves as *klikushi* were being told that they were actually suffering from some form of hysteria.

Commission members investigating Pitirim's miracles, for example, examined a case that as late as the nineteenth century would have been labeled *klikushestvo*. It involved "the healing of the peasant girl Pelagiia Kliueva of hysteria," an ailment that expressed itself in "shouting and hiccups," symptoms associated with possession. According to the report, this Kliueva of the village Epanchino had written the senior priest of the Tambov Cathedral on 20 August 1912, informing him that she had been cured of a two-year bout of hysteria through Pitirim's mediation with God. However, the commissioners did not specify who labeled the ailment hysteria, Kliueva herself or the priest who informed church authorities of the miracle. In any case, the description of the so-called hysteria coincides with that of which was usually considered demon possession: initially Kliueva yelled involuntarily for two to three hours at a time, after which she began to hiccup without interruption for several days. She became so ill from the fits that she had to abandon all heavy labor. In January 1912 Kliueva reported having a vision of an elderly man who looked like St. Nicholas and who told her that she was to embark on a pilgrimage to Pitirim's grave in Tambov. Eventually Kliueva did just that, arriving in Tambov on 19 June 1912. "In the Cathedral she prayed at the relics of St. Pitirim, took the sacraments, took anointing oil from the lamp at this sepulcher and drank it to take away the hiccups." Subsequently, the hiccups did not return and Kliueva could resume heavy work.[118]

In the church's investigation of Kliueva's case, the priest Gavriil Sokolov, accompanied by a policeman, questioned Pelagiia Kliueva under oath on 4 November 1912. Confirming what she had written in the letter, Kliueva provided a more detailed account of the illness that had struck her at age 30. She also revealed that she had communicated with the elder Anatolii at the Optina Hermitage about her illness and subsequently visited him in the summer of 1911, asking his advice about "whether she should receive [medical] treatment. The elder did not give his blessing for the treatment, and Kliueva suffered as before from her illness." Witnesses, including the peasant women Ol'ga Tenina, who had lived with Kliueva for 12 years, and Feodosiia Penina; the priest's widow Ol'ga Ivanovna Zarubkinskaia and her daughter Taisiia; and the parish priest of the village Epanchino, Mikhail Eleonskii, all corroborated Kliueva's description of her illness and miraculous cure at Pitirim's grave.[119]

Meanwhile, lay and clerical investigators appointed by the bishop of Tambov asked Dr. Pushkarev, a doctor with the provincial Staro-Iur'evskaia Hospital, for his expert assessment of Kliueva's sickness. Since Kliueva had not once consulted doctors during her illness, but had sought spiritual advice instead, Pushkarev had to base his medical assessment of her previous condition on her testimony and on eyewitness accounts. Noting that it was impossible to state categorically whether the woman had been cured, he provided the opinion that Kliueva must have suffered from a severe form of hysteria. Pushkarev went on to explain that although cases in which individuals were completely cured of their hysterical behavior did exist, there were also instances in which some of the illness's symptoms, such as Kliueva's hiccupping or characteristics associated with *klikushestvo,* disappeared, only to resurface at some other time in different forms. Interestingly, Dr. Pushkarev was the only person cited in the commission report to use the term *klikushestvo.* Even patients whom doctors believed were fully cured, Pushkarev added, lapsed into the illness once again. From this expert testimony, the priest Sokolov concluded that in the doctor's judgment hysteria "in the majority of cases, but especially in a severe form, does not yield to a cure by way of medical methods." Lay commissioners confirmed this opinion, stating even more categorically that "hysteria is not cured not only in the majority of cases but never by medical means. Medicine can only relieve some manifestations of 'hysteria,' and even with that lengthy and persistent treatment and regime, medicine is powerless to defeat that disease completely." Having established that Kliueva was once ill but now completely cured, that she never turned to doctors for aid, and that medicine was ineffectual with regard to hysteria, the commission charged with investigating miracles ascribed to Pitirim agreed with Father Sokolov that Kliueva had been cured by divine intervention.[120]

By consulting doctors and including their diagnoses and at times details of hospital logs in the reports of miracles, the Russian Orthodox Church had acquiesced, at least to a certain extent, to the authority of medical science. Had Kliueva sought help from medical doctors prior to her cure at Pitirim's relics, there is little doubt that the commissioners would have reached a different conclusion, as they had in the case of the Tambov townswoman Elizaveta Kononova Troshina. Doctors had diagnosed Troshina as having "a serious nervous disorder." However, Troshina herself claimed that the medicines she had been prescribed in the insane asylum were ineffectual until she drank holy water from St. Pitirim's well. Unable to determine conclusively whether the holy water or doctors' prescriptions affected Troshina's cure, commissioners did not include it among the miracles officially attributed to Pitirim.[121] Miracles had to rest on incontrovertible evidence.

While cognizant of the advances of science, the church could not accept the rationalist argument that miracles were impossible. To have done so would have undercut its doctrine. Thus ecclesiastical writers defended the notion of the miraculous in religious journals, especially after scandal erupted over the poor condition of Serafim of Sarov's remains and subsequent doubts were raised about his canonization among educated circles. Sergei Goloshchapov wrote a powerful polemic against modern skepticism in the religious journal *Vera i razum*. Defending biblical miracles against the attacks of skeptics, he rejected the Enlightenment notions of God as the supreme watchmaker and the universe as a mechanism, arguing that "a miracle is a manifestation of God's powers in the spiritual or material world" and that "nature itself, its complete harmony and beauty is a miracle." Goloshchapov warned rationalists not to dismiss miracles as the product of natural causes and rejected scientists' penchant to relate so-called miracles to whims of the human psyche that could be controlled through hypnotism, the power of suggestion, and the power of belief acting on the nervous system. "Why is it," he asked, "if a doctor returns vital activity to a sick person with the help of medicine, that we do not consider this contrary to nature, but if Jesus Christ, as the All-Powerful God, as the Creator of healing elements and the powers of nature said to a sick person—stand up and walk, we consider this a violation of the laws of nature?" Conceding that the biblical miracles were extraordinary, Goloshchapov noted that "God's powers to act in the world did not end. . . .God gave the world eternal miracles" through Christ, his miraculous resurrection, and ultimately Christianity. Subsequently, miracles occurred through the mediation of saints. "It is sufficient," argued Goloshchapov, "to recall the saints closer to our times—Tikhon of Zadonsk, Feodosii of Chernigov, Serafim of Sarov and the now canonized Ioasaf of Belgorod [1911] and their miracles—healings of a completely evangelical nature."[122]

The fact that, in the early twentieth century, possession still enjoyed a place among the ailments that received divine intervention surfaced in another article in the religious press. According to V. Vinogradov, demon possession was not a mere superstition, and there was no better authority for this claim than the Gospels. Christ, he pointed out, had recognized the demon possessed among the sick who were brought to him for healing. "A person, who has become a home for devils can be counted among the ill since he endures cruel torments, not only physical but also moral [ones]." Such an illness had nothing to do with nervous illness or derangement, Vinogradov argued. "In possessing a person demons do not destroy but distort" the psychology of an individual; "they become the managers and administrators of a person's nervous system during the time when the sick person's soul is completely active." Defending Christ's miraculous ability to exorcise demons and to cure the possessed, Vinogradov, like Goloshchapov, rejected the ideas of modern psychiatrists, who preferred naturalist explanations to spiritual ones. Even then, Vinogradov reminded his readers, no one could be sure what happened to patients discharged from medical clinics: "no one knows what happens after the ill person leaves the clinic, whether he was cured or received more or less relief."[123] He would have agreed with the premise that miracle cures, including the healing of the demon possessed, occur not because of medical science, which is limited in its scope, but through an individual's burning faith in God and his saints, the intercession of a saint on behalf of an individual, and God's infinite mercy.

Although possession appeared only rarely in the miracles attributed to the new Orthodox saints of the early twentieth century, ecclesiastical writers nonetheless continued to mention demoniacs in their general descriptions of canonization celebrations. For example, they acknowledged the presence of *klikushi* among the throngs of pilgrims at the canonization ceremonies at the Sarovskaia Hermitage in 1903. Writing about his pilgrimage, Archimandrite Evdokim remarked that, at the Arzamas train station, he overheard pilgrims relating a story about a possessed woman being healed at Serafim's spring at the hermitage. His description of worshipers at the spring included another reference to demoniacs: "Here it is possible to see the blind, and the lame, and the demon possessed, and the paralyzed, and the mentally ill, and the sick."[124] The conservative Orthodox journal *Vera i razum* provided the following bleak description of the sick along the road to the spring: "one can see a multitude of ill [persons]. Here on a stretcher—two sticks with a cloth stretched over them—they are carrying an ill girl; in a cart they are leading a sick man whose legs are paralyzed; a pale, weak, sick woman, having put her arms around the shoulders of two women, hardly moves her legs, every minute using up her breath from exhaustion; a hunchbacked old woman goes on two crutches; holding the stick of a boy-leader, a blind man walks with his head high; behind him a boy hops on a crutch . . . ; a woman moves on her arms and legs, like a four-legged [animal]." The reporter subsequently noted the sounds of shriekers amidst a cacophony of human voices at Serafim's spring: "the loud cries of those with falling sickness, the demon possessed and *klikushi,* the groans of the ill, the joyous exclamations of those healed."[125] By pointing out God's mercy and the numerous miraculous cures that occurred at the spring as a result of Serafim's prayers, he tempered this dismal picture.

Descriptions of demoniacs at the grave of Ioasaf of Belgorod also colored religious publications. Father Skubachevskii's poignant account of an exorcism, presented at the beginning of this chapter, is a case in point. A year later, during the first anniversary of Ioasaf's canonization, the priest Porfirii Amfiteatrov noted that the crowd accompanying the procession of priests who carried the saint's coffin around the exterior of the church included in its ranks women possessed by demons, whose cries and shouts resounded in the midst of the priests' chanting.[126]

Clerics and ecclesiastics could not ignore the presence of demon-possessed women at saints' shrines, for it signified the church's relevance in a secular world and provided testimony to preternatural forces. While the Russian Orthodox Church could not completely dismiss medical science in an increasingly skeptical world and indeed co-opted it to a certain extent, the church stressed the limitations of medicine in a world that God continued to govern. Priests and monks, like Christ before them, were just as much physicians of the body and soul as were medical doctors.

Throughout European Russia monks were renowned for their counseling and healing abilities. The tremendous growth in monastic establishments in the second half of the nineteenth century meant a proliferation of nuns and monks who specialized in thaumaturgical cures.[127] Monasteries famous for exorcisms included among others the Sarovskaia Hermitage in Tambov province, the Kalochskii Monastery in Smolensk province, the Simonov Monastery in Moscow, the Monastery of the Caves in Kiev, the Lavrentiev Monastery near Kaluga, the Trinity–St. Sergii Monastery in Sergiev Posad, the V'iasskaia Vladimirskaia Hermitage in Penza, and the Tikhonova Hermitage in Kaluga.[128] Finally, both the sick and the well flocked to the Optina Hermitage to seek the advice of its elders.

At the parish level priests either ministered to *klikushi* or tried to control their behavior by turning them over to medical authorities. Here the debate among representatives of the church played itself out. Because the *klikushi* did not confine themselves to shrieking in church or in the presence of holy objects, but also attacked neighbors they believed responsible for bewitching them, parish priests often found themselves in the role of mediator. Better educated priests, who had adopted some rationalist ideas, were more likely to castigate *klikushestvo* as a superstition and to look askance at parishioners who disturbed the liturgy and community order and sought the aid of monks at nearby or distant monasteries.[129] In so doing, they strictly followed the precepts of the Spiritual Regulation and the advice of ecclesiastical writers who viewed the treatment of possession as belonging to the domain of medical specialists. They chose to ignore those church writings that reinforced beliefs in the machinations of evil spirits through sorcerers and witches.

Among the few parish priests who gained national reputations as exorcists figured Father Ioann of Kronstadt (1829–1908).[130] Father Ioann's ministrations to the possessed as well as his clerical role demonstrate the continuing relevance of the miraculous and possession in late Imperial Russian society. Enjoying an immensely popular following that provoked sensational interest in both the religious and secular press from the 1880s onward, Father Ioann was intent upon becoming a living saint. He ministered to the poor through charitable works, emphasized the importance of the confessional and communion by introducing public confessions, and enjoyed an ability to cure illnesses through intense prayer. He not only regularly exorcised demons from *klikushi* but also employed some of the characteristics associated with possession in stirring up popular piety.[131] A charismatic priest, Father Ioann infused his church services with an unprecedented intensity and zeal. According to the testimony of the lawyer Anatolii Koni, Father Ioann's "manner of performing the liturgy was utterly extraordinary . . . when he began to read the Gospel, his voice took on a harsh and commanding tone and he began to repeat the holy words with a kind of hysterical shriek."[132] During mass public confessions this energetic priest encouraged thousands of people to scream out their sins. As they did so, "there was a fearful unimaginable noise," commented another eyewitness. "Some wept, others fell to the floor, others stood stock-still in a frozen wordless state. . . . The huge cathedral was full of moans, shrieks, and howls; it seemed as if the whole church was shaking from the shattering wails of the people."[133] Thus, the congregation took on the characteristics of *klikushi,* who had to wait for quieter moments in church services, such as the presentation of the communion cup to confessed believers, for their screams to be heard.[134]

Father Ioann railed against the ubiquitous presence of the devil and declared that exorcism was proof of the beneficence of God and power of the cross. He cautioned the faithful to be ever vigilant against the devil. He wrote,

> As long as we lead a carnal life, and do not wholeheartedly draw near to God, so long will the demons hide themselves within us, concealing

> themselves under the forms of various vices: greed for food and drink, lust, pride, and arrogant free thought concerning the Church and her teachings; malice, envy, avarice, covetousness and so on, so that we live in accordance with them; but as soon as we begin truly to serve the Lord, and thus provoke and strike the demons nesting in us, then they attack us with infernal malice, and manifold, burning attachments to earthly things, until we drive them out of us by fervent prayer, or by partaking of the Holy Sacrament.

For Father Ioann the devil and evil spirits were not simply symbols of evil but actual beings who possessed individuals and who in the presence of sacred objects were repulsed by them: "they blaspheme and spit at it, and scream. That is why those possessed with evil spirits scream in church during divine service, or when they approach relics; it is because the demons are then met by the blessed power, which is hateful to them, and stronger than them; and which burns, oppresses and strikes them with righteousness, and drives them out of those in whom they dwell."[135]

CONCLUSION

Father Ioann's comments epitomize Russian Orthodoxy's understanding of the devil and demon possession. Ultimately, the belief in the devil's ability to possess individuals won out over attempts on the part of the church and state to unmask those who feigned their demon possession to wreak vengeance on others. The intent of the eighteenth-century regulations had been to uncover shamming *klikushi;* yet neither the state nor the church was rigorous in its prosecution of the demon possessed. The belief in the devil's ability to persuade individuals to do his bidding by acting malevolently against others was still strong even among the highest members of Russian society in the eighteenth century. The laws themselves, however, by identifying the demon possessed as women who were potential impostors, began the process of casting doubt upon the possibility of demon possession. The devaluation of *klikushestvo* in part explains the feminization of the demoniacs in the miracle stories that attested to the sanctity of eighteenth- and nineteenth-century holy persons. While psychiatrists in the nineteenth century labeled them hysterics, the church generally had a much more benevolent attitude toward them. They were accorded attention and treatment through public exorcisms, often through the mediation of saints' prayers.

The church's acceptance of demoniacs does not mean that it was immune to secularization. The church found itself having to counteract what it deemed the pernicious influences of Old Belief and to give credence to some scientific thought as medical doctors became important members of educated society in the nineteenth century. It had become much more reticent in sanctioning local cults of saints. Yet it did not try to deemphasize demon possession and its relationship to the miraculous until the early twentieth century. The fact that demon possession had enjoyed a prominent place in the miracle stories and saints' vitae published in the religious press until 1903 and continued thereafter to resurface in relation to discussions of the miraculous suggests that forces within the church and Russian society still attached importance to the role of the devil in the secular world. The monasteries and urban chapels famous for their exorcisms of the devil reflect not only the continuing religious beliefs of monks and urban clerics, like Father Ioann, but also the ongoing beliefs of a significant portion of Russian society.

Chapter Two

PEASANT VIEWS

✦ Historically an affliction of both men and women of all social estates, demon possession in Imperial Russia had become a largely peasant and overwhelmingly female phenomenon by the 1820s. An examination of *klikushestvo* among postemancipation Russian peasants provides a window into prerevolutionary peasant culture. Peasant views of possession demonstrate how peasants appropriated Orthodox understandings of the devil and his minions and interacted with the clergy in a cosmic drama in which good triumphed over evil. These views also illuminate the connection that villagers made between possession and witchcraft. While using images of witchcraft and sorcery for didactic purposes, peasants also targeted real and alleged malevolent individuals whom they held responsible for unleashing demons. By comprehending misfortune as either God's wrath or, more often than not, the machinations of unclean spirits who dispensed harm through human intermediaries, they mixed the sacred with the profane. At the same time, parish clergy and monks who ministered to demoniacs subscribed to a similar myth. They emphasized the cosmic battle between good and evil, although they did not necessarily reject the premise that malevolent individuals who practiced the black arts acted as demons' deputies. The complementary myths rendered intelligible the behavior of possession victims and underscored what peasants and representatives of the church viewed as the causal relationship between bewitchment and possession.

Klikushi and their kin beseeched sympathetic priests and monks as well as healers and sorcerers to employ countermagic against demons and evil individuals. The thaumaturgical arsenal of Orthodox ritual, prayers, incense, communion, consecrated bread, holy water, grasses, and oils could be concentrated on both the exorcism of demons and the identification of individuals responsible for malefic action as monks and parish clergy's coupling of possession with bewitchment legitimated peasant understandings. Offering supplementary services in the battle against malevolence, lay healers or sorcerers similarly ministered to the possessed with incantations, counterspells, potions, and herbs. Demons, malefic individuals, priests, healers, victims, and witnesses all enjoyed roles in a ritual drama of possession and the possibility of redemption through exorcism. The drama accordingly had the potential to resolve or at least relieve personal and community tensions and reinforce religious values.[1]

Subscribing to an Orthodox Christian cosmology, peasants framed their lives according to Christian precepts. Their understanding of demons, the timing of demoniacs' initial fits and seizures coinciding with major holidays in the religious calendar, the public display of possession seizures in the midst of the holy liturgy, and pilgrimages to holy sites for miraculous relief from possession reveal aspects of popular Orthodoxy that have been little studied. In trying to settle the contest between the demons and their victims in favor of the latter, the possessed, spectators, and clerics assumed various roles in the possession drama.

In their search for the causes of possession, peasants looked to their belief in witchcraft. Common to tribal and agrarian societies the world over, malefic witchcraft was the perceived ability of an individual to harm or injure people and animals by supernatural means, words, spells, and potions. Living at the mercy of the environment, exploitative classes, and the state, peasants in the preindustrial world had a wealth of beliefs and practices that explained their circumstances, provided them with safeguards against adversity, and enabled them to counteract the calamities that befell them. Blaming a delinquent neighbor, relative, or stranger for causing possession or long-term illness; making a woman barren and a man impotent on their wedding day; depriving a cow of her milk; or bringing about a drought, hailstorm, or severe thunderstorm personalized misfortune and made it comprehensible. It also allowed the victims to combat their suffering by taking action against the perceived perpetrator. Furthermore, beliefs in sorcerers and witches clarified the tensions inherent in closely knit communities, whose existence depended upon a semblance of harmony and rooting out of deviance.

Faced with the skepticism of medical science, a well-meaning elderly peasant woman's explanation to N. V. Krainskii, the psychiatrist who traveled to Ashchepkovo in 1898 to halt an epidemic of *klikushestvo,* captures the essence of peasants' understanding of the adversity in their midst: "What can I tell you? They say that there are no sorcerers now. In the cities they don't believe in them. Then why is it, I say to you, that a person buys a cow from another and she [the cow] begins to dry up? Or a maiden when she marries is healthy, but after the wedding ceremony she begins to dry up, and everything dries up. . . . She becomes bewitched . . . it happens quite frequently!" With that preamble, the old woman immediately switched the conversation to Ashchepkovo's problems. She identified the woman Siklitin'ia as the source of the outbreak of possession, noting that with Siklitin'ia's departure from the village for the safety of Moscow, Siklitin'ia's daughter, who initially stayed behind, would not remain alive if the symptoms associated with bewitchment continued. In other words, Siklitin'ia's daughter was also under suspicion of being a witch.[2]

Once peasants had identified a witch or sorcerer as the cause of possession and other ailments, they tried to convince the individual to reverse the spell, or, if this failed, they sometimes beat the alleged evildoer.[3] If they did not seek retribution immediately, they closely monitored the malevolent individual's activities and reflected on past encounters with the sorcerer or witch that might have led to illness or strange sensations. Only when they perceived the evildoer to be caught off guard or in a vulnerable position did they avenge themselves.

The peasants' understanding of both *klikushestvo* and witchcraft suggest that the rural *klikusha* represented the counterimage to the rural witch and sorcerer. In the opposites of good and evil, passive and active, victim and agent, and innocent and guilty, the demoniac captured the positive attributes, the witch the negative characteristics. These attributes were not absolute, however. Once a victim of demons—through no fault of her own—the woman demoniac did not remain passive. She actively sought to identify the source of her affliction. By remembering an event in the distant past that could provide a plausible explanation for her vulnerability to possession, she historicized her condition. Or she identified the alleged witch or sorcerer who had violated "the boundaries of the moral community" by placing a hex upon her or by breaking the sacred trust of community and family by poisoning her food.[4] Indeed, once the signs of possession appeared, the possessed and her family sought justification for the ailment or the perpetrator responsible for the demons.

While *klikushi* represented the counterimage of witches and sorcerers, they also shared attributes with them: after 1861 both demoniacs and witches tended to be women (87% of those identified as possessed and more than 66% of those targeted as witches in the Russian village between 1861 and 1917), and both played the role of a liminal personage within the community.[5] Alleged witches and sorcerers held precarious membership in their villages. Perceived by their neighbors to have transgressed shared norms and values, they were in a position of limbo until neutralized by countermagic, reincorporated into the community by way of repentance and reconciliation, or rooted out by violent means. The demoniacs' liminality stemmed from their infirmity and victimization by demons. Taking on other personas during their seizures, they were no longer responsible for their actions and found themselves in a state of limbo as well. Family members and neighbors permitted *klikushi* to play the sick role and to relinquish, at least temporarily, their family and community obligations. Freed of everyday responsibilities, demoniacs could leave the village to seek cures either in other rural settlements or at monastic institutions renowned for their ability to help the possessed, sick, and crippled. If healed by way of saints' intercession, exorcisms, or countermagic against the alleged witch or sorcerer, they abandoned their liminal position, regained membership in the Christian community, and resumed full adult responsibilities; if not, they continued to assume the sick role, explaining their fate either as predetermined by God or resulting from a misstep in the rituals of exorcism or other types of countermagic.[6] Finally, the danger that both *klikushi* and witches posed to people around them accentuated their liminal positions within their communities. Although peasants sympathized with the plight of demoniacs, they also feared them as sources of contagion. The dread that they had of witches led to forebodings at weddings and at certain times of the year when they believed witches' powers to be at their height.

While Russian peasants believed possession to be an outcome of bewitchment, their equation of possession with bewitchment, however, was never exact. First of all, peasants understood that God rather than a malevolent individual might be punishing their sins through possession; God's role in allowing evil to overcome good constituted one of life's intangibles. Second, bewitchment did not always correspond with possession. In other words, not all allegedly bewitched individuals in the Russian village identified themselves as or were perceived to be demoniacs. Demoniacs, as opposed to bewitched individuals who were not possessed, exhibited symptoms that were part of a culturally prescribed script or "a culturally organized diagnostic system of bodily signs."[7] During religious services, in the midst of an icon procession, or in contact with holy objects, they began to convulse uncontrollably, to writhe on the floor, to make animal or bird sounds, and in the midst of other villagers, to cry out the name of the individual they thought had bewitched them. They ended in a state of temporary unconsciousness. In some cases, they shouted obscenities and blasphemed, tore at their hair and clothing, and developed uncontrollable hiccupping. Community witnesses believed these public demonstrations to be involuntary, a product of the demons inhabiting the victims' bodies, rather than manifestations of mental illness. Attacks of possession rarely occurred outside religious settings; when they did, they were largely confined to wedding celebrations, a common time for witches to strike. On these occasions the symptoms were identical, but holy objects did not provoke the demons' antics, and men were just as likely as women to be targets of possession. Those who suffered bewitchment, but not possession, either shared with the possessed physical ailments such as impotence and stomach pains or exhibited entirely different symptoms, including hernias and abscesses.[8] But their debilities, with the exception of epilepsy, did not manifest themselves in public displays of body contortions and writhing on the floor. Nor did they erupt in reaction to religious services and objects. The sick generally took to their beds, leaving to community gossip the responsibility of spreading the word about their illness and raising the issue of there being a witch or sorcerer in the community.

✦ Russian and Ukrainian peasantries shared a popular Orthodox cosmology, and both occasionally attributed family discord, barrenness, impotence, droughts, and economic tensions to witchcraft and sorcery. Despite these similarities, however, postemancipation Ukrainian villages were less prone than Russian villages to have shriekers. Ukrainians accounted for only 5 percent of *klikushi* in the postemancipation period. Lower rates of labor migration for men for substantial periods of a given year and underreporting partly explain the discrepancy. In the central and northern Russian provinces, higher rates of off-farm labor for men resulted in greater agricultural responsibilities and stress for the women left behind in the villages; women who could not cope with the additional burdens became prime candidates for *klikushestvo.* Underreporting of possession cases was greater among Ukrainian than Russian peasants, because there were fewer trained psychiatrists in the region at the end of the nineteenth century to report on epidemics of possession. Undoubtedly, Ukrainian ethnographers also omitted possession cases from their portraits of rural life. Battling a dominant Russian culture and restrictions on the use of the Ukrainian language in print, they touted the virtues of the Ukrainian peasantry in comparison with its Russian counterpart. In a flourish of national pride, they ignored domestic discord and preferred to idealize the Ukrainian family and peasant mother. Discussion of peasant beliefs, including those regarding witchcraft and sorcery, which they perceived as relics of a pagan past and outside the tenets of the Russian Orthodox Church, entered ethnographers' records. However, they ignored the victims of bewitchment.

While largely absent from secular accounts of *klikushestvo,* Ukrainians are also underrepresented in the stories of individuals who received miraculous cures. That omission suggests that cultural differences between Russian and Ukrainian peasantries may have existed. Very few

Ukrainians appear among those cured of possession or other ailments in the miracle tales for the 1896 canonization of Feodosii of Chernigov, a late-seventeenth-century Ukrainian monk who became part of the reforming Russian Orthodox ecclesiastical hierarchy. The scarcity of Ukrainians among those benefiting from the miraculous is curious as the ceremonies occurred in a Ukrainian province. Besides, the church had hoped to demonstrate the organic connection between the Great and "Little" (as Ukrainians were called) Russians and would not have purposely excluded Ukrainians from the miracle stories. In addition to the church campaign being unsuccessful, it is also likely that Ukrainian peasants did not seek aid from the same monasteries that Russian peasants frequented. In the case of the Monastery of the Caves in Kiev, which attracted both Ukrainian and Russian pilgrims, Ukrainians may have viewed the shriekers' behavior as distinctly "Muscovite," that is, Russian. While both peasantries had to confront the nonvernacular Church Slavonic in religious services, Ukrainian peasants at times had to communicate with Russian-speaking monks. According to the 1897 census, about 50 percent of clerics in Ukraine were native Russian speakers.[9]

Even though the issue concerning the existence of possession among Ukrainian peasants cannot be resolved conclusively, one can speculate that Ukrainian peasants preferred dealing with healers who spoke their own dialects of a language related to, but nonetheless different from, Russian. The fact that clerics were largely absent from the rituals surrounding bewitchment in the Ukrainian countryside serves to deemphasize possession.[10] The paucity of examples of *klikushestvo* among Ukrainian peasants, even when underreporting and low rates of prolonged labor migration on the part of men are taken into account, serves to highlight the cultural underpinnings of the phenomenon within the Russian context.

POPULAR ORTHODOXY

Before the components of the ritual drama of possession in the Russian Orthodox parish can be identified, the religious context for the drama must be explored. The ways in which Orthodox teachings about demons and possession played out at the local level in the postemancipation period require investigation because peasants' understanding of possession and the reactions of priests and monks were key to the elaboration of similar myths of possession.

Traditionally, the study of popular Orthodoxy has focused on pagan remnants and superstitious elements within the peasants' belief system. Rejecting that traditional emphasis, the viewpoint presented here is predicated upon the revised understanding of popular Orthodoxy as communities of believers following Christian teachings.[11] This approach does not negate the tensions that existed between the Holy Synod and peasants over religious practices.

The campaign by the church bureaucracy to centralize its authority and to control local practices was relaxed but not abandoned in the nineteenth century. Intent upon trying to bring some uniformity to local practices, the church imposed standards that often met resistance from peasants.[12] The negative rhetoric of the ecclesiastical hierarchy regarding the beliefs of the "dark" and "superstitious" masses, however, must be viewed in light of a church asserting a monopoly over mediation with supernatural forces. As in other cultures "religion as practiced" did not always meet the ideal of prescribed religion.[13]

A closer look at peasant beliefs regarding possession reveals that Russian peasants followed Orthodox teachings regarding demons and the struggle between good and evil, the power of the living cross, the magical properties of holy water, the authority of saints, as well as faith healing and exorcism. Seeking spiritual help, demoniacs regularly went on pilgrimages. They not only found such help at monasteries and saints' shrines, but also found confirmation in the rite of exorcism that a link between bewitchment and possession existed as that rite asked them to identify the individuals who had bewitched them.

Nineteenth-century Russian peasants embraced Orthodox precepts regarding the pervasiveness of sin and demons and the constant vigilance needed by mere mortals to offset temptation. Through self-control and symbolic confessions of faith such as making the sign of the cross, wearing a cross, and invoking God's name or that of his Son, they believed that they could save themselves from the devil's powers. Yet they also knew that as a result of humans' propensity for error, demons sometimes won their struggle over human souls, at least temporarily.

In accordance with Orthodox teachings, peasants understood the meaning of the Orthodox cross correctly as not only a signifier of the faith, but also as a talisman against demons. According to a manual for priests, making the sign of the cross protected a person from evil spirits.[14] Conversely, not making the sign of the cross left an individual exposed to demons. The seventeenth-century secular Muscovite tale about Savva Grudtsyn and his contract with the devil, popularized by eighteenth- and nineteenth-century chapbooks, warned accordingly, "If only he [Savva] had made the sign of the cross, then all those devilish temptations would have vanished like a shadow."[15] It is little wonder then that Russian Orthodox peasants crossed themselves before they undertook any task. Making the sign of the cross in locations they associated with demons or unclean spirits, including forests, crossroads, mills, and bathhouses, and in the presence of demoniacs also served in their mind to ward off assaults by demons.

If neglecting to make the sign of the cross increased a person's vulnerability to demon invasion, so too did the misplacement of the baptismal cross that peasants wore round their necks. While the deliberate act of removing the cross amounted to a renunciation of God, the involuntary loss of the same holy object meant a forfeiture of God's protection and an individual's vulnerability to demon possession or sudden death.[16] How else can one explain that on 4 July 1881 the forty-year-old carpenter Gavrilo Vasil'ev became convinced that he had committed a grave sin by losing his baptismal cross while washing in a dirty place? For several hours he prayed with his eyes fixed on one spot; he could not sleep, eat, or do anything, believing that demons had besieged his unprotected body.[17] Similarly, late-nineteenth-century peasants in Viazniki district, Vladimir province, told ethnographers that they avoided bathing without a cross around their necks for fear of unclean water spirits or demons.[18] Clearly, negligence did not always result in possession, but if disaster did strike, peasants had a ready explanation for it.

Given the frequency of accidental drownings in the countryside as well as the Orthodox Church's emphasis on the curative and protective powers of consecrated water, Russian and Ukrainian peasants feared natural sources of water.[19] They believed that their rivers, streams, and lakes were populated with *rusalki* (water nymphs)—the souls of the drowned, unbaptized, and stillborn babies who, it was believed, sought revenge by attacking mortals. Scores of water demons infested these waters and haunted wells. Only water purified during the Epiphany rites in commemoration of Christ's baptism in the River Jordan was free of unclean spirits and of the dangers these demons posed to humans. Such beliefs complemented the Orthodox Church's liberal use of holy water and the supernatural properties it ascribed to water that had undergone ceremonial purification. Evident in its opening statements, a popular incantation from Smolensk province against possession, for example, rests on belief in the curative powers of water from the Jordan River: "Lord God! Jesus Christ, the Lord's Son, came away from the Jordan River with crosses and blessed water."[20] The church's reporting of miraculous healings associated with holy wells and streams, endowed by the benevolence of individual saints, further distinguished the sanctity of holy water from the impurity of ordinary water.[21] Following Orthodox teachings, peasants took precautions against the unclean forces in unconsecrated water. They felt protected when they made the sign of the cross and said a prayer before washing or taking up well water.

The linkage between water and demons is clarified by a popular late-nineteenth-century Russian didactic tale. Recorded by the ethnographer D. N. Ushakov, it emphasizes the dangers of an individual's not taking appropriate measures to neutralize evil spirits in wells. Not even monks dedicated to the life of contemplation were immune from human frailty and the devil's wiles. The narrative begins with a monk carrying out the ordinary task of fetching well water. The unfortunate monk forgets to pray or cross himself before drawing the water, and the unclean spirits lurking in the well begin to plague him. His first mishap befalls him on his way back to the monastery when he spills the bucket of water. Having no choice but to return to the well for more water, the monk once again forgets to pray as he takes up the bucket. The second misfortune (although undetected at this point) awaits the holy man as he heads once again for the monastery: he notices a child crying on the spot where he spilled the water, and, filled with Christian charity, he takes the boy to the monastery where he is brought up, educated, tonsured, and made an expert on the Scriptures. As it turns out, the orphan is really a demon who patiently waits several years before attempting to wreak havoc in the monastery by distorting the Gospels. Realizing the orphan's true identity before the demon can do too much damage, the monks successfully banish him from their midst.[22]

If a monk devoted to a life of serving God could repeatedly forget to say a prayer over well water, were not mere mortals more vulnerable? A Ukrainian demoniac named Agafiia in the sloboda Gorodishche (near the Russian Don Cossack Host) must have believed so when her demon greeted a priest who came to minister to her in the 1850s with the following words: "I will make Agafiia suffer again; she did not cross herself when she drank water from the well; that's when I jumped inside her."[23] No doubt Agafiia, in searching for a reason for her malady, seized upon a plausible incident that might or might not have happened.

While Russian peasants believed that all humans were vulnerable to demonic assault, they regarded women as more susceptible to possession than men. Women's helplessness stemmed from the natural sexual impulses of demons who were invariably male. Peasants' images of demons came from iconographic and religious woodcut representations. They accordingly described them as having horns, wings, tails, and claws, but human faces and torsos. And whatever shapes the demons took, their tails, according to peasants in Olonets region, remained visible. While the victims of possession and demonic torments on icons and woodcuts were most often male, the occasional representation of debauched women or prostitutes being tortured by serpents and snakes emphasized these women's nakedness and weighty breasts.[24] The depiction of an evil wife on a late-eighteenth-century woodcut also stresses women's sexuality: with her hair hanging loose, she is akin to a prostitute. Furthermore, she sits on a bed with a man at her feet, demon-serpents and a devil to her right, and Adam and Eve in the background.[25] The connection that peasants made between demon possession and women's sexual organs is thus understandable. As a peasant explained to an observer, a witch's hex laid under a porch was less likely to take effect on a man than a woman because "he wears pants and therefore it doesn't seize hold [of him]." The peasant was alluding to the fact that because women did not wear underwear, their genitals were exposed to demons released by the spell when they crossed over the porch.[26] The literal understanding of demons' sexual penetration of women reveals a larger "cultural perception that women's bodies were open and men's sealed."[27]

While peasants believed women to be in greater danger of possession, they also subscribed to Orthodox notions that specific times in the religious calendar heightened the possibility of demon invasion. The primary stage for the drama of *klikushestvo* was the village church during services, particularly during the most highly charged periods of the Orthodox calendar—from Christmas through Epiphany and Lent. In the Ashchepkovo epidemic of possession, the first victim experienced her initial attack during Epiphany 1898, while the epidemic itself unfolded during Lent. A smaller 1909 epidemic in Moscow province likewise began before Easter, the most important holiday in the Orthodox calendar.[28] Both religious periods highlighted battles between good and evil and the ultimate triumph of good.

The purification of water during Epiphany to celebrate Christ's baptism signified a cosmic victory over demons. In the prayer that priests or bishops intoned in the "Great Blessing of the Waters," they asked God to "make it [the water] a source of incorruption, a gift of sanctification, a remission of sins, a protection against disease, *a destruction to demons,* inaccessible to the adverse powers and filled with angelic strength."[29] Youths who had participated in holiday masquerades—which the Russian Orthodox Church associated with the devil and his minions because they epitomized false identities—had symbolically allowed demons to invade their bodies. They subsequently purged their bodies of evil by swimming in the ice holes that had been cut for the rite of purification.[30] Other worshipers joined them, hoping to cleanse away their demons or sins.[31] Many felt susceptible to the invasion of angry demons around the time of Epiphany, especially on the eve of that holiday, when peasants believed that witches possessed stronger powers.[32]

Lent, or the Great Fast, a period in the Orthodox calendar when a struggle occurred between God and the devil as well as between life and death, also signified a time when humans were more defenseless against the devil's wiles.[33] Repeated references to individuals succumbing to demons or becoming servants of demons as well as denunciations of evil spirits in the Lenten services raised expectations among worshipers and clerics that demons would attack at least one vulnerable woman in their midst.[34] It was not coincidental that peasants believed that witches remained invisible in church during the Easter morning services only until that point when the priest emerged from the Royal Doors carrying the Holy Gifts and vanquishing evil.[35]

Outside the post-Christmas celebrations and the period of the Great Fast, women experienced seizures of possession during the regular liturgy. As the *Kheruvimskaia* or Cherubikon hymn began, demoniacs hissed, meowed, howled, and cawed. An 1890 newspaper reporter's account of a shrieker in the Smolensk village of Egor'-Bunakovo described the woman's fit at that point in the liturgy as consisting of "a horrible inhuman shout" that crescendoed into five minutes of screaming before she fell down exhausted and sobbing.[36]

Commemorating Christ's walk to Golgotha, the Cherubikon accompanies a dramatic moment of the liturgy, the so-called Great Entrance. At this point the officiating cleric carries the communion cup and the deacon the tray with consecrated loaves from the Prothesis chapel to the altar. Following the structure of the ancient church's liturgy, the Orthodox liturgies of Basil and of Chrysostom have two parts. The didactic first section is designed for both the baptized and unbaptized (catechumens). Halfway through the service, however, the catechumens are dismissed because they are not entitled to witness the mysteries of the Eucharist.[37] The Cherubikon hymn, accompanied by the priest's exhortation against the unworthiness of "those who are bound by carnal desires and pleasures," occurs shortly after the dispersal of the unbaptized.[38] By the nineteenth century and even earlier, when the distinction between baptized and unbaptized had lost its relevance, the celebration of Christ's Resurrection and of the triumph of good over evil, nonetheless, was believed to provoke the demons' fear and hence the fits of the shriekers.

Not only did the beginning of the Eucharist portion of the divine liturgy torment demons, but so too did special prayer cycles, such as the *akafist* (doxological prayers) and holy objects of any kind. The presence of the Almighty, icons, incense, communion bread, and holy water aroused the ire of demons. Thus, *klikushi* were also prone to have seizures and to shriek in animal voices during icon processions, early morning services for the possessed, blessings with holy water, and contact with holy relics.

Such public demonstrations of demon possession solicited a variety of responses from parishioners who could draw upon a range of behaviors in the possession drama. According to the Novgorodian psychiatrist Krainskii, worshipers at the end of the nineteenth century in Moscow's St. Panteleimon Chapel were moved by the seizures and screams of the possessed. The chapel attracted demoniacs from various regions of Russia because of the popular veneration of St. Panteleimon and because of its special early morning services for victims of possession. According to Krainskii, the *klikushi*'s screams began at the end of the service when the priest began to chant the doxological prayers in front of an icon of the Mother of God. A witness to one demoniac's seizure in the chapel,

Krainskii described her as a young woman who "stood calmly and prayed diligently, not paying attention to anything." All of a sudden, however, she began to scream. He noted, "The sounds [she makes] become varied, more frequent, although sometimes quieter. One hears a clear hiccup, then a snort. . . . These sounds alternate with quiet groans and deep breaths." Krainskii described "the surrounding crowd" as "quietly listen[ing] to the *klikusha,* observing her with compassion and pity. . . . With every sound the people in the chapel began to cross themselves earnestly, while the *klikusha,* sensing all the attention and sympathy of the crowd on her, became even more posed."[39] By virtue of being present at a service specifically held for the possessed and expecting to hear *klikushi*'s anguished cries, worshipers at the St. Panteleimon Chapel had prepared themselves psychologically for the spectacle they witnessed. However, not all believers remained calm when a woman experienced a demonic seizure.

The body contortions of a possessed person provoked fear and anxiety among unsuspecting witnesses. In 1890 a Smolensk newspaper columnist reported that when a woman began to scream in the midst of the Cherubikon hymn, several observers fled the church, others fainted, and still others clustered around the afflicted woman. Distressed by the demoniac's disruption of the service as well as by the panic her seizures had caused among members of the congregation, the parish priest asked the consistory if he should continue to allow the *klikusha* to attend services.[40]

Another observer captured the fear that gripped a group of Old Believers who witnessed the demonic fits of 15 shriekers in 1910. According to his account, the demoniacs' "appearance and shrieks terribly agitated [people], especially the women. The latter during the *klikushi*'s shouts looked around uneasily [and] made the sign of the cross over their mouths, then tightly clenching their lips placed two fingers on them and stood that way for the entire service. Afterwards, I found out that they did this so that the devil leaving a shrieker did not enter one of their mouths."[41] Obviously, the witnesses believed possession to be contagious. By expressing fear and anxiety and acknowledging the existence of evil spirits who tortured their victims with abandon, witnesses played a critical role in the possession drama.

The drama also required that, as with any form of illness, kin and friends react collectively to minister to the victim.[42] According to the 1861 testimony of parents, brothers, and acquaintances of the possessed young woman Anna Stefanova Dvurechenskaia from Tambov province, the sight of Anna attacking herself drove them "out of compassion to restrain her from injuring herself; but she developed such strength that it was difficult for two or three healthy men to subdue her."[43] A *klikusha*'s unfeminine physical strength illustrated the male demon's control of her body and her lack of will, and became an indispensable trope in miracle stories and other reportings of possession.[44] Consequently, it was not unusual for several men to rush to a shrieker's aid in the midst of a church service and encourage her demons to resist their efforts to restrain her. By transforming their function as spectators to participants in the possession drama, these male helpers further legitimated the demoniac's affliction.[45] Once they had her in tow, they carried the possessed woman to the front of the holy gates to receive communion.

Giving Holy Communion to the possessed publicly proclaimed the fact that the victims of possession were not responsible for their situation. A mid-nineteenth-century primer for parish priests included church father John Chrysostom's sermon regarding the sacrament of communion in which he distinguished between the possessed who were worthy of communion and those individuals whose actions made them unworthy of the sacrament. In the words of Chrysostom, "Let no one inhuman, no one rough and unmerciful, least of all any one unclean approach here. This I say not only to you, who seek to receive the Communion, but also to you, whose ministry it is to give it. . . . *They that be possest in that they are tormented of the devil are blameless and will never be punished with torment for that:* but they who approach unworthily the holy Mysteries shall be given over to everlasting torments."[46] Suspecting that she was possessed and fearing that her demons would not allow her to take communion, a peasant woman from the village Khomutovo in Moscow province at the turn of the twentieth century ordered her husband to see to it that she was forcibly taken up to the Holy Gifts, if necessary.[47] Focusing on the demons, she absolved herself of responsibility for her possession, a sentiment that was acceptable to her community of Orthodox believers.

Parishioners' participation in the unfolding drama of possession did not end with forcing communion upon a *klikusha*. They took a variety of other steps to minister to the possessed and expel her demons. When the *klikusha* began to calm down upon receipt of communion, the same men who had taken her before the iconostasis carefully led her out of the church and placed her on the ground. Women of the congregation became actors in the ritual drama by covering the shrieker with blessed Easter tablecloths and linens. Others offered their Epiphany water for her to drink even though it was extremely precious, saved as it was for unexpected illnesses within the family.[48] In addition to these remedies for possession, concerned parishioners and priests chanted the Lord's Prayer, prayers of exorcism, and other prayers such as *"Dostoino est"* (Worthy is He), *"Da voskresnet Bog"* (Indeed, God raises from the dead), and the Jesus prayer.[49]

Outside the church Russian peasants had at their disposal an arsenal of countermagic to drive away a shrieker's demons. Such means included special prayer sessions conducted by a priest, deacon, *chernichka* (a woman who renounced the secular world for the contemplative life without, however, entering a monastery), or village healer in the home. Even the incantations that secular healers employed against possession were modeled on Christian prayers. An 1892 incantation from Smolensk province invoked the help of God, Christ, and the Mother of God in expunging demons from all parts of the body:

> Lord God! Jesus Christ, the Lord's Son, came away from the Jordan River with crosses and blessed water. He came to a halt and became [quite] still. The convulsions of (some sort of) blessed animal with (some type of) wool in the belly, stomach, bones, skeleton, turbulent head, bright eyes, dark eyebrows, [and] veins made him come to a halt and become still. And the Blessed Mother came with the twelve apostles, and she came to a halt and became still. The convulsions (naming the wool of the animal [in order to identify the type of animal]) made her come to a halt and become still. Our most holy Protector, have mercy on us in our youth, our old age, for the rising moon, and for eternity. Amen.[50]

The incantation's references to animals and animal wool or fur stemmed from the belief that demons took the shape of small animals when they inhabited an individual's body. Since it was believed that evil spirits usually entered a demoniac through her mouth, it was not unusual for a *klikusha* to expel them from the same aperture by coughing up animal fur. At Easter in 1909 in the village Khomutovo (Moscow province), for example, a woman who believed herself to be possessed spit out sheep's wool in her neighbors' presence. The witnesses were terrified by this sign that the sheep-devil possessing Klavdiia's body was trying to escape her body.[51] Incantations could provoke violent behavior on the part of the demons inhabiting a woman's body, threatening her and others with injury. In such an event Nizhnii Novgorodian peasants of Vasil' district bound reclining shriekers' hands and feet to benches so that they could apply appropriate countermeasures.[52]

Other exorcism practices involving sympathetic magic or countermagic related directly to the shrieker's person. Family members or healers might flail demoniacs with birch twigs mixed with cuttings of salutary herbs and grasses (Gzhatsk district, Smolensk province) or give them an infusion that contained as a critical ingredient incense that had been used during the singing of the Cherubikon hymn during the divine liturgy (Orel province). Choosing to feed *klikushi* such substances as cocks' heads or scraps of horses' hooves from the blacksmith's floor, villagers in Griazovets district, Vologda province, and Karachev district, Orel province, hoped to appease the women's demons. In Kaluga district and province, peasants turned to sympathetic magic by cutting off a piece of a shrieker's hair from her right temple as well as part of the underseam of her left shirt sleeve, which they then burned, while their Zhizdra neighbors favored a variation of the ritual of *opakhivanie* (plowing) that was meant to ward off evil spirits who brought epidemic diseases such as cholera. In the latter event peasants tied a shrieker to a plow and pushed the plow across the soil in a symbolic attempt to drive away her demons.[53] It was also common for peasants in various areas of Russia to dunk demoniacs in a baptismal font or ice hole used for the blessing of waters at the Epiphany or to pour water from those sources over their heads. The most extreme method of chasing away a shrieker's demons, recorded by ethnographers in Melenki district, Vladimir province, involved tying shoes to the woman's feet and then branding the shoes with a hot iron.[54]

Still other procedures of countermagic were intended to control a *klikusha*'s demons as well as to compel her to identify the individual who had bewitched her. Pressure on a shrieker's ring finger on her right hand or on the little finger of her left hand, peasants believed, would produce the desired results.[55] A horse collar or yoke was the most common device for harnessing a possessed victim's convulsions and making it safe for her to divulge the bewitcher's name. Thus, at the end of the nineteenth century, Arzamas peasants of Nizhnii Novgorod province either placed a horse collar around a *klikusha*'s neck or wrapped the rope from a bell around her waist. Before putting a harness or a horse collar over a shrieker's head, Orel peasants tried placing a cross on her head as a supplementary measure to counteract the demons' powers.[56]

According to the nineteenth-century ethnographer Ushakov, peasants in Tula province explained that it was the horse collar's crosslike shape that neutralized demons.[57] What Ushakov did not note, however, was the peasants' faithful appropriation of the cross, which, according to the Orthodox Church, acted "as guardian and protector and driver away of demons."[58] Given Russian peasants' penchant to punish deviant behavior by placing a harness or yoke over the offender, the supposed salutary effect that the same device had in the case of *klikushestvo* testifies to the multiple uses and symbols that the limited number of material objects enjoyed in the nineteenth-century village.[59]

Still another measure of countermagic had the salutary effect of releasing a demoniac's powers of divination. Villagers in Nikolaevsk district, Samara province, and areas of Kaluga, Penza, Orel, and Viatka provinces sometimes hung a lock and key in lieu of the horse's collar around the woman's neck.[60] The symbolic meaning of these objects may have originated with an eighteenth-century woodcut entitled "The Chasing Out of Three Devils by a Certain Saint." The print's text portrays the demons possessing a man as locksmiths: "One locks the man's heart so it cannot break; one locks his lips so they cannot confess his sins; and one locks his money-bag to teach the sinner greed so that he will accumulate money and take care it is not stolen."[61] In the peasants' literal reading of the didactic print, the key unlocked not only the truth about the identity of the witch who had bewitched the demoniac but also what the future held for others.

Like their Western European counterparts, Russian demoniacs were believed to be clairvoyant and thus could advise peasant girls about future husbands and could help others purchase healthy animals, find lost objects, or identify thieves.[62] The announcement by two *klikushi* during the 1898–1899 Ashchepkovo epidemic in Smolensk province that people were on their way to disturb the village made quite an impression on villagers when a psychiatrist and the police chief arrived the next day; Ashchepkovo peasants became convinced that these demoniacs could predict the future.[63] Gifts of divination empowered female shriekers in ways that were otherwise impossible in the everyday life of the patriarchal village.

While peasants reacted sympathetically to demoniacs and employed countermagic against their demons, they did not believe that all *klikushi* were genuinely possessed. Before entering the possession drama as willing participants, they had to be sure that a demoniac's seizures were authentic. If peasants suspected a shrieker of feigning possession, "the meaning of the whole event becomes subverted and the scenario falls apart in shame, anger, and recriminations."[64] At the end of the nineteenth century, for example, villagers of Ashchepkovo did not take Vasilisa Alekseeva's claim of possession seriously until she had experienced more than one seizure and the seizures became increasingly severe. In accusing a well-respected community member of being a witch and casting a spell on her, Vasilisa did not possess a great deal of credibility. Furthermore, she had offended some of her neighbors with the superior airs that she had assumed because she had lived in Moscow. Once other villagers began to experience the symptoms of possession, however, most, if not all, lingering doubts about Vasilisa's possession were dispelled.[65]

The government's debunking of the myth of possession by asserting that shriekers were malingerers also influenced Russian peasants, especially when they had to deal with state officials and members of educated society. Attempting to ward off a negative attitude toward *klikushestvo* and to present herself as a truthful and God-fearing soul, one of the Ashchepkovo victims told the investigating psychiatrist, "others say that we [shriekers] are pretending . . . God preserve us from that." When the same physician tried to gain another shrieker's trust by assuring her that everyone believed in bewitchment and in the resulting affliction of possession, Khavron'ia Appollonova responded, "Hey, *barin* [Lord]! How can they not believe when I was healthy for four years and was not afraid of anyone, but look at how thin I have gotten now! During a holiday I do not sleep; I shake all night."[66] In another case, Dar'ia Fedorova Dolganova of the village Malolevinko in Penza province, who visited the Sarovskaia Hermitage in 1903, attributed her affliction of possession to the fact that God was punishing her for having dismissed the possibility of devil possession and for having thus presumed that the *klikushi* in her village were frauds.[67] Could Dolganova have been warning the psychiatrist who interviewed her that skeptics like himself were not immune from *klikushestvo*?

When a peasant official expressed doubt about the genuineness of a shrieker's possession, he could find himself in a minority position. An 1886 incident that wound up before the Moscow circuit court provides an example in which a parish priest attempted to restore a woman's identity as a demoniac after it had been boorishly challenged by a village policeman named Kamenskii. The officer had beaten a shrieker during a church service because he believed her to be an alcoholic who was feigning her possession. Walking into the Predtechenskaia Church on 26 November near the conclusion of the divine liturgy, Kamenskii found a woman named Semenova attending a cossack wife, Evdokia Pestova. The latter had experienced a seizure prior to the main service and was lying unconscious on the church floor. Ignoring the pleas of people nearby, Kamenskii told Pestova that she was a malingerer and began to beat her. The officiating priest, Father Sareevskii, sent two ushers to quell the disturbance. An unrepentant Kamenskii ordered one of the ushers to carry Pestova out of the church to the jail, where he beat her again and sent her home. In a formal denunciation of the policeman, the angry priest contended, "I consider this transgression of the constable Kamenskii to have been an offense against the spiritual atmosphere and an insult to the moral sensibility of everyone present in the Church."[68] The police officer not only had displayed disrespect for the divine liturgy but also had questioned Pestova's representation of herself as a shrieker. He may have known from personal experience that she was a drunk and malingerer or may have had some other bone to pick with her. By denouncing Kamenskii, the priest revealed his sympathy for the possessed woman, a member of his congregation under his spiritual care, and the importance of the possession myth.

Not all Orthodox priests believed in the possibility of possession in the modern era, especially among uneducated peasants. At the turn of the century, the ethnographer Sergei Maksimov cited an unusual example of a new young parish priest refusing to accept the idea that a shrieker was possessed. According to Maksimov, the cleric informed his parishioners that he would take any woman who dared interrupt his service to the provincial hospital, and, if the doctors declared her to be shamming illness, he would hand her over to the authorities. Maksimov added that this threat had the salubrious effect of silencing three *klikushi* in the village. In another village, he noted that a priest strongly reprimanded a shrieker, embarrassing her in front of the entire congregation.[69] The priests in question may have been better educated than their predecessors or at least chose to enforce the strictures of the Spiritual Regulation against possession and to ignore other church writings about the possibility of possession. Their threats, nonetheless, demonstrate the cultural underpinnings of *klikushestvo*. By questioning demoniacs' credibility and refusing to participate in the possession drama by ministering to their needs, priests shattered the peasant myth of possession and effectively silenced demoniacs. They also risked undercutting their authority among parishioners, upon whom they were economically dependent.

Some peasants were able to salvage the myth of possession from their priest's questioning eye. As the epidemic of possession in Ashchepkovo unfolded, the parish priest found himself sympathetic to both the *klikushi* and Siklitin'ia, the woman who had been accused of witchcraft and unleashing demons in the parish. He subscribed to most components of the possession myth except for the alleged causal relationship between possession and bewitchment. While providing the shriekers with communion bread and saying prayers on their behalf, he also tried to convince them that Siklitin'ia was not responsible for their affliction. Because the priest legitimated the shriekers' possession by ministering to them, the demoniacs and other parishioners were able to turn his solicitude toward the alleged witch to their advantage and to salvage the integrity of the possession drama. They did so by counting the priest among Siklitin'ia's victims: they concluded that she must have secured the priest's protection by adding a potion to the tea she served him at her home. Subsequently, rumors circulated that the priest's bewitchment manifested itself in a variety of ways: during church services he often did not emerge from beyond the royal doors of the iconostasis with the Holy Gifts of bread and wine, and he was unable to raise the cross for a blessing.[70] The act of explaining away the priest's support of the alleged bewitcher as a sign that he, too, was possessed sanctioned further mistreatment of the alleged witch Siklitin'ia.

In most cases priests served a critical role in the possession drama. Ultimately, they or monks performed exorcisms against demons. In pitting the power of God against demons, religious exorcisms were far more important than the holy water, prayers and incantations, horse collars, and other means used to control and vanquish evil. These were terrifying battles that did not always succeed in expelling the unclean spirits. In 1901 a priest by the name of Lev Matveev witnessed the successful exorcism of a possessed woman by the popular healer-priest Ioann of Kronshtadt. He noted in his report not only a description of the exorcism and miraculous cure but also his personal experience with the possessed woman. In this case the cured woman had been Matveev's parishioner for eight years, during which time she "was unable to kiss the cross or take holy communion voluntarily." When her relatives approached him to perform an exorcism, he agreed. In spite of his 17 years of clerical experience and his dealing with many instances of *klikushestvo,* however, the exorcism failed and provoked a frightening response on the part of the woman's demons: "The sick woman hissed like a snake, meowed like a cat, barked just like a dog, and shouted in the voice of various birds, whistled, and shouted in an inhuman voice, 'I am coming out.' Her stomach became extended by three-quarters of an *arshin,* forming a sharp point like a cone. She rolled around the floor in the church. It was a horrifying sight for those present."[71] That demonstration convinced the priest of the demons' strength and stubbornness. He may have been the one to suggest to the suffering woman that she seek the ministrations of Ioann of Kronshtadt.

Indeed, shriekers and their families did not confine their search for treatment to villagers' remedies, but they also sought the aid of miracle-working icons, monks, and other spiritual healers. They joined the sick and those who sought spiritual solace or had made vows to God on pilgrimages during the spring or summer when travel was easiest, but labor in the fields was intensive.[72] The release of *klikushi* from domestic and agricultural labor further testifies to families' compassionate response to possession. Informed by word of mouth about successful exorcisms and religious publications that recorded miraculous cures of the possessed at holy places and before miracle-working icons, the sufferers left the security of their villages and traveled with relatives and friends to settlements that possessed miracle-working icons or to neighboring and distant monasteries.[73]

Pilgrims regularly traversed the countryside, heading for various religious sites. At the turn of the twentieth century, "hundreds of thousands of pilgrims" each year "descended upon Kiev [and its various monasteries] from all corners of the empire."[74] A June 1891 Smolensk newspaper reporter described the scores of pilgrims who visited a village in Dorogobuzh district: "On the Day of the Ascension people, sometimes [numbering] up to four or five thousand, gather in the village Rybki. . . . However, the Orthodox people come here not so much for the market as for the opportunity to pray before the miracle-working icon of the Mother of God. A lot of women, in particular, come on pilgrimage; many of them hail from a hundred or more versts away. . . . Each of these pilgrims comes here with a strong belief in [being able to] obtain . . . a cure; a few are seeking help from various difficult life circumstances."[75] Another reporter for a Smolensk newspaper also commented on the annual pilgrimage of "several thousands of peasants, mainly women," from various neighboring provinces to the city of Smolensk to bow and pray before a miracle-working icon of the Mother of God (the Smolenskaia-Odigitriia), also on the Day of the Ascension.[76] As important social occasions during which friendships were forged and gossip exchanged, pilgrimages served as part of the healing ritual.[77] Pilgrims returning to the site of their healing to give thanks for their recovery provided hope to those who were making the trek for the first time.

Religious newspaper and journal reports encouraged villagers to time pilgrimages to coincide with canonization and relic translation services. For example, the testimony of the miraculous cure of the *klikusha* Mariia Kos'mina Mikeshina of Penza province indicated that the 1896 proclamation of the opening of Feodosii of Chernigov's grave (in preparation for his canonization) prompted Mariia's husband, Filipp Mikeshin, to pledge that "he would take the sick woman to Chernigov to pray at the new saint's relics."[78] Similarly, in 1903 a young *klikusha,* subsequently healed at the grave of Serafim of Sarov in Tambov province, explained, "When news that our Father the Tsar ordered . . . that the holy remains of the elder Serafim be opened reached our village Novo-Kurchak (Bobrov district, Voronezh province), our peasants, both young and old, decided to go to Sarov on pilgrimage. They seized me, I was ill at the time, and my godchild Kostia," who had been blind since birth.[79] The lists of similar miracle stories published by the church in popular religious magazines and pamphlets to coincide with canonizations convinced shriekers and their families as well as peasants suffering from other afflictions that they needed to take advantage of the opening of saints' relics to seek out new cures. Indeed, the testimony regarding the 1861 miraculous healing of the possessed Anna Stefanova Dvurechenskaia contained the observation: "Unwittingly, the thought arises that the saint somehow intentionally suppressed his healing powers until the day of the ceremonial opening of his relics so that all those who, by the grace of God, are glorified by their incorruptibility can see the source of the rich gift of miracle-working."[80]

While canonization celebrations attracted large crowds of pilgrims, demoniacs did not always have the luxury of waiting for these irregular events and chose instead to travel to monasteries that had reputations for exorcising demons. Before arriving in Sarov in 1903, Elena Afanas'eva Shibakova, a married peasant woman from the village Slobodka in Moscow province, had visited four monasteries in Kaluga and Moscow provinces and a Suzdal church. She sought help at the Lavrentiev Monastery (Kaluga), the Tikhonova Hermitage (Kaluga), an almshouse church in Suzdal, the Simonov Monastery in Moscow, and finally the Trinity–St. Sergii Monastery in Sergiev Posad.[81] Nowhere was she turned away, as monks subscribed to the possession myth and ministered to demoniacs with a host of remedies.

Similarly, after Epiphany 1898 the *klikusha* Vasilisa Alekseeva of the Smolensk village Ashchepkovo made the rounds of several holy sites, where monks confirmed that she was possessed and chanted special prayers and masses for her. First, her family took her to the village Leshkovo, where a holy man said prayers over the sick, especially demoniacs. Subsequently, Vasilisa and her family went to the Tikhonovskii Prepodobnyi Monastery. There the monks "gave her communion, bathed her, and wanted to administer extreme unction, but she refused." When the numerous masses the monks performed for Vasilisa did not vanquish her demons, the demoniac's relatives took her to the Kalochskii Monastery, where 12 masses were said for her. From the Kalochskii Monastery Vasilisa and her entourage traveled to two other monasteries, including the Luzhetskii Monastery in Moscow province before returning home temporarily.[82] Vasilisa's travels to several monasteries and her pattern of departing before the full regimen of exorcisms had taken hold reflected her desire to prolong the liminal status that possession provided her. Vasilisa's shrieking may also have reflected her frustrations of being an urbanized woman accorded the diminished status of daughter-in-law in her husband's household and larger community. Everywhere she turned, monks confirmed the genuine nature of her possession and provided her with the requisite attention.

At about the same time, Pelageia, a *klikusha* from the Mokrovskii parish in Kaluga province, told a zemstvo doctor that she too had sought help from monks. Unlike Vasilisa, however, she blamed herself for neglecting to follow the strict regimen for demoniacs. After numerous pilgrimages and bathing in baptismal fonts failed to relieve her of her demons, she sought the aid of an elderly religious woman, a *bogomol'naia* (a woman who prays to God), who had a reputation for helping shriekers like herself. The holy woman, "dressed all in black just like a nun," counseled Pelageia not to eat or drink anything for three days of fasting. But Pelageia lost the battle with the demon and surreptitiously ate some dry bread after only two days. Having suffered from possession since she was 16 or 17, she philosophically concluded, "Indeed, clearly God decided to torment me my entire life."[83]

Not quite so philosophically resigned, Vasilisa sought help at the Simonov Monastery in Moscow, which housed between 30 and 40 shriekers at any one time. There Father Mark, like others before him, affirmed Vasilisa's belief that she was possessed and advised her to stay at the monastery for six weeks. During that interval she was to attend special services from 3 A.M. until 1 P.M. each day and to take his treatment of grasses, oils, and communion bread. Once again, however, Vasilisa refused to stay at the monastery for the full six weeks.[84]

Another woman, thirty-three-year-old Mar'ia Fedorova of the village Zhikharevo (located just three kilometers from Vasilisa's village of

Ashchepkovo), described Father Mark's therapeutic method in some detail and noted that the ritual involved soliciting the name of the individual who had bewitched her. "I went to see him [Father Mark] in his cell," Mar'ia told a visiting psychiatrist. "When he initially came to me, I could not control myself; I fell down, cried and sobbed and was not conscious. . . . After some time I came round. . . . He brought communion bread to me, and once again I could not control myself. Then he asked if he could hold me; he smeared me with tree sap and put a piece of communion bread in my mouth." Mar'ia commented further that when Father Mark administered a mysterious substance to the shriekers, they would begin to shriek out the names of the individuals who had bewitched them. According to her mother, Mar'ia did not identify her bewitcher, so the clerical staff tried other means. They held her by the appropriate finger to elicit the information, but to no avail. Nuns then placed icons against her chest and talked about religious objects consecrated by Father Ioann of Kronshtadt, but they also failed to make Mar'ia speak.[85] Until the truth about the bewitcher's identity was revealed, it was believed, Mar'ia could not be healed.

Whether monks and clerics always demanded that the possessed name their bewitchers is difficult to determine. Understandably, materials about miraculous healings at the instigation of saints, which focus on the saints' divinely endowed powers rather than the causes of possession, are silent on the matter. Only a few discrete descriptions of exorcisms, involving attempts on the part of clerics to gain control over unruly women, mention the identification of the bewitcher as part of the ritual drama and remedy. Father Ioann of Kronshtadt demanded that a possessed woman name her bewitcher in the middle of a seizure. This request was one of several the priest asked a woman's demon in the question and answer period of the exorcism.[86] Almost three decades earlier in 1870, a Smolensk anchorite treated a *klikusha* with grasses, holy water, communion bread, and holy oil. When her demon would not identify her bewitcher, he ordered the woman's father to take her to the village crossroads—a spot believed to be the haunt of evil spirits. There, the anchorite presumed, the evil spirit would divulge the appropriate information and leave his victim's body.[87]

The practices at the Simonov Monastery and elsewhere suggest that the naming of a *klikusha*'s bewitcher was an integral part of the exorcism ritual, the intent of which was to impose order upon disorder. The more information the exorcist could acquire in the course of "cajoling and commanding the demon to leave," "the greater his control over the spirit."[88] As Robin Briggs points out with regard to cases of suspected witchcraft in early modern Europe, "the notion that illness might be related to the breakdown of interpersonal relations . . . was far from absurd. If the sickness resulted from a broken relationship with the witch, then the natural inference was that a formal display of reconciliation was a necessary part of the cure."[89]

WITCHCRAFT

As in other cultures, the beliefs and practices of late-nineteenth-century Russian and Ukrainian peasants regarding witches and sorcerers underscored three functions.[90] First, their oral culture, rich in its imagery of witches and sorcerers, had a didactic purpose. It taught community members about evil, deviant social behavior, and the danger of female sexuality. These "were stories anyone could tell, drawing on a great reservoir of shared beliefs and fantasies, endlessly recycled as part of everyday experience." Second, the belief that antisocial community members violated familial responsibilities or norms of neighborliness allowed peasants to restore their communities' equilibrium by securing confessions or counterspells from or by avenging themselves on suspected enemies.[91] Third, the cultural construction of witchcraft permitted weaker members of communities to take advantage of the powers ascribed to witches and sorcerers. By presenting themselves in this guise and threatening to hex co-villagers, they gained authority otherwise denied them. In the complex world of the village, where interpersonal relationships were vital and concerns about the natural world were paramount, peasants alternatively shunned witches and sorcerers and sought them out so that their powers could be directed against supernatural forces.

The three functions of witchcraft beliefs sometimes overlapped and supported each other. For example, when peasants charged others with bewitchment, they used traits from folktales of witches and sorcerers to legitimate their claims. Persons eager to play the role of witch or sorcerer also adopted stereotypical characteristics attributed to malevolent individuals. On other occasions, however, there existed little relationship between the cultural attributes of witches and the individuals identified as possessing malevolent powers. As Robert Rowland points out regarding early modern European witchcraft, "the aggrieved person asks, not 'Who has been behaving like a witch?', but 'Who can have been wishing me harm?'"[92]

The folkloric material concerning witches and sorcerers recorded among late-nineteenth-century Russian and Ukrainian peasants merits exploration, as do actual cases in which individuals were denounced or defined themselves as witches or sorcerers. Over 80 percent of the 80 cases identified from ethnographic, psychiatric, juridical, and newspaper accounts stem from the last three decades of the nineteenth century, a period that witnessed the effects of industrialization, population pressures, perceived land hunger, and increase in temporary migrant labor for Russian male peasants. These socioeconomic factors caused tensions that could be relieved in part through charges of witchcraft. The fact that tensions within households as well as fears of infertility and impotence could still result in such charges, however, suggests that socioeconomic causes should not be overstressed. Witchcraft continued to be relevant in a developing society that had to cope with problems of everyday life.

Some of the witchcraft charges could be negotiated and resolved; others required more extreme action. In 48 percent of the cases involving the identification of witches, communities erupted with anger and brutality against their own members. Another 6 percent involved collective action against all or some women of individual villages. In such cases men seeking to identify witches in their midst forcibly searched the women for tails, stripped and dunked them, or forced them to climb through horses' collars. Because incidents of violence tended to leave paper trails in the criminal court system, one can assume that their high percentage among the recorded cases amounts to a distortion of historical reality. Robin Briggs has astutely reminded scholars in his study of European witchcraft that societies subscribing to witchcraft beliefs possessed a variety of coping strategies vis-à-vis malevolent individuals. "There were many techniques for limiting one's personal exposure, and for controlling the suspect's behaviour,"[93] not all of which involved violence. Had rural folk always reacted violently against alleged witches, they would have destroyed their society and lived in anarchy. Since violent acts attracted the attention of the authorities and outside observers, while nonviolent actions often remained hidden from their gaze, the picture of village life presented by elite records is skewed and exaggerated.

The fact that the 80 cases of witchcraft occurred in 34 diverse provinces and regions of European Russia and Russian-ruled Ukraine, ranging from the most industrialized to the most remote, with 73 percent emanating from Russian-populated villages or towns, suggests several realities about the late-nineteenth- and early-twentieth-century Russian and Ukrainian countryside. First, witchcraft beliefs did not disappear with encroaching modernization but, as in other developing European societies, underwent refinement because of socioeconomic changes. Second, it was the rare Russian and Ukrainian village in the late nineteenth and early twentieth centuries that had direct experience with witches and sorcerers, although fear of witches was widespread. According to anthropologist Gananath Obeyesekere, "While cultural ideas may be almost universally believed in, personal confrontation with these ideas is highly variable."[94] Third, a charge of witchcraft constituted only one type of denunciation that peasants could employ against individuals who represented a threat to their lives and communities. Migrant workers who returned to their native villages to make land claims, for example, might be denounced on religious grounds if they had abandoned Orthodoxy and joined a religious sect, sympathized with Old Belief, converted to another Christian faith, or were atheists. Peasants possessed a myriad of institutions to mediate and resolve village conflicts, including their village assemblies, informal courts, and cantonal courts. Charges of witchcraft represented only a small fraction of disputes that peasants effectively dealt with in other ways. As with charges of horse theft and immorality, those having to do with witchcraft were usually subjected to extralegal justice. The empire's legal code did not recognize the validity of witchcraft, and peasants were reluctant to use the cantonal courts to try witches for fear that the courts' lenient sentences would result in the accused seeking revenge against their accusers.[95] Finally, the preponderance of witchcraft cases among Russian peasants may be explained by the high incidence of *klikushestvo* that was largely absent from the Ukrainian provinces.

Women figured prominently both in the cultural definitions and actual identification of witches and sorcerers. Male sorcerers and warlocks did exist in the belief system of the late-nineteenth-century Russian and Ukrainian countryside, but women accounted for more than 70 percent of those charged with witchcraft and sorcery between 1861 and 1917. While peasants physically attacked one in every two men and women they identified as sorcerers, sometimes with fatal results, they did not subject groups or entire villages of men to physical tests to determine if they were sorcerers as they did groups of women. All women were potential witches and seemingly less overt in making their powers known. This feminization of sorcerers reflected a growing identification of women and unrestrained sexuality as potentially dangerous to the patriarchal world. The dependence of elderly women on family and community for food and shelter, the availability of which was perceived by peasants to be increasingly shrinking by the late nineteenth century, also ensured their higher visibility among the ranks of those accused of malefic witchcraft. Lastly, women themselves figured more prominently than men as victims of bewitchment, maleficence, and sorcery. More often than not they identified other women as their bewitchers. Those accused of witchcraft and subject to popular violence, whether female or male, tended to be weaker members of their communities or poverty-stricken strangers, and the alleged witches' assailants were more powerful than the sorcerers' supposed magic.

✦ Because of the different historical traditions of areas of Ukraine that had been under the political domination of Poland in the early modern and modern periods, Ukrainian peasants were not immune from the lingering cultural influences of the European witchcraze of the sixteenth and seventeenth centuries. The rich lore of Ukrainian and Russian peasants in the last decades of Imperial Russia reveals a cultural borrowing of European precepts: the witches' sabbath, witches' apostasy, and the general demonization of evil that educated elites had superimposed upon the popular beliefs of European peasants in an effort to create a more rational religious and political order.[96] That oral culture also bears the stamp of the Russian and Ukrainian educated elite, who went out to the countryside to study the peasants with preconceived notions about their beliefs. The questions that ethnographers and physicians asked of peasants stemmed from their familiarity with Western European works on witchcraft. References to the witches' sabbath, for example, might have originated with the observers rather than the peasants themselves, helping to explain why peasants did not always have well-developed notions of ideas that were mistakenly attributed to them. In talking to different audiences about their afflictions, peasants might have varied their explanations to suit their interlocutors' presuppositions. For example, Russian peasants would not have been opposed to talking about the human source of misfortune with ethnographers, but they would stress the demonic side of possession when addressing a priest or monk upon whom they depended to exorcise the demons afflicting them. Getting to the reality of peasant mentalities is a difficult task, permeated as those ideas were by their reporters' biases as well as by peasants' awareness of their audience.

The ethnographic materials of the nineteenth and early twentieth centuries suggest that Russian and Ukrainian peasants did not distinguish between witches and sorcerers. Unlike African tribal societies, they lumped the "innate psychic powers" of the witch together with the sorcerer's ability to inflict harm on others through injurious medicines and incantations.[97] Peasants, or at least the educated elite in describing peasant beliefs, used the feminine terms *"ved'ma"* and *"vid'ma"* ("witch" in Russian and Ukrainian respectively) and *"koldunia"* (female sorcerer) interchangeably with a decided preference for the latter and referred to a male sorcerer chiefly as a *"koldun."* Ultimately, anyone within or outside the village had the potential of becoming a witch. Suspecting an individual of having dabbled in sorcery did not provide the accuser immunity from suspicion from the same charge in other circumstances.

At the same time, healers in Ukrainian and Russian villages were more vulnerable to charges of witchcraft and malefic intent. According to ethnographic accounts, nineteenth-century Russian peasants sometimes referred to a witch or sorcerer as a *znakhar'/znakharka* or *lekar'/lekarka* (male or female healer); a *sheptun/sheptun'ia* (male or female whisperer); or a *zagovornik* (incanter), among other things.[98] Ukrainian peasants in Khar'kov province also confused witches and sorcerers with healers, suggesting that there existed a thin line between black and white magic, magic with or without the aid of evil spirits.[99] Since the peasants thought disease came from the realm of the supernatural, those who could access the supernatural had to be sought out.

Indeed, healers and witches had a good deal in common. To ensure the full efficacy of their curative and fortune-telling powers and their ability to reverse spells, they shrouded their practices in secrecy, whispering and mumbling incantations over remedies and potions, making it difficult for patients to know when the healer was beseeching the help of God, the Mother of God, and saints or that of the devil.

V. Mansikka, an early-twentieth-century scholar of Russian popular beliefs, argued on the contrary that the healer and witch or sorcerer were polar opposites. While the healer beseeched God's help, the sorcerer relied on the aid of the devil. The sorcerer, according to Mansikka, specialized in abortion, destroying amorous relationships, undoing hexes, making individuals ill, and bewitching newlyweds. Evidence suggests, however, that a rigid distinction between witches and sorcerers, on the one hand, and healers, on the other, did not exist. Both performed abortions, reversed spells, and made individuals ill, although peasants normally did not accuse healers of bewitching newlyweds. Mansikka was closer to the mark in pinpointing individual intent: should healers wish harm upon someone, they became in the peasants' minds sorcerers and their powers evil.[100]

The outcome of a cure might determine a peasant's interpretation of the healer as either a good or evil person. While peasants did not rush to ascribe all failures of healers to sorcery, a series of misfortunes at a healer's hand might lead them to that conclusion. For example, in 1880 in Penza province, an old woman healer experienced a downturn in her fortunes when she supposedly hexed two of her patients; villagers subsequently blamed her for causing a series of stomach disorders.[101]

The common potions and herbs that healers and sorcerers administered to their clients for various ailments and requests further blurred the line between beneficial and malefic magic. Some of those potions had clear demonic implications and could only be associated with evildoers, while others could be administered by either witches or healers. For example, a story from the town of Kupiansk in Khar'kov province identified the salve that empowered witches to fly as a mixture made from dogs' bones, cats' brains, and human blood.[102] These sources of witches' powers were common to European witchcraft as well and might reflect Western influences on Ukrainian folklore. Other witches' salves, however, were concocted from plants commonly used by healers. In the 1870s Russian peasants explained to the ethnographer M. N. Parunov that witches used henbane, thorn-apple, *helleborus, parnassia palustris,* and *aconitum napellus* for their ointments.[103] These plants with their poisonous and narcotic properties were part of a healer's remedies to treat patients for rheumatism, gout, lumbago, bruises, asthma, lice, and, in the case of hellebore, to cause miscarriages.[104] Could not a salve found in a healer's arsenal of potions have been easily interpreted as proof that the healer was actually a witch?

While Russian and Ukrainian peasants at times identified healers with sorcerers and witches, or vice versa, they kept their definitions of evildoers sufficiently broad to encompass anyone in the village. They claimed that witches and sorcerers either inherited their powers or learned their trades by choice or accident.[105] According to Russian and Ukrainian peasants, sorcerers often had no choice but to transfer their powers to an unwilling individual. This notion stemmed from their shared belief that as instruments of the devil or unclean spirits, learned witches and sorcerers were tormented on their deathbeds until they passed their talents on to someone else, normally a relative. Dying witches and sorcerers might also imbue a stick or other inanimate object with their strength so that an unsuspecting passerby, thinking that the stick was harmless, would pick it up and immediately become a witch. Both peasantries characterized natural witches as being superior to and more benevolent than those who consciously chose to break the rules of the moral community by learning the ways of sorcery. These latter witches and sorcerers made pledges with the devil or his emissaries, thus invoking the idea of the demonic common to Western European witchcraft, but that had largely been absent from beliefs in witchcraft and sorcery in medieval Muscovy.[106]

The steps to becoming a sorcerer were identified in a May 1815 court case in which nineteen-year-old Mikhail Petrov Chukharev of Pineg district, Archangel province, was charged with casting a spell over his cousin Ofim'ia Aleksandrova Lobanova. Chukharev confessed to the court that the peasant Grigor'ev Krapivin had taught him how to become a sorcerer. According to the defendant, Krapivin had advised him, first, to abjure the Christian faith. After removing his baptismal cross from his neck and carrying it in his shoes for 12 hours, he was to say, "I renounce God and his life-giving cross; I give myself into the hands of the devil." Then he was to whisper over salt the name of the person he wished to harm and describe the manner in which the harm was to manifest itself. Having done all that, he was to take the cross from his shoe and hang it up on the wall. Unprotected by the forces of God, he would immediately become possessed by devils and become an evildoer.[107]

The prescription for becoming a witch or sorcerer through apostasy and crossing the boundary between morality and immorality continued to prevail in post-1861 Russian and Ukrainian villages. In the late nineteenth century, Russian peasants from Makar'ev district, Nizhnii Novgorod province, told an ethnographer that persons wishing to learn the secrets of sorcery should walk at night to the crossroads, a place of liminality between the known and unknown. By removing their crosses and renouncing Christ; their relatives; and the earth, sun, moon, and stars, they could invoke Satan's minions. They subsequently had to pledge their allegiance to the dark spirits and beg these devils for instruction in sorcery. A declaration written in blood to obey Satan sealed the pact.[108]

A detailed prescription for becoming a *viritnik*—a powerful sorcerer whose spells could not be undone—comes from Bolkhov district, Orel province. Persons were advised to walk at the dead of night to a crossroads outside the village where six roads in honor of six devils (identified as Beelzebub, the Prince of Darkness, and one spirit each for guile, lies, sickness, the evil eye, and malice) converged. Standing in the middle of the point at which the roads converged, the individual wanting to become a sorcerer was to call upon one of the devils, who in turn would ask him to bring a succession of sacrifices to that location. The first sacrifice was a cock stolen from a priest during mass. Upon receipt of the sacrifice, the unclean spirit would tear it into six pieces and throw the parts onto the different roads for each of the devils. Night after night the initiate had to bring other sacrifices, including a sheep, human bones, and finally his shirt. A contract written in the new sorcerer's blood sealed the pact whereby his body and soul in life and in death belonged to the devil.[109]

Late-nineteenth-century Ukrainian peasants of the village Kolodezhnaia in Kupiansk district, Khar'kov province, still talked about witches learning their craft from natural witches by removing the cross they wore around their necks and placing it in their boots. In the same district peasants took the renunciation of the Christian faith a step further, noting that a woman wishing to become a witch should take the icon of the Mother of God with which her parents had blessed her on her wedding day down to the mill or riverbank, favorite haunts of demons and sites of clandestine meetings. There, away from observation, the witch-to-be had to trample on the icon, while reciting the Lord's Prayer three times backwards. The reversal of the prayer would summon unclean spirits who would continue the witch's education. The woman's schooling would be completed atop Bald Mountain in Kiev at a witches' sabbath—the institutional expression of social deviance.[110]

The belief among nineteenth-century Russian and Ukrainian peasants in witches' sabbaths reflected Western European influences coming through Ukraine from Poland, beginning in the seventeenth century with Muscovy's acquisition of Left-Bank Ukraine. Those influences were popularized in prints and chapbooks in the following two centuries, with literature about witches and sorcerers still influencing peasant readers in the late nineteenth century. By the fin de siècle, authors of these stories hoped to dissuade peasants of their beliefs by providing scientific explanations for illness and debunking the powers of witches and sorcerers. Paradoxically, they may have encouraged beliefs in sorcerers and witches by drawing attention to malevolent individuals and thus legitimating their existence.[111] Descriptions of the witches' sabbath in print literature undoubtedly also influenced peasant oral culture.

One of the more detailed accounts of the witches' sabbath comes from an 1891 folktale recorded in the Russian province of Smolensk, variations of which were popular in areas of Russia and Ukraine. Like its Western European counterparts, it refers to the witches' salve and implies that sexual intercourse occurs between female witches and demons. The tale focuses on a soldier's discovery that his wife and mother-in-law are witches. Suspicious of their frequent nocturnal forays from the hut, the soldier chooses the night of Ivan Kupalo, the summer solstice, when peasants believed witches to be most active, to spy on the women from his bed. At midnight, as if on cue, the two women get out of bed, dress themselves, and throw a potion onto the hearth fire. When a voice orders them to fly, the two women disappear up the stovepipe. Copying the women's actions, the husband follows them up the chimney and finds himself flying off to Karmilitskii mountain. At the mountaintop the soldier sees numerous witches and a large seven-headed serpent sitting on a chair. When the serpent whistles, the witches start to dance and sing. Observing his disheveled mother-in-law dancing with an old man who wore no pants, hat, or belt, the soldier attracts the unwelcome attention of the orgy's participants by laughing out loud at the odd scene. Before he can come to harm, however, his wife orders him to fly home, and he does as he is bidden. When his spouse and mother-in-law return home, the soldier promises that he will refrain from using their special potion.[112] A variant of this story from Kupiansk, Khar'kov province, identifies the king of the sabbath as a devil, sporting a tail and horns. Yet another Ukrainian tale comes closest to its Western European counterpart by referring to the devil as Lucifer and as presiding over a table covered with human skulls filled with blood.[113]

Ukrainian peasants told ethnographers that at sabbaths witches flirted with devils without engaging them in sexual intercourse, no doubt sanitizing their descriptions for the ears of outsiders.[114] Convinced that sexual orgies were part of the peasants' definition of the witches' sabbath, early-twentieth-century ethnographer Vladimir Hnatiuk may have been influenced by Ukrainian tales of devils appearing before girls in the guise of their boyfriends engaging them in sexual acts as well as by tales of demons draining women's blood by sucking at their breasts.[115] The wasting away of a woman as a result of what today would be diagnosed as anorexia thus may have been explained by Ukrainian peasant culture as possession.[116]

Similar tales about women having sexual relations with devils circulated in late-nineteenth-century Central Russia. However, there the focus centered on widows and young women whose migratory-worker husbands were gone for significant periods of time as prime candidates for serving the devil. Seduced by demons who appeared before them in the shape of their dead or absent husbands, these women sometimes became pregnant. Stressing the demonic, such stories provided an acceptable explanation of pregnancy among women whose husbands were in absentia, as well as of the origins of natural sorcerers and witches.[117]

The Russian tales also reflected peasants' mixed reactions to the increase of off-farm labor on the part of adult males. By the 1890s nearly every household in the Central Industrial belt had a family member who worked outside the village, usually in St. Petersburg and Moscow. Migrant laborers, while coveted by young peasant girls as marriage partners because of their urban ways and access to material goods, could also arouse village suspicions. They had abandoned demanding agricultural labor for a supposedly less responsible lifestyle in the tainted city. Leaving behind their wives and parents to take care of the farming and to meet communal dues and obligations, they were perceived by their envious neighbors as shirking their responsibilities, especially if they were delinquent in sending cash back to their families. When the laborers returned to live in the village between jobs or to retire there, peasants who had remained in the countryside criticized the individualistic and antipatriarchal ways their former neighbors had adopted in the city. They sometimes went so far as to denounce them to the authorities as having infected the community with "pernicious moral influences" and religious nonconformity. While retaining older, time-honored suspicions of women as likely candidates of devils' sexual interest, peasants shifted their attention to migrants' wives as individuals they suspected of witchcraft. Attacking these vulnerable women who did not have the protection of their spouses was relatively easy. Peasants chose to attack male migrant laborers through official channels of denunciation.[118] Peasant institutions were simply not equipped to track down migrants in faraway places.

Russian peasants' readiness to accept male demons' sexual attraction toward women also resulted in a feminization of witchcraft victims that corresponded with the greater identification of women as witches and sorcerers among Ukrainian peasants. The tendency of seventeenth-century Muscovites to target men as witches more frequently than women had changed by the nineteenth century, when women were far more likely to be denounced than men in the Russian village (at a ratio of more than 2:1). Among Ukrainian peasants in the post-1861 period, women's predominance over men as alleged witches by at least five to one is consistent with the figures for the earlier European witchcraze.

Approximately 80 percent of so-called witches in significant areas of Western Europe and Poland between 1500 and 1700 were women.[119]

In addition to ascribing carnal knowledge of the devil to female witches, Russian and Ukrainian peasants also identified natural witches as genealogical freaks, sometimes the result of sexually deviant behavior.[120] For example, Russian peasants of the village Bariatinskoe in Meshchovsk district, Kaluga province, characterized a natural witch as the bastard of another illegitimate child's grandchild.[121] By believing that the tenth daughter or the thirteenth child (male or female) of a woman who had previously given birth only to female babies was a witch or warlock, Russian peasants of Chern' district, Tula province, chose to interpret an unnatural number of pregnancies that produced a string of girls as evidence of supernatural intervention and sexual aberration.[122] Too many daughters, in the Russian peasants' minds, constituted a financial drain on patrilineal households, because parents had to provide them with dowries when they married and could not depend upon them to look after them in their dotage, an obligation that fell instead to the eldest or youngest son. Ukrainians viewed either seven daughters or seven sons as abnormal and assumed that the seventh daughter was sure to be a witch and the seventh son a vampire.[123]

Russian and Ukrainian peasants not only perceived natural witches to be products of unusual sexual practices, circumstances, or pregnancies, but also claimed that the natural witch herself was sexually deviant. The identification of witches with sexual misconduct was not distinctly East Slavic. Western European courts in the medieval and early modern period were prone to charge witches and heretics with sexual nonconformity, including homosexuality.[124] According to Ukrainian and Russian popular lore, a natural witch, like the folktale witch Baba Iaga, possessed a physical abnormality in the form of a tail. Unlike the witch's teat or devil's mark described by Western European elites in early modern Europe as succoring the devil's appetite, the tail denoted the witch's animal-like nature and suggested genitalia that were akin to the male penis. In fact, the witch was a personification of a demon. She could be guilty of sodomy and bestiality. The image of male sexual arousal is evoked in the nineteenth-century Ukrainian peasant belief that a witch's tail appeared at night but disappeared during the day. Like male genitalia, the natural witch's bald tail was thought to be hairless at birth, but gradually became covered with hair as she aged. The sexual appetite of the unnatural witch was evidenced by the length of the penis-tail. Russian peasants of Chernsk district, Tula province, claimed that by the time a witch had reached the age of 40 or 50, her tail measured 5 *vershkov* (anywhere from 5 to 8.75 inches).[125] In other words, a female witch was the most sexually dangerous to the patriarchal order when she was near or at the end of her childbearing years.

Suspected witches needed to be rooted out, even if it meant a humiliating physical examination for the offending tail.

At the turn of the twentieth century, Russian and Ukrainian peasants were still searching alleged witches for tails. Suspecting a woman of being a witch because she had threatened to put a hex on a neighbor with whom she had just quarreled, villagers in Bolkhov district, Orel province, in 1899 attacked her, hoping to yank her tail out. When they did not find the desired appendage, they resumed beating her. No doubt they assumed that she had the ability to make the dangerous member disappear or at least to conceal it effectively, as witches, like demons, were expert masqueraders. In the worst case, she was not a natural, but learned witch.[126] The peasants clearly did not require "a high degree of proof for what they already believed to be true."[127] Another instance of an attempt to examine a woman for a tail occurred near the end of the nineteenth century in Bratslav district, Podolia province, when a Ukrainian household found that its cows would not give milk. Ignorant of theories of bacteriology, the residents turned to a visiting healer, Kiprian Pukas, who informed them that a witch had hexed the animals. Needing to find the culprit in order to maintain his credibility, Pukas asked his clients a number of leading questions that prompted him to point his finger at their next-door neighbor. He suggested to the concerned peasants that they search the woman for a tail. When it proved impossible to examine the woman's backside, the healer asked a peasant woman for a candle that she had saved from Passion Week, noting that a witch would be deprived of all her powers if her eye was burned. The neighbor shrieked so loudly when her neighbors and the healer came after her with the candle that some factory workers came running to her rescue.[128] In yet another instance at the turn of the twentieth century, a Russian peasant woman in self-defense "went to a doctor for a certificate to the effect that she was built like other women and did not have a tail."[129]

In addition to depicting witches with tails, late-nineteenth- and early-twentieth-century Russian and Ukrainian folklore also underscored the sexual prowess and unnatural sexual propensities of female witches. The folkloric character Baba Iaga is always depicted as traveling with the phallic symbols of a pestle and broom or mop.[130] As in Western European lore, the image of the flying witch, using an animal or person as her broom, was ubiquitous. Woodcuts portraying the devil riding a male sinner as if he were a horse clearly influenced a Russian folktale from Orel province in which a soldier billeted with a witch became her victim.[131] But in this case, the sexual inferences are more explicit: "the witch used to take a bridle, throw it on the soldier, mount him, and ride right up until the rooster crowed." It is the woman's reversal of normal sexual relations by presuming to mount the man that makes her such a threatening character. In restoring his rightful position as the sexual aggressor and making the woman the passive receptor, the soldier reasserts the traditional patriarchal order.[132]

A tale from the village Sovetsk in Iaransk district, Viatka province, recorded in the 1920s but undoubtedly dating back to the prerevolutionary period, used sexual imagery to describe the transferral of power from a sorcerer to a layperson. According to the female narrator, a woman agreed to receive an ill sorceress's powers. Following instructions, the novice arrived at the bathhouse (a traditional hiding place for demons) on the designated day to find the old witch, a female intermediary, and a frog larger than a human. The sorceress ordered the initiate to undress and to climb into the frog's mouth, which, like a woman's vagina, expanded to accommodate her. The initiate did as she was told. She went in and out of the frog's mouth three times, and in this fashion became a sorceress.[133] Once again, a woman assumed the characteristics of a phallic symbol, but this time an animal constituted the object of desire. Nothing was said of the frog's gender. However, the popular association of female witches with cows, their supposedly insatiable desire for cow's milk and cheese, as well as the imagery of witches having milk pails and strainers on their heads in Ukrainian and Russian folklore suggest a belief that women witches had a proclivity toward bestiality.[134]

All witches, whether natural or learned, also betrayed their sexual deviance by wearing their hair loose rather than braided and covered in the manner of respectable married women. In this respect they were akin to prostitutes portrayed on religious icons depicting the torments of hell. If a woman wished to intimidate her neighbors by making them think that she was a witch, she could wear her hair down and uncovered. In 1880 Agrafena Dmitrieva Chindiaikina of the village Mordovskie Marki, for example, took the description of a witch literally by walking about her neighbors' yard at night with her hair loose. Found in a neighbor's cellar, she was apprehended as a witch—either on suspicion of theft or laying a hex—and was beaten to death.[135]

Female witches, according to Russian and Ukrainian peasants, possessed other physical properties that made them repulsive. Again like the folktale witch Baba Iaga, they were said to have large blue noses or broad snub noses, bony arms, protruding chins, and some physical deformity such as a humpback. A Ukrainian story from Kupiansk district described a witch as an "old woman with a completely disfigured and scarred face."[136] According to a Russian folktale from Tula province, a witch as the epitome of evil was "a woman as old as old can be, a taught sorceress-witch, gloomy to look at, yellow as a mushroom, with wrinkles on her face two feet long, and with a nose like that of a dog sniffing for bones."[137]

While in practice a woman's malevolent conduct rather than her physical appearance led her to be identified as a witch, stereotypical images of witches were imbued with meaning.[138] Anne Llewellyn Barstow interprets the fear of overassertive and sexually active elderly women among Western Europeans at the height of the early modern witchcraze as men fantasizing that "old women still fancied them and [finding] . . . the idea grotesque."[139] In interpreting Baba Iaga in Freudian terms, Andreas Johns suggests that by endowing Iaga with such ugly features, men may also have been subconsciously counteracting their Oedipal tendencies: "Fantasies about phallic women are especially significant for men who have an insufficient sense of self separate from the mother. Thus in a culture where male children are exclusively taken care of by women (like Russia), one might expect the development of phallic women fantasies."[140]

The sexual powers that Russian and Ukrainian peasants in the late nineteenth century ascribed to male sorcerers were not so extensive as those they attributed to female witches. They had neither tails nor grotesque physical features. Because peasants firmly believed that sorcerers, like witches, could adversely affect fertility, however, it is quite plausible that they sometimes associated sodomy and bestiality with sorcerers.[141] The 1887 charge of sorcery against two peasants, Andrei Arkhipov and Nikifor Dorofeev, exemplifies the popular belief that sorcerers caused infertility of both women and crops. Peasants of the villages Novinki and Durino near the town of Torzhok threatened mob violence if the local priest did not cooperate in requiring all villagers to take an oath of faith in God as a way of identifying the two sorcerers. A subsequent legal inquiry indicated that the peasants had already singled out Arkhipov and Dorofeev as the culprits. Local peasant girls had reportedly postponed marriage out of fear of being bewitched by one of these two men. Indeed, Dorofeev made a living by treating bewitched women; at other times he allegedly bewitched women through his breath or kiss. The fact that Arkhipov and Dorofeev's grain harvest was abundant while the other peasants suffered poor harvests provided more incriminating evidence. Peasants who thought in terms of equality of opportunity were resentful of neighbors who were able to better themselves. They accordingly accused the two men of adversely affecting everyone else's harvest. By making *perezhinki,* twists or knots in the grain out in the fields, and saying incantations over them, Arhkhipov and Dorofeev had released ergot, a fungus on rye, that resulted in poor yields and food poisoning.[142] By ridding their community of the alleged culprits, peasants hoped to restore the pattern of early marriage and to ensure bountiful harvests.

Ukrainian and Russian peasants' imbuing witches and sorcerers with dangerous powers over the sexual activities of others provided all sorts of pretexts for holding community members responsible for the impotence and infertility of humans, animals, and land. More than a quarter (26%) of all of the recorded incidents of alleged witchcraft available dealt with impotence and infertility or fears thereof. In drought-prone areas of Russia and Ukraine (Saratov, Samara, Ekaterinoslav, Podolia, Kherson, and Khar'kov provinces), peasants tried to reverse the weather patterns by disinterring bodies of alleged witches and sorcerers or by pouring water into their graves, and by dunking suspected living witches into water.[143] Since all humans were susceptible to impotence or infertility, the witch or sorcerer's power in this regard was particularly alarming. In an extreme example in 1890, a twenty-one-year-old male of the village Sychevka, Karachev district, Orel province, killed his seventeen-year-old bride on the pretext that she used witchcraft to make him impotent.[144]

Weddings constituted particularly vulnerable times for the sexuality of newlyweds and their guests as Russian and Ukrainian peasants believed that sorcerers sought revenge for having been wronged either before or during the marriage festivities, or worse yet, for not having been invited to the wedding. Fantastic tales about witches or sorcerers turning entire wedding parties into wolves circulated among the peasants. In theory any community member, either invited or uninvited to a wedding, could become a witch or sorcerer.[145] Peasants could explain a bride's barrenness, a groom's impotence, and, in the case of the Russian village, demon possession at a wedding as a result of a grudge that the malevolent individual bore against the bride's or groom's family. Not surprisingly, weddings increased stress levels among the wedding party and other guests as they expected misfortune to befall them.

Among Russian peasants brides believed themselves to be especially prone to the invasion of evil spirits because of the dramatic change taking place in their lives. The boundaries between being a maiden and being a wife (a woman with sexual experience) and between living in the home of her parents and living in the home of her in-laws were temporarily suspended. She was not yet wife or in-law, nor was she any longer a maiden and her parents' ward. That lack of definition and the anxiety produced by the public celebration and scrutiny of the consummation of the marriage made her ripe for believing in the machinations of evil spirits.

The story of twenty-six-year-old Natal'ia Ivanovna Levakova of the village Chaslitsa in the Kasimov district of Riazan' province poignantly illustrates the dangers that a bride believed threatened her as well as the causal relationship in the peasants' mind between bewitchment and demon possession.[146] In an interview with a psychiatrist at the Sarovskaia Hermitage, where she had gone on pilgrimage in 1903, a childless Natal'ia explained that she had been a *klikusha* for seven and a half years. Asked about her initial signs of physical distress, the woman dated the beginning of her problems to her wedding day. Reconstructing the events of this occasion that attested to her bewitchment, Natal'ia recollected that on the morning of her nuptials she became unnerved momentarily when she went outside to get fresh air and noticed Semen, a villager with a reputation for bewitching people, talking to two men out on the street. Knowing that she had already taken the proper precautions against sorcery by inserting three pins in the hem of her skirt, she forgot the incident. The pins supposedly protected her genitalia against demon invasion and counteracted the pins that sorcerers used to cause infertility and impotence.[147] That night, after the wedding feast when she and her husband were alone, however, she noticed with horror that the pins were missing. She immediately thought that they might have dropped out in the morning when she saw Semen looking at her. Agitated by this news, Natal'ia's husband helped her look for the pins, but to no avail. Their thoughts about Semen's hexing Natal'ia, however, disappeared when they were able to consummate their marriage. Another sign of trouble, nonetheless, occurred on the second day of the wedding festivities when Natal'ia felt a pain in her foot; taking off her footwear, she noticed three blue spots outlined in red on her skin. Since nothing adverse happened, she thought no more about the omen. After a year and a half of marriage, however, Natal'ia began to complain about pains in various parts of her body. Her discomfort rekindled suspicions that Semen might have bewitched her and planted a demon inside her on her wedding day. Natal'ia did not explain why the demon waited to afflict her with a seizure until her father-in-law brought her some paper flowers that an old woman pilgrim had given him. Taking the bouquet from her father-in-law, Natal'ia suddenly fell to the ground, screaming and beating herself as the demon inside her reacted adversely to the religious power of the flowers that had been sanctified with holy water at a monastery. When a witness grabbed Natal'ia by her ring finger so that she would name her accuser, she yelled out Semen's name. Recurring periodically, Natal'ia's seizures intensified when her husband was away from home earning money as a laborer. Only a visit to St. Serafim's grave at Sarov in 1903 freed her of her demons.[148]

Other peasants had direct experience of demon possession during wedding celebrations. Two epidemics of *klikushestvo* serve as examples of this phenomenon. Both occurred during weddings in Molodinskaia canton of Podol'sk district, Moscow province, one in February 1895, the other almost three years later in January 1898. Peasants attributed the two episodes to the malevolence of neighbors they identified as witches or sorcerers. The first began on the third day of the marriage feasts when the bride, Dar'ia Dmitrieva, had a nervous fit associated with demon possession during which she accused her neighbor Natal'ia Vasil'eva of bewitching her. The groom was the second person to experience convulsions. In the end, a total of 15 persons (6 men and 9 women) believed themselves to be possessed because of Vasil'eva's hex. Vasil'eva and her mother-in-law enjoyed reputations as sorcerers, but this time attention fell squarely on Vasil'eva as she had justifiable cause for disliking the bride: Dmitrieva had spurned Vasil'eva's son as a suitor. When the examining doctor pointed out that Vasil'eva could not be the culprit as she was experiencing similar convulsions as the possessed, the peasants remarked that the coincidence only confirmed that she was a sorcerer, "If it hadn't happened to her, it would not have been that evident that she knows how to bewitch people." Initially, the villagers wanted to kill Vasil'eva, but she outsmarted them by scrambling on top of a stove and hurling bricks down upon the angry mob. When the village constable appeared, he was able to get Natal'ia down, whereupon he began to beat her.[149]

In the second epidemic a few years later, the victims of possession included only four persons (one man and three women). What is striking about this epidemic was that it affected the groom's father, his sister, his sister-in-law, and his cousin's wife, but not the bride or the groom. Like the members of the previous wedding party, these four individuals believed that they were susceptible to the wiles of an evil person. Artemii, the groom's father who had previously experienced a demonic seizure at his uncle's wedding, accused his eldest son's mother-in-law of bewitching him. The women demoniacs pointed their fingers at a villager by the name of Stepan. Two years earlier one of the demoniacs had targeted him as having bewitched her. Now it appeared to the wedding guests that Stepan was getting back at the woman and her family members. As word spread throughout the village that Stepan was causing an epidemic of *klikushestvo,* peasants headed out to his home to force him to reverse the spell cast on the wedding guests. Stepan refused, however, and barricaded himself in his hut armed with an axe. After breaking some windows, the peasants gave up, but went away convinced that Stepan's refusal to halt the epidemic of possession constituted an admission of guilt.[150]

The notion that witches or sorcerers were avenging past wrongs done to them or their family members was common in the cases of witchcraft accusation from 1861 to 1917. In the 1895 Molodinskaia episode, wedding guests were apprehensive that Natal'ia Vasil'eva would punish them for the bride's spurning of her son; in the 1898 episode they were convinced that Stepan was seeking retribution for having been accused previously of bewitching one of the guests. Broken love affairs might also result in a witchcraft accusation against the mother of a spurned lover. For example, in fall 1883 a young man in the small Ukrainian market town of Brailova in Podolia province attacked his former girlfriend's seventy-year-old mother as she walked by his family's farm. Suspecting the woman of taking action against him because he had refused to marry her daughter, with whom he had had sexual relations, he turned the tables on her. He shoved her against the fence and yelled out that he had apprehended a witch. When his shouting brought his relatives to the scene, he pointed out that the woman had to be a witch because she wore her hair loose and he had caught her pouring a potion out onto the ground, presumably in order to rekindle his love for her daughter. The relatives' subsequent taunting of the woman in turn caught the attention of neighbors who proceeded to beat her senseless.[151] The fact that the old woman lived with her son and daughter at the edge of town along a street that led to the railway station suggested that she was indigent and thus the classic victim of the type of witchcraft accusation that occurred during the seventeenth-century European witchcraze. One can certainly picture the elderly woman cursing and threatening the young man for having ruined her daughter's reputation, as words were her only defense against the more powerful. The increase of poverty and growing disparities between the indigent and their more prosperous neighbors in the late-nineteenth-century Russian and Ukrainian countryside ensured that those seeking charitable handouts would sometimes be charged with witchcraft or sorcery.

Late-nineteenth-century European Russia was undergoing tremendous change as a result of a rapidly increasing population and mounting land shortages, economic difficulties resulting from periodic famines, and increased off-farm labor. While the debate about the peasants' standard of living is ongoing in Russian historiography, it is evident that the countryside was in flux.[152] On the road to commercial agricultural estates, factory and mining towns, and cities, where they hoped to find jobs to supplement farm earnings, peasants moved from village to village seeking temporary lodging and sustenance. Hundreds of thousands of peasants engaged in begging, some on a professional basis. According to the 1897 census, which underestimated the total numbers, more than 400,000 individuals identified themselves as beggars, while another 100,000 sought welfare relief from institutions in the empire.[153] In the countryside this meant that peasants faced increased demands on their resources from the indigent within the village as well as from strangers who knocked on their doors. In 1890 in the Russian north a correspondent on peasant life remarked that a peasant woman, left on her own, was afraid to extend hospitality to a stranger, even if the outsider was a woman.[154]

Rising requests for handouts and shelter challenged both the Orthodox dictum to provide charity to all who asked for bread in Christ's name and village notions of mutual aid. By accusing individuals to whom they denied aid of being witches and sorcerers, Russian and Ukrainian peasants could assuage their own guilt feelings. According to Alan Macfarlane in his study of early modern England, the "accusation of witchcraft was a clever way of reversing the guilt, of transferring it from the person who had failed in his social obligation under the old standard to the person who had made her fail."[155] At the same time, villagers-turned-beggars placed themselves outside the community by challenging natural expectations of reciprocity contained in well-developed forms of mutual aid.[156] They still expected better off peasants to help them, but no longer felt obliged to return the favor at a later date. Placed in a humiliating position by the act of begging, peasants might utter threats against their neighbors at the outset, pronouncing even more colorful curses once they were turned away at the door. Neighbors subsequently attributed any illnesses or misfortunes to the curser, who became in their minds a witch or sorcerer. Once again, the cultural imagery of the witch came in handy, further convincing the victims of witchcraft that they had acted properly by refusing the beggar alms and that they needed to counter the witch's malevolence before further harm came to pass. Individuals suspected of witchcraft need not have possessed any of the stereotypical physical characteristics of a witch; their actions were sufficient proof of identity.

Of the 80 cases of witchcraft accusation isolated for this study, 11 percent involved individuals specifically identified as poverty-stricken or as wanderers and strangers. The projection of guilt onto a beggar is evident in an incident that occurred in 1879 in the Novgorod provincial village of Vrachevo. Inhabitants burned alive fifty-year-old Agrafena Ignat'eva, a beggar and soldier's wife, on the premise that she was a witch. Suspicions about Ignat'eva had surfaced during Epiphany of that year when the Kuz'mins' daughter became ill after the family had denied Ignat'eva Christian charity. As she experienced convulsive fits, the daughter shrieked that Ignat'eva had bewitched her. Two other women who became ill, one from Vrachevo and one from neighboring Perednikovo, also claimed that Ignat'eva had hexed them. One of these women subsequently died. When the deceased's sister, Ekaterina Ivanova Zaitseva, succumbed to illness after refusing to allow her son to chop wood for Grushka, as the peasants called the beggar, Zaitseva's husband Nikiforov begged the villagers of Vrachevo to save his wife from the beggar woman-witch. The peasants locked Ignat'eva in her hut, boarded up the windows, and set it on fire. Nearly 200 peasants from Vrachevo and Perednikovo witnessed the murder.[157]

In an 1891 case in the village Znamenskii, Zvenigorod district, central industrial Moscow province, a woman's seeking charity for which she was not deemed sufficiently grateful confirmed a long-held assumption that she was a witch. In this case the accuser, Luker'ia Ivanova, extended Christian charity to the seventy-three-year-old beggar woman Dar'ia Vasil'eva from the neighboring village Buzulina, but concluded from the woman's frown that Vasil'eva had hexed her. So convinced was Luker'ia that Vasil'eva had bewitched her that she immediately began to have convulsions and to scream out the beggar woman's name. Other villagers came running to her aid and beat Vasil'eva so severely that she died of multiple internal wounds in the Zvenigorod hospital. During the ensuing trial at the Moscow circuit court, villagers of Znamenskii defended their actions by pointing to the fact that Vasil'eva had been bent on destroying their community. Rybin, the village police officer, noted that eight years earlier, the woman had unsuccessfully attempted to bewitch a bride and groom at their wedding. Observing her with a knife in her hands, the guests had beaten her badly at that time. Since the woman had not suffered from the first beatings, Rybin could only conclude that she possessed supernatural powers.[158] Thus, Dar'ia had been accused of witchcraft at least once before the 1891 incident that resulted in her untimely death.

Searching the past for episodes that confirmed peasant suspicions that a neighbor was a witch or sorcerer was not uncommon. When the alleged sorcerer Egor Gromozkov was murdered in the village Ivanovka in 1879, about 35 versts from the town Nikolaevska in Samara province, 12 of 13 witnesses testified to Gromozkov's evil powers. These charges ranged from episodes that occurred three years earlier when Gromozkov had supposedly made a villager's daughter barren and ill, had hexed another person from whom he had begged alms, and had caused dysentery and even birth pangs among men. After piecing a series of events together, the peasants of Ivanovka became convinced that Gromozkov was an evildoer. One witness testified that every time he met the sorcerer on the street he said a prayer to the Mother of God as a precautionary measure. The villagers clearly believed that Gromozkov had received his just rewards when brutally murdered by their co-villager Tavunshchikov.[159]

The epidemic of demon possession that raged during 1898–1899 in the Russian village of Ashchepkovo, Gzhatsk district, Smolensk province, also involved villagers jogging their memories for instances when their neighbor Siklitin'ia Nikiforova might have hexed them, once they became convinced that she was responsible for the epidemic of *klikushestvo*. When the number of possessed victims reached five, those villagers who had previously eaten bread or hotcakes at Siklitin'ia's home became extremely apprehensive as it was thought that a hex could involve the intentional poisoning of food. A simple stomach pain was all that was necessary to make a woman believe that she too had been bewitched by Siklitin'ia. This confirmation of Siklitin'ia's transgression of the trust community members associated with hospitality and the sharing of food had a ripple effect as more and more individuals experienced convulsions. Eventually 15 persons—13 women and 2 men—became *klikushi,* claiming that Siklitin'ia Nikiforova, now a widow, had bewitched them. Thirty-two-year-old Marfa Petrova, one of the possessed, connected the beginning of her illness to a visit that Siklitin'ia had made to her home: "Sikliukha came to me and when she drank kvas in the kitchen area, my heart began to hurt, and my chest and stomach began to have spasms. Only I did not think of her other than [someone who lives according] to God's [commandments] and thought nothing of it. Then there were no rumors about her among us. Vasilisa shrieked, but we did not believe. . . . I, my sinful self, did not believe." Another *klikusha,* Mar'ia Alekseeva, claimed that while she did not harbor any ill feelings toward Siklitin'ia, she had refused to give Siklitin'ia some clothes for her daughter Marina. Accusing Siklitin'ia of hexing his cows, the village shepherd Frolov connected his misfortune to the fact that he had made Siklitin'ia some shoes for which he charged her 50 kopecks instead of the 20 kopecks she had offered to pay.[160] The last two cases were once again classic examples of persons who had denied a neighbor charity, and in the face of rumor and gossip about Siklitin'ia, came to believe that she was taking revenge by bewitching them and planting demons inside them.

More than the widowed Siklitin'ia's dependence on her neighbors' charity was at play in the Ashchepkovo epidemic of demon possession, however. A majority of the demoniacs had substantial household responsibilities as their husbands were either deceased and absent from home. All 13 women had been married at one time or other, while 9 were either widows (3), soldiers' wives (1), or had migrant husbands (5), which meant that they were maintaining their household economies with only the aid of children or elderly in-laws. In Neonila Titova's case, the demonic convulsions, severe depression, and inability to work that she connected to Siklitin'ia's bewitchment brought her husband back home to manage the household economy. The husband of Vasilisa Alekseeva, who had first denounced Siklitin'ia as a witch, also returned to the village. Increasing off-farm labor for men, which took them far from their native villages, could have negative consequences on the women who were left behind to shoulder all responsibility for the agricultural and domestic work, often under the eyes of critical in-laws.[161]

The Ashchepkovo epidemic was not an isolated phenomenon. N. V. Krainskii estimated that there were several thousand, if not tens of thousands, of women shriekers who believed that they were bewitched and consequently possessed by the devil in regions of Iaroslavl', Moscow, Novgorod, Smolensk, Tula, Tver, Vladimir, and Vologda, all of which, with the exception of Vologda, had significant portions of their male population working in cities.[162] Another psychiatrist estimated that in 1893 there were more than 1,000 shriekers in Orel province alone where out-migration was limited to a few districts.[163] By contrast, neither temporary male labor migration to cities and industrial sites nor *klikushestvo* was common in Ukrainian provinces.[164]

Fights within families could also lead to charges of witchcraft. Denunciations of this type account for almost one-quarter of the cases available—a fraction that should be seen as a minimum as the sources do not always identify the relationship between accuser and accused. Only 3 in 19 cases involved charges against male relatives (2 brothers-in-law and 1 unidentified relation). The others were fairly evenly distributed among wives (3), sisters-in-law (3), mothers (2), mothers-in-law (2), daughters-in-law (2), aunts (2), a stepmother (1), and a female in-law (1). The economic dependence of some of the elderly women (who were likely to outlive their spouses) on their families may have been the source of the accusations, although the records are silent on this matter. Tensions and the power struggles between relatives, especially between in-laws in extended family households, that involved transgressions of family solidarity, contributed to charges of witchcraft.[165] By questioning the hierarchical power structure of extended households, allegations of sorcery against mothers-in-law and sisters-in-law may have altered untenable situations, especially when the accuser claimed to be possessed. Those in positions of authority, especially mothers-in-law, could employ similar charges as a way of stifling independent-mindedness among subordinates. Even if reconciliation among kin occurred, their relationships were likely altered by such accusations.

Whatever the source of difficulty between Petr Briukhanov's wife and mother, it proved sufficient to persuade Briukhanov and his neighbors in a village in industrial Iaroslavl' province that his mother was a witch. In the spring of 1895 Briukhanov's wife became a *klikusha*. On Easter Sunday, in the presence of his mother Mar'ia and neighbors, Briukhanov gave his wife some holy water and asked her to name the person who had bewitched her. The woman named her mother-in-law, Briukhanov's mother. "At the sight of her mother-in-law standing before her, her face suddenly became transformed; she jumped, lifted up her hair, sang something, and with convulsive movements lunged at the seventy-year-old woman, threw her to the ground, began to drag her by the hair and to strike her all over her body." The wife also demanded that her mother-in-law reverse the spell. Briukhanov joined his wife in the beating as the other peasants looked on and prevented Mar'ia's husband from defending his spouse. Finally, the peasant Vinogradov suggested that the old woman be tossed in a grave where she could break the spell by digging up earth. Fetching a rope, he tied it around Mar'ia's neck and dragged her among a crowd to an open grave in the cemetery. When the beaten woman could not dig any longer, the peasants left her in peace. In the meantime, neighboring villagers, who had heard about the beatings, arrived in Sinitsy. One of them advised Petr Briukhanov to heat up an iron bar for the purpose of branding the witch. By that time, however, Briukhanov's mother had died. His wife, who had been experiencing demonic convulsions ever since she identified her mother-in-law as the person who had bewitched her, responded to the news of the death by dancing and grabbing some incense. In the end she claimed that the spell was dissipating. At the testimony before the Kashinskii circuit court, the peasants of Sinitsy justified their actions by claiming that they had all been bewitched at the time of the beatings and murder of Mar'ia. They argued that they had only wanted Mar'ia to reverse the hex and had not intended to kill the woman. The victim's son, Petr Briukhanov, explained that when he became convinced that his mother was a witch, it became necessary to struggle with this evil being (who was no longer his mother) in order to save his suffering wife.[166]

The Sinitsy peasants' assertion before judges that they had only intended to have the witch Mar'ia counteract her spell may have constituted their way of trying to lessen their punishment, or it may have reflected what they sincerely believed. As has been demonstrated repeatedly, priests and lay healers employed a variety of measures to help the *klikushi* identify their persecutors. There were also numerous stratagems that peasants concocted for detecting and making witches appear. These involved such actions as holding cheese in the mouth during church services, making an insulting hand gesture under the armpit in the midst of a group of women, sprinkling warm fresh milk in the yard, spitting behind oneself on the street where a witch lived, or heating milk from a cow that a witch coveted.[167] Through these means peasants hoped to force alleged witches to counteract their spells and restore harmony to the village. Only when malevolent individuals denied dabbling in witchcraft and refused to cooperate did peasants resort to violence.[168]

Witchcraft beliefs and practices in late-nineteenth-century Russian and Ukrainian villages underscore the presence of social tensions that were upsetting the countryside's equilibrium. Communities and households could become contested sites when violations or perceived transgressions of the trust placed in personal and social relationships occurred.[169] Traditionally defined as a largely female skill in the Ukrainian countryside, witchcraft in the Russian village had by the second half of the nineteenth century become predominantly associated with the malevolent actions of women. Notions of the witches' sabbath had percolated from the West and from the basic preconceptions of educated observers of the peasants. Yet the emphasis on the demonic in Russian peasant culture fit nicely with popular misogynistic beliefs that identified witches as misfits, sexual deviants, and, at times, the products of illicit love affairs. Russian and Ukrainian peasants used their cultural symbols of evil to identify and either neutralize or root out malevolence in their midst, attributing impotence and illness to witches and sorcerers. Given the broad-ranging attributes and activities that peasants ascribed to natural and learned witches, identification of witches became easy. In the end, practically all villagers—especially women and healers—who crossed the moral boundaries of neighborliness and family obligations as well as those who made economic demands upon households, became witches. That the powers of witches and sorcerers could be overcome through countermagic and periodic mob violence allowed peasants to redeem themselves and to restore some semblance of equilibrium to their lives.

The Russian peasants' cultural repertoire of witchcraft and sorcery also had a strong religious component in the form of *klikushestvo,* offering a different kind of redemption, one that was spiritual. The sympathetic attitudes toward the possessed attest to the ways Russian peasant culture allowed individuals to play the sick role and to be relieved from obligations. Subscribing to a cosmology where evil spirits were ever present, the possessed could take advantage of the liberties their society provided them. They sought relief from their demons at the hands of spiritual healers, often at distant monasteries, and by denouncing individuals they thought were responsible for bewitching them. The ritual dramatization of possession allowed demoniacs to communicate their inner turmoil to others and to seek immediate relief from their afflictions. As in the case of every illness, however, not everyone could be cured. The shrieking of the possessed, however, was not confined to the village or monastery, but reached far beyond, attracting the attention of writers, ethnographers, psychiatrists, and jurists.

Chapter Three

LITERARY AND ETHNOGRAHIC PORTRAYALS

✦ The nineteenth-century Russian intelligentsia's discovery and subsequent investigations of the Russian peasantry had a profound impact on the ways in which educated Russians grappled with their national identity. The same inquiry shaped the growing cultural chasm between the intelligentsia and the peasantry. The renowned Slavophile-Westernizer debates of the 1830s and 1840s permeated much of the thinking of the nineteenth and early twentieth centuries as writers, ethnographers, jurists, doctors, government officials, and revolutionaries repeatedly reevaluated Russia's history, the Russian position on the world stage, and Russia's future international and domestic roles. Critical analyses of Russia's governmental, economic, and spiritual institutions sparked important controversies over the path on which the Russian Empire found itself and over the effects of the westernization and secularization that the Petrine revolution had set in motion. Faith in Russia's exceptionalism clashed with a conviction that Russia had to be harnessed even more to the advances of Western European civilization. Whichever way Russia's intelligentsia turned, its members had to consider the millions of peasants who were unfree until 1861 and who were the least affected by westernization.

Influenced by German romanticism and the central role that German philosophers assigned the *Volk* in defining a nation, Russian literati and intellectuals set out in the early nineteenth century to acquaint themselves with the world of the Russian peasantry. What began as study from the comfort of their armchairs became by the 1840s forays into the countryside to collect folk poetry, tales, customs, and beliefs. Interest in daily peasant life produced a rich body of fiction and nonfiction that at times idealized the peasantry as the repository of true Russianness and the key to Russia's uniqueness. At other times, it merely borrowed elements of peasant culture to convey a sense of otherness, a sense of the exotic. And at other times the discourse in the periodical literature raised the specter of a backward and "dark" mass that in its ignorance and drunken stupor acted as a decisive brake on Russia's progress toward becoming a modern Western nation. The interests of Russian literati and ethnographers in the phenomena of *klikushestvo,* witchcraft, and the supernatural must be understood within this context.

Published mainly in substantial journals of various political representations, nineteenth-century fictional and ethnographic portrayals of the Russian peasant not only coexisted but also infused each other. Indeed, ethnography seemed to know no limits as amateur ethnographers became fiction writers and literati turned to ethnography to authenticate their works and at times to raise important social issues. Still other members of the Russian intelligentsia, at least in the postemancipation period, used ethnography to buttress their claims about a peasantry that confronted them with a conundrum. The abolition of an exploitative economic system had not been the panacea that intellectuals had hoped for, in part because emancipation did not go far enough in bringing the peasants freedom. But another outcome of emancipation confronted the intelligentsia: the peasants still remained largely unknown and impenetrable. The rift between the intelligentsia and peasantry had not disappeared. Further ethnographic study of the rural masses was absolutely necessary if Russian society was to be healed.

The fairly rigid separation between professions that one would expect in the twentieth century did not characterize nineteenth-century intellectual Russia—or Western Europe, for that matter. In fact, even when professionalization and specialization took root in turn-of-the-century Imperial Russia, the mixing of genres continued. The great dramatist and short-story writer, Anton Chekhov, was, after all, trained as a physician. Not only could he not separate his medical, scientific persona from his fiction, but as a positivist committed to the need for a systematic collection of empirical data, he also wrote important nonfiction pieces. His sketches of the penal colony on Sakhalin Island (serialized in 1893–1894), which provide an interdisciplinary tour de force of statistics, a detailed account of everyday life and individual experiences, and a collection of historical and geographical reflections, stand as a monument to the responsibility that Russian writers felt they owed society. By raising painful issues, they sounded the warning signs of an emerging civil society disdainful of a tyrannical government.

Lesser known jurists and physicians in the late nineteenth and early twentieth century also tried their hand at collecting ethnographic data, either in the field or culled from newspaper accounts. Trying to understand the peculiarities of the extralegal practices and healing regimens of the Russian peasants, for example, they uncovered a world that some of them believed exposed the peasants' brutality. Most did not agree with Feodor Dostoevsky, who, in reading the same newspaper reports of what appeared to be a rising number of violent rural crimes, viewed the peasants' brutality to be a product of centuries, worth of slime imposed upon them. The dirt could be washed away, according to Dostoevsky, not by enlightenment but through the baring of the peasant soul.[1] However, jurists, ethnographers, and doctors despaired of what they viewed as ignorance and backwardness. Enlightening the peasants became a formidable responsibility for these specialists. Yet, they too had to understand so-called peasant superstitions to be able to penetrate and reshape the peasant mind. In 1890 the jurist Petr N. Obninskii declared that "a certain evolution of juridical intellect and a broad erudition in anthropology, ethnography, and the history of epic popular beliefs" were necessary to unravel the complexities of crimes committed as a result of what he termed "superstitious convictions."[2]

While the intelligentsia's interest in popular demonology and witchcraft beliefs were especially pronounced in the first half of the nineteenth century and the last decades of the imperial regime, accounts of *klikushestvo* and demoniacs are limited. Indeed, the prodigious amount of literary criticism of Russian literature in the Golden Age barely mentions representations of possession in belles lettres. A closer look at the literary canon, however, reveals several portrayals. Writers such as Aleksei Pisemskii and Nikolai Leskov, as well as the luminaries of Russian fiction, Dostoevsky and Leo Tolstoy, addressed the subject to varying degrees. Although these writers held different and often opposing attitudes toward Orthodoxy and formal religion, they did speak with one sympathetic and understanding voice about *klikushestvo* and the mental and emotional anguish that peasant women experienced in their daily lives. Viewing shriekers as victims of their environment and men's brutality, they rejected the legal stand on possession as a form of malingering. Pisemskii and Leskov, writing in the 1850s and 1860s, also used *klikushestvo* to castigate the inhumane system of serfdom and to raise critical questions about westernizing trends associated with urbanization and scientific method. Dostoevsky's shriekers represent different stages in his life as he grappled with the contradictory messages of positivism and religious faith. Eventually rejecting Western idealism and secularism, Dostoevsky not only viewed the *klikusha* as a victim, but also as a paragon of virtue and suffering akin to the Mother of God.

Given Russian intellectuals' interest in the Russian peasantry, it may appear surprising that the demoniac does not figure more prominently in

Russian belles lettres. Several explanations can be offered for this puzzling reality. First and foremost, it is important to keep in mind that in the Golden Age of Russian fiction, not one important novel tackled the subject of the peasantry. According to Donald Fanger, the peasant constituted a myth in the eyes of literati, who were content to use the peasant "as an instrument, the image varying with the writer's social and moral preoccupations."[3] Most heroines in Russian fiction, whose tortuous lives epitomized the suffering of Mother Russia, hailed from classes other than the peasantry. Given that "the elevation of the Russian woman" was "matched only by the self-abasement of the Russian man," the tormented, possessed woman could not act as an appropriate foil to the restless "Byronic types," "superfluous men," and "underground types."[4] As urbanization and the attendant ills of city life attracted the attention of social critics, the prostitute rather than the peasant woman became a symbol of virtue and wisdom. Victimized by men too enamored with the intellectual fashions of the day that elevated reason and science over ethical and religious concerns, she could always maintain the moral high ground. The *klikusha,* seemingly unaffected by westernization and urbanization, did not constitute an appropriate subject to explore larger political issues affecting men. In fact, when Dostoevsky chose to focus an entire novel around the subject of demoniacs, he defined them not as rural women but rather as Russian revolutionaries, captivated by Western positivist, materialist, and atheistic ideas.

With such notable exceptions as Nikolai Gogol, Dostoevsky, and Leskov early in his career, most Russian intellectuals disdained the Russian Orthodox Church; this disdain also removed *klikushi* from the intelligentsia's purview. Although monasteries and their saints played pivotal roles in the possession drama, when writers and ethnographers wrote about the peasants' religious beliefs, they emphasized elements that they believed represented remnants of a pagan culture untainted by Orthodoxy and the institutional church. Seeking to bridge the gap between themselves and the rural masses and increasingly committed from the 1850s onward to a scientific worldview, they fashioned for themselves and their reading public an image of a peasantry divorced from formal religion.[5] *Klikushestvo* did not fit into such an image, whereas selected peasant beliefs in witchcraft that avoided the subject of demon possession did. Even the writers of the Silver Age, who looked to religion and spiritual rejuvenation as a panacea for the sterility of materialism and who returned to the countryside to uncover the essence of peasant beliefs, steered away from *klikushestvo.* The shriekers' ties to the institutional church made them a suspect subject for poets and prose writers fascinated with primitivism and the exotic rites and rituals of Russian sectarian groups. At the same time, the turn-of-the-century Silver Age's preoccupation with satanism suggests the influences not only of occultism among Western European intellectuals but of indigenous sources as well.

Finally, strictures of the Russian Orthodox Church, which prohibited depictions of all Orthodox subject matter in theatrical productions, guaranteed that the *klikusha* would not appear on stage. Imperial censors viewed "portrayals of the . . . church, its rituals, its doctrines, or its clergy (and in opera any monks or clergy at all) . . . as inherently blasphemous." If Alexander Pushkin's drama *Boris Godunov* (1825) could be produced for the first time in 1866 without the patriarch or monks appearing on the stage, and if Modest Mussorgsky's opera on the same subject (1868–1869) could be performed in 1870 stripped of the scene set in the monk Pimen's cell, then the absence of theatrical representations of *klikushestvo* is less surprising.[6] So ingrained was Orthodoxy's aversion to representations in drama of religious matters that when Sergei Diaghilev, the ballet impresario of the Ballets Russes, approached Igor Stravinsky in the 1910s to write music for a liturgical ballet, the composer refused. He could not approve of the staging of the Passion, Annunciation, Ascension, and Resurrection.[7] Ironically, the church's prohibitions promoted the exploration of so-called pagan themes and folk superstitions in the theater. That *klikushi* appeared at all in Russian fiction and ethnographic accounts gives them more importance than might appear on the surface.

ROMANTIC IMAGES

In the first decades of the nineteenth century, until the 1840s, Russian writers who tackled the subject of peasant beliefs were attracted to elements of Russian and Ukrainian folklore as well as folktales from other countries, especially material dealing with the supernatural. "Romantic theory exalted ethnography and folk poetry as expressions of the Volksgeist."[8] To express solidarity with the peasantry and empathy with their wretched lives, Alexander Pushkin was among the first major Russian writers to don peasant clothing. In his writing his intent was not to portray the actual world of the peasant, but rather to bridge the chasm between the intelligentsia and rural folk "by infusing a derivative literature based on Western models with the vitality of folklore and epic, popular language, and ritual, and by using the mythological paradigms contained in Russian folk culture to make his own work resonate with the myriad sounds emanating from that 'Mother Lode.'" In so doing, he brought respectability to folk poetry and tales.[9] Other writers followed suit.

The Ukrainian witches' sabbath beckoned Pushkin and other literati. The fascination with "Little Russian," or Ukrainian, folklore among St. Petersburg literary circles in the Nikolaevan period (1825–1855) can be explained by a migration of Ukrainian and Russian-Ukrainian gentry to the capital in search of a distinctive pan-Russian culture that would meld Russian and Ukrainian elements. With "the concept of the Russian nation . . . still relatively open," "Russian" had not yet become identified with "Great Russian."[10] Ukrainian subjects appealed to St. Petersburg audiences as more exotic than Russian ones, and the supernatural world of the Ukrainian peasant was no exception. Ukraine was "a country both 'ours' and 'not ours,' neighboring, related, yet lending itself to presentation in the light of a semirealistic romanticism, a sort of Slavic Ausonia."[11] Forays into the exploration of the theme of Ukrainian witches came from the pens of Pushkin, the Ukrainian Orest Mikhailovich Somov (1793–1833), the Russified Ukrainian and master of the supernatural, Nikolai Gogol, and the composer Modest Mussorgsky.

Pushkin's short ballad "The Hussar" (1833) introduced Russian audiences to a Kievan soldier's journey to a witches' sabbath, modeled upon Ukrainian tales, with some European overtones. The soldier is billeted with a recently widowed woman "comely and good," who disappears at night by drinking a bitter substance. Rather than call her a witch, as peasants would have done, Pushkin prefers to refer to her as a *basurmanka* (infidel). He thus takes one of the early definitions of witches as heretics from the Western European model of witchcraft. Again following the story line of the Ukrainian tale, Pushkin has the hussar drink the potion as well, only to find himself on a mountain where "Pots are boiling; they are singing, playing. / They are whistling and engaged in some vile play." Pushkin, however, takes the image of the infidel a step further by introducing anti-Semitic undertones. He ends the stanza with "They are marrying a Jew to a frog." When Marusen'ka sees the hussar and warns him to return home, Pushkin has her give him a *kocherga* (poker), an implement specifically identified with a woman and her domination over the hearth. In Ukrainian tales witches rode either brooms or oven forks. The poker, which witches in Ukrainian tales periodically rode, turns into a horse. "When he [the hussar] looked, he saw that he was riding not a horse but a bench."[12] Pushkin thus ends the tale invoking reality and the fantasy-like world of dreaming that is not so frightening or grotesque because it is illusory and fleeting.

Somov's attraction to the theme of the witches' sabbath, in "Kievan Witches," also published in 1833, stemmed from his desire to preserve Ukrainian folklore and customs that he feared would disappear once peasants became exposed to education and once the written word displaced oral culture.[13] The supernatural and popular demonology particularly appealed to him as evidenced by such tales as "Rusalka" (1829), "The Werewolf" (1829), "Stories about Treasures" (1830), and "The Evil Eye" (1833). While Pushkin's ballad about the witches' sabbath is fairly faithful to the story line of Ukrainian tales about a soldier billeted at a witch's home, Somov's piece is more complicated and detailed.

In "Kievan Witches" Somov takes another popular version of the witches' sabbath theme in which a dashing soldier marries a beautiful young woman, only to discover that she and her mother are witches who frequent witches' covenants on Bald Mountain. To set the stage for the Cossack's visit to the mountain, he provides encyclopedic information about Ukrainian witchcraft lore. At the beginning of the story, women peddlers at the Kiev market gossip about the Cossack Bliskavka's love for Katrusia Lantsiugovna, noting that the girl's mother is reputedly a witch. Readers learn about the woman flying out of her chimney, sucking a neighbor's cow dry, poisoning a neighbor's dog because it had the ability to detect and bite witches, and revenging herself on another peasant for engaging her in a quarrel. To add more drama, Somov has one of the gossipers note that another of the old woman's sins of sorcery involved bewitching someone's daughter. He uses the popular verb *isportit'* (to spoil or hex) to refer to the bewitchment, but avoids the noun *klikusha* to describe the bewitched daughter. Instead, he delineates her ailments, which indicate that she was indeed a demoniac: "Now poor Dokiika incessantly meows like a cat and scratches the wall, and barks like a dog and shows her teeth, and chatters like a magpie and jumps on one foot."[14] Finally, there is a reference in the story to witches having tails. Somov's detailed descriptions of witches' actions and attributes, down to the long list of disturbing human and animal ingredients in the witches' salve, create a foreboding about the story's outcome.[15] Even the description of the devil, an amalgam of Eastern and Western European folkloric depictions and poetic license, is frightening: "On it [the scaffolding] sat a huge bear with a double ape-like snout, goatlike horns, a serpent's tail, hedgehog bristles all over his body, with skeleton hands and cat's claws on his feet."[16] The very fact that Ukrainian and Russian peasants believed that devils could take the shape of humans or animals allowed Somov to bring many forms into one creature.

Anticipating the works of Nikolai Gogol, upon whom Somov had influence, "Kievan Witches" has a horrific romantic ending. Because the Cossack had found out his wife's true identity as a witch before Passion Week, when "she would have thrown herself at the feet of monks and begged them to lock her up for the last three days in the Pecherskaia Lavra [the Monastery of the Caves] until Easter morning" and vanquish her "devilish hallucinations," the couple was doomed.[17] The wife had taken an oath to the devil that she would drink the blood of any relative who had unwisely observed the rituals of the witches' sabbath. Lantsiugovna kills her husband by sucking his breast, an image not associated with witches but rather with demons in both Ukrainian and Russian folklore. She herself is later rumored to have been burned by her own sisters for trying to leave the covenant and enter a women's monastery. The horror of the story is mitigated by Somov's reminding his readers that Bald Mountain, having been abandoned by the witches, is no longer anything but a sandy hill.

The master of the short story and supernatural elements was, of course, Nikolai Gogol. Rejecting Peter the Great's attempts to westernize Russia and their lingering effects, he sought to capture the essence of Russianness, which included Little Russian elements. Like Somov, he used Ukrainian folklore initially in his "rural" stories to set up situations and events that delighted his audiences who were already familiar with the fiction of other Ukrainian writers. Gogol himself did not study the peasantry, but relied on information gleaned from ethnographic collections as well as material he solicited from family members.[18] In a 30 April 1829 letter to his mother asking for graphic details about the clothing that Ukrainians of different ages and occupations wore, he also asked for "a few words about caroling, about St. John the Baptist, about water nymphs. If there are, besides, any spirits or house goblins, then about them, as precisely as possible, with their names and what they do; among the simple people there are a great many beliefs, terrifying legends, traditions, various anecdotes, and so on."[19] Gogol requested too that his mother send him copies of his father's farcical plays, based on the Ukrainian *vertep* (puppet theater). The folktale elements appear in Gogol's early stories, in which he presents demons vanquished by the sign of the cross, witches taking on animal shapes, witches with tails, the identification of old women as witches, the small hut on chicken legs, and witches riding men as if they were horses.

At the same time Gogol borrowed from Ukrainian folklore, he also tapped the writings of German romantic writers for plot outlines, as he could not escape Western influences. A case in point is the gothic melodrama "A Terrible Vengeance," which appeared in the 1831–1832 collection, *Evenings on a Farm Near Dikanka*. The "plot of the wicked sorcerer who suddenly appears to his daughter's family, tries to lead his son-in-law into a life of brigandage, and kills his daughter's son, is taken from E. T. A. Hoffmann's tale 'Ignaz Denner,' with some amplifications from Tieck's 'Pietro von Abano.'"[20]

Gogol embellished his folkloric borrowings by creating new images and adding attributes that were not part of popular lore. "Viy" (from the 1835 collection *Mirgorod*), the most terrifying of Gogol's rural stories, involves a witch who, together with a monster, takes revenge on a Cossack seminarian by the name of Khoma Brut. The Viy is a completely made-up figure. Covered in black earth and having a face of iron, he has no counterpart in either Ukrainian or Russian folklore. But, as if to give him authenticity, Gogol declared: "The 'Viy' is a colossal creation of the imagination of the simple folk. The chief of the gnomes is called by such a name among the people of Little Russia: the eyelids over his eyes reach to the very ground. All this tale is popular tradition."[21] Ultimately, however, Gogol's main concern "was the quality of storytelling rather than ethnographic accuracy."[22]

If the character of the Viy had no counterpart in folklore, the witch in the same story certainly did, although even there Gogol embellished her attributes. The situation from popular tales in which a witch has sexual experiences with a mortal by riding him like a horse, only to be outwitted by her victim, is replicated in "Viy." Khoma Brut is able to gain control over the old witch by saying prayers and exorcisms against evil spirits; he not only rides her, but also beats her with a log. The woman slowly metamorphoses into a beautiful girl with exquisite hair and long eyelashes. Like the devil, a witch could take on other forms in Ukrainian and Russian folklore. But by moving from old and ugly to young and beautiful, the witch plays with Brut's mind, making him temporarily doubt his initial assumption that she was a witch. When Brut is summoned to say prayers for the dead over the coffin of the daughter of a wealthy Cossack, who had died of mysterious bodily injuries, he meets the witch once again. She is none other than the deceased daughter, who in a vampirelike state comes alive in her coffin when Brut begins to read prayers in church. She torments him until the Viy appears on the third night and kills him. Like Somov's Katrusia, the witch had reputedly been a vampire before her death; she sucked the blood of a child as well as that of several girls in the village. The vampirelike witch also appears in Gogol's "St. John's Eve."

In "Viy" the witch's victory over Khoma Brut is all the more hair-raising as Gogol turns the world upside down by having evil vanquish good. It is as if he is reminding his audience that God periodically allows evil to triumph. Brut's exorcisms and precautions protect him from the flying coffin on the first night and from the demons' claws on the second night. On the third night, however, Christian supplications lose their power before the monstrous creatures who enter the sanctuary. Lest readers think that God had abandoned his place of worship, the demons miss the cock's warning crow and are plastered against the church's windows and doors. Gogol's later stories, set in a St. Petersburg firmly in the clutches of demonic forces, no longer relied on ethnographic materials. However, their exploration of the supernatural and the message that it is difficult "to discern the boundaries between a world apparently governed by" reason and science "and the realms of dream, fantasy, the supernatural, poetry, the spirit" had roots in that lore.[23]

Gogol's rural stories involving evil spirits and witches (as well as other subjects) influenced one of Russia's most original composers, Modest Mussorgsky. Late in 1858 he contemplated writing an opera based on Gogol's "St. John's Eve," and then near his death he began working on *Sorochintsy Fair,* another Gogol-inspired opera. Although neither was completed, they illuminate the fact that for his entire life, Mussorgsky was interested in the theme of witchcraft. As a populist and admirer of the peasants, he infused his work with peasant subjects as he searched for a purely Russian art form of music that would stand up to Western models, but also articulate Russia's distinctiveness.[24]

Mussorgsky's famous *St. John's Night on Bald Mountain* constituted his attempt to capture the grotesque in music, based solely on what he believed to be Russian sources. Conceived in 1860 as a result of Mussorgsky's having read a libretto called *The Witch* by Goerg Mengden (which has been lost), *Bald Mountain* was to include "a witches' sabbath, individual episodes for the wizards, a ceremonial march of all this rabble, the finale—a glorification of the sabbath, for which Mengden has personified the sovereign of all the festivities on Bald Mountain."[25] In 1866, after hearing a performance of Franz Liszt's *Totentanz* and after reading Matvei Khotinskii's historical discussion of magic, witchcraft, and mesmerism (mainly in Western Europe), Mussorgsky finally began to plan the work.[26] In June 1867 on Minkino Farm, he took all of 12 days to compose the piece. Upon completing it, he made it very clear in a letter to his friend Nikolai Nikolskii that the work would convey a distinctive Russian (rather than "Little Russian") flavor: "I am probably chattering a lot about my *Night,* but this, I suppose, stems from the fact that I see in my sinful prank an original Russian composition, one not having a profound and routine German cast, but like [the song] 'Savishna,' molded in our native fields and nourished on Russian bread."[27] It is fitting that in the context of describing his new composition, Mussorgsky referred to his song "Svetik Savishna." The song's text features a holy fool, whose "tongue-tied laments interspersed with shrieks convey" his suffering for having been spurned by a beautiful woman.[28] It is as though Mussorgsky consciously chose to portray the shrieking of a man rather than a woman, a holy fool rather than a *klikusha,* and to focus the musical study of witchcraft on the witches, rather than on their victims.

Mussorgsky's understanding of the witches' sabbath contained elements of Western European lore about witches. In letters to both Nikolskii and Nikolai Rimsky-Korsakov, he explained that he envisioned witches assembling on the mountain "gossiping, playing lewd pranks, awaiting their superior-Satan." Upon the he-goat's appearance, the witches began to honor him. "In B minor—these are the witches glorifying Satan—as you can see, stark naked, barbarous, and filthy." "When Satan became frenzied enough at the witches' glorification, he would order the start of the sabbat, whereupon he would select the witches that caught his fancy to satisfy their needs."[29] The obvious sexual overtones of the sabbath come from Mussorgsky's reading of a court case in Khotinskii's book in which a woman accused of being a witch described the covenant of witches graphically in her testimony and "who had confessed to the court that she had had romantic flings with Satan himself."[30] Concerned about his interpretation, Mussorgsky asked Nikolskii whether or not he had accurately rendered folk fantasy. Given the influence of Western European folklore, Mussorgsky may have been guilty of embellishing the folkloric content. Even so, his musical rendition of "a scattered and continuous outcry up to the final merging together of the whole witches' riff-raff" has captivated audiences since 1968 (when the original score was published and performed for the first time, minus Rimsky-Korsakov's 1886 revisions).[31] Like Somov's ending to his short story about the witches' sabbath, Mussorgsky's conclusion to *Bald Mountain* does not exalt "the primacy of the sacred over the profane; [his] . . . treatment abandons itself to the orgy and ends not when the sacred has ordered a halt, but only when the profane has abruptly spent its strength."[32]

IMAGES OF SERFDOM

While the period of romanticism saw efforts to create a distinctive Russian literature that at times incorporated and embellished ethnographic elements about demons and witchcraft, the next period of realism did not eschew these ethnographic themes but stripped them of their supernatural force to concentrate on what writers believed was closer to the harsh realities of village life. And the "Little Russian" element was abandoned in favor of Great Russian examples. In the realist genre, the Russian *klikusha* took center stage in a few stories and a less pivotal role in fiction.

Two early representatives of realism, Aleksei Feofilaktovich Pisemskii (1821–1881) and Nikolai Semenovich Leskov (1831–1895), wrote about possessed women fairly early in their literary careers when the evils of serfdom were paramount in the eyes of learned Russian society. No doubt familiar with journal articles about bizarre cases of witchcraft in the countryside and nascent medical understandings of *klikushestvo* and informed by their own observations, these writers seized upon *klikushi* as epitomizing the victimization of serfs at the hands of their landowners, bailiffs, and government officials.[33] For Pisemskii and Leskov abuse of peasant women symbolized nothing less than the molestation of Mother Russia.

Born in the provinces, Pisemskii, the son of a poverty-stricken Kostroma noble family, and Leskov, the son of a minor Orel government official, were both intimately familiar with rural Russia. In fact, Leskov had personal experience with conditions on serf estates. In 1857 he left his government position as clerk in Orel's criminal court for employment with an uncle who managed several estates and who participated in the resettlement of serfs from the central to the eastern provinces. Sensitive to peasant dialects, customs, and beliefs, both Leskov and Pisemskii adopted a folk idiom. In the end, however, it was Leskov who mastered the genre of the Russian *skaz* (tale), while Pisemskii largely abandoned the short story for the novel.[34]

Seeking to avoid the romanticization of the countryside that had trapped earlier Russian writers, both writers accompanied harsh indictments of serfdom with bleak descriptions of peasant life. Critics championed Pisemskii's early peasant pieces as refreshingly devoid of a "condescending sentimentality" and the product of a "dispassionate observer."[35] Of the two writers, Leskov was far more critical of the peasantry, if within self-prescribed boundaries. "I studied the people in the meadows of the Gostomlia [Orel province]," wrote Leskov in 1863, "with a copper pot in my hand, on the dewy grass where horses pastured for the night, beneath a warm sheepskin coat, and in the mill of Panino, behind circles of dusty chaff; so it is indecent for me either to place the peasants on a pedestal or to trample them beneath my feet."[36] Precursors of the populists of the 1870s and 1880s who depicted peasants as noble savages, Leskov, Pisemskii, and ethnographers of the 1860s subscribed to the notion that "the more horrifying the conditions depicted, the more powerful the impression on the reader would be, and therefore the more effective the message."[37]

Pisemskii's and Leskov's stories about shriekers constitute fascinating portrayals of contemporary elite, popular, and medical perceptions of *klikushestvo*. Taking on a largely peasant phenomenon to illustrate the ills of serfdom, these writers viewed *klikushestvo* as an ailment that struck serf women as a result of the oppressive environment in which they lived. Influenced by a materialist, scientific worldview, however, they decoupled *klikushestvo* from demon possession and preferred to view popular beliefs in possession and bewitchment as mere superstitions. At the same time, neither author championed aspects of Western culture that seemed to be intruding upon the Russian village. Pisemskii blamed urbanization as well as serfdom for corrupting the countryside, while Leskov criticized the excesses of modern medicine.

Fascinated by and yet skeptical of peasant beliefs in evil spirits, Pisemskii's foray into the subject of *klikushestvo* resulted in the short story "Leshii: Rasskaz ispravnika" (The wood demon: The story of a district police officer). It appeared in 1853 in the leading liberal journal *Sovremennik* (The contemporary), which had an impressive paid readership of almost 6,000.[38] Set on an isolated estate of an absentee landlord in Pogorelka canton of Kostroma province, the story focuses on a district police officer's investigation of the mysterious disappearances of the beautiful Marfa, a young, unmarried peasant woman. Suspicious of Marfa's explanation upon her return that a wood demon, an evil spirit that peasants believed inhabited the forests of the area, had kidnapped her, the narrator-policeman uncovers the bailiff's sexual exploitation of Marfa and other serf women. Pisemskii is thus able to demonstrate that Marfa's experience with *klikushestvo* stemmed not from the wood demon's sexual impositions upon her, as the peasants would have it, but rather from those of the bailiff Egor Parmenov. Newly arrived from the city, Parmenov brings the destructive and immoral ways of modernity upon the already blighted rural landscape. Marfa is not, however, totally blameless for her suffering. While it is clear from the narrative that Parmenov seduces Marfa, Pisemskii avoids using the verb *nasilovat'* (to rape) and softens Parmenov's image by suggesting that Marfa had fallen in love with the bailiff before their relationship became sexual. Nonetheless, Marfa's error involved faulty judgment rather than any lack of virtue on her part.

In presenting Marfa as a *klikusha,* Pisemskii documents some elements of the peasant ritual drama surrounding possession. He introduces his readers to *klikushestvo* fairly early in the story. They meet Marfa for the first time when, like scores of other demoniacs, she experiences a fit of possession at the beginning of the Cherubikon hymn during the Sunday liturgy. After covering her with a cloth, the parishioners leave her alone and claim that to do otherwise would be detrimental to her. As the previous chapter explained, Russian peasants believed that such a cloth (either from an icon or from an altar), having been blessed with holy water and censed, would exert beneficent powers over the demons possessing the woman.[39] Having rendered faithfully the timing of a demoniac's seizure and villagers' sympathetic responses to her, Pisemskii subsequently debunks what he considered to be two myths of *klikushestvo.*

Through the voice of his narrator Pisemskii identifies two diametrically opposed characterizations of shriekers: one popular and the other elite. According to "the simple people," as the narrator condescendingly refers to the peasants, these women are the victims of bewitchment. The villagers, the bailiff informs the narrator, tend to accuse elderly landless peasant women of being witches who taint their victims' food or drink or send their spells through the air, "as far as 5,000 versts."[40] He also points out that a woman might have hexed Marfa because she was jealous of her beauty. Pisemskii's exaggeration of peasant beliefs in Parmenov's remarks not only demonstrates the bailiff's duplicity, but also ridicules those beliefs as far-fetched. On the other hand, the narrator notes that the landlords reject any causal relationship between bewitchment and *klikushestvo* and prefer to see demoniacs as feigning possession or playing pranks.

Aleksandr Ivanovich Klementovskii (1822–1882), a physician at the Moscow Foundling Hospital[41] and contemporary of Pisemskii, was also cognizant of the serfowners' perception of *klikushestvo* as insincere behavior. Writing about demoniacs among Russian peasants in 1860, he explained that when *klikushi* were threatened or punished, they ceased the behavioral patterns connected with demon possession. Pointing out that fear could produce such a result on the sick, he argued that these women were genuinely suffering from mental stress.[42] Although Pisemskii may not have been aware of this explanation, he did subscribe to the medical theory that *klikushestvo* constituted a form of mental illness. In "The Wood Demon" he summarily rejected the popular and elite understandings of the phenomenon, declaring that the affliction was akin to the hysteria that befell Russian noblewomen.

While pinpointing similarities between different classes of women, Pisemskii conceded that a peasant woman's lot was worse than that of her upper-class counterpart and that her circumstances contributed to her hysteria. According to the narrator-policeman of "The Wood Demon," "her [the peasant woman's] father-in-law compels her to submit, her mother-in-law makes life miserable, and possibly her husband also batters her: thus she is depressed, she pines, week in and week out, goes to church, begins to pray, is deeply moved, and here [in the church] there is also burning incense [and] stuffiness; well, and she falls with a thud."[43] This explanation for *klikushestvo* bears an uncanny resemblance to an 1841 description of peasant women's life, published in a provincial newspaper: "Any young woman *[babenka],*—they say,—lives in an absolute [pig]sty, the husband beats [her], no one in the home loves her, for every trifle all of them simply curse and beat her; the poor soul has nowhere either to sit or lie, and she, sobbing, sobbing, begins to shriek *[klikat'].*"[44] By the 1850s images of abusive husbands and in-laws were becoming tropes in elite narratives about victimized women. *Snokhachestvo,* or incest between fathers-in-law and daughters-in-law, which sometimes occurred in multigenerational serf households (and to which Pisemskii alluded), had become a symbol of the inhumanity of the serf system in which oppression begat oppression.

Despite Pisemskii's use of an unmarried woman in "The Wood Demon" to illustrate the cruelty of bailiff-serf relations, he acknowledged the tendency of married women to become *klikushi.* His shrieker, Marfa, having involuntarily forfeited her maidenly purity, approximates the position of a married woman more closely than that of a maiden. In fact, Pisemskii does not have her undergo the ritual shaming to which peasants subjected unchaste maidens. Ultimately, Marfa bears Parmenov's child and insists on raising the illegitimate child in spite of community censure. Shunned by her neighbors, she communicates only with God through prayer.

In "The Wood Demon" Pisemskii thus drew upon peasant lore about *klikushi,* wood demons, and witches to construct his morality play about the evils of serfdom and the vices that urban-born estate managers brought to the countryside. Through the shrieker Marfa, who achieves redemption through communion with God, he idealized simple and chaste peasant women as exemplars of virtue, indeed of Mother Russia herself, in a world turned morally upside down by serfdom. Marfa is a shrieker not because she is possessed but because *klikushestvo* constitutes the only way that she can effectively express her trauma and outrage at being sexually abused. Ultimately, the peasants' understanding of possession acts as an unfortunate cover for the evil of the greasy-faced, shifty-eyed, and foppishly dressed bailiff Parmenov whose lust creates misery in an isolated part of the country. Abolition of serfdom and its cruel demands on the peasants, according to Pisemskii, would restore Mother Russia's equilibrium, vanquish her oppressive environment, and render peasant superstitions moribund.

Pisemskii did not, however, limit his discussion of popular beliefs in bewitchment to female victims. In his 1855 story "Plotnich'ia artel'" (The carpenters' artel), also set during the era of serfdom, he extended his portrayal of popular beliefs by making his male protagonist a casualty of bewitchment on his wedding day.[45] Bewitchment during wedding celebrations as a result of the hosts' slighting or insulting a sorcerer or witch, as the previous chapter illustrated, constituted another topos in the peasants' arsenal of explanations for misfortune. In writing about the bewitchment of a man, Pisemskii stayed far closer to the peasant script than he did in "The Wood Demon."

The witch in "The Carpenters' Artel" is identified as the carpenter's stepmother who had previously made unsuccessful amorous advances toward her stepson and had threatened him with misery should he marry. In defiance of his stepmother, Petr marries. During the wedding celebrations he defies the protocol of hospitality by not offering the stepmother liquor. Shortly thereafter, he begins to suffer from depression. A powerful sorcerer in the village, Pechurakh, to whom peasants, merchants, and even lords turn for treatment of illnesses and bewitchment, claims that the stepmother is responsible for Petr's morose state. Identifying the stepmother-witch in a cup of water, he extends the list of her victims by noting that the woman had bewitched Petr's father's first wife, the girl Variushka Nikitina, and more recently Petr's father. Pisemskii is a careful observer of peasant life, implying the ways in which village rivalries played themselves out: the so-called sorcerer was only confirming his clients' suspicions. All the peasants need is plausible evidence of the stepmother's dabbling in witchcraft. When they find herbs in her possession, a sure sign in their minds that she is capable of maleficent acts (even though herbs were part of any peasant women's arsenal of natural medicines), they turn her over to the lord, who in turn exiles her. Thus the evil is exorcised from the community, but her victim Petr continues to suffer from depression. Never once in the story does Petr lose control, as did Marfa in "The Wood Demon" by experiencing a seizure or convulsions, because Pisemskii subscribed to the cultural distinctions between masculine and feminine forms of mental anguish. Indeed, Pisemskii preferred the desexualized term *depression* to the decidedly feminine *klikushestvo* (or hysteria) to describe Petr's symptoms.

A far darker indictment of serfdom and modernity and their destruction of the peasantry than Pisemskii's "The Wood Demon" may be found in Nikolai S. Leskov's portrayal of a shrieker in his 1863 "Zhitie odnoi baby (iz Gostomel'skikh vospominanii)" (The vita of one woman [out of memories from Gostomlia]).[46] Following the structure of an Orthodox hagiographical tale, the vita traces the serf woman Nast'ia's tragic martyrdom. Unlike a saint's life, however, the story, in true realist fashion, is devoid of miraculous elements. Nast'ia's victimization proceeds from the brutal environment in which she lives, and her mental health depends upon her removal from that setting. Only through the portrayal of a peasant woman "foredoomed by fate to lifelong misery," as Dmitrii Grigorovich had done before him in his 1846 physiological sketch, "The Village,"[47] could Leskov despairingly ask his readers, "Oh, my Rus', my native Rus'! . . . Isn't it time to wake up, to put oneself in order? Isn't it time to unclench the fist and to come to one's senses?"[48] Published two years after the emancipation, Leskov's story may have been alluding to the continuing, even if temporary, obligations that peasants owed their former masters and thus suggesting that the oppressive nature of the serf system remained intact. Once actual emancipation took effect, however, conditions in the countryside were bound to improve.

Leskov's plot, highlighting the consequences of a peasant girl's lack of freedom in determining her marital status and lack of choice in marriage partner, is fairly simple: a greedy and unprincipled entrepreneurial brother arranges Nast'ia's marriage to the village idiot, the son of a wealthy peasant. While disdainful of her betrothed, Nast'ia has no choice but to go through with the marriage. It is not consummated, a sure sign for the peasants that a sorcerer had hexed the couple. The miserable Nast'ia becomes ill, increasingly depressed, and ultimately a *klikusha*. After having been successfully treated by a kind religious healer in town, Nast'ia returns to the village, falls in love with a married man, and has an affair with him. She and her beloved Stepan flee the village but are arrested as runaway serfs by the authorities. Nast'ia subsequently gives birth in jail to Stepan's child. Unfortunately, the frail progeny of this ill-fated relationship lives only a few days in the unsanitary jail. Thereafter, both Stepan and Nast'ia are whipped and sent back to their owner. En route to the village, Stepan dies of typhus. Of course, the calamities cannot end there: Leskov has Nast'ia return home insane and become a wandering beggar in the tradition of holy fools in Christ. The protagonist is finally released from her misery by freezing to death in a forest.

The bitter tragedy of Stepan and Nast'ia's love affair itself would have been sufficient to win over the hearts of Leskov's readers. However, by making Nast'ia a *klikusha* and having her break mentally under the strain of emotional traumas, Leskov drives his points home with poignancy. The reader's attention is solely focused on this industrious, gentle, and virtuous woman driven to despair by a village community that is tainted by the cruelties of serfdom, by her owners' callousness, and by the inhumanity of modern medicine, which ascribes mental breakdown to her female organs rather than to the rural environment.

Leskov's construction of Nast'ia's *klikushestvo* combines his materialist understanding of the phenomenon with elements of peasant beliefs. Like Pisemskii, he provides an environmental explanation for *klikushestvo,* casting doubt upon the peasants' assumption that *klikushi* were actually possessed by demons. Determined to demonstrate that shriekers were not malingerers or shirkers of strenuous labor, as often claimed by serfowners, he portrays Nast'ia as a consummate laborer.[49] Describing her as "accustomed to men's work" because of her owner's excessive demands, Leskov lists her skills in painstaking detail. "Nast'ia knew how to mow, rake, tie sheaves, steer a horse, break hemp, spin, weave, bleach cloth; in a word, she knew all peasant work, managed everything adroitly, and she was not afraid of the chicken coop. Even her hut was nicer than the entrance of the manorial cottage." But it was precisely because of women's arduous labors on serf estates that they, in Leskov's opinion, became shriekers. Leskov understood shrieking to be not the result of demon possession but rather a coping mechanism for overworked peasant women: "That is why when . . . life knocks a *baba* about, she endures—she endures, from the heart, and manages somehow, and screams in voices—well, as if it becomes easier [for her this way]." In describing her aversion to having sexual relations with the husband she did not love, Leskov likens Nast'ia to "a demon running away from incense."[50] In so doing, he uses the popular belief that a demoniac's evil spirits react negatively to holy objects to emphasize that Nast'ia is not literally possessed but rather is repulsed by the spouse she has been forced to marry. Leskov also borrowed from the possession drama the timing of Nast'ia's first attack of *klikushestvo*. It occurs just before Easter, a point in the Orthodox calendar of heightened demonic activity. Yet Leskov avoids the term *klikushestvo,* preferring instead the medical designation of "hysteria." He also limits the characteristics of the attack to guffawing, crying, laughing, hair pulling, and rolling about on the floor. By eliminating any references to Nast'ia's shrieking or mimicking the voices of animals, Leskov chooses to dismiss two critical characteristics of *klikushestvo;* his clinical description of a hysterical fit emphasizes a woman's extreme mood swings and theatricality. It is only when Nast'ia describes the sensation she feels in her heart before the convulsions as something like a "snake, a fiery snake" sucking at her heart that Leskov makes a concession to popular depictions of demons.[51]

By setting up the premise that Nast'ia is not possessed, in contrast to her neighbors' conviction, Leskov shaped his narrative to criticize peasant practices regarding the treatment of *klikushi*. He had nothing but contempt for the lay healers upon whom peasants depended. The healer summoned by Nast'ia's family to help the hysteric confirms the peasants' suspicions that Nast'ia is possessed. He explains that a great sorcerer had bewitched the woman and that the implanted demon is particularly difficult to exorcise as it had been released by means of fire. Despite the healer's incantations and rituals of exorcism, Nast'ia's illness worsens. Leskov paints a picture of a charlatan who is only too willing to take money for his unsuccessful medicines and incantations and then to blame the stubbornness of the demon and the intensity of the spell for his inability to cure the poor woman. Nast'ia understands correctly, in Leskov's view, that she is not possessed and begs the healer to stop torturing and frightening her with his stupidity. Leskov clearly had little patience with rural healers who took advantage of the peasants' beliefs. Neither did he have much faith in the Orthodox Church's claim to be able to cure *klikushestvo* through exorcism, a rite that, in Leskov's assessment, could not alleviate a peasant woman's dire circumstances.

Leskov's description of an unsuccessful religious exorcism performed on Nast'ia inverts the traditional descriptions of possession. Stereotypical accounts suggest that demons are so afraid of exorcism that they imbue possessed women with such strength that several strong men must restrain them in the presence of priests and holy objects. In keeping with his rejection of peasant beliefs in possession, Leskov gives Nast'ia complete agency and sets out to prove that her ailment is not connected to possession: First, she does not want to have prayers said over her, claiming that devils do not inhabit her body; after all, she is able to pray to God on her own, a sure sign that she is not possessed. Second, once in church, she moves to an open window to escape the claustrophobia she feels in the church and the heavy incense that permeates the air. "She just wanted to stand in the window, breath in fresh air, look at God's free world, but four strong hands grabbed her and dragged her back."[52] It is at that point that Nast'ia becomes frightened and tries to flee her tormentors. When the poor woman submits to the chanting of the exorcism prayers, she loses consciousness.

Rejecting the treatment of rural healers and exorcisms of the Orthodox Church, Leskov finds Nast'ia's savior in Sila Ivanich Krylushkin. He is a kind and devout self-proclaimed religious man, the antithesis of the charlatan and greedy lay healer. Until Leskov began to question Orthodoxy and ultimately became a Tolstoyan in the 1880s, he was captivated by Russia's holy people.[53] He describes Krylushkin as a former merchant who upon his wife's death gave up his trade for a five-year pilgrimage to holy sites in Palestine, Turkey, Solovki, and finally Georgia. In Georgia a holy elder taught Krylushkin how to treat the sick successfully. Once having returned to his hometown, Krylushkin began to take in the sick, refusing payment from the poor and accepting only enough money from the rich to cover the costs of his patients' subsistence. His success with Nast'ia lies in his gentleness and kindness. It is in Krylushkin's home, which is far away from her village and her daily circumstances, that she finds peace and happiness. Nast'ia feels as though she is in heaven, in a house where "there were never any quarrels, fights, [and] squabbles," in contrast to life among the peasants and their masters.[54] A cured Nast'ia returns to the village only in time to bid farewell to her dying mother, but cannot maintain her virtue or sanity back in the brutal rural environment.

Leskov has Krylushkin return twice in the story, each time to expose the inhumanity of institutions that propped up the serf system. It is only after Nast'ia's initial bout with *klikushestvo* and subsequent cure at Krylushkin's hands that she falls in love with a married man. When her ill-fated relationship culminates in the tragic death of both her illegitimate child and the man she loves and she is returned insane to the village under armed guard, her neighbors once again declare her to be demon possessed. Nast'ia's family seeks out Krylushkin's help, and within a year Nast'ia regains her sanity, but not respite from persistent miseries. Village gossip that she had been sexually promiscuous during her spell of mental imbalance reaches her ears, and a shamed Nast'ia begs Krylushkin to arrange for her to be confined in a women's monastery "where she could find joy for her lacerated soul." Given the strict rules barring a married individual from entering a monastery, however, the consistory secretary forbids the Mother Superior of a monastery to provide shelter for Nast'ia. Nast'ia's responds to this cruel action on the part of the Orthodox church by noting that "this marriage . . . plagues me everywhere."[55]

Leskov also exposes the culpability of the government in Nast'ia's situation. Near the end of the novel he has the authorities question Krylushkin's right to practice medicine without a license. Medical officers take advantage of Krylushkin's absence from his home to whisk away Nast'ia and other women in his care to the offices of the medical administration. Krylushkin arrives too late to save Nast'ia from what Leskov describes as medical rape, the doctors' scrutiny of Nast'ia's sexual organs with a surgical instrument. He reproaches these so-called educated men in extremely powerful language: "Ekh, gentlemen! Gentlemen! And you still call yourselves learned doctors. You were in the universities. Doctors! Healers! How can you rape [*nasilovat'*] a woman, and a sick woman at that! For shame, for shame, gentlemen! Doctors don't do this, but butchers do. . . . May God forgive you and may you not pay for this by having the same thing done to your daughters or wives."[56] Here Leskov decisively rejects an influential strain in contemporary medical opinion that targeted woman's sexual organs as the source of mental illness.[57] His indictment of contemporary medical practices rounds out his harsh critique of serfdom and the dangers that so-called progressive thinking devoid of ethical considerations held for Russia.

While critical of gynecological explanations for women's psychological torments, Leskov was not out of step with professional doctors who believed environmental causes and emotional shocks were responsible for Russian peasant women's mental stress; in this respect he and Pisemskii were in agreement about the deplorable conditions that peasant women faced, driving some to the breaking point. It is possible that Leskov was influenced by Klementovskii's 1860 article on *klikushi* in *Moskovskaia meditsinskaia gazeta* (The Moscow medical newspaper) that appeared as a separate publication shortly thereafter. Klementovskii attributed the phenomenon of *klikushestvo* to the physical and mental circumstances that befell peasant women, including poor diets, insufficient sleep, arduous work, cramped and unsanitary living conditions, numerous pregnancies, and poor treatment of illness. Since all peasant women shared these problems but not all of them became shriekers, Klementovskii emphasized the additional burdens of mental stress that occurred as a result of "depressed mental influences, the loss of tranquility [and] hope, the destruction of family happiness, unsuccessful love, and everything else that strikes the human heart."[58]

Increasing familiarity with the poverty of the countryside on the part of the small Russian intelligentsia fostered a sensitivity to lower-class women's lives that was unusual in the European context. The sufferings of Russian peasant women, these observers implored, were genuine and merited humanitarian considerations. The victimized peasant woman symbolized an exploited Russian peasantry. Pisemskii's and Leskov's portrayals of rape in their tales about *klikushi* added a sexual dimension that placed the burden of deviant sex practices upon the shoulders of husbands, rapacious bailiffs, landlords, and doctors—all of whom sought mastery over women.

AN ETHNOGRAPHIC-HISTORICAL ACCOUNT

The disturbing fictional accounts of *klikushestvo* during serfdom by Pisemskii and Leskov were soon supplemented by a fascinating historical and ethnographic analysis of the phenomenon that appeared in

1868 in the influential liberal journal *Vestnik Evropy*.[59] The author of this premier scholarly account was Ivan Gavrilovich Pryzhov (1827–1885), better known for his history of Russian taverns and exploits as a revolutionary. The son of a former household serf belonging to the Stolypin family,[60] he, like his contemporaries Pisemskii and Leskov, deplored serfdom and felt obliged to study the peasants in order to improve their lot. While Pisemskii and Leskov rejected nihilism—popular among Russian radicals in the mid-nineteenth century—Pryzhov traveled in the opposite direction. At the end of the 1860s he joined the revolutionary cell around the notorious Sergei Nechaev, who in 1869 arranged for the murder of a fellow revolutionary and student Ivan Ivanovich Ivanov.[61] Pryzhov was arrested as an accomplice in the murder.[62]

According to his memoirs, in the villages and district towns of Moscow, Tver, and Vladimir provinces, Pryzhov copiously collected information about priests and monks, serfdom, medieval folk beliefs, material life, "the history of Russian women, the history of begging in Russia, sects, heretics, Old Belief, and Little Russia [i.e., Ukraine]," some of which he destroyed on the eve of his arrest. Disdainful of the Orthodox Church, Pryzhov described monasteries as dens of iniquity, full of "the worst drunkenness, blasphemy, open trade in innocence, fantastic raucous [*rykanie*] songs, prayers, hysterics, the reading of written and sorcerers' incantations."[63] Given his fascination with popular religion and the circumstances of Russian women's lives throughout Russian history, it is not surprising that his attentions turned to *klikushi*. He blamed the Orthodox Church's attitudes toward women, Peter I's extension of serfdom, and the postemancipation imperial government's legal restrictions on peasants for what he perceived to be a growing frequency of possession among peasant women.

Curious about the origins of *klikushestvo,* Pryzhov looked for both foreign and domestic roots. At the outset of his 1868 article, Pryzhov stated that shriekers existed among all societies and throughout the ages; therefore, they were not unique to Russian society. However, it was only fairly recently that the phenomenon had, in Pryzhov's opinion, been correctly identified as pathological, ensuing from women's oppressive environment. Universalizing possession and witchcraft, Pryzhov began his historical account with a brief discussion of possession in ancient Greek and Roman societies, which, in his opinion, were tainted by Eastern notions: "Dark superstitions of the East crossed into Europe through Africa, Rome, and Byzantium, and thus, little by little, shaped the monstrous period of medieval witchcraft." Having laid the blame for witchcraft on forces outside Russia, Pryzhov subsequently traced the historical roots of *klikushestvo* in Russia back to an eleventh-century Old Church Slavonic translation of a Byzantine manuscript.[64] Pryzhov found the next reference to demon possession among Russian women in a fifteenth-century

Muscovite tale about a woman named Matrena. She became possessed by a legion of devils because she had defied God by entering his church unclean, having engaged "in carnal lust with her husband" and not having undergone ritual purification through bathing. However, the first actual shriekers, that is, women who shouted out the names of witches or sorcerers who had planted demons inside them, Pryzhov argued, did not appear until the seventeenth-century Muscovite witchcraze. Like many of his fellow radicals, Pryzhov was a proponent of women's liberation. He accordingly characterized the seventeenth century as the low point in the peasants', especially in peasant women's, social lives because of widespread beliefs in witches and unflattering portrayals of women by churchmen as evil wives. Even the late Muscovite image of the "good wife," Pryzhov noted, was not beneficial to women as they remained unprotected by law. Subject to their husbands' control and whims, women, according to Pryzhov, were obliged to be humble and silent as well as to suffer their husbands' beatings.[65]

Continuing his study of the historical evolution of *klikushestvo,* Pryzhov cited court cases and descriptions of shriekers in seventeenth- and eighteenth-century documents. He linked cases of possession in these two centuries to the church schism of the mid-seventeenth century and to state oppression of Old Belief. The schism occurred when the Orthodox Church hierarchy introduced reforms in ritual, which were rejected as heretical by priests and their followers who called themselves Old Believers. Highlighting the revolutionary changes wrought by Peter I (1682–1725), Pryzhov contrasted the diametrically opposed position of Peter's sister, Sophia, who served as regent from 1682 to 1689, regarding the possessed. Although Sophia also embraced Western European ideas and culture, she represented, according to Pryzhov, "a link between old and new Russia"; in fact, she was a reputed healer of *klikushi.* In rejecting the old Russia entirely, Peter viewed demoniacs as malingerers and ordered them expunged from Russian society. Peter's decrees against *klikushestvo,* Pryzhov argued, were ineffective because the tsar's expansion of serfdom worsened women's position. Sardonically, he noted, "But the devils . . . continued to howl and shout as before: the now evolving serf order multiplied them."[66] Thus, like Pisemskii and Leskov, Pryzhov saw women demoniacs as crying out against their oppression. Contrary to Leskov, however, he did not view the emancipation of the serfs as bringing with it an amelioration of the peasant women's position and a corresponding decline in the number of *klikushi.*[67]

Pryzhov suggested that the evolving humanitarian order that produced emancipation should have brought more humane treatment on the part of the government and medical authorities and a subsequent dramatic decrease in incidents of possession. In chronicling court cases involving shriekers in the first half of the nineteenth century, he discussed an 1861 case involving an epidemic of *klikushestvo* among the *odnodvortsy* (peasant freeholders) of Bukreev *khutor* (hamlet) to illustrate his point. The medical experts, consulted by the judges of the Ekaterinoslav court, noted that the shriekers' convulsions resulted from hysteria. Citing a hereditary explanation for hysteria for the first time, the doctors claimed that these "full-blooded [and] passionate" women were susceptible to hysteria, having inherited nervous temperaments from their mothers. They concluded that even completely healthy women could succumb to hysterical fits in the wake of seeing hysterics' convulsions. On the basis of this expert testimony, the court ruled that "all the accused deserve not to be punished for their delusions but [merit] appropriate understanding that would dispel these delusions." Clearly supporting the court's decision, Pryzhov noted that the phenomenon of *klikushestvo* should have disappeared with the appearance of such progressive thinking. The fact that it did not dissipate, he attributed to Article 937 of the new Criminal Code. By continuing to connect possession with deceptive and dangerous behavior, that article, he argued, recreated the brutality of the sixteenth through early eighteenth centuries. Only now, rather than suffer torture, malingerers were to be whisked away to insane asylums: "To our horror we find a cantonal policeman here [in the new court] who, afflicted by the savagery of investigating prophets, dragged shriekers to the police, we see doctors who undress and examine these women and who decide that they are normal and that they are more or less pretenders, and the court, finding them guilty of 'evil deception' sentences them to be locked up in an asylum."[68] Pryzhov's reference to doctors' subjecting *klikushi* to an improper physical examination harkens back to Leskov's outrage at some of the practices of modern medicine.

In identifying the ethnic and class origins of demoniacs as well as the Russian Orthodox Church's pernicious hold on these women, Pryzhov concluded his article by pinpointing the value of both enlightenment and economic improvements in wiping out the phenomenon. He pointed out for the first time in the literature the distinctive Russianness of possession, claiming that it existed everywhere in Russia, but not in Little Russia, except in the Kievan churches and monasteries that attracted Russian pilgrims.[69] *Klikushestvo*'s absence from Ukraine subsequently became a theme in ethnographic and psychiatric writings.[70] Pryzhov then made a direct link between shrieking and Orthodoxy. "All over the northeast," he notes, "you will come across *klikushi* in all the monasteries and churches where there are saints, relics, or miracle-working icons." These women were more often than not peasants. A shrieker, he surmised, is a healthy woman who cannot endure moral insults from an abusive husband without cracking and "in the midst of wild superstitions around her becomes a *klikusha*." Pryzhov was sympathetic to these women whose betterment, he believed, depended on the erosion of religious superstitions, especially beliefs in witches, through enlightenment of the peasants and through an improvement in their living standards.[71]

Pryzhov's compassion did not, however, extend to those few *klikushi* he characterized as malingerers who because of poverty made a trade out of feigning this illness. This lack of sympathy squares with his censure of individuals he labels savages, pathological types, or basic swindlers in another of his seminal pieces on popular belief entitled "Twenty-Six Moscow Prophets, Holy Fools, Female Fools, and Fools."[72] In that book, which sold out its initial printing of 2,000,[73] he scorns such individuals as Tat'iana Stepanovna Bosonozhka (*bosonozhka* means "barefooted") who "exploit[ed] the gullible public with their predictions and cures."[74] Bosonozhka became a holy fool in Christ in 1840s Moscow after experiencing an unsuccessful love affair and joining up with individuals Pryzhov describes as being hypocritical and sanctimonious. In Pryzhov's account the "Barefooted" became quite the entrepreneur when a rumor spread that she had acquired a miracle-working icon; she welcomed people into her flat, sold them candles to place before the icon, sold phials of holy oil from the same icon, and accepted donations. After the authorities closed down Bosonozhka's business and dispatched the icon to a Moscow monastery because of the disorderly conduct and unproven miracles reported at the woman's apartment, Bosonozhka abandoned her religious trade in favor of marriage, further proof in Pryzhov's mind that she was a swindler.[75]

FEODOR DOSTOEVSKY

Pryzhov's fascination with shamming holy fools may have been sparked by Feodor Dostoevsky's 1859 Gogolesque tale "The Village of Stepanchikovo." In that story Dostoevsky modeled his character, the buffoon Foma Fomich Opiskin, on the holy fool Ivan Iakovlevich Koreish (1817–1861), one of the individuals later described by Pryzhov. Koreish bore the ignominy of being the first holy fool incarcerated in a mental asylum—the Preobrazhenskaia Hospital in Moscow. Once the church began in the late seventeenth century to distance itself from individuals who declared themselves to be holy fools, considering them deceivers, these self-proclaimed holy people became suspect in the eyes of the law. By the early nineteenth century, physicians classified what had previously been accepted as a religious vocation to be a form of mental imbalance. In spite of the fact that Koreish officially had been declared mad, members of the upper class nevertheless flocked to the asylum where he was incarcerated to seek his advice and blessings, which they believed came directly from God.[76] Because at the time religious mysticism enjoyed a revival within some elite circles, the attention that Koreish received from these quarters is understandable. Dostoevsky exposed Koreish's charlatanism through the downfall of his character Foma Fomich. A self-proclaimed holy man, "Fomich would give readings from devotional books and hold forth with eloquent tears on Christian virtues" and dutifully attend religious services twice a day. Yet his egotism would get the better of him as he would "recount his life story and achievements" and was "a past-master at running down his fellow-men."[77]

Dostoevsky's contempt for religious charlatans who masqueraded as holy fools in his early 1859 work, however, contrasts sharply with his later depictions of saintly holy fools, exemplified best by his Christlike character, Prince Lev Myshkin, in *The Idiot* (1869). Myshkin's innocence and spiritual superiority doom him in the modern world. Indeed, his schizophrenia as both a Russian and a European, whose Russian side embodied Christian truths that battled the evils of modern European rationalism, guaranteed his ultimate exclusion from European society and confinement in a Swiss hospital for the insane.[78]

A master of psychological insights and intrigued by the contradictions in human beings in general and in the Russian culture's hybrid of Western and Eastern characteristics and values, Dostoevsky joined realist writers in giving attention to the *klikusha*. As in the case of his portrayals of holy fools, his characterizations of demoniacs and popular religion changed with the development of his philosophical ideas. Dostoevsky's revulsion against self-proclaimed religious men, who, he believed, at heart were evil, is replicated in his 1847 story "Khoziaika" (The landlady). The story also features a shrieker, Katerina, who is sexually abused by the sorcerer-cum–holy man Murin. Katerina possesses only a few characteristics commonly attributed to demoniacs, whereas the shriekers in Dostoevsky's masterpiece of more than 30 years later, *The Brothers Karamazov* (1879–1880), are easily recognizable because of greater attention given to the Orthodox context of the possession drama. The demoniacs seek treatment at a monastery from Father Zosima, the novel's saintlike spiritual elder. Dostoevsky's depiction of Alesha's mother in *The Brothers Karamazov* as akin to the Mother of God makes her more memorable than Katerina despite her hardly appearing in this novel in which men engage in a battle over Christian and atheistic principles. The two masterpieces document Dostoevsky's progression from his radical phase when he was enamored with materialism and positivism (i.e., with what the West had to offer Russia) to his later revulsion toward Western philosophies and profound faith in the Russian *narod* (people) as the country's saviors. The *klikushi* in each of the stories are victimized women, but in "The Landlady," the abuse of Katerina exposes the dark side of popular religion, which in the course of the story escapes the humanizing efforts of the rational and materialist philosopher Ordynov. In *The Brothers Karamazov,* the maltreated Sof'ia Ivanovna, through her suffering and tears, is a paragon of the beauty and strength that Orthodoxy presents to the world in contrast to the destructive tendencies of cold rationalism and materialism.

Literary critics have not identified "The Landlady"'s central character, Katerina, as a *klikusha*. They have generally been content to discuss this undervalued story as an early expression of Dostoevsky's fascination with a philosophical discussion of opposing ideas, in this instance utopian socialism versus a Manichaean popular worldview that pits good against evil.[79] Victor Terras, for example, labels "The Landlady" "an artistic failure," but concedes that "it contains the seed of some of Dostoevsky's deepest ideas, including the Grand Inquisitor theme of *The Brothers Karamazov*."[80] R. Neuhauser chooses instead to see the short story as illuminating contemporary revolutionary ideas, referring to it "as a socio-political allegory reflecting the intellectual scene of 1846–47." At the same time, he places the heroine Katerina within the context of Dostoevsky's other female protagonists who embody the qualities of "life-giving mother earth" and the Mother of God. Standing for ideals of love and beauty, Katerina, according to Neuhauser, nevertheless cannot remain uncorrupted "by evil . . . in a perverted society."[81] Although Neuhauser's interpretation is persuasive, it is not a complete picture of the one central character who identifies herself as being possessed.

At the outset of "The Landlady," Dostoevsky presents his female protagonist as suffering from some undefinable malaise for which she seeks spiritual help. It is only gradually that the reader learns that the beautiful Katerina believes herself to have been bewitched by her lover, the elder Murin. Murin had previously been her mother's paramour. Dostoevsky foreshadows Katerina's revelation about her possession by introducing her within the setting of a Russian Orthodox Church, a traditional site for the seizures of demoniacs. Her seizure, however, is rather mild. She does not experience convulsions, shriek in animal voices, or lose consciousness as would be expected of a shrieker; she merely sobs and sheds tears of contrition. Her fit is provoked not by a religious service, as vespers have long ended, but by the cloth from a resplendent icon of the Mother of God that her companion Murin places over her head. Once Katerina regains her composure, she lifts her head, the icon lamp illuminating her tear-stained face: "There was a small smile on her lips but her face had traces of some kind of childhood terror and secret horror. She timidly pressed herself up to the old man, and it was clear that she was trembling from emotion." Katerina appears a second time in the same church prior to the start of the evening service. And like a *klikusha,* who must join her fellow sufferers on pilgrimage to holy sites in search of solace and miraculous healings, she finds herself in the midst of a "dense mass of indigent, elderly women in rags, the sick and disabled, waiting for alms at the church doors." Excluded from the main sanctuary because of her uncleanliness, she prays on her knees fervently in the entrance. "Tears flowed onto her cheeks as if washing away some sort of terrible crime."[82]

Further evidence of Katerina's possession comes during the unfolding of her story. In a conversation with the intellectual Ordynov, who has taken a room in the St. Petersburg flat she shares with Murin, she remarks that books can spoil or bewitch a person. Invoking the image of a priest or healer reading prayers of exorcism over demoniacs, she also suggests that books can have beneficial properties, as evidenced by the religious texts that Murin reads aloud to her. Katerina's identity as a *klikusha* is confirmed when she experiences a seizure in response to Ordynov's request that she tell him her life story. This time the seizure replicates the fit of a demoniac as she makes a terrifying animal sound—"a piercing howl"—and utters words in a staccato-like fashion, akin to the hiccuping of demoniacs plagued with *ikota*. Finally, she loses consciousness. It is only upon waking that Katerina confesses that she has been "bewitched."[83] Restating the contradictory images of books as having both beneficial and malevolent outcomes, Katerina presents Murin as her bewitcher (the man who mutters indistinct words over her) and her savior (the man who at times reads an Old Believer religious text over her). "Here Murin, the seducer, Satan, assumes the form of the savior, Christ: a strange metamorphosis foreshadowing the grim figure of the Grand Inquisitor, the antichrist himself."[84] Katerina cannot extricate herself from the person to whom she has sold her soul. Estranged from the western and alien St. Petersburg, she and her lover return to the countryside.

While Katerina's behavior fits the cultural narrative of *klikushestvo,* her claim that she sold her soul to Murin represents a departure. In this regard a young Dostoevsky may have been influenced by Goethe's *Faust,* the stories of E. T. A. Hoffmann, and other Western European tales about contracts with the devil. However, it is also possible that he borrowed the idea from Russian sources.[85] According to Russian scholar O. D. Zhuravel, the motif of contractual arrangements with the devil was not unknown to ancient Rus'; it appeared in the Old Church Slavonic translations of the Byzantine vita of St. Basil and Balkan apocryphal tales concerning Adam and the devil. The popularization of the idea, according to Zhuravel, began only in the mid-seventeenth century when it appeared in trial records and the 1660s tale "The Story of Savva Grudtsyn." The author of the fictional Savva Grudtsyn's life merged ancient Byzantine notions with Western images that came into Muscovy from Poland and Ukraine. Zhuravel concludes that by the late seventeenth century and certainly throughout the eighteenth century, popular Orthodoxy had subscribed to the notion of the devil's being as powerful as God. This dualism imbued the devil with an intelligence and cunning that had been absent from stories of saints' lives and gave him authority over such earthly matters as "sexual love, relations among people, the goodwill of masters and officials, success, and wealth." In return for earthly happiness, mortals had to pay an extremely high price by selling their souls.[86] Dostoevsky later subscribed to the newer vision of the devil in *The Brothers Karamazov* in which the Grand Inquisitor describes him as "a terrible and intelligent spirit, the spirit of self-annihilation and non-being."[87] In "The Landlady" Katerina's entry into a pact with the devil-Murin would thus have resonated with Russian readers as consonant with their cultural understanding of apostasy.

If Dostoevsky painted an impressionistic portrait of a *klikusha* in "The Landlady," then 30 years later, convinced that Russia's salvation lay in her popular Orthodoxy, he was prepared to accept most of the tropes of possessed women in his characterization of shriekers in *The Brothers Karamazov*. He introduces his readers to the shrieker Sof'ia Ivanovna, Fedor Karamazov's second wife, in an early chapter (book 1, chapter 3). Like Katerina in "The Landlady," she is exceptionally beautiful. Her Christlike "phenomenal humility and meekness" provide a direct contrast to her husband Fedor's debauchery and habit of abusing his wife. Identifying her as a shrieker, Dostoevsky's narrator explains that, in response to her husband's cruelty, "the unhappy young woman, frightened since childhood, contracted some type of nervous women's illness that is found most often amidst the simple people among village women who are called *klikushi*. . . . Because of that sickness, [accompanied by] terrible hysterical seizures, the ill woman sometimes even lost her reason." A few pages later, the novel's hero Alesha remembers his mother kneeling in front of an icon of the Mother of God, with the rays of the setting sun complementing the light from the icon lamp. "Sobbing as if in hysterics, with screams and shrieks," she held Alesha before the icon as if he were under the protection of the Mother of God and prayed on his behalf.[88]

What is missing from these descriptions of Sof'ia Ivanovna is any mention that she is a demoniac. However, if one relates her shrieking to Fedor Karamazov's mistreatment of her and to his blasphemous behavior in the monk Zosima's cell, it becomes clear that Fedor himself is a devil. Just as Murin bewitches and possesses Katerina, Fedor possesses his own wife. But through her possession and suffering, Sof'ia Ivanovna attains a higher spiritual truth, which she passes on to Alesha, who too becomes a shrieker.

Alesha's identification with his *klikusha*-mother is absolute. Her saintliness and communion with the Mother of God envelop the character of this highly religious son, who announces that he will enter a monastery and "whose dominant trait is seeking after truth."[89] The servant Grigorii, who loved and tried to protect Sof'ia when she was alive and who paid for her cast-iron gravestone (because her husband Karamazov could not be bothered), frequently remarks to Alesha that he bears an uncanny resemblance to his mother. Alesha himself refers to Sof'ia as "his shrieker-mother." And to seal the comparison between son and mother, Alesha later experiences an *"istericheskii pripadok"* (hysterical fit) when his father relates to him an incident during his first year of marriage to Alesha's mother. At that time Fedor Karamazov had the audacity to spurn his wife's religiosity and mysticism by threatening to spit on her icon. The threat caused her to experience convulsions. It is as if the father replicated his very actions in telling the story to his son because "Alesha suddenly jumped up from the table, in the spitting image, according to the story, of his mother, clasped his hands, then covered his face with them, fell on the chair as if he had been mowed down, and shaking all over from a sudden hysterical fit, simply [released] unexpected, quivering, and inaudible tears. His uncanny resemblance to his mother struck the old man [Fedor]."[90] And like his mother, Alesha achieves a higher spiritual truth. He ultimately becomes a *kheruvim* (cherub), who, according to his brother Ivan, is the only one who can exorcise Ivan's demons.[91] The shrieker is thus able to vanquish his own and others' demons.

Dostoevsky's religious depiction of Sof'ia deepens with his linkage of *klikushestvo* and other ailments to the holiness and curative powers of the elder Zosima at the monastery where Alesha becomes a novice. Here the narrator provides a generic but sympathetic portrayal of shriekers in a chapter entitled "Devout Women." The chapter is set outside one of the hermitage walls, the only area of the monastery where women are permitted. When the elder Zosima emerges on the veranda and dons his stole, the 20 women waiting there lead a *klikusha* to him. At first the narrator describes the demoniac as squealing in a ridiculous fashion, hiccuping, and trembling as if she were experiencing birthing pains. Once the elder is able to calm her with a prayer, the narrator provides background information about *klikushestvo* in order to counteract any prejudices educated readers might have toward *klikushi* and to share the latest medical thinking on the subject.

The narrator points out that as a child he frequently came across shriekers in villages and monasteries (an autobiographical comment on Dostoevsky's part).[92] He describes them as having yelped or barked like dogs during church services but reports that as soon as they were brought up to the communion cup, they always became quiet. "However, at that time I heard from some serfowners and especially from my urban teachers, [in answer] to my queries, that it was all of a sham to avoid work, that it was always possible to eradicate [it] with suitable severity, and various anecdotes were told as proof." The narrator immediately overturns this elite theory that *klikushi* were not genuinely ill, as the narrator in Pisemskii's "The Wood Demon" had done. He claims that medical specialists have dismissed the possibility of these women feigning their illnesses, arguing instead that *klikushestvo* constitutes a serious illness. According to doctors, the sickness occurs mainly among Russian peasant women because of their difficult lives, especially "the illness that develops from exhausting work [that is undertaken] too soon after difficult, abnormal birthings without any type of medical help." The narrator also points to peasant women's "uninterrupted misery" and beatings as contributing to the illness.[93]

However, medical and environmental explanations for *klikushestvo* were not enough for Dostoevsky, who also subscribed to the religious aspect of the possession drama. Through their suffering and genuine possession, he believed, demoniacs reached a higher state of spiritual ecstasy generally reserved for only the holiest of people. The narrator explains the shriekers' cures before the communion cup as being directly related to their belief in the power of Christ's Body over the demons possessing them. "And that is why it always happened (and should have happened) that the nervous and, naturally, also mentally ill woman," in anticipation of a miracle, felt a momentary shaking of her entire body at the moment when she bowed before the Holy Gifts. The experience of the miraculous is shared by the female witnesses who shed "tears of tenderness *[umilenie]* and ecstasy."[94] In describing their tears, Dostoevsky consciously chose the highly complimentary Old Church Slavonic word *umilenie,* "untranslatable because of the richness of sense inherent in it," to refer to emotions invoked by God's grace.[95] Later in the novel Dostoevsky uses the word again, this time, to describe the elder Zosima's gift of tears.[96] The image of the famous *Umilenie* Mother of God of Novgorod icon, which reportedly shed tears when the icon had fallen from the iconostasis in July 1337, comes readily to mind.[97]

Dostoevsky's sympathetic portrayals of shriekers stem from his personal religious experiences and his Slavophile belief that true religiosity lay with the Russian peasantry. As early as April 1876 he commented on the intelligentsia's ridicule of popular beliefs: "About the faith of the people and about Orthodoxy we possess merely a couple of dozens of liberal and obscene anecdotes, and we delight in scoffing stories about how an old woman confesses her sins to the priest and how a peasant prays to *Piatnitsa* [Mother Friday]." In August 1880 Dostoevsky made a plea to disregard this kind of thinking. Acknowledging that peasants did not know the catechism, he asserted,

> that our people have long been enlightened, having embraced in their hearts Christ and his teachings. . . . The[y] . . . acquired their knowledge in churches where, for centuries, they have been listening to prayers and hymns which are better than sermons. They have been repeating and singing these prayers in forests, fleeing from their enemies, as far back as the time of Batu's invasion; they have been singing: *Almighty Lord, be with us!* It may have been then that they memorized this hymn because at that time nothing but Christ was left to them; yet in this hymn alone is Christ's whole truth. And what is there in the fact that few sermons are preached to the people and that chanters are muttering unintelligibly? . . . As against this, the priest reads: "God and Lord of my being," etc.—and in this prayer *the whole essence of Christianity* is contained, its entire catechism, and the people know this prayer by heart. Likewise, they know by heart the life-histories of many a saint; they relate them and listen to them with emotion.[98]

Dostoevsky voiced his faith in the *narod*'s religiosity after he had visited the Optina Hermitage and the famous spiritual elder Amvrosii (after whom Dostoevsky modeled his character Zosima) in June 1878, having just lost his three-year-old son Alesha, the prototype for his hero in *The Brothers Karamazov*.[99] According to Dostoevsky's wife Anna, her husband "recorded many of my doubts, thoughts, and even words in the chapter of *Brothers Karamazov* called 'Devout Women.'" Here Anna referred to a scene that complements the healing of the shrieker in which the elder comforts a woman who has just lost her child.[100]

Dostoevsky's highlighting of the religious component of *klikushestvo* and of the role that miracles played in Russian Orthodoxy in affirming the faith and easing the burdens of suffering peasant women marks a departure from the purely secular understandings of Pisemskii, Pryzhov, and medical observers such as Klementovskii. The elder Zosima's ability to calm the shrieker at the hermitage recalls the healing powers of Leskov's noble character, Krylushkin, with the notable distinction that Father Zosima enjoyed the imprimatur of the Russian Orthodox Church, while Krylushkin did not. Both the characters of Zosima and Krylushkin symbolize individuals within the Russian Orthodox faith who provided people of all classes, especially the indigent, with psychological help. The Russian hermitages and monasteries with their relics and shrines attracted pilgrims who sought cures or at least relief from their afflictions. Like French pilgrims to Lourdes after 1868, they "discovered a spirit of hope, equality, and communal suffering" at sites "where powerful (if unacknowledged) psychological forces were at work."[101] Dostoevsky was less enamored with the upper classes who sought the help of elders such as Father Zosima because of what he viewed to be their egotism and less sincere faith but nonetheless portrayed the hermitage in this positive spirit of communal suffering.

LEO TOLSTOY

Even Leo Tolstoy, while highly critical of the ritual of the Orthodox Church,[102] admired the psychological aid that a hermitage such as Optina provided the faithful. In reply to an 1899 letter from a Kievan woman, Zinaida Mikhailovna Liubochinskaia, who asked Tolstoy's advice on her right to commit suicide, Tolstoy wrote,

> For more than 30 years a monk, crippled with paralysis and only having control of his left arm, lay on the floor in the Optina Monastery. The doctors said that he was bound to suffer greatly, but not only did he not complain about his situation but, crossing himself, gazing at the icons and smiling, he constantly expressed his gratitude to God and joy for the spark of life which glowed in him. Tens of thousands of visitors came to see him, and it's difficult to imagine all the good which was spread about the world by this man, deprived of all possibility of action. Probably the man did more good than thousands and thousands of healthy people who imagine that in their various institutions they are serving the world.[103]

Although Tolstoy rejected Orthodox rituals as superstitious and was excommunicated by the church for heretical beliefs, he shared not only Dostoevsky's understanding of the spiritual importance of suffering but also his sympathy for *klikushi*. Viewing the ailment as the direct result of women's sexual victimization by men in his controversial and sensational "Kreutzer Sonata" (1889), he closed the circle that began with the stories by Pisemskii, Leskov, and young Dostoevsky that also posited a sexual etiology for *klikushestvo*. Disgusted by men's insatiable sexuality, Tolstoy in "Kreutzer Sonata" focuses not on peasant women, but Russian women of all classes, who in marriage are subjected to their husbands' repeated demands for sexual intercourse when they are pregnant and breastfeeding. He asserts that man's inability to practice continence saps the strength of both woman and child. The spontaneous abortions that women sometimes experience as well as the trauma their bodies experience during intercourse at times when sexual relations should be taboo, Tolstoy explains, results in the weakening of women's minds. "This is what causes nerve troubles and hysteria in our class, and among the peasants causes what they call being 'possessed by the devil'—epilepsy. You will notice that no pure maidens are ever 'possessed,' but only married women living with their husbands. That is so here, and it is just the same in Europe. All the hospitals for hysterical women are full of those who have violated nature's law. The epileptics and Charcot's patients are complete wrecks, you know, but the world is full of half-crippled women."[104] Cognizant of Jean Martin Charcot's treatment of hysterics at the famous Salpêtrière Hospital in Paris, which received wide press attention in European and Russian journals, Tolstoy suggests that all women, regardless of their class and nationality, become hysterics and epileptics because of the sexual abuse they suffer at their husbands' hands. Returning to a sexual etiology for demon possession, which he incorrectly equates with epilepsy, Tolstoy decries the barbarity of an indulgent society in which men act solely for their pleasure.

THE DARK SIDE OF PEASANT BELIEFS

By the end of the nineteenth century, the figure of the *klikusha,* who had received a sympathetic hearing in the works of the realist writers Pisemskii, Leskov, Dostoevsky, and Tolstoy, largely became displaced by the witch as a result of the intelligentsia's growing fascination with the occult and the darker side of peasant beliefs. The exception to the rule lay in the more specialized and new writing of psychiatrists, who sought to uncover the mental properties of the *klikusha*. But even the psychiatrists were part of a new intellectual and cultural era. The period from 1890 to the eve of World War I, Russia's noted Silver Age, witnessed cultural and intellectual experimentation in response to an increasingly fragmented and perilous world brought about by Western science and materialism. The social unrest attendant upon the development of industry, the inundation of cities with uncultured peasants, and the rise of venereal disease marked a society that was "marching inexorably toward world war and revolution."[105] While pornography, vulgarity, drug addiction, sexual experimentation, and anti-Semitism were all the rage among the educated middle and upper classes at the turn of the century, there existed among the same groups an attraction to and a simultaneous repulsion toward Russian peasant culture, epitomized by its allegedly superstitious belief system and its barbarous crimes against witches and sorcerers.

Influenced by Western European fads of spiritualism and occultism and a questioning of a positivist worldview, Russian intellectuals reembraced the supernatural and the fantastic without, however, rejecting scientific principles. In the first half of the nineteenth century, romantic writers had identified belief in the supernatural to have been a positive attribute of Russian peasant culture that could be used to explore the complexities of human nature as well as the distinctive qualities of Russian culture. By contrast, Silver Age writers and ethnographers were captivated by the village's darkness and peasant beliefs that suggested the existence of a primordial world in which violence and destruction were pervasive.

Swayed by Western European accounts of witchcraft, these writers concentrated on beliefs in witches and sorcerers at the expense of the witches' victims, the *klikushi*. When demoniacs were portrayed in literature, they were not *klikushi* but Western European demoniacs in historical dramas set in Western countries infused with Roman Catholic, not Orthodox, imagery. Mirra Aleksandrovna Lokhvitskaia's play *In nomine Domini* and Valerii Briusov's 1907–1908 novel *The Fiery Angel* are representative of this new genre. Although Russian demoniacs did appear in some of the graphic representations of the Silver Age, they depicted the sexually assaulted modern urban woman, a new allegorical representation of Mother Russia, not the peasant woman out of control.[106] Witches, on the other hand, largely came from the Russian village context. The pockmarked rural witch Matrena of Andrei Belyi's 1910 *The Silver Dove,* who, together with her sorcerer-master, destroys the novel's hero Darialsky, is modeled from ethnographic accounts and Belyi's observations of peasant life. Within the novel's struggle between Western and Eastern civilizations, the folk culture of the East "proves more potent and ultimately brings entrapment and destruction."[107] The darkness of the village, it implied, might overrun Russia.

The images of the "dark masses" and the "darkness" of the Russian village were not creations of the turn of the century. Nineteenth-century journals impress upon readers the continuity of those images over time, punctuated as they periodically were with far fewer voices that championed the peasantry. Even the realist writers painted a bleak picture of the Russian village and corruption of the peasants under serfdom. When the environment did not noticeably change with emancipation and the idealistic picture of the countryside painted by the Populists cracked with their failed attempt to rouse the peasants to revolt in the heady days of the summer of 1874, the dark representations of Russian village life resurfaced with a vengeance. Even Dostoevsky, who viewed the peasantry as the vessel of the true faith and Russian soul, spoke of rural folk in terms of their brutality and barbarism. At the same time, he believed that the negative features of peasant culture would disappear on their own and warned repeatedly against the corrupting influences, the "falsehood and darkness," of so-called civilization.[108] The jurists-cum-ethnographers and physicians-cum-ethnographers, on the other hand, championed the benefits of modern civilization. Seeking to understand the dark side of peasant culture, they viewed themselves as enlighteners and civilizers. "Darkness" became symbolic of anything these middle-class professionals deemed superstitious, Orthodox, traditional, stagnant, ignorant, primordial, and primitive.

Concerns about growing lawlessness among Russian peasants that had been voiced in the 1870s increased in the 1880s and 1890s. Nobles returning to the countryside to practice agrarian capitalism demanded greater protection against peasants from the state. At the same time, the urban upper and middle classes felt threatened by the increase in peasant migrants to Moscow and St. Petersburg, who seemingly brought with them brutal ways and a lack of respect for middle-class culture. Reports about growing rural crime against individuals and a comparable escalation in hooliganism, or petty crimes committed by the lower classes against property and individuals of the middle and upper classes, intensified educated society's fears of peasant barbarism. An apocalyptic mood seized some of the professionals as their quest for greater knowledge about the relationship between crime and peasant beliefs in witchcraft and demonology became "colored by a deep fear that a powerful primeval force might be tapped into and released," a fear vindicated by the Revolution of 1905.[109]

Rather than focus upon "the lack of a police presence at the village level" and the reluctance of the imperial government to protect peasants from other peasants, legal specialists collected ethnographic evidence to support their claims that superstition and immorality drove peasants to attack their own kind in fits of collective rage.[110] In the postemancipation period, the peasants' extralegal justice, involving murders—including burnings of witches and sorcerers—captured the legal specialists' attention and imagination. In order to understand the burning of a woman alleged to have been a witch in Novgorod province in the late 1890s and to illuminate similar "savage and insufferable events," the lawyer N. P. Karabchevskii, for example, felt obliged to examine cases in the early nineteenth century involving bewitchment and "other evil doings." In so doing he could demonstrate a disturbing continuity in practices over time.[111] Likewise, the jurists A. A. Levenstim, P. A. Tulub (also a former justice of the peace), and L. Vesin culled comparable incidents for the postemancipation period from newspapers and, in some cases, from their own juridical case files.[112] Only through the insights derived from such investigation, they reasoned, could they try to solve the problems of rural Russia and alleviate the burdens that peasant migrants were imposing on the cities. However, as long as these jurists concentrated on brutal violence and bloodshed rather than the issue of causality and "the complexity of relations between victim and assailant," as Stephen Frank has persuasively pointed out, they perpetuated the image of "the pitch-black darkness and helpless impotence of . . . village people."[113] Like children, ignorant peasants "could not be held fully accountable for the insult and violence they inflicted upon one another."[114]

Not to be outdone by jurists, physicians, who accumulated ethnographic materials about peasant medical practices, turned their venom against self-proclaimed religious healers who reportedly enjoyed curative powers against a variety of ailments, including *klikushestvo*. À la

Pryzhov, they exposed the healers as charlatans preying upon peasants' ignorance. In a scathing description of a woman who earned a reputation in Smolensk province for healing and providing God-given advice, A. Kushnerev began his newspaper article pointing out that "rude ignorance and prejudices, deeply lodged in the midst of the dark peasant people, serve a favorable soil for clever scoundrels to manage their dark affairs." He focused on what he termed the bogus saint's penchant for giving foolhardy advice and predictions that injured gullible peasants, in return for which she took money and gifts. Matushka Avdot'ia's hypocrisy, Kushnerev underscored, was demonstrated by her hiding "small luxuries (bread rolls and fruit liqueur) so as to appear abstemious."[115] Similarly, the zemstvo doctor Nikolai Rudinskii in his discussion of shriekers and individuals suffering from mental illnesses focused on the holy fools who treated them. He described Masha Mykhanovskaia of the village Mukhanovo in Dankovsk uezd, Riazan province, whose outward appearance, he claimed, was "simply horrifying": "her hands are always convulsing; she is always grimacing; her body leans over; her fingers are always moving, her eyes wince. Saliva constantly runs out of her mouth. Her chin and clothing are thus always wet." Another so-called holy fool from Dankovsk uezd, Rudinskii noted, was more of a self-taught gynecologist than a healer. He concluded from stories he had heard but could not share with his readers in print that this man was something of a Don Juan.[116] The psychological comfort that religious and secular healers provided is forgotten in such stories that were meant not only to expose charlatanism but also to paint dark pictures of healers who were not certified doctors of medicine.

The doctor and ethnographer G. I. Popov was one of the few observers of the peasantry at the turn of the century who provided a more nuanced and balanced picture of peasants' religious beliefs and medical practices. His 1903 book is mentioned here because of his attempt to grapple with aspects of bewitchment and *klikushestvo* that most of his learned colleagues ignored. The study constitutes a fairly sophisticated attempt to comprehend popular medicine by amassing data reported by 350 correspondents from across 23 provinces in European Russia. These correspondents included rural priests, teachers, students, landowners, land captains, medical aides, and peasants who had participated in the 1890s ethnographic program sponsored by Count Tenishev to collect material on all aspects of peasant life and who periodically wrote for local publications. Using the familiar theme of darkness, Popov introduced his volume by pointing out to his readers that they knew little about the Russian peasantry:

> The people's poetry [*narodnaia poeziia*] . . . and fragmentary newspaper reports about various things, mainly the dark side of the people's lives,

> comprises almost the single source of knowledge about the people for a significant portion of our educated society. If we exclude the few scholarly investigations of some of the spiritual and economic sides of popular life, we have very few other sources about the *narod*'s worldview, superstitions, prejudices, customs, and those new conditions that have arisen in the last forty years. Thus, the majority of us are inclined to form an opinion about the people only superficially.

That opinion, based on perceptions of the peasants' poverty, coarseness, ignorance, and savagery, continued Popov, could only be negative. To balance the picture, he believed, educated society had an obligation to search beyond the stereotypes to seek out both the positive and negative traits of the peasants' worldview. Quoting Gogol, Popov emphasized "the need to know the past, the inner nature of the Russian in order to decide what exactly we should borrow from Europe." For rural doctors, in particular, Popov argued that an intimate understanding of the peasants' thinking and the limitations that their living conditions imposed was critical for the physicians' prescriptions to be effective. Until scientific medicine understood village reality, physicians' attempts to cure the sick would be stymied. According to Popov, physicians needed to be cognizant of the severe limitations of their therapeutic methods in dealing with victims of *klikushestvo*.[117]

In his discussion of *klikushestvo* and bewitchment, Popov underscored that Russian peasants were actually advanced in their thinking. While he attributed peasant understanding of nervous, psychological, and organic illnesses to superstition, he nuanced his negative assessment by noting that it was no wonder that peasants believed in the ability of witches and sorcerers to harm them when villagers' knowledge about the existence and origins of illnesses and the impact of bad water and foods on health was so weakly developed. More important, from Popov's point of view, however, was that Russian healers were practitioners of sophisticated psychiatric thinking that they had intuitively developed on their own. Indeed, he argued, they already understood the power of suggestion in creating epidemics of *klikushestvo*. In other words, they were aware of the impact of the peasants' foreboding about bewitchment that accompanied the onset of illness and every wedding celebration. Although he characterized rural healers as charlatans, Popov was willing to concede that they inspired confidence in their patients by being sensitive to their needs and by giving them peace of mind through their incantations and other practices that worked on the premise of suggestion. Popov expressed astonishment that the concept of suggestion, which had only been recently acknowledged by scientific medicine, had been around for centuries in Russia. Yet educated society, medical practitioners in particular, only gave such a method credence when it surfaced in the latest thinking of Western European specialists and thus appeared to have Western European origins. Asserting, "It is startling too that those methods [a reference to other therapies practiced by peasants] came to us from the West, when they have been among us, right under our noses, for a long time," Popov ascribed this blindness to the scorn with which educated society treated the peasantry and to the resulting ignorance of peasant ways.[118]

At the same time Popov praised some therapeutic methods of the Russian peasantry, he held to the general notion that the peasants needed spiritual enlightenment and more specific knowledge of the ways in which syphilis, alcoholism, and heredity were linked to mental illness. However, Popov firmly believed that communication between educated society and the peasantry had to be a two-way street. Once more taking a nationalistic approach and expressing an opinion with which Dostoevsky would have agreed, he concluded, "If our *narod,* with its less cultured nature, and despite its outer, sometimes even coarser, shell, is infused with more humanism and less egotism than, for example, representatives of the Teuton or Anglo-Saxon races, then it is" because the *narod* has embraced "the true spirit of Christianity." The church never had "inquisitional bonfires for heretics, did not investigate, torture, and burn the mentally ill and insane, as" did its counterpart in "fifteenth-, sixteenth-, and seventeenth-century Western Europe."[119] Here was a rare assertion that the Orthodox Church had had a positive impact in helping to shape a distinctive Russian culture.

CONCLUSION

As beneficiaries of education and the latest intellectual currents of Western Europe, Russian writers and ethnographers sought to use the peasantry as a barometer that would help them decide whether Russia had a unique destiny or a destiny that should follow the example set out by the most advanced countries of Western Europe. At the same time, they infused ethnographic detail about peasant beliefs with their own notions often shaped by knowledge of Western European lore as well as their own prejudices. Consequently, representations of Russian peasants were often removed from village reality. The hopefulness of the romantic period, the faith that uncovering the essence of the Russian peasantry might bridge the gap between the intelligentsia and the masses of people, did not last long. Even before emancipation the darkness of the Russian village had been laid bare and continued to intrude upon the intelligentsia's consciousness as more information about the countryside became available. What had appeared in the first half of the nineteenth century to be quaint beliefs appeared by the second half of the century to reflect a peasantry so ignorant, backward, primitive, and destructive that it had the power to destroy everything that was progressive and Western in Russian society. The colonization of the city by the village, as hundreds of thousands of peasant migrants flooded into St. Petersburg and Moscow, frightened members of educated Russian society. The few voices championing the Russian peasantry tended to belong to those who had embraced Russian Orthodoxy. These individuals tempered their portrayal of the Russian peasantry by looking at their religious belief system in its entirety. They emphasized popular Orthodoxy rather than simply noting remnants of what intellectuals had identified anachronistically as pagan beliefs.

Chapter Four

PSYCHIATRIC DIAGNOSES

✦ As pioneering practitioners of the newly emergent and as yet not clearly delineated therapeutic sciences, Russian psychiatrists and neurologists at the turn of the century were, not surprisingly, fascinated by *klikushestvo* and wrote extensively about it.[1] Through their theories and case histories they participated in two conversations: European scientific disputes over the classifications and definitions of mental illness and the understanding of mass psychoses, on the one hand, and the national debate over the Russian peasantry, on the other. Psychiatrists and neurologists were well versed in European theories about what constituted abnormal and normal behaviors. Many had attended lectures and observed experiments by renowned psychiatrists, psychologists, and biologists in France and Germany.[2] Furthermore, they kept abreast of the latest European discoveries in translated articles of European psychiatrists and neurologists published in Russian medical journals. Thus, it is little wonder that Russian specialists of the mind and brain found themselves caught up in wider European medical, social, and cultural obsessions with female hysteria and gender stereotypes as they tried to understand the phenomenon of *klikushestvo*.

In order to categorize *klikushestvo* Russian psychiatrists and neurologists turned to the multiple theories that their European counterparts had advanced with regard to hysteria. Among nineteenth-century medical specialists, hysteria constituted a pathological disorder that defied precise definition, "whereby nonspecific distress was given somatic contours."[3] Believed to afflict women far more than men because of their biological makeup, it became a catchall term to categorize what medical specialists perceived to be abnormal female behavior.[4] Because the emotional and physical characteristics of *klikushestvo* fell within the parameters of the wide-ranging symptoms associated with hysteria, a majority of Russian psychiatrists and neurologists believed that *klikushestvo* was a special form of hysteria, a Russian version of aberrant and irrational behavior on the part of women. While acknowledging that men could be victims of *klikushestvo,* they downplayed men's participation, preferring to focus on female shriekers and women's supposedly vulnerable emotional nature.

A markedly small minority of Russian psychiatrists preferred to diagnose *klikushi* as suffering from somnambulism rather than hysteria. That diagnostic category, borrowed from the writings of Alfred Maury, Jean Martin Charcot, Pierre Janet, and other prominent nineteenth-century European psychiatrists, denoted, as in the case of hysteria, a pathological condition. Somnambulism was abnormal in that it was an intermediary condition between the usually distinct states of waking and sleeping. In that middling position, "memory, imagination and the senses are, as it were, exercised imperfectly, or in a state of partial activity."[5] By adopting the term "somnambulism" to describe *klikushestvo,* a minority of Russian psychiatrists were suggesting that *klikushi* were suffering from genuine ailments. These experts differentiated the positive character traits of peasant women from the negative characteristics that psychiatrists had noted among hysterics. The negative traits included inflated ego, love of theatricality, mendacity, and misguided cleverness. By implication, this minority of Russian psychiatrists felt that hysterics were faking their illness at least to some extent, while genuine shriekers were not.

Whether proponents of the diagnosis of hysteria or of somnambulism, Russian psychiatrists agreed that *klikushestvo* constituted a mild and curable form of mental illness among peasant women that was to be distinguished from insanity and diseases of the brain. However, physicians' "boundaries between . . . milder forms of nervous prostration and out-and-out madness were . . . [so] fluid and ill-defined" that they could also argue that untreated *klikushestvo* could eventually lead to mental degeneration in the next generation.[6] Both analyses provided Russian psychiatrists with the rationale they needed to argue that their medical expertise would profit Russian society.

Russian psychiatric and neurological specialists hoped that their studies of *klikushestvo* would have several benefits. They wished, of course, to advance European science as well as to convince other Russian physicians that psychiatry and neurology were respectable medical subfields. They also set the ambitious goals of unlocking the psyche of Russian peasants and improving their lives. Equipped with a storehouse of modern scientific arguments, humanitarian Russian psychiatrists and neurologists viewed themselves as knights in shining armor who would combat and eradicate what they perceived to be the superstitious, unenlightened ideas of the "dark masses." These medical experts, like ethnographers and other educated observers of the Russian peasantry, believed that *klikushestvo* in particular epitomized Russia's backwardness. While ambivalent about some features of modernity, including urban prostitution and labor unrest, they were nonetheless committed to radically changing the belief structure of a rural society that understood its world in religious and supernatural terms in favor of a secular and medical understanding of illness. Their mission to civilize the Russian peasants was just as much cultural as it was medical.[7] The psychiatrists' first step in the realization of this goal involved wresting control of the diagnosis and treatment of mental illness from popular healers, especially from monks and other spiritual healers. The modern crusade of scientific rationalism had no room for alternative interpretations and competing sources of power.

The psychiatrists' battle against *klikushestvo* and other aspects of Russian peasant culture was very much a contest for absolute authority; it was directed against religion and its hold over the minds of peasants. The Russian Orthodox Church, perceived to be the bulwark of the autocratic state, bore the brunt of the psychiatrists' attack. Particularly suspect in the eyes of Russian medical experts were those Orthodox monks who provided special services for *klikushi* and supported these women's conviction that they were possessed. By confirming peasant beliefs—grounded in scriptures, tales, and so-called superstitions—monks were, in the view of medical and secular rationalists, encouraging individual cases of demon possession that had the potential of erupting into epidemics of hysteria. Such epidemics were particularly troubling at the end of the nineteenth century when apocalyptic beliefs propelled non-Orthodox sectarian groups to engage in what psychiatrists and other educated members of Russian society perceived to be sexual deviance as well as ritual murder and mass suicide. The coupling of epidemics of *klikushestvo* with those of non-Orthodox religious manifestations underscored for Russian psychiatrists the irrational and pathological nature of the Russian peasantry that could lead to social and political disaster unless properly harnessed or directed by scientific rationalism.

The psychiatrists' concern with epidemics of hysteria, including those involving demon possession, led to the elaboration of theories concerning mass psychoses. These theories took on greater social and political significance with the Revolution of 1905. In responding to workers' strikes, rural violence, pogroms against Jews, and government repression, government-employed Russian psychiatrists and neurologists found themselves divided. A majority were appalled by the tsarist government's reestablishment of control through punitive means, including the incarceration of political prisoners in insane asylums. These psychiatrists sought to redirect the anarchy of the lower classes into orderly opposition to the tyrannical state. Repressive government measures also served to reverse these psychiatrists' argument for greater institutionalization of the mentally ill in favor of deinstitutionalization and the establishment of foster care programs for the mentally ill in rural communities.[8] A smaller group of psychiatrists sided with the government against what they believed to be the uncontrollable anarchic and psychopathological masses, who were led by pathologically ill liberals and radicals.

Regardless of their political positions, Russian psychiatrists were united in their modernity crusade against what they understood to be Russian backwardness and traditionalism. Armed with an ideology of progress, they set up binary categories of absolutes, delineating the positive from the negative aspects of society and culture; that is, the civilized from the primitive, the modern from the traditional, the rational from the irrational, the scientific from the religious, and the normal from the abnormal. Their categorization of what constituted abnormal behavior grew appreciably as mental illness became "an amorphous, all-embracing concept."[9] Irrational religion embraced superstition and fanaticism, while manifestations of *klikushestvo* amounted to pathological female behavior, the antithesis of orderly and controlled conduct.

When Russian psychiatrists ventured out into the countryside as emissaries of both the state and scientific rationalism, they confronted a completely different worldview that had no understanding of demon possession as a pathological illness requiring the ministrations of urban, educated doctors. Consequently, finding patients suffering from what the rural populace defined as possession proved to be a formidable problem. By examining Russian psychiatrists' perceptions of demon possession and mental illness in the Russian countryside, historians can come to a fuller understanding of the dynamics of Russian society at the turn of the twentieth century and of the tensions between scientific and popular culture.

THE SEARCH FOR *KLIKUSHI*

While madhouses in Russia had first been established by Catherine II in the late eighteenth century, the emergence of psychiatry as a medical speciality in that vast empire coincided with the earliest stage of the Alexandrian reform period in the mid-nineteenth century. At that time, as a result of the crushing defeat in the Crimean War (1853–1855), the Russian government and educated society had begun to reassess Russia's institutions and place in the European family of nations. Following the lead of Western European scientists and with government permission, Professor Ivan Mikhailovich Balinskii (1827–1902) founded Russia's first independent department of psychiatry at the Military Medical Academy in St. Petersburg in 1857 and founded the empire's first psychiatric clinic in that city in 1867. The graduates of the Military Medical Academy filled academic positions as new departments of psychiatry were established in universities in other cities, including Khar'kov (late 1870s), Kazan, and Kiev, all before the creation of a similar department at Moscow University in 1887. The growth of the psychiatric profession was particularly marked in the last two decades of the Romanov dynasty. Although in 1887 only 93 specialists attended the first professional meeting of psychiatrists in Moscow, by 1905 psychiatrists and neurologists numbered 350; seven years later the Union of Russian Psychiatrists and Neuropathologists boasted 538 members.[10]

The creation in 1867 of zemstvos gave these institutions of local self-government, among other mandates, responsibility for providing education and health care for the peasants. This gave a temporary boost to the establishment of asylums for the insane in various Russian provinces. The zemstvo reform also resulted in the transfer of existing asylums and psychiatric wards of general hospitals in provincial towns to supervision by zemstvo personnel. Russian psychiatrists, however, were not satisfied with the zemstvo-operated asylums because they did not enjoy fiscal control over them. With most provincial zemstvos at the beginning of the twentieth century employing fewer than five psychiatrists, not all of whom had specialized training, psychiatric specialists found themselves outnumbered by general medical practitioners who scrambled for the same inadequate resources from government coffers.[11] Psychiatric care continued to be centered in large provincial mental hospitals rather than in wards of smaller general hospitals in outlying districts.[12]

While visible in urban centers and on the pages of the general and specialized press by the end of the nineteenth century, Russian psychiatrists had hardly made their presence known in the Russian countryside. It should be no surprise then that these specialists did not contribute substantially to the dialogue among members of Russian educated society about the phenomenon of *klikushestvo* until the turn of the century. Their assessments and theories depended upon access to individuals suffering from possession.

Complicating matters for psychiatric specialists interested in demon possession was the fact that *klikushi* rarely graced the doors of newly established urban psychiatric wards and clinics. Indeed, they generally did not even figure among the patients of older insane asylums and psychiatric hospitals, who in about two-thirds of all cases were men. The predominance of men in madhouses reflected heavy male in-migration to cities, army doctors' identification of mental illnesses among soldiers, and the inclination of urban police to incarcerate individuals they believed posed a danger to the rest of society. Some Russian psychiatrists' views that men were more prone to insanity than women also served to increase the number of male patients in Russian asylums.[13] Believing that scientific medicine was powerless against the force of witches and sorcerers' spells, peasants and rural police officials (who also came from the peasantry) generally did not view demon possession as either a mental illness or a form of deviant behavior. Those few *klikushi* whom psychiatrists examined in the cities were urban residents (recent migrants from the village among them) or visitors to the city, picked off the streets for disturbing the peace. Only a small number of possessed came from social groups outside the peasantry, and these people were more likely to accept psychiatrists' notions of what constituted mental illness and nervous disorders.

The peasants' lack of understanding of *klikushestvo* as abnormal and pathological and their unwillingness to dispatch demon-possessed women to insane asylums meant that Russian psychiatrists had to venture out to the countryside for patients. These medical experts hoped to convince the peasants that the shriekers were mentally ill and that only they could restore these women's mental health. Limited by their small number and insufficient governmental funds to expand their ranks of trained medical personnel, psychiatrists had three means to address the problems of mentally disturbed peasants in general and the *klikushi* in particular.

One response depended upon the occurrence of spontaneous rural epidemics of hysteria, including those involving demon possession. According to past and current medical theory, "epidemic" or "mass hysteria" is recognized as "the occurrence of a constellation of physical symptoms suggesting an organic illness but resulting from a psychological cause in a group of individuals where each member experiences one or more of these symptoms."[14] When several women began to shriek that they were possessed, the potential for other women to join the ranks of *klikushi* appeared imminent. Because epidemics of demon possession not only disrupted the equilibrium of everyday life but also sometimes erupted in violence against individuals accused of bewitchment, the tsarist government felt compelled to send psychiatrists to the countryside. The personal testimony of N. V. Krainskii of the Komovo Psychiatric Hospital in Novgorod illustrates the government's and Krainskii's concerns about a case of mass hysteria turning into a violent revolt:

> At the beginning of February 1900 I was ordered by the Novgorod provincial administration to go [to] the village Bol'shoi Dvor in Tikhvin district where, according to [recently] acquired information, an epidemic of hysteria had arisen and it was taking a serious turn, threatening a popular uprising. This epidemic arose in Tikhvin district some thirty to forty versts from the spot where in 1879 [and] under similar circumstances the peasant woman Agrafena Ignateva had been burned, [a precedent] that does not make one too optimistic about this epidemic.[15]

Medical experts were charged to quell the outbursts before they claimed more victims or at least to investigate their causes after they had been repressed by the police. Courts might also call upon psychiatrists as expert witnesses in cases where an epidemic led to a criminal action.

Table 4.1 Epidemics of Mass Hysteria in the Countryside Investigated by Psychiatrists

Date	*Location*	*Type*	*Presence of* "Klikushi"
1887	Tver province	*folie à deux*	no
1889	Iampol' district, Podolia province	hiccups	no
1891–92	Vasil'kov district, Kiev province	sectarian movement	no
1893	Zhizdra district, Kaluga province	demon possession	yes
1895	Podol'sk district, Moscow province	bewitchment at a wedding	yes
1896	Tarusa, Kaluga province	religious ecstasy among *khlysty*, a Russian sect known as the Flagellants	no
1897	Podol'sk district, Moscow province	*folie à deux*	no
1897	Tiraspol', Kherson province	mass live burials among Old Believers	no
1898	Podol'sk district, Moscow province	bewitchment at a wedding	yes
1898–99	Gzhatsk district, Smolensk province	demon possession	yes
1899–1900	Tikhvin district, Novgorod province	demon possession	yes
1901	Briansk district, Orel province	religious movement involving Baptists and *khlysty*	no
1907	Gorets district, Mogilev province	apocalyptic movement	no
1909	Moscow province	demon possession	yes
1911	Kherson and Bessarabia provinces	religious movement	yes

Reported epidemics of hysteria involving either *klikushi* or religious enthusiasts among sectarian groups and Old Believers between 1887 and 1917, while not numerous, were extremely important for Russian psychiatrists in their quest to devise theories of mass psychoses (see Table 4.1). They hoped to be able to control "'the pandemonium of insanity' that threatened the foundation of the social order."[16] Once dispatched by government officials to villages experiencing mass hysteria, psychiatrists took full advantage of being in the field and studying the etiology of the epidemics as well as the victims' mental and physical health. They conducted interviews and examinations, writing up detailed case histories and biographies of the victims. Wedded to organic medicine and to the belief that all illnesses have somatic origins, psychiatrists borrowed the term *epidemic* to categorize uncontrolled psychological disturbances that involved several individuals who behaved in similar ways, subconsciously imitating the behavioral patterns of others as if infected by some germ. The common traits of *klikushi* included shrieking, convulsions, *globus hystericus* (spasms in the esophagus and throat), speaking in voices different from their own, and temporary loss of consciousness. If the contagion only affected a couple of people, psychiatrists used the French term *folie à deux* to identify more circumscribed incidents in which the second victim of a pathological disturbance imitated the initial victim's symptoms. By grouping epidemics of hysteria involving demon possession with episodes of mass hysteria involving

---

Sources: V. N. Ergol'skii, "O sudebno-psikhiatricheskoi ekspertize v sektantskikh delakh," *Vestnik obshchestvennoi gigieny, sudebnoi i prakticheskoi meditsiny* 30, no. 2 (May 1896), pt. 3: 1–42; Ergol'skii, "Prestuplenie pod vliianiem demonomanicheskikh galliutsinatsii. (Sudebno-psikhiatricheskii sluchai)," *Arkhiv psikhiatrii, neirologii i sudebnoi psikhopatologii* 24, no. 2 (1894): 61–76; E. A. Genik, "Sluchai '*folie à deux*,'" *Nevrologicheskii vestnik* 5, no. 4 (1897): 59–72; Genik, "Vtoraia epidemiia istericheskikh sudorog v Podol'skom uezda, Moskovskoi gubernii," *Nevrologicheskii vestnik* 6, no. 4 (1898): 146–59; P. I. Iakobii, "'Antikhrist': Sudebno-psikhiatricheskii ocherk," *Sovremennaia psikhiatriia* 3 (June–August 1909): 288–301, 337–55; Iakobii, "Religiozno-psikhicheskiia epidemiia: Iz psikhiatricheskoi ekspertizy," *Vestnik Evropy,* nos. 10–11 (October–November 1903): 732–58, 117–66; I. Iakovenko, "Epidemiia istericheskikh sudorog v Podol'skom uezda, Moskovskoi gub.," *Vestnik obshchestvennoi gigieny, sudebnoi i prakticheskoi meditsiny* 25, no. 3 (March 1895): 93–109, 229–45; Vladimir Ivanovich Iakovenko, *Indutsirovannoe pomeshatel'stvo ("folie à deux") kak odin iz vidov patologicheskago podrazhaniia* (St. Petersburg: Tip. M. M. Stasiulevicha, 1887); V. S. Iakovenko, "Psikhicheskaia epidemiia na religioznoi pochve v Anan'evskom i Tiraspol'skom uezdakh Khersonskoi gub.," *Sovremennaia psikhiatriia* 5 (March–April 1911): 191–98; A. D. Kotsovskii, "O tak nazyvaemom 'Baltskom dvizhenii' v Bessarabii," *Trudy Bessarabskago obshchestva estestvoispytatelei i liubitelei estestvoznaniia* 3 (1911–12): 142–80; N. V. Krainskii, *Porcha, klikushi i besnovatye, kak iavleniia russkoi narodnoi zhizni* (Novgorod: Gubernskaia tipografiia, 1900); M. Lakhtin, *Besooderzhimost' v sovremennoi derevne: Istoriko-psikhologicheskoe izsledovanie* (Moscow: Tipo-litografiia T-va I. N. Kushnerev, 1910); I. A. Sikorskii, "Epidemicheskiia vol'nyia smerti i smertoubiistva v Ternovskikh khutorakh (bliz Tiraspolia)," *Voprosy nervno-psikhicheskoi meditsiny* 2, no. 3 (July–September 1897): 453–511; Sikorskii, "Psikhopaticheskaia epidemiia 1892 goda v Kievskoi gubernii," *Universitetskiia izvestiia [Universiteta sv. Vladimira, Kiev],* no. 4 (April 1893) pt. 2:1–46; and K. P. Sulima, "Epidemiia ikoty (*Singultus*) v selenii Ketrosy, Iampol'skago uezda, Podol'skoi gubernii," *Vestnik obshchestvennoi gigieny, sudebnoi i prakticheskoi meditsiny* 4 (October–December 1889): 36–40.

other religious manifestations such as apocalyptic forebodings and religious ecstasy, psychiatrists were categorizing all types of religious fanaticism as pathological occurrences. They were emphasizing not only the imitative quality of the victims' abnormal behavior but also the contagion of mental illness, which if left unchecked had the potential to destroy the social fabric.

The second means of eliciting facts about mental illness and demon possession in rural Russia required psychiatrists to take a more active role in the countryside by isolating the mentally ill from the general population. Initially that task entailed conducting systematic psychiatric censuses of the mentally ill at the provincial level. Only with concrete information about individuals' mental health could psychiatrists effectively intervene in the peasants' daily life.

In the spirit of a statistic-gathering age, provincial zemstvos sponsored censuses of the mentally ill. Psychiatrists who designed the surveys concerned themselves with gleaning accurate information from a rural population hesitant to talk to strangers. Discontented with the results of initial censuses in the late 1880s, they devised sophisticated questionnaires to guide census takers in their work and to elicit answers from a broad range of people. With a goal of conducting an accurate census in Moscow province in 1893, for example, Vladimir Iakovenko, director of the Pokrovskaia Psychiatric Hospital, dispatched to the countryside census takers with some psychiatric training. The inspectors had instructions to query village elders and priests about the mental health of local inhabitants; through individual interviews with peasant leaders and religious authorities, who had intimate knowledge of local peasants, Iakovenko believed that the inspectors would be able to sort out contradictory information. According to the census's questionnaire, the mentally ill were broadly defined to include "those who are insane, mad from birth, those with fits (falling sickness), the feebleminded, imbeciles, *klikushi, iurodivye* [fools for Christ], chronic drunkards, and those with suicidal tendencies." Thus, victims of demon possession were lumped together with individuals believed to be chronically ill and dangerous members of Russian society. The surveyors then forwarded to zemstvo doctors for their input and correction the information they culled from the testimonies of the elders and priests. In the district towns the census takers interviewed doctors, priests, administrators, and local police. Once all information had been gathered, psychiatrists were to follow up with examinations of those individuals the census had identified as mentally disturbed and to decide which ones needed to be incarcerated and treated in asylums.[17]

The Moscow census results were mixed. They revealed that at least 90 percent of the populations' mentally ill came from the peasantry, a figure matched by similar surveys. That high percentage fed Russian psychiatrists' fears about the dangers that the unenlightened masses posed to society's order if they were left without professional care.[18] On the other hand, the number of individuals suffering from mental illness identified by the census, in Iakovenko's opinion, was far too low. In spite of the precautions taken, carrying out accurate village censuses that pinpointed and classified mentally disturbed and insane individuals proved difficult. Nonscientific understandings of mental illness among the rural populations posed their own set of problems to the census takers. According to Iakovenko, the Moscow assessors identified few individuals suffering from *klikushestvo* and chronic alcoholism because of the peasants' and priests' refusal to regard either phenomenon as a mental illness. At the same time, Iakovenko pointed out that both illnesses were ubiquitous and easily detected.[19]

Russian peasants' wariness of outsiders compounded the problems census takers faced in identifying the mentally disturbed. Villagers knew from long experience that censuses were serious undertakings that might have negative consequences, whether in the form of new or higher taxes or, in this case, incarceration in distant mental hospitals. It is little wonder that zemstvo statistician F. A. Shcherbina, in compiling information for household budget studies in the late 1890s, reported that Voronezh peasants viewed the collection of such data as "evil signs indicating . . . if not the anti-Christ, then in any case unclean forces" and tried to counteract the evil by using crosses, prayers, and charms.[20] In Nizhnii Novgorod in 1889 and 1890, peasants cleverly responded to psychiatric census takers' queries about the existence of *klikushi* in their villages, illustrating their strong sense of family and community solidarity as well as their ability to outsmart their interlocutors. According to P. P. Kashchenko, the psychiatrist in charge of the Nizhnii Novgorod census, male heads of households acknowledged the fact that shriekers lived in the village. Nevertheless, they immediately dashed the hope that response generated by noting that the statisticians would have to list all peasant women in their census if they wished to have a complete enumeration of *klikushi*.[21]

What did the Nizhnii Novgorodian peasants' reply to the census takers mean? Were they saying that all the women were crazy? Were they bowing to the elite notion that women used *klikushestvo* to avoid work? Or were they subverting the census by protecting women and other village folk from prying psychiatrists and ultimately from incarceration in asylums? Given the peasants' tendency to dissemble before authority figures so as to safeguard their own interests, it is reasonable to assume that they were employing the elite's rhetoric to isolate themselves from the outside world. By identifying all peasant women as demon possessed, the Nizhnii Novgorod peasants unwittingly seized the psychiatrists' notion that all women were potentially hysterical. They realized that, as individuals, none in the village were safe from the psychiatrists and their penchant for institutionalization.[22] The peasants were determined to neutralize the harm that these urban professionals represented in their daily lives.

Peasant resistance to psychiatric censuses continued into the Soviet period. As late as 1931 (when the government still permitted medical specialists to compile such surveys and to report the findings in medical journals), N. L. Ostapovich, a member of a medical brigade in Voronezh province, noted a similar problem with eliciting information from peasants about the existence of mentally ill family members. She reported that peasants may have been afraid of the social stigma attached to the identification of mental illness. Since peasants did not generally share physicians' wariness of mental illness and had a far narrower definition of what constituted mental illness, Ostapovich was imposing her own educated notions on the villagers by making such a supposition. Her observation that the rural folk feared that the enumerators' primary goal entailed delivering individuals they identified as being ill to asylums "where they would be beaten," however, more accurately reflected peasants' thinking.[23] In 1929 psychiatrists Strel'chuk and Rumshevich had reported a similarly hostile reaction to asylums and psychiatric hospitals among Ukrainian and Belarusian peasants in Podolia. In their discussions with the Podolians, it became clear that the rural population viewed such institutions as places of last resort where the incurable would be poisoned.[24]

In spite of the difficulties plaguing the compiling of censuses of the mentally ill, psychiatrists interested in *klikushestvo* felt compelled to produce statistics on the phenomenon. Concrete cases of demon possession rendered the peasantry less opaque.[25] They also gave psychiatrists the ammunition they needed to convince their medical peers and government officials of the seriousness of what they considered to be a mental affliction and with which they, the psychiatrists, should deal. Leading psychiatric specialists on *klikushestvo* estimated there to be at least tens of thousands of shriekers in the central and northern Russian provinces of Moscow, Smolensk, Novgorod, Orel, Tula, Tver, Vladimir, and Vologda.[26] In terms of provincial breakdown, Kashchenko, clearly frustrated with the Nizhnii Novgorodian male peasants' lack of cooperation in identifying individual shriekers, thought that the estimate of two *klikushi* per district in that province sorely underestimated reality.[27] Pavel Iakobii provided more precise figures for Orel province, noting that there were at least 1,000 in the entire region, with shriekers numbering between 1.30 per 10,000 inhabitants in Sevsk district and 21.21 per 10,000 in Dmitrovsk district.[28] The higher percentages of shriekers in a district such as Dmitrovsk, Iakobii argued, could be attributed to the area's isolation and therefore its relative backwardness.

At the turn of the twentieth century, medical personnel at Moscow's Pokrovskaia Psychiatric Hospital, convinced of the hereditary nature of mental illness and *klikushestvo*'s danger to Russian society if left untreated, went beyond gathering census information by asking patients suffering from a variety of mental disturbances to identify relatives who were *klikushi*. In 1899 about 5 percent of all male patients and less than 12 percent of all female patients claimed to have had shriekers in their families. Among patients admitted to that hospital in the years from 1899 to 1902, more than 8 percent of men and almost 8 percent of women claimed to have *klikushestvo* in their family.[29] "Hereditary models" of mental illness, popular among the European psychiatric profession at the end of the nineteenth century, served to "marginalize individuals on the basis of their family history."[30] The variant claiming the degenerative nature of mental illness suggested that the disease intensified with each generation. The offspring of untreated *klikushi*, in other words, were destined to suffer more severe mental problems than their mothers.[31]

The third and least frequent way for psychiatrists to learn about demon possession and to confront individuals they believed should become their patients required the psychiatrists to visit monasteries with reputations for miraculous cures of demon possession. It was rare, however, for an overworked psychiatrist to have time to visit monasteries and shrines for a chance meeting with a *klikusha* and to convince her and her relatives that she required psychiatric treatment rather than spiritual aid. Of the group of psychiatrists who wrote about demon possession in the countryside, only N. V. Krainskii and M. P. Nikitin sought out *klikushi* at pilgrimage sites. Krainskii went out of his way to visit monasteries in the aftermath of examining victims of the 1898–1899 epidemic of possession in the Smolensk village of Ashchepkovo. He recorded his general impressions of shriekers witnessed during religious services in Moscow and Smolensk monasteries renowned for their treatment of the possessed. Nikitin was more thorough in his investigations of individual shriekers. Rather than wait for an epidemic of *klikushestvo*, he traveled in the summer of 1903 to the Sarovskaia Hermitage in Tambov province to investigate the healings of shriekers and individuals suffering from a variety of psychological disorders. His visit coincided with celebrations connected to the glorification of Serafim of Sarov, whose relics the faithful and Holy Synod considered miraculous. Nikitin wrote careful accounts of the faith healings he witnessed, supplementing them with biographical information that he obtained from interviews with the cured pilgrims, as well as medical data recorded from the few physical examinations he was able to make.[32]

Having determined that there were thousands of shriekers in the Russian countryside, Russian psychiatrists felt compelled to account for *klikushestvo*'s existence and to combat it with scientific knowledge. They also had to classify what they believed to be a pathology akin to hysteria, a psychological affliction or neurosis they defined as striking mainly women. Before turning to the various theories to explain *klikushestvo* and its place among disorders that produced epidemic hysteria, one must first deal with the psychiatrists' desire to achieve absolute control over the treatment of the phenomenon and over mental illness in general.

SCIENTIFIC RATIONALISM VERSUS POPULAR PRACTICES

In their determination to control the treatment of mental illness, Russian psychiatrists waged their battle against peasant practices and beliefs in the specialized and popular press. They informed educated Russian society of the latest scientific discoveries of the mind and body as well as the dangers of allowing peasants and untrained healers to continue to care for the mentally ill. Supplementing their census data with horror stories, psychiatrists expressed their incredulity and anger at the ways in which peasants treated individuals suffering from nervous problems and various types of mental illness, including *klikushestvo*. Their attacks on the Orthodox Church, especially monks who ministered to victims of demon possession, were particularly venomous.

The shrill tone of the polemics derived in part from psychiatrists' desire to impress upon Russian society the need for the supposedly more benevolent and humanitarian care that they could provide the mentally disturbed. Psychiatric specialists wanted both the psychotically ill and *klikushi* to be under their supervision and treatment within the confines of hospital wards or insane asylums. The psychiatrists' battle of words, however, was prompted as well by the abysmally low cure rate in insane asylums and by the negative press reports about asylum conditions. Finding themselves on the defensive, they painted a bleak picture of traditional society's treatment of the mentally ill. They also responded to press accusations that they employed "harsh and sadistic methods of treatment" by casting blame on the public for misunderstanding the nature of psychiatry and listening instead to the rantings of the mentally disturbed.[33] One prominent psychiatrist even remarked defensively, "Dishonorable individuals are beginning to assert that [we] are inventing the insane in order to enhance our reputations."[34] Public knowledge of mind-numbing and sleep-inducing drugs—sulphonal and chloral hydrate, barbiturates, bromides of potassium and ammonia—administered by psychiatrists to their patients, often with adverse physical and mental effects, also posed problems for psychiatrists' image.[35]

Vladimir Iakovenko, for example, used the publication of the 1893 Moscow provincial census of the mentally ill to denounce what he considered to be a high percentage of families (20%) that cruelly treated mentally disturbed relatives by regularly beating, tying, or chaining them. To illustrate his outrage and the callous behavior of peasants, he cited figures regarding these practices. For instance, Iakovenko noted that census takers found 76 of 1,744 (4.4%) mentally ill persons they registered in Nizhnii Novgorod chained up; in Moscow and Tambov provinces the figures were 75 out 3,072 (2.4%) and 169 out of 3,834 (4.4%) respectively.[36] By citing comparable figures for beatings and other violence against the mentally disturbed, he may also have been implying, contrary to some of his peers' opinions, that the peasants, like other social classes, feared the mentally ill and would welcome the opportunity to be unburdened of the care of dangerous family members. While Iakovenko's humanitarian concerns are to be applauded, the fact remains that Russian psychiatric wards and asylums also physically bound their patients. In spite of Sergei Korsakov's campaign to do away with such restraints, Russia's institutions for the mentally ill regularly used shackles, not only in 1900 when Iakovenko published his assessment, but also in 1912 when psychiatrists complained of the abuse at the First Congress of the Union of Russian Psychiatrists and Neuropathologists.[37]

Besides providing statistical data about peasant maltreatment of the mentally ill, Iakovenko, intent upon striking a humanitarian note with his readers, graphically described numerous individual cases of cruel treatment. For example, he noted that in the village of Maksimovo in Bogorodskii district, Moscow province, census takers had discovered thirty-nine-year-old P. G-va in a small locked storehouse. G-va, when they found her, was almost naked, and her body was covered with bruises as a result of the beatings she had received from her husband. Upon making inquiries, the census takers learned that the husband had frequently abandoned his wife, leaving her without care and adequate provisions. As a consequence, G-va was often dirty and soiled with her own excrement.[38] Here, for Iakovenko, was a perfect example of a woman who could be cared for in an asylum safe from the actions of an abusive and neglectful spouse.

Iakovenko's most graphic story in his catalog of barbaric peasant practices involved an eighteen-year-old youth who eventually landed in Moscow's Pokrovskaia Psychiatric Hospital and who was cured of his ailment. The account reads like a didactic tale, outlining the horrors that the mentally ill faced in the countryside. Like a saint in the hagiographical literature, the hero of this story had to undergo numerous humiliations at the hands of both family members and uncivilized local healers. At the end of a long tortuous road, however, there was light, provided not by God but by trained psychiatrists. According to Iakovenko, the youth suffered from severe headaches that hampered his ability to work. Thinking that he was simply lazy, however, his parents frequently beat him. When it finally dawned on them that he was insane, they turned repeatedly to healers who had reputations for curing mental illness. On one of these occasions, when the youth resisted a healer's remedy, his father slapped his face several times and almost dislocated his jaw in trying to pry it open to insert the potion. The youth rebelled further by spitting out the liquid poured into his mouth; he was rewarded by a severe beating. The family had also turned to other healers—a thirteen-year-old girl, an elderly woman, and a nobleman (described by Iakovenko as a charlatan)—who all specialized in saying prayers over the mentally disturbed. Each visit ended with the boy running away and his father catching and beating him. Finally, the man decided to take his son to the zemstvo hospital, where the medical staff suggested that the youth required the specialized care of experts at the Pokrovskaia Psychiatric Hospital. On the road to Moscow, the boy escaped when his father and a medical attendant stopped at a tavern for a drink. Eventually, he returned to his village, where his father caught up with him, beat him, and tied him up. When the youth took flight again, this time from another nobleman healer, he headed for his sister's village in Pushkin. The sister's family members, according to Iakovenko, were even less charitable than the boy's parents; indeed, they proceeded several times to throw the youth into a manure hole, hoping thus to rid him of his illness. The boy fled to the zemstvo hospital where luckily the doctors assigned a feldsher to accompany him to the Moscow Pokrovskaia Hospital. Iakovenko finished the tale by boasting that when the boy was released from the hospital after three and a half months of successful treatment, he was completely cured.[39] Psychiatric treatment not only secured the boy's mental health but also spared him further savage handling by family and charlatan healers.

Other doctors were more sympathetic than Iakovenko in assessing the peasants' treatment of mental illnesses, including *klikushestvo,* although they shared with him a distaste for popular healers. Writing about his observations on this subject in Podolia in the southwest, the district doctor K. P. Sulima noted that peasant families turned to both the clergy and healers (whom Sulima called charlatans) for help with the demon possessed. While repulsed by the healers' treatments, Sulima at least understood these actions to be tied directly to peasants' understandings of the devil. The healers required the possessed to drink, Sulima wrote, "a myriad of potions [and] Epiphany [i.e., holy] water, bathe [them] with various essences, burn a host of substances, and in general do whatever in their opinion would be repulsive to Satan. Each healer applies his own special method of treatment to the patient, and these methods are horrible. They force the patient to leap over a bonfire, frighten him, lock him in a cellar for a long time, and sometimes torture him in a special manner on the supposition that only in that fashion can the devil be made to suffer."[40] Drawing upon the 1889–1890 Nizhnii Novgorod census, Kashchenko reflected on cases in which epileptics and persons suffering from other mental illnesses (contemporary medical thinking classified epilepsy as a mental illness) were tied, chained, and locked up. Unlike Iakovenko, however, Kashchenko thought that peasants were generally neither cruel nor indifferent to ill family and community members but that they were "helpless and defenseless when it comes to mental illness."[41] While more sympathetic to the peasants' handling of the mentally disturbed, Sulima and Kashchenko nonetheless would have agreed with Iakovenko that individuals suffering from mental illnesses, ranging from the mild form of *klikushestvo* to serious forms of psychotic illnesses, were better off in psychiatric hospitals, where they enjoyed the benevolent care of trained psychiatrists.[42]

In their discussions of *klikushestvo,* psychiatrists saved much of their rancor for spiritual healers whom, they felt, were largely responsible for encouraging the phenomenon and refusing to view it as pathological behavior. A 1908 census of the mentally ill in St. Petersburg province reported 233 instances in which peasants turned to exorcists for treatment of mentally ill family members.[43] The fact that self-proclaimed healers—monks and members of the parish clergy—were not peasants, but supposedly educated individuals, most vexed the psychiatrists. The clergy, according to Vladimir M. Bekhterev (1857–1927), professor of psychiatry and neurology at the highly respected Military Medical Academy in St. Petersburg, should have been "eliminat[ing] crude superstitions from the people's faith and . . . disseminat[ing] . . . healthy religious notions among the simple people," rather than promoting irrational beliefs.[44] In their zeal to civilize the Russian peasantry, however, Russian psychiatrists were undercutting their argument that *klikushestvo* constituted a pathological illness that only they could cure. If the expulsion of irrational beliefs from the peasants' worldview resulted in the elimination of *klikushestvo,* possession was no more than a cultural artifact.

The quest for authority over treatment of the shriekers propelled Russian psychiatrists forward in their attacks on the Orthodox Church. They especially opposed monks' ministrations to *klikushi.* By offering special prayers, holy water, oil, and herbs, and by performing exorcisms, these spiritual confessors, according to the medical specialists, convinced shriekers that they possessed exceptional God-given powers to drive away the shriekers' demons and to relieve their suffering souls. In his influential 1900 book on the subject of *klikushestvo,* N. V. Krainskii concluded from his sojourn at the Kalochskii Monastery in Smolensk province that, "in general, the monastic clergy protects *klikushi,* acknowledges them as possessed, looks after them, and allows them to have fits, often accompanied by shrieks, sacrilege, and struggles with the elements possessing them during services." More damning, Krainskii suggested that the monks had greater interest in profits than in the care of tortured souls. After all, he pointed out, despite the special prayers that monks said for a fee over the shriekers, these poor women were rarely cured.[45] Perhaps most galling to the psychiatrists was that peasants did not hold monastic clergy accountable for their actions. When the clergy's treatment worked, the healers and healed ascribed the cure to God's infinite mercy; in the event of unsuccessful exorcisms, the victims of possession pointed to their own sinfulness rather than to the failure of holy individuals to purify them.

Psychiatrists also attacked self-proclaimed spiritual healers who were not connected with monasteries. At the 5 December 1910 meeting of the Psychological Society, Mikhail Lakhtin directed his enmity against a Moscow healer named Brother Iakov. In his investigation of a 1909 epidemic of *klikushestvo* in the Moscow provincial parish of Troitskoe, Lakhtin discovered that victims of possession and hysteria sought the help of Iakov, whose fame as a spiritual healer was widespread in the province. He portrayed Iakov as a

> severe cripple, a feeble-minded old man who throughout his life has gone from monastery to monastery and mixed with beggars and the crippled. He can only imitate those rites and prayers that he heard in church. Those who go to him do so for help and advice and they receive both from him, since Iakov's words are so quiet and imprecise but so benevolent that everyone finds in them what they want [to hear].
>
> If he only prayed and gave advice, his actions would be beneficial; but he tries to treat the illness and instructs others. He only affirms the people's superstitious belief in the strength of the devil. It is obvious that it is not enough to fight a psycho-pathological epidemic with a police investigation of individuals. There will always be paranoiacs, maniacs and the mentally ill, and another or several individuals will replace the one who has been removed. The fight must be directed towards those conditions that allow for the existence of such phenomena as the activities of brother Iakov, and before anything else this means the broad enlightenment of the masses.[46]

Lakhtin was thus ready to leave theology and praying to clerics, monks, and nuns, as well as to self-appointed religious figures such as Brother Iakov, but he certainly did not condone medical and psychological treatments by these individuals.

A 1911 scandal involving a monastery in Bessarabia provided further grist for the psychiatrists' mill. Their image of a disreputable church had been shaped by tales of the scandalous faith healer Grigorii Rasputin, who was ministering to the heir to the throne, Alexis; to his mother Alexandra; and to a small circle of people from Petersburg high society.

When news broke of epidemics of religious hysteria among peasants in Bessarabia and Kherson, accompanied by rumors of sexual improprieties between Orthodox monks and pilgrims, medical specialists had reason to castigate the church. As early as 1909, pilgrimages to the Baltskii Monastery in the southern part of Kishinev district became popular mainly among Moldavian peasants from the provinces of Kherson and Bessarabia. Stories soon spread that miraculous cures had occurred upon the uncovering of the relics of Feodosii, a former priest, at that monastery. Newspaper reporters, curious to see the miracles for themselves, traveled to the religious site and found quite a different set of circumstances. They reported that, contrary to rumor, ill pilgrims were not being healed and furthermore, that many worshipers returned to their villages in Kherson and Bessarabia with a new ailment that resulted in epidemics of a neuropsychological nature: "Everywhere in the villages appear these dark persons, who on the pretext of redeeming sins mislead the village people, urging them to uncover [holy] springs, build up wells, supposedly with miracle-working water. Crowds of dark village people are thronging to these wells and springs [and] are holding funeral services, prayer services, etc. . . . As a result, many young people, young girls and often old peasants have started to show signs of abnormality."[47]

The psychological assessment of these epidemics came from psychiatrists who served as government emissaries charged with sorting out the situation to quell the disturbances. In his investigations of the Baltskii Monastery, psychiatrist A. D. Kotsovskii blamed the actions of individual monks for exploiting gullible pilgrims. He charged the ieromonakhs Gerasim, Gennadii, and Feodosii with being crude charlatans who took advantage of young women who had come to the monastery for cures. He found Ieromonakh Gerasim, whom he labeled a drunk and "a coarse, uneducated *muzhik* [peasant]," the most loathsome. "Pale and emaciated, because of all [his] excesses, with cunning, small, roaming eyes, Gerasim produces a repulsive impression," Kotsovskii wrote. The psychiatrist accused the monks of committing sexual improprieties with the faithful, pointing out that the ieromonakh Innokent had received worshipers in his underwear and forced these young girls to scratch and caress his body with kisses.[48]

Russian psychiatrists' negative portrayals of religious and lay healers had some validity. Indeed, the Holy Synod itself set up a commission of ecclesiastics and laypersons to investigate the charges leveled against the Baltskii Monastery.[49] Furthermore, as the church hierarchy adopted a narrower understanding of the miraculous (as discussed in chapter 1), it welcomed medical doctors onto its commissions to verify miraculous cures.

However, as champions of scientific knowledge and their own expertise, Russian psychiatrists generally concentrated on objectionable examples at the expense of successful cures by popular healers.[50] Like their counterparts in the rest of Europe, they refused to acknowledge or failed to understand the psychological comfort that monks and lay healers offered the population at large and railed against the superstition they believed was at the root of spiritual healing. They were not prepared to share the stage with these healers and their nonscientific remedies. Rather, they sought to extend the authority of modern science over care of the body and the mind at a time when science's cure rates were no better than those of "alternative psychotherapeutic cultures."[51]

Feeling themselves under siege, psychiatrists raised their voices against the dangers of governmental control and the possibility of scientific reason losing out to a repressive autocratic system. Not surprisingly, their offensive against the Orthodox Church—long thought to be a bulwark of the state—increased at the same time. By attacking spiritual healers and by claiming to have the humanitarian solution, psychiatrists could win some credibility with educated society and thus deflect attention from their own failings. At the same time, they had to devise credible theories about mental illness and *klikushestvo* to demonstrate their sincere desire to help the population at large.

HYSTERIA VERSUS SOMNAMBULISM

Having staked out their territory as experts, then, how did Russian psychiatrists diagnose *klikushestvo* and propose to treat the phenomenon? Here the debate centered around the classification of demon possession either as a form of hysteria or a manifestation of somnambulism as Russian psychiatrists engaged various European theories regarding hysteria. Hysteria was by far the most enigmatic diagnostic category as "it hovered elusively between the organic and the psychological" and as it discredited itself by suggesting that hysterics might be feigning their ailments. The symptoms of hysteria "were heterogeneous, bizarre, and unpredictable: pains in the genitals and abdomen, shooting [from] top to toe, rising in the thorax and producing constrictions in the throat *(globus hystericus);* breathing irregularities; twitchings, tics, and spasms; mounting anxiety and emotional outbursts; breathlessness, and floods of tears; more acute seizures, paralyses, convulsions, hermiplagias, or catalepsy—any or all of which might ring the changes in dizzying succession and often with no obvious organic source."[52] The *klikushi*'s symptoms of convulsions, abdominal pains, throat constrictions, and catalepsy fell easily into the category of hysteria. The fact that most of Russia's possessed were women also prompted doctors to diagnose the illness as a form of female hysteria, which underscored nineteenth-century medicine's misogynistic discomfort with the female body and its attribution of hysteria's causality to women's sexual organs. Even those Russian psychiatrists who preferred to diagnose *klikushestvo* as a form of somnambulism, an abnormal state between waking and sleeping in which individuals do not remember their actions upon waking, could not escape the assumptions that uterine or menstrual irregularities and either sexual overstimulation or sexual repression were responsible for mental disorders among women. The label of somnambulism robbed *klikushi* of agency, as doctors believed that their subconscious controlled their actions once they found themselves in a somnambulistic state. Hysteria as a diagnostic category, on the other hand, endowed *klikushi* with some responsibility for their actions; physicians assumed that hysteric symptoms were "often faked—a characteristic foible of a sex whose entire demeanor was pockmarked by dishonesty, deceitfulness, and emotional waywardness."[53]

By the mid-1890s, a consensus had emerged among Russian psychiatrists that environmental conditions as well as the low spiritual and intellectual development of the Russian people had resulted in cases of hysteria or *demonomania* (the Latin term that psychiatrists sometimes used for demon possession) among peasants. Drawing upon the writings of earlier medical observers, they argued that poor material conditions and the psychological strains of daily life induced women who subscribed to superstitious ideas about demons and bewitchment to become *klikushi*.[54] Two epidemics of possession in the 1890s allowed psychiatrists in the field to elaborate their theories. These incidents validated the French psychiatrist Charcot's theory that men could be victims of hysteria just as easily as women. Russian psychiatrists, however, argued that "hysteria had different causes that depended on gender."[55] They declared that men were susceptible to possession only under exceptional circumstances, such as weddings, which led to an excess of the masculine behavior of drinking. Women, on the other hand, were biologically predisposed to hysterical episodes.

An example of the different causations attributed to hysteria on the basis of gender was given by Moscow psychiatrist I. Iakovenko. In 1895 in the village Novgorodovo, Podol'sk district, Moscow province, he served as the Russian government's psychiatric investigator of an outbreak of possession that affected both men and women at a wedding. He discovered that 60 percent of the male guests as opposed to only 43 percent of the women had taken ill, although the number of women stricken outnumbered men in a ratio of 3:2. Iakovenko attributed the men's hysteria, including the groom's convulsions, to their consumption of too much alcohol over a three-day period with little sleep. In his mind they had no natural predisposition to mental illness. Yet even with the information concerning binge drinking and lack of sleep at hand, Iakovenko cast the bride as the culprit in sparking the epidemic as she was the first to experience hysteric symptoms. Assuming incorrectly that peasant women did not imbibe alcohol as they were too busy with food preparation, he looked for other causes of the hysteria among the women, centering his attention mainly upon the bride. The bride, Iakovenko wrote, suffered from more than extreme exhaustion from the three-day feast. Iakovenko cast her as a trollop with an insatiable sexual appetite. Having accused her of having indulged in sexual excesses during the wedding festivities, he also attributed her shrieking to a pathological imitation of the antics of *klikushi,* whom Iakovenko assumed she had seen at an earlier time, and to a strong superstitious foreboding that a disgruntled guest/sorcerer would cast a spell on her during the wedding celebrations. Using a double standard, Iakovenko refrained from attributing sexual excesses, imitation, or foreboding to the groom.[56]

In a study of another epidemic of *klikushestvo* at a wedding three years later in the same district, the psychiatrist E. A. Genik also preferred differential explanations for possession among men and women. This time two men and four women experienced convulsions during the festivities when they became convinced they had been bewitched by other guests. In his interviews of the victims, Genik discovered that a significant quantity of alcohol had been consumed over the course of one day and night—2 1/2 buckets of vodka for 20 guests (amounting on average to 1 1/2 liters per person).[57] He chose to ignore that discovery when he searched for reasons for the women's pathological behavior. Like Iakovenko, he paid relatively little attention to the men, stressing that one of them, the bride's father, had been drinking heavily and had previously experienced a fit, also at a wedding. Genik gave far more notice to the women, pinpointing in two cases hereditary dispositions to *klikushestvo* because their mothers had been *klikushi.* Subscribing to the sexual etiology of mental illness among women, he recorded the possessed women's regularity of menses, childbearing experiences, numbers of miscarriages, and in the case of one woman, a painful right ovary (that is, when he applied pressure in that area).[58] Genik presumed that excessive alcohol consumption, physical exhaustion, and beliefs in the possibility of bewitchment and possession occurring at weddings were insufficient to explain hysterical outbreaks among women. Hereditary predisposition among women to *klikushestvo* and the rhythms and cycles of their reproductive organs were also held responsible.

N. V. Krainskii challenged the conclusions of these earlier doctors who had determined *klikushestvo* to be a type of hysterical behavior, preferring to understand demon possession as a form of somnambulism. He stressed the amnesic state in which shriekers found themselves after they experienced convulsions as proof of their being somnambulists. Krainskii's study of *klikushestvo* was so extensive and his book so influential, they merit attention here.[59]

Krainskii sought to legitimize his understanding of the phenomenon of *klikushestvo* by historical inquiry and by making retrospective diagnoses of the possession cases contained in the historical record. Since medical science in the nineteenth century was committed to the discovery of nature's universal laws, it stood to reason that those laws were immutable through the ages.[60] Taking a cue from the earlier writings of the ethnographer-cum-revolutionary Ivan Pryzhov and the French psychiatrists' historical studies of mental and nervous diseases, Krainskii placed possession and shrieking in their medieval Muscovite context.[61] He subsequently charted *klikushestvo*'s historical evolution, providing verbatim passages from court cases, law codes, and other scholarly writing. Having identified the characteristics of the phenomenon—the belief in possession, revulsion toward holy objects, screaming in animal voices, and convulsions—as being the same over the course of centuries, he began his discussion of the Smolensk village of Ashchepkovo and the epidemic of demon possession that developed there in 1898.

From the outset, Krainskii sought to persuade his medical colleagues against an environmental approach to demon possession and mental illness in general. He pointed out that Ashchepkovo, contrary to expectation, was not an isolated backwater cut off from enlightened urban life; rather the village was located 27 versts (about 18 miles) from the town of Gzhatsk and a mere 7 versts (4.6 miles) from a railway station on the Moscow-Brest railway line. Furthermore, almost half of the male population was employed in Moscow or Petersburg. These laborers left their wives behind in the village either on their own or with in-laws. "Because of that [urban experience]," Krainskii concluded, "the population has a bit of a town flavor and in general is fairly enlightened." Not only was literacy widespread, but alcoholism was not a problem. The villagers of Ashchepkovo, according to Krainskii, had even opposed the opening of a tavern in their village. Despite those positive signs, he detected a high incidence of syphilis and nervous diseases among the inhabitants of Gzhatsk district.[62] Furthermore, Ashchepkovo's progressivism had not prevented an epidemic of possession.

Indeed, Krainskii was not sure that modernization necessarily produced positive results. In his analysis of the Ashchepkovo epidemic, he reacted most negatively to the most urbane of the shriekers, Vasilisa Alekseeva. As the chief instigator of the epidemic, Vasilisa, in Krainskii's view, was faking her possession and enjoyed "the attention and sympathy focused on her." He also described her as presenting "the appearance of an urban woman." Having spent considerable time in Moscow with her migrant husband, "she wears city clothing, she is fairly advanced for her circle, she speaks in a fairly witty fashion and knows how to justify her beliefs. She is literate and learned some things in Moscow so that she gives the impression of an intelligent and fairly enlightened woman." Under that veneer, however, Vasilisa still subscribed to peasant notions about witchcraft and followed the example of her mother who reportedly was a shrieker as well. In a note of antimodernism, Krainskii inferred that Vasilisa, in having a taste of city life and prized individualism, had appropriated traditional beliefs in order to corrupt her village.[63]

After examining Vasilisa, Krainskii turned his medical attention to the other victims of demon possession. He separated out one of the women, whom he also identified as a malingerer, and the two men. He judged one of the men to be psychologically normal but gullible to the general rumors of bewitchment and the other to be "naturally stupid, almost retarded." The latter's claim to be possessed, according to Krainskii, was totally imaginary. Like his contemporaries, Krainskii was not interested in the men who believed that they were possessed and preferred to concentrate on the women, whom he thought to be more susceptible to believing they were possessed. While the psychiatrist characterized the remaining women as being superstitious, he found most of them to be well-meaning. He carried out tests to determine whether their somatic conditions matched those defined by Charcot, with whom he had studied. Thus in the case of twenty-four-year-old Mar'ia Alekseeva, Krainskii reported that "outside the seizures, Mar'ia did not exhibit any of the symptoms characteristic of hysteria: her eyesight did not change, there was no change in her pupils or vasomotors. Her reflexes and tactile sensations were normal; she did not have any spinal injury. She had strong stomach pains. Her ovaries were fine, and the seizures had no effect on them. Her face reflected a trace of *globus hystericus,* and she complained of heart pains and melancholy."[64]

Like Charcot, Krainskii rejected genital etiologies for hysteria, but could not get away from sexualizing his diagnosis of the female *klikushi.*[65] He must have asked Vasilisa, the woman he identified as a malingerer, about her menstruation cycle to elicit the response that she began menstruating during all high holidays or when she traveled to monasteries, meaning that she would not be able to attend church services and face the holy objects that made her shriek. Vasilisa's responses to questions concerning her sexual relations with her husband led Krainskii to conclude that, because of her husband's living in Moscow, she was sexually frustrated.[66]

Krainskii argued that three of the genuine victims of *klikushestvo* (thirty-six-year-old Neonila Titova, twenty-four-year-old Mar'ia Alekseeva, and thirty-three-year-old Mar'ia Fedorova), whose husbands were absent from the village either as laborers or soldiers, were also victims of sexual frustration. In Neonila's case, Krainskii noted that her sexual activity had declined dramatically with her spouse's departure. He attributed Mar'ia Alekseeva's "absence of sexual need and her continuing frustration" to "her husband's lengthy absence," whereas in the case of Mar'ia Fedorova, he observed that she had a crushed ovary. It is clear from his notations that Mar'ia Fedorova told Krainskii that she had deliberately not had sexual relations with her husband for the three months of her illness because she did not want to infect him or the child she might bear if she became pregnant.[67]

Krainskii, who understood patriarchy to be the natural order, projected unnatural sexual practices upon the women he examined in Ashchepkovo. Blinded by patriarchal notions, like his medical counterparts, he was unable to make "objective" diagnoses. At times, he struggled between notions of women's heightened sexuality that needed periodic release and the Victorian notion of women's discomfort with sex. Refusing to entertain the notion that Neonila Titova and Mar'ia Fedorova might have been practicing birth control, Krainskii preferred instead to conclude that they were sexually frustrated. It also does not seem to have occurred to him that these women might have been reacting negatively to their husbands' prolonged absences, not because of sexual frustration, but because of the overwhelming burdens they faced in managing their household economies. Krainskii attributed another of the Ashchepkovo *klikusha*'s ailments to her fear of sexual relations, a conclusion that he reached when thirty-two-year-old Akulina Semenova told him she had been ill since her wedding day.[68]

While Krainskii followed the lead of contemporary European and Russian psychiatrists in finding sexual etiologies for women's behavior and ailments, he did not focus solely on women's sexual organs and sexual experiences. He compassionately elicited the family histories and, in some cases, the tragic experiences of the shriekers he examined. Russian psychiatrists subsequently correlated the onset of *klikushestvo* with the timing of traumas, not all of which were connected to sexual experiences.[69] Krainskii also concluded that some of the shriekers' physical ailments had organic roots. He thus attributed their chest pains, for example, to dyspepsia and the effects of an inadequate diet. Some of the women, he found, exhibited symptoms of emaciation, anemia, and other disorders that "last years, sometimes even a lifetime, when suddenly they get the idea that they are bewitched . . . and they become *klikushi,* copying those phenomena they had witnessed among other shriekers."[70]

More important than the organic explanation for some of the shriekers' physical ailments was Krainskii's conclusion that the physiological roots of their mental illness were grounded in somnambulism rather than hysteria. In determining whether the Ashchepkovo *klikushi* were somnambulists or hysterics, Krainskii began with two premises: hysterics are not amnesic, will not react to artificial stimulants during their seizures, and cannot be hypnotized, while somnambulists can easily be hypnotized because hypnosis duplicates the essential features of somnambulism. All the *klikushi* whom Krainskii identified as nonpretenders and somnambulists took to hypnosis well and always reacted to the ammonia he made them sniff during their episodes of possession. "The fact that after being hypnotized," Krainskii posited, "all the *klikushi* had no recollection of what had happened to them corresponds to their claim that they do not remember anything about their fits. This gives reason to think that during a fit a *klikusha* is in a somnambulist state." Having made his diagnosis of *klikushestvo* as a form of somnambulism, Krainskii cautioned psychiatrists against lumping everything that did not have an organic source under the rubric of hysteria.[71]

In stressing the somnambulistic nature of *klikushestvo,* Krainskii distinguished between the positive character traits of shriekers and negative qualities of hysterics. In this respect, he subscribed to the notion of the "hysterical constitution" or "hysterical temperament" whereby hysterics exhibited unpleasant characteristics, a concept favored by the contemporary German psychiatrists Paul Möbius and Otto Weininger and by leading British psychiatrists.[72] "A *klikusha,*" according to Krainskii, "does not have the ego of a genuine hysteric; on the contrary she is meek and tolerant." Again, unlike a hysteric, a shrieker exhibited neither characteristics of mendaciousness and cleverness nor feelings of anger; furthermore, "her consciousness and all mental processes are normal." While shriekers shared with hysterics a tendency toward theatricality during their seizures, Krainskii argued that the *klikushi*'s gestures resulted from genuine suffering. At the same time, Krainskii contradicted his characterization of *klikushestvo* as a type of somnambulism by noting that during their fits shriekers were always in control of their movements and had a specific goal in mind for their behavior—the easing of their lot in life. Somnambulism stresses actions involuntarily performed through the subconscious. Krainskii's diagnosis of somnambulism was actually focused on the period when a shrieker lost consciousness, which lasted from several minutes to several hours, and on her memory loss regarding her behavior upon waking.[73]

G. B. Grossman of the Khar'kov University's Orshanskii Polyclinic was one of the few psychiatrists to come to the defense of Krainskii's conclusion that the shriekers were not hysterics. Based on his examination of a single woman (an accepted practice in psychiatry), he too concluded that shriekers did not experience changes in feeling, movement, or vasomotor systems. He claimed that "there are no hysterical zones. All psychological functions remain in a normal state: One does not find the lying, deceit, or anger that one often observes among hysterics. The sick are well fed and do not have any signs of degeneration. They are not unstable, unbalanced, capricious, irritable; they do not have ravings and hallucinations typical of grand hysteria." Furthermore, Grossman argued that hypnosis was effective in ridding them of their stomach pains and fear of holy objects, at least temporarily.[74] Thus, he shared with Krainskii the notion of the "hysterical temperament." Both psychiatrists also agreed that shriekers did not experience hallucinations.

Vladimir Bekhterev figured among the psychiatrists and neurologists who did not agree with Krainskii's diagnosis of *klikushestvo* as a form of somnambulism. In rejecting Krainskii's refusal to classify *klikushestvo* as a hysterical neurosis, he argued first that the stereotypical behavioral patterns of the shriekers over time and large geographical distances proved that *klikushestvo* was a pathology rather than feigned illness. Not a proponent of the notion of a hysterical personality, Bekhterev likewise characterized hysteria as a genuine ailment. Then he determined that all medical observations of the phenomenon led one to conclude

> that the illness . . . develops on hysterical grounds. We are speaking here not only of the epileptic character [of the illness], marked by shrieks, falling [to the ground], and a whole series of disruptive actions, not only of the existence of full amnesia concerning the entire fit, but [also] a series of other disorders, such as spasms in the esophagus and throat *(globus hystericus),* belching, hiccuping, vomiting, quickening of breath, a more or less abrupt quickening of the pulse, anaesthesia of the body during the course of the fit as verified by several authors, trembling of one or other muscular groups, pain in the pit of the stomach and other parts of the body, a feeling of numbing in the limbs, *the development of the illness among mainly women,* and finally, a striking tendency for an epidemic of the illness. All of the just enumerated physical phenomena can hardly raise doubt that this is an illness, the foundation of which is hysterical neurosis.[75]

Thus both the symptoms of the shriekers and the high incidence of women among possession victims suggested to Bekhterev that *klikushestvo* constituted a form of hysteria. Believing autosuggestion to be the cause of an epidemic of demon possession in the countryside, he recommended that in future psychiatrists needed to separate the ill women from the healthy population and the stimuli that encouraged beliefs in possession. Only then would they be able to cure the demoniacs with hypnotism. Bekhterev also advocated the need to enlighten the peasants and expunge their worldview of crude and irrational superstitions. Until the peasants became rationalists and accepted scientific and medical understandings of the universe, beliefs in bewitchment and demon possession would continue to trigger the illness as women previously exposed to the frightening antics of shriekers would continue to imitate those behavioral patterns.[76] No doubt influenced by Pierre Janet, Bekhterev was proposing the psychogenesis of hysteria and thus rejecting Charcot's somatic origins of the illness.

Subsequently, other doctors questioned Krainskii's conclusion that *klikushestvo* was merely a somnambulistic phenomenon M. P. Nikitin's examination at the Sarovskaia Hermitage and nearby Serafimo-Diveevskii

Monastery of shriekers and women who suffered from forms of psychosomatic illnesses, led him to reject Krainskii's appraisals. "It appears to me," Nikitin wrote, "that Dr. Krainskii's objective investigations of the nervous systems of the *klikushi* can hardly be considered sufficiently complete to prove that there is no relationship between *klikushestvo* and hysteria." Nikitin criticized Krainskii for having been sloppy in his physical examination of the shriekers and for coming to conclusions without empirical evidence.[77]

The lecturer V. P. Osipov at Bekhterev's Petersburg clinic took up his mentor's attack on Krainskii's insistence that *klikushestvo* was not a manifestation of hysteria.[78] He argued instead that it was more fruitful to categorize it as a "distinct hysterical psychological neurosis." Krainskii, he insisted, was wrong in his assumption that because these women could be hypnotized they were not hysterics. Osipov pointed out that Krainskii's sample was too small and that every practicing neuropathologist had experiences with hysterics who could be hypnotized and who thus "easily developed a state of somnambulism."[79]

Osipov went on to discuss two cases, one of a peasant woman and the other of a male telegrapher on the Warsaw railway line, both of whom thought that they had swallowed snakes. Class, not gender, distinctions influenced Osipov's diagnosis. He determined that the peasant woman was superstitious and believed literally in the legends of devils changing their shape and entering the body as snakes or other creatures. The telegrapher, on the other hand, had an education and lived in a more cultured place; while he had heard stories about possession and had a familiarity with a variety of superstitions, he was appropriately critical of them when he was healthy. It was only after his various stomach ailments had proved impervious to treatment that he came under the influence of tales about people who became ill because they had swallowed snakes and believed himself to be in such a hopeless state. The telegrapher took well to treatments of bromides, hot baths, and hypnosis, whereas the peasant woman resisted hypnosis, claiming that such treatment was not for her but for the mentally disturbed. The woman had been in the clinic for almost a year and a half without any change in her condition. Osipov believed here was clear proof that classes with dissimilar cultural experiences might, in some cases, have the same psychological problem but differing results. By ascribing their ailments to their having swallowed snakes rather than to demon possession, members of educated society, Osipov suggested, had a greater scientific understanding of the universe than did their peasant counterparts.[80] Unfortunately, Osipov did not speculate as to whether educated women of the upper classes were privy to this male rationalism. Nonetheless, the very fact that the doctor took the male telegrapher's complaints seriously and treated him suggests that he did not subscribe to the belief that only women were hysterics.[81]

Osipov might also have taken a step further his conclusion about the dissimilar cultural experiences of the peasant woman and the telegrapher. The latter responded well to the psychiatrist's treatments precisely because he had faith in the psychiatrist's abilities and had accepted the medicalization of his ailment. The peasant woman, on the other hand, understood her affliction in spiritual rather than medical terms and consequently was unable to see herself as being mentally ill. Consequently, scientifically based remedies proved useless. A dialogue between the peasant and psychiatrist over possession was virtually impossible when they subscribed to two distinct and unequal cultures, one of which claimed superiority over the other.[82] "The doctor's authority flowed directly from his mastery of a language of science, empowering him to instruct, diagnose," and prescribe treatment. The peasant woman, "lacking such a language, could only express [her] beliefs at the risk of seeming a 'simpleton.' No communication, no defense of belief was possible across this cultural divide."[83]

As late as 1926, N. P. Kazachenko-Trirodov, a Leningrad psychiatrist, had difficulty communicating with a forty-six-year-old peasant woman, identified only as M., from Smolensk province. Diagnosing her as suffering from hysteria in the form of *klikushestvo,* in addition to diabetes, he eventually cured her *klikushestvo* through hypnosis.[84] According to Kazachenko-Trirodov, M.'s problems began at the end of 1924 when she stopped menstruating and at the beginning of 1925 when she began to show initial signs of diabetes and lost her ability to work. Constantly thirsty and hungry from the diabetes, the woman began to imbibe alcohol, thinking that "some kind of ill spirit that begs for food, drink, and merriment possessed me." No doubt, M.'s diabetic comas produced by dangerously low blood sugar levels brought her to the attention of the medical authorities. Kazachenko-Trirodov initially treated his patient, whom he described as being severely depressed and emotional, with a strict diet, bromides, and psychoanalysis. Psychoanalysis, however, proved to be unproductive: doctor and patient talked past each other, unable as they were to bridge the cultural barrier between scientific and popular culture. After trying one hypnotic method, Kazachenko-Trirodov abandoned it in favor of another. Twenty sessions of sleep hypnosis with pre- and post-hypnotic suggestion finally succeeded in convincing the patient of the validity of the doctor's arguments that she was not possessed by an unclean spirit and that her seizures were related to the diabetes. Kazachenko-Trirodov claimed that he was also able to persuade M. that her spells in church developed from the strong impressions that the ceremony and rituals made on her rather than from actual possession.[85]

In the end, Kazachenko-Trirodov concluded that M.'s *klikushestvo* constituted a form of hysteria. He credited Bekhterev and Nikitin with having been correct in their diagnoses but also noted that Krainskii's observations about the shriekers' somnambulistic states in and out of hypnosis were accurate as well. According to Kazachenko-Trirodov, "the hysterics, who are partially cured, become classic somnambulists who easily manifest emotional automatism not only in relation to their hypnotist but also to daily life." Thus, women who thought that they were demon possessed were both hysterics and somnambulists.[86]

In the debate over whether *klikushestvo* constituted a form of hysteria or somnambulism, Russian psychiatrists (with the partial exception of Kazachenko-Trirodov whose case argued against the role of heredity) agreed on the vital roles that suggestion and imitation coupled with superstition and biological and hereditary predisposition played in causing the phenomenon. All these causes were potentially dangerous when epidemics occurred, drawing in individuals who were perfectly healthy at other times. The epidemics at weddings and in Ashchepkovo were cases in point, as was a bizarre incident in the town of Zhizdra, Kaluga province, in May 1893, that ended in a *klikusha*'s murder.

Summoned by the Kaluga Circuit Court as an expert witness in the 1893 case, Dr. V. N. Ergol'skii characterized the crime as having a psychopathic basis that was "a complete anachronism at the end of this century, recalling the dark era of the middle ages." At the same time, he felt the macabre story reflected everyday life. The case involved a widowed petty townswoman, fifty-seven-year-old Pelageia B. of Zhizdra, who, along with her daughter Agaf'ia (who was married to a peasant and lived in the countryside), had been charged with murdering eighteen-year-old Mar'ia, another of her daughters. When Mar'ia became a *klikusha,* the mother and sister turned to various healers and religious exorcisms for help. Ergol'skii painted both Pelageia and Agaf'ia as being uneducated and superstitious women who up to the time of murdering Mar'ia had been completely healthy, although burdened by a hereditary predisposition to mental illness. Mother and daughter sincerely believed that Mar'ia was possessed, a fact reinforced not only by Mar'ia's experiencing the classic symptoms of a shrieker, but also by the opinions of neighbors and healers. According to Ergol'skii's analysis, the shrieker's seizures, which involved attacking her mother and sister and insulting them with offensive language, "caused physical unpleasantries and moral sufferings for the two women, as a result of which a severe nervous strain overcame the two. . . . With their nerves destroyed and perhaps being a bit hysterical themselves, they were open to suggestions of all kinds." Ergol'skii believed the women's heightened nerves and their failed attempts to find a cure for Mar'ia set the stage for the events of the night of May 3 and 4 when they became psychologically infected by the shrieker.[87]

On that fateful night an exhausted mother and daughter began fumigating Mar'ia's body by burning charcoal and blessed thistle in a pan under Mar'ia's head, all in an attempt to drive out the devil. Once the room began to fill with carbon monoxide from the burning charcoal, they experienced visual hallucinations of demons flying in and out of Mar'ia's body and having intercourse with her. Out of desperation they subsequently attacked the demons head-on, hoping to prevent them from entering the poor woman's body again by applying the burning thistle directly to Mar'ia's body as well as stuffing her vagina and mouth with it. Ergol'skii concluded that the quick onset of the mother and daughter's illness represented "an example of induced hallucinatory insanity" among two individuals (the so-called *folie à deux*) "with a definite hysterical basis." The women egged each other on until they resolved the issue of Mar'ia's possession by murdering the poor woman. Ergol'skii attributed the continuing illnesses of mother and daughter Agaf'ia to the lingering effects of carbon monoxide poisoning they suffered during the fumigation: the mother went insane, while Agaf'ia died three weeks later in the Kaluga zemstvo hospital.[88]

Epidemics of *klikushestvo,* whether confined to two individuals or more broadly based among a village population, had potentially dramatic and dangerous consequences for Russian society, according to Russian psychiatrists. While not all of the epidemics ended in violence, the possibility of savagery among a pathologically predisposed and superstitious population was tremendous. The roles of suggestion and imitation in these epidemics that reached a frenzied pitch of emotion needed further investigation as psychiatrists were determined to use "their medical expertise in the policing and disciplining of lower-class religiosity."[89] By raising the specter of the social menace that popular religion represented to society at large, the medical specialists were warning educated Russians that epidemics might in future not be confined to isolated areas of the countryside, but would merge into mass movements that would spill into the cities. Only psychiatrists' monopoly over the treatment of mental illness, they argued, could prevent anarchic mass revolution. In strengthening their arguments, Russian psychiatrists linked epidemics of *klikushestvo* to epidemic hysteria among Old Believers, sectarians, and Baptists; indeed, hysteria appeared to be on the rise at the turn of the twentieth century. The 1905 Revolution provided additional ammunition for the psychiatrists' quest to present themselves as Russia's saviors. The ways in which they tied *klikushestvo* to these other epidemics of religious hysteria, rather than the specifics of the epidemics, are of interest in understanding the theories of mass psychology that Russian psychiatrists developed.

MASS PSYCHOLOGY

The most extreme interpretation of *klikushestvo* and mass psychology of religious movements was introduced by psychiatrist Pavel Iakobii

(1842–1913) in 1903 and 1909, two pivotal years on either side of the revolution.[90] Iakobii had lived several years in Western Europe and became active in radical political circles among Russian émigrés.[91] After returning to Russia to practice psychiatry in Orel and Moscow, he sparked furor within the psychiatric community for his denunciation of insane asylums. He characterized the asylums as prisons for the poor. Psychiatrists, in Iakobii's opinion, had taught the middle and upper classes to fear the disadvantaged members of society. Considered a social pariah for accusing fellow physicians of supporting what he termed "police psychiatry," Iakobii nonetheless succeeded eventually in persuading psychiatrists that institutionalization of the mentally ill and insane might not have been the panacea they had envisioned.[92] With regard to epidemics of religious hysteria, he was a scientist of his times, caught up in biological and social Darwinism, the emerging eugenics movement, and anthropology. Iakobii's ideas represented a synthesis of the latest European and Russian thinking. The appearance of his first article on religious hysteria epidemics in the widely circulated and influential liberal journal *Vestnik Evropy* attests to the popularity of some of these ideas among educated Russians.

Iakobii's fascination with *klikushestvo,* which he felt remained understudied and its extent sorely underestimated, appears to have been stimulated by an incident involving mental instability and epidemic hysteria. In 1898 in Suponev canton, Briansk district, Orel province, under the leadership of Vasilii D., a religious movement with Baptist tendencies developed. Shortly thereafter, it evolved into *khlystovsto* (sectarian movement of the flagellants) and then into an epidemic of hysteria in 1901. The peasant Osip Potapkin, whom psychiatrists identified as suffering from paranoia and hysteria, had gained control of the movement from Vasilii D., who had been arrested by government officials. Potapkin shifted the group's focus away from seeking the grace of the Holy Spirit toward the attainment of brotherly and sisterly love through sexual intercourse. Reported sexual improprieties between Potapkin and some of his women followers attracted the attention of the judicial system. Other women had participated in the holy rites that involved "singing, the clapping of hands, stamping of feet, kissing, the summoning of the Holy Spirit, all of which took them to a level of heightened exaltation" and ultimately hysteric reactions. Iakobii made fascinating, if alarming, connections between these events and cases of demon possession, as he was convinced that Russia had a far higher incidence than other areas of Europe of religious hysteria. Like other Russian psychiatrists, he believed such epidemics to be evocative of the European Middle Ages rather than of the early twentieth century.[93]

For Iakobii the Suponevo incident could only be understood in the context of *klikushestvo,* a mental illness he defined as striking mainly women and endemic within Orel province. Looking at the statistics for the mentally ill in the province for 1893 on a per district basis (see Table 4.2), he was horrified by the thousands of registered *klikushi* whom he felt Russians had ignored. He also noted a correlation in certain districts between a higher incidence of mental illness and a greater frequency of *klikushestvo* among women than men (see Tables 4.2 and 4.3). He explained the geographic bunching of possessed women in Karachev, Bolkhov, and Dmitrovsk districts as a reflection of those areas' isolation from towns and major communication links. Although Suponev canton, the site of the religious movement involving the *khlysty,* was more modern because of its two railway lines and proximity to the greater industrial center of Briansk, it was underdeveloped. According to Iakobii, it was "wild [and] neglected, without roads, education, [and] local industries," but with two monasteries that attracted pilgrims—all factors that facilitated "the rise of a mass degenerative hysteria and other, mainly degenerative, forms of psychiatric dysfunction." The same psychological and psychiatric bases and environmental conditions that allowed *klikushestvo* to arise in other parts of Suponev canton, Iakobii argued, fostered the epidemic hysteria of the sectarians in the village of Suponevo. "I must say," Iakobii further reflected, "that it was only in the Salpêtrière where I saw such a rich collection of hysterical degenerates with severe anatomical and physiological stigmata."[94]

Table 4.2 Number of Women Classified as Mentally Ill in Orel Province in 1893

District	*per 100 mentally ill men*
Sevsk	78.64
Trubchevsk	75.00
Briansk	85.35
Elets	65.93
Livny	90.80
Maloarkhangel'sk	100.71
Kromy	185.64
Mtsensk	107.32
Orel	104.71
Bolkhov	166.00
Karachev	187.60
Dmitrovsk	300.00

Source: P. Iakobii, "Religiozno-psikhicheskiia epidemiia: Iz psikhiatricheskoi ekspertizy," *Vestnik Evropy,* no. 10 (October 1903): 737.

Table 4.3 Number of Women Classified as *Klikushi* in Orel Province in 1893

District	*per 10,000 inhabitants*
Sevsk	1.30
Briansk	1.64
Trubchevsk	2.44
Livny	2.08
Elets	2.17
Maloarkhangel'sk	3.27
Orel	5.30
Kromy	6.35
Mtsensk	6.69
Karachev	10.32
Bolkhov	16.00
Dmitrovsk	21.21

Source: P. Iakobii, "Religiozno-psikhicheskiia epidemiia: Iz psikhiatricheskoi ekspertizy," *Vestnik Evropy,* no. 10 (October 1903): 738.

Taking the environmental argument a step further and adding a cultural spin to it, Iakobii blamed economic and social conditions and cultural primitiveness for creating pathological traits among the Russian population of Suponev and Orel, in particular, and of the Russian north and east, in general. He noted that the poor agricultural soils had the undesirable consequences of encouraging men to leave the canton in pursuit of paid labor elsewhere and of leaving women in control of farming (in this case, market gardening for the town of Briansk). Iakobii did not view these changes as indicative of a modern economic transition that had stressful consequences for individuals, particularly for women, whose responsibilities were substantially broadened. Rather, he was obsessed with what he regarded as the retrogressive development of "perverse conditions" whereby a "gynecocracy" inverted healthy and normal patriarchal relations. Using a term that emphasized rule by the womb rather than by the brain and underscoring, as Krainskii had done before him, the sexual frustration that women experienced because of their husbands' lengthy absences, Iakobii concluded that women's rule had a "destructive influence on the psyche and morals of the population." It would have been one thing if Suponevo had constituted an isolated phenomenon. However, such was not the case, Iakobii argued, because "women of the

Russian north and east already for a long time have been suffering from moral discontent, poverty of ideas, and that 'dearth of [positive] influences'[, on the one hand,] and too early sex . . . , on the other."[95]

For Iakobii, the peasants' supposedly retrogressive sexual behavior went a long way toward explaining the pathological illness of *klikushestvo* and other manifestations of religious madness. He was clearly influenced by the writings of the famed criminal anthropologist Praskov'ia Tarnovskaia on the negative consequences of marriage at early ages among Russian peasant women, by her theories about the Russian peasantry's evolutionary and psychological primitivism, and by major German writings on the concept of sexual degeneracy.[96] Accordingly, Iakobii lambasted loose sexual morals among the peasants as indicative of a pathological regression to primeval sexual behavior. Employing gross generalizations to support his view of sexual anarchy in the countryside, he suggested that peasant women did not maintain their virginity until they married and engaged in adulterous behavior, while peasant men accepted illegitimate children into their families. According to Iakobii, certain peasant practices—ranging from the custom whereby a bride removed a groom's footwear before consummation of the marriage to *snokhachestvo* (incest between father-in-law and daughter-in-law)—represented other holdovers of ancient, uncivilized sexual practices. Given all the social, economic, moral, and cultural problems besetting the countryside, there was little wonder, as far as the misogynist Iakobii was concerned, that hysteria and *klikushestvo* were rampant among the peasants.[97]

While environmental, social, and economic issues were critical in creating the preconditions for hysteria and mystical sects, Iakobii ultimately gave preeminence for causation to race. Race became a convenient way to account for *klikushestvo* appearing to be geographically bound to the north and east. By finding a purely Eastern-Finnish ancestry for the Russian population of Suponev canton and for the populations of the three districts of Orel province where he calculated that close to 95 percent of the *klikushi* originated, Iakobii could deflect the presence of racial impurities from the Russian stock. Southern Russia, by contrast, had no Finns and therefore fostered only rational sectarian movements. The only exceptions to the latter were those migrant communities of *khlysty* who had fled to the south during the eighteenth century. The consequences of racial impurity for the north and center were horrifying, Iakobii warned: "the poor, ravaged, and hungry center is leaving Christianity and returning to shamanism, [it] is giving up individual marriage, the family, and returning to the society of women and hetaerism. Without a doubt, these symptoms are very dangerous." Only in a healthy population, Iakobii pointed out, did a psychological epidemic subside immediately; conversely, an epidemic of this type spread more easily in "a nervous, exhausted, physically, morally, and mentally weakened degenerate population," which also produced more psychopaths.[98]

Iakobii's explanations for psychological problems among the Russian population had yet two other dimensions: one organic and the other, by far more important, political. According to Iakobii, that the Suponevo population suffered from endemic goiter problems—which affected the nervous system—had to be a partial, if minor, explanation for the inhabitants' predisposition to epidemic hysteria.[99] An opponent of the autocratic regime, Iakobii followed the lead of J. J. Bachofen and Eduard Reich, the German proponents of models of sexual degeneracy, by blaming the immoral state for corrupting its population.[100] Iakobii contradicted his racial explanation for the peasantry's mental degeneracy by directing his fury toward the Muscovite government for imposing its power over the north and center and thus supposedly arresting the biological and psychological development of its subjects. Russia, according to Iakobii, was nothing but a wasteland of "psychological illnesses [and] degeneration." And the state's penchant for responding to these illnesses by placing the victims under police custody only exacerbated the problems. Iakobii accordingly held tsarist officials responsible for the Suponevo epidemic. Repression of non-Orthodox religious stirrings and a legal investigation, he argued, had driven the residents to a higher state of agitation. They had also removed the one person, Vasilii D., the original religious leader of the movement, who could have stopped the drift toward sectarianism and the attraction to the paranoic-erotic Potapkin, who, in the name of the Holy Ghost, enticed women to have sexual relations with him. If a psychiatrist had been summoned earlier, Iakobii claimed, the specialist would have halted the epidemic.[101] Thus, despite all the factors that militated against a psychologically healthy population, including race and cultural primitivism, as well as organic, environmental, social, and political problems, he held out hope for the Russian people: through the demise of the autocratic regime and under the benevolent care of psychiatrists, they would be liberated and well looked after.

A similar prospect came from Bekhterev who, unlike Iakobii, viewed hysteria epidemics as part of a universal phenomenon, rejected racial explanations, and emphasized the role of suggestion in psychological epidemics among both the uneducated and educated classes. In a synthetic sociological study about the collective psychology of the Russian people, Bekhterev repeated his earlier conclusions about epidemics of *klikushestvo* and the role that superstition played in provoking these incidents. However, this time he placed them in a larger world context. He set out to demonstrate that manifestations of demon possession were not unique to nineteenth-century Russia and were not simply holdovers from a medieval past, as Iakobii and others had argued. The epidemics of demon possession among young girls taking their first communion in Savoy in 1857–1864 and later among the urban population of Vertsenis in northern Italy in 1878–1879 provided proof for Bekhterev that Europeans were not immune to the negative effects of superstitious thinking.[102]

Bekhterev, as Iakobii before him, linked epidemics of possession to epidemics of religious ecstasy. Before launching into a discussion of epidemics among religious sects in late Imperial Russia, Bekhterev once again provided non-Russian examples. He cited cases in 1800 Kentucky, the Oneida commune, and the Second Great Awakening in the United States, as well as religious movements among Jews linked to a belief in the coming of the messiah. Having demonstrated that epidemics of religious hysteria were not peculiarly Russian, he discussed in turn the religious epidemics among the Legovites east of the Urals, in Ufa province and the northern Caucasus in the 1830s and 1840s; the Tatar Muslims in Kazan province in the 1880s; the Malevantsy in southern Russia in the 1890s; and the *khlysty* in Orel province in 1903. Here were examples of religious movements whose leaders, argued Bekhterev, were "notorious hallucinators and paranoiacs who through suggestion" could "cultivate foolish ideas among people and give rise to psychopathological epidemics of a religious content." Bekhterev concluded that all such epidemics, including epidemics of *klikushestvo,* had a psychological basis, "characterized by extreme ignorance, spiritual needs that have not been fulfilled, the absence of moral guidance, and insufficient intellectual development that borders on pathological imbecility." Together with specific physical conditions such as anemia and exhaustion, this psychological basis created "the conditions for an unusual suggestibility among individuals who accept the most distorted fantasies of the mentally ill as faith." By utilizing the broad and slippery term "psychopathy," coined by German psychiatrists in the 1880s, Bekhterev placed a host of indeterminate behaviors "beyond the mental tests' measure—eccentricities, peculiarities, oddities, quirks" in the category of the abnormal. Rejecting theories of the peasants' primitivism, however, he reminded his readers that the deviant behaviors associated with psychopathological epidemics were not the exclusive preserve of the peasants.[103]

Educated society, according to Bekhterev, could and did become enveloped by psychopathological epidemics. While more cultured populations disdained crude beliefs, they had fads of their own. As proof, Bekhterev again provided foreign illustrations by pointing to the example of the hold that mesmerism had on eighteenth- and nineteenth-century Parisian society. The popularity of magnetic cures in St. Petersburg at the end of the 1870s, the attraction of religious mysticism at various times in nineteenth-century Russia, and the contemporary epidemic of "free love" and sexual freedom among Russian educated circles were, in his opinion, psychopathological phenomena.[104]

What were definitely not pathological epidemics, according to Bekhterev, were the revolutionary stirrings of the Russian people against an oppressive regime in 1905. As in the epidemics of *klikushestvo,* suggestion and autosuggestion played major, but this time positive, roles. "All that is necessary" in creating monumental revolutionary disturbances, wrote Bekhterev, "are two to three bombastic words by an orator at a meeting or educational gathering or a few revolutionary pamphlets given out by agitators." Thus for Bekhterev, the greater Russian populace was versatile: "the courses of suggestibility of the masses can be directed both toward the most immoral and cruel actions as well as huge historical victories." Revolutionary stirrings consequently represented the opposite of *klikushestvo* and other emotional expressions that Russian psychiatrists defined as aberrant and potentially violent. Once again, Bekhterev argued, the Russian masses were not unique in the directions they chose; all societies had examples of barbaric behavior as well as progressive actions. How else, he posited, could one explain the actions of an American lynch mob in a supposedly advanced country or the successes of such great historical figures as Joan of Arc, Mohammed, Napoleon Bonaparte, and Peter the Great?[105]

With leadership that deflected attention away from superstition and other irrational beliefs, the Russian people's collective mentality, in Bekhterev's opinion, could be harnessed to progressive activity. Enlightened individuals, namely revolutionaries and psychiatrists together, could lead the Russians into a better future. Displacing the adjective "dark" from describing the masses to describing the realm as a whole, Bekhterev reminded his fellow psychiatrists in 1909 "of your duty to spread rays of spiritual life in our realm [*tsarstvo*] of darkness. Only by the harmonious cooperation of all the country's forces will light spread to the horizons of the gloom that presses in on us from all sides. And we will go on hoping that we will yet live to see better days for our unfortunate native land."[106] Implicit here was a sense that what Russian psychiatrists had identified as a rise in moral degeneration through alcoholism, prostitution, homosexuality, venereal disease, and criminality was not conditioned environmentally but politically. In this regard, Bekhterev sympathized with Russian socialists, and it is little wonder that he welcomed the Bolshevik Revolution.

Bekhterev's radical views, expressed in his publications and in his speeches at professional meetings, were well received by many psychiatrists. Some had been actively involved in the left-wing politics of 1905, and many more were appalled at the tsarist government's repression of revolutionary activity. During the heady revolutionary days, the staffs of psychiatric asylums and hospitals in Moscow, St. Petersburg, Khar'kov,

Nizhnii Novgorod, Voronezh, and Kazan hid illegal literature and weapons and held political meetings. These same institutions, however, found their beds being taken up by political prisoners whom the government, not psychiatrists, deemed pathologically deranged. Numerous psychiatrists, including Vladimir Iakovenko, lost their positions in government-financed institutions in the aftermath of the revolution.[107]

These same liberal psychiatrists also agreed with Bekhterev in applauding the 1905 Revolution as a mass phenomenon that had positive ends. As clinical psychiatrists, their focus, however, tended to be narrower. They were interested in the effect of the revolution on mental disorder, testing the view of the German psychiatrist Wilhelm Griesinger and French psychiatrist J. E. D. Esquirol that revolutionary events did not cause an increase in mental illness.[108] Through case studies of individuals whose mental illness began during revolutionary events, psychiatrist N. I. Skliar argued that all the illnesses fell into conventional categories, proving that there was no such thing as a political psychosis.[109] Some psychiatrists such as I. S. German, F. Kh. Gadziatskii, and A. N. Bernshtein agreed that those who experienced nervous and psychological problems during the political turmoil were already predisposed to such problems through unstable minds.[110] Whether such individuals were active or passive in the revolutionary events remained an open-ended question, but according to the specialists they might have remained healthy in normal nontraumatic circumstances. In contrast to these interpretations, Vladimir Iakovenko argued for the categorization of behavior as a mirror of political extremes in contemporary society: "neurasthenics, hysterics, and generally the unstable more often side with the innovative tendencies in society, whereas the simple-minded, the senile, epileptics, and degenerates with moral defects or defects in sexual feelings side with [those with] conservative tendencies," often taking part in the punitive military expeditions against various groups in society.[111]

In reaction to the high-minded opinions of their liberal colleagues, conservatives disdained the revolution as an expression of a mass social pathology. Forensic psychiatrist V. F. Chizh took umbrage at Iakovenko's claims that the hopelessly deranged elements of society were tools of the regime, pointing to psychopathy, dementia, chronic paranoia, epilepsy, and degenerative forms of mental illness among revolutionaries.[112] While S. Iaroshevskii shared the opinion of his liberal colleagues that predisposition to mental illness made individuals more likely to succumb to illness during revolutionary trauma, he also saw the masses as a whole predisposed to neuropsychological illnesses and the revolution as provoking "the appearances of atavism that remind us of our wild ancestors." In this manner he brought Iakobii's musings about race and the primitive nature of the peasants' culture to their logical conclusion. Iakobii would have been appalled. Iaroshevskii did not share Bekhterev's opinion of the revolution as a psychological epidemic: "The diversity of the described forms [of mental illness], starting with relatively mild forms of hysteria and ending with deep hallucinations and maniacal insanity, although they stem from one general cause, show that we do not have a psychological epidemic, but mass illnesses of neuropsychologically unstable elements, created by one general cause: political events."[113]

Trying to maintain a more balanced opinion of the revolutionary period and its participants on both sides of the political divide from the hindsight of 1907, A. N. Bernshtein linked 177 clinical cases of mental illness during 1905–1906 in Moscow to the role that suggestion played among individuals who already suffered from depression and paranoia. In the early stages of insanity, Bernshtein argued, individuals seized on popular ideas of the day, a characteristic not only of revolutionary but also of nonrevolutionary times. Ideas transmitted through the press, gutter literature, literary and scholarly writings, involving "the gramophone and wireless telegraph, Boer and Japanese military leaders, the Sarov and Chernigov miracle workers, the Jewish and Armenian pogroms, political assassinations and expropriations," became obsessions. "Strikers, cossacks, Semenovtsy, Social Democrats, and Black Hundreds have only just appeared as new personages in the ranks of the persecutors and creators of fear and have played the very same role that unqualified spies, foreigners, petty thieves played before." And such *idées fixes* were observed among long-term residents of hospitals as well as among those who appeared at the clinic door for the first time.[114] Coming full circle to Bekhterev's emphasis on the role of suggestion, Bernshtein linked women who had become *klikushi* after hearing about the miracles occurring at the shrines of St. Serafim of Sarov and St. Feodosii of Chernigov to mentally disturbed individuals in the traumatic period of 1905–1907.

CONCLUSION

The psychiatrists' political opinions, on one level, seem far away from the discussion of *klikushestvo* in the Russian countryside and, on another level, remind historians of the disquiet that preoccupied Russians of all classes at the turn of the twentieth century. The *klikushi* and epidemics of possession were real and not the creations of psychiatrists hoping to justify their existence. However, caught up in their own professional insecurities and convictions that scientific rationalism would save Russia, they attacked *klikushestvo* as an aberrant female behavior unacceptable in a modernizing society. Just as hooliganism had become for educated society a haunting specter of deviant conduct among unruly male youths and male peasant migrants, *klikushestvo* became for psychiatrists a metaphor for a pathological phenomenon among rural women with residual effects in the towns as well. Although none of the psychiatrists endorsed in writing Iakobii's declarations that *klikushestvo* signified a regression to primitivism, perversion of patriarchal relations, and rule by the womb, they nonetheless viewed women's sexuality as predisposing them to irrational thought and behavior. They differed in their diagnoses, borrowing various ideas from their European colleagues who likewise could not agree on the etiologies of hysteria and other forms of what they defined as mental illness. Ultimately, Russian psychiatrists hoped to move the village into the modern age by challenging the religious beliefs of peasants and the Orthodox Church, which they deemed superstitious and fanatical. Little did they understand that the triumph of scientific rationalism and psychiatrists' control over what they classified as mental illness would in turn result in the codification of hitherto tolerated behaviors as abnormal and new illnesses. At the same time, by providing detailed studies of individual *klikushi* who emphatically believed in the possibility of bewitchment and demon possession, these men of science served historians who can analyze that information anew.

Chapter Five

SORTING THROUGH MULTIPLE REALITIES

✦ Much of the preceding discussion has focused on the ways in which *klikushi* in Imperial Russia became a contested subject. Attacked by the state, beginning with Peter the Great, as malingerers and deviant members of society, these women also attracted the notice of the Russian Orthodox Church. Writers, ethnographers, psychiatrists, and physicians also developed an interest in *klikushi*. The church used them to validate the possibility of miracles and its own relevance in an increasingly scientific and materialist age. Mid-nineteenth-century writers called attention to the difficult conditions of peasant women's lives by viewing possessed women as symbolic of Mother Russia, either tainted by serfdom or noble and heroic. Ethnographers and other observers of the peasantry focused on what they perceived to be deviant behavior that could be rooted out only by enlightening the peasants and by demonstrating to them the folly of their superstitions and ignorance. Psychiatrists at the turn of the twentieth century engaged the Russian Orthodox Church in a battle of words as they attempted to wrest control over the shriekers and to expand their authority over the countryside. What might have been an insignificant feature of Russian peasant life, that is, demon possession, took on much greater importance in a state that was struggling to modernize.

Klikushestvo became one of many aspects of peasant life that for educated Russian society symbolized backwardness, deviance, disorder, suffering, irrationality, and ignorance. Such traits represented the otherness of the Russian peasants that had to be conquered either by the state's or professional cadres' progressiveness, normality, order, rationalism, and knowledge. Even those such as N. V. Krainskii, who did not embrace all aspects of modernity as being beneficial to Russia and her peasantry, complained about the obscurantism of village thought and culture. Still other voices, such as those of Dostoevsky and representatives of the Orthodox Church, cautioned against the rigidity of understanding the world in bipolar terms and found spiritual solace in some of the supposedly negative features of the peasantry.

Given the complicated rhetoric and the voices of the *klikushi,* heard indirectly through scripts written by professionals and monks, is it possible for the historian to uncover the identity of these possessed individuals and to provide plausible explanations for their behavior without being charged with academic arrogance? It may be impossible to avoid the latter, but it is necessary for historians to uncover the ways in which past societies functioned and understood the world around them. Like anthropologists and scientists, historians seek to pinpoint the universal as well as the unique features of different societies.

Although the debate between cultural relativism and universalism has raged for centuries, it has had particular resonance in the modern period. As the concept of nationalism became defined, Enlightenment and German romantic philosophy tackled the issue of whether specific national groups possessed inherent characteristics. Within the Russian context, the Slavophile-Westernizer controversy opened a Pandora's box of disputes regarding Russia's historical destiny that to this day has not been closed. Questions of whether Russia should become a part of Western Europe or whether the country, possessing the best of both cultures, should aim for a unique position between East and West, continue to haunt the Russian psyche as a fledgling democracy grapples with the pains inflicted by the dismantling of a centralized economic system and the unrelenting demands of a global capitalist economy.

Late-nineteenth-century Russian intellectuals, attempting to understand *klikushestvo,* were divided in their assessment of demon possession as either a unique cultural artifact or a phenomenon shared by other societies. Ethnographers and jurists decided that witchcraft and possession among the peasantry demonstrated a primitivism in Russian culture that could be rescued only by modern Western European civilization. At the turn of the century, they were, however, casting doubt on the possibility of rescue. The so-called dark countryside appeared to be colonizing the city; this was manifested most noticeably by the increasing number of rural migrant arrivals and by urban violence. A superior urban bourgeois culture, from the ethnographers' and jurists' point of view, had hardly made a dent in village culture. Most Russian psychiatrists, while also crusaders for progress and civilization, had greater faith in the more optimistic universalist approach. By studying non-Russian cultures they discovered that demon possession and outbreaks of witchcraft hysteria had marked the tortured histories of other societies, including those in seemingly more advanced Western Europe. If *klikushestvo* represented an illness or the beginnings of a pathological disease that affected the minds of weak women, it could be conquered, they reasoned, both by scientific expertise and by cultural enlightenment.

Such discussions hold relevance today, although historians, influenced by anthropologists and literary critics, are less comfortable with the unilinear evolutionary scheme that developed out of scientific discussions in the second half of the nineteenth century. That scheme proposed that all cultures and societies must follow the same trajectory toward progress or fall by the wayside in the process. Wishing to avoid the pejorative value judgments of modernization theory as well as notions of superiority connected to Western colonialism, some historians are drawn to cultural relativism that emphasizes the historical and cultural particularism of individual societies. While such an approach has considerable merit, the historian must nonetheless avoid the trap of exaggerating continuities over time and succumbing to historical determinism.

In the case of Russian *klikushestvo,* the temptation to view that phenomenon and its flip side, witchcraft, in isolation, solely according to the dictates of cultural relativism, has the potential of advancing a theory of linear evolutionism in Russia/Soviet history. Perhaps the late-nineteenth-century ethnographers' and jurists' pessimistic predictions for Russian history, based on their study of the "backward" peasant masses, were prescient. After all, the identification and persecution of witches, among other forms of indictments in the turn-of-the-century Russian village, foreshadowed the denunciations of the 1920s and especially the purges of the 1930s in the Soviet Union. By manipulating peasant beliefs in witches and sorcerers, as Bernice Glatzer Rosenthal has pointed out, the Soviet propaganda machine could harness the masses to its campaigns against unclean forces.[1] The Russian historian Boris Mironov has argued for the existence of an evolutionary linkage between the authoritarianism of the Russian peasant family and commune and the success of the Soviet dictatorship.[2] Such an argument could easily accommodate the *klikushi*'s accusations against family and community members by pointing to the ways a repressive social system begets accusatory practices.

On the other hand, by the second half of the nineteenth century, the witchcraft accusations of the *klikushi* and other villagers constituted a facet of internal village politics rather than denunciations of individuals to the state or church. When, after emancipation, priests or monks carrying out exorcisms demanded that the possessed identify their bewitchers, they did not take the next step of prosecuting the named sorcerers or witches. Eighteenth-century state and church hierarchs had been more vigilant in this respect, but church officials were reluctant to report *klikushi* to the state bureaucracy as the law demanded.

A comparative approach avoids the pitfalls of using cultural analysis to pinpoint the defects of Russian society. Not all peasant societies or past societies that subscribed to witchcraft and possession beliefs succumbed to repressive authoritarian systems. Given the ideological commitment to capitalism, Western scholars have resisted comparing the seventeenth-century English enclosure movement with Stalin's twentieth-century forced collectivization of Kazakhs, as well as the Russian, Ukrainian, and Belarusian peasantries. While the methods differed, both the English and Soviet reform movements were propelled by ideological motivation that called for the destruction of the traditional village in the name of a superior goal: agricultural capitalism in the case of England and agrarian socialism in the case of Stalin's Russia. Both attacked a class of people. Furthermore, the dramatic transformations that occurred as a result produced thousands of peasant rebellions that provoked state repression.

The furious resistance with which peasants raged against the Stalinist regime's philosophical class warfare does away with the theory of "Russian" (not to mention Ukrainian, Belarusian, Georgian, Kazakh, and other ethnoses') political passivity and the notion of unbroken continuities in authoritarianism. Stalinism's attempt to annihilate peasant life highlights the disastrous consequences of a rigid utopianism that ruled out other more humane paths toward economic modernization. It also illustrates the Bolsheviks' ideological animus toward various peasantries' strains of collectivism. The phenomenon of *klikushestvo* helps one to understand Russian society in both its complex cultural and historical contexts as well as within a comparative framework, thereby combining the best features of both cultural relativism and universalism.[3]

The phenomenon of *klikushestvo* did not represent a fleeting moment in Russian history. It made its appearance as early as the eleventh century but became a common occurrence only in the sixteenth and seventeenth centuries. From the eighteenth through early twentieth centuries, the study of demon possession increasingly centered on women who stemmed almost exclusively from the peasantry. As they expressed their anguish and suffering, these women periodically attracted the attention of individuals who enjoyed the benefits of learning. Whether sympathetic or unsympathetic, state officials, clerics, professionals, and amateur intellectuals recorded the plight of possession victims and their ritualized conduct. Driven underground by the Soviet regime, demon possession among women has resurfaced in a Russia that, while championing freedom of expression, has raised economic and social anxiety levels.[4] Reports of miraculous healings at reopened monasteries are legitimizing the resurgence of religious beliefs, while the deafening shrieks of the possessed are interrupting those very church services that had for the seven decades of the Soviet regime been the preserve of increasingly shrinking, elderly, and female crowds of believers. Fearing that these disturbances might unleash uncontrollable emotions, the Russian Orthodox Patriarch in the summer of 1993 banned *klikushi* from attending the main services at the Trinity–St. Sergii Monastery in Sergiev Posad and directed them to other, less public sites within the monastery for spiritual guidance and aid.[5]

Given the high literacy of post-Soviet society, how does one explain the resurgence of a phenomenon that, according to educated men at the turn of the century, could be eradicated with enlightenment? Readers may still wonder if *klikushestvo* is in fact a distinct pathology, a mental disorder peculiar to Russian society, or perhaps a consequence of purely biological factors. In order to delve further into the nature of the phenomenon and the issue of causality, it is necessary to examine the age, sex, and marital profiles of *klikushi* as well as their experiences in the historical past. Doing so leads to a rejection of both pathological and biological explanations for demon possession in favor of the conclusion that the phenomenon constituted a sociocultural expression that allowed social actors, in this case weaker members of the society, to release stress and readjust their life circumstances.

The available database of 260 shriekers for the period between 1820 and 1926 suggests that the possessed were overwhelmingly women (88.1%). Even given the underreporting of men, the cultural attributes peasants and the church ascribed to the *klikushi* suggest that women were far more likely than men to identify themselves or to be identified as possessed. These women tended to be married (50.7%) or widowed (3.1%), while single women accounted for 12.2 percent and women with unknown marital statuses accounted for 34.1 percent of the 229 women shriekers. Most of the women in the significantly large grouping for whom marital status was not recorded were likely married, because of the distinction in nomenclature that Russians make between married and unmarried women.[6]

The *klikushi*'s mean age (of the recorded ages available) at the time they first experienced demon possession varied between 26 years and 33 years. The lower figure reflects those women who had personal and individual experiences of demon possession; that is, they were not involved in epidemics of possession. Individual cases account for 42.8 percent of the total. Their victims suffered possession symptoms for as little as a few weeks and in some instances for as long as several decades before they were cured. For a woman to suffer her entire adult life as a demoniac was a rare occurrence. The higher mean age at onset reflects epidemic demon possession. It corresponds to women involved in 18 separate episodes of possession that claimed more than one victim within a village or parish. In all instances, whether an individual or mass phenomenon, a majority of women (75% in solitary cases and

66.6% in instances of epidemics) began to shriek in the prime of their childbearing years, that is, between the ages of 18 and 40. Postmenopausal women were more often represented among victims of epidemics than among individual cases (25.5% as opposed to 4.8%). While 57 percent of the women manifested signs of possession in the course of epidemics, a higher percentage of men (65% of the total) were victims of such collective experiences. The predominance of women among the victims of possession in the Russian context mirrors the pattern observed in the contemporary developing world. Explanations for that gender imbalance vary.

The gendered nature of *klikushestvo* and its periodic collective manifestation, according to current neurobiological psychiatric thinking, fit neatly into a typology favoring a pathological explanation of hysteria or "mass hysteria," a typology already developed by Russian psychiatrists at the turn of the twentieth century. Modern psychiatrists would not accept a diagnosis of Tourette's syndrome, a genetic disease, in part because that syndrome does not discriminate between men and women and does not result in epidemics. Nor do all of its characteristic features—"onset before age 21, multiple motor and one or more vocal tics (involuntary cursing or shouting), the tics occurring many times a day (usually in bouts), nearly every day or intermittently through a period of more than a year, and changes over time in the anatomic location, number, frequency, complexity and severity of the tics"—correspond with those of possession.[7] Rather than a sporadic outburst amenable to religious or supernatural suggestion, as in the case of *klikushestvo,* Tourette's syndrome is fairly constant and chronic. By subscribing to a theory of "mass hysteria," modern psychiatrists view the behavior prevalent in epidemics of demon possession as aberrant, "resulting from a malfunctioning 'proper' social order."[8]

The cultural relativists among anthropologists are critical of such an assessment as it imposes bourgeois cultural notions of highly urbanized and industrialized European and North American societies on others. They note that the rigidly scientific approach erroneously reduces behaviors that do not "fit within the autonomous parameters of [their] . . . Western-biased culture model," as "deviant, irrational or abnormal." By subsuming a variety of culturally unique behaviors under the pejorative rubric of "mass hysteria," psychiatrists and some social scientists, according to their critics, suggest that "seemingly diverse social phenomena as witchcraft, 'cargo cults,' mass clay eating and the diagnosis of masturbation" all reflect mental disorders or pathologies among specific groups. The anthropologists implicitly charge the psychiatrists with having a class bias for assuming that groups "of low social and/or economic status, 'primitive' or tribal peoples, [and] those from developing countries" share "an innate female susceptibility" to collective psychopathology. By ignoring the cultural and social features of these communities, contemporary psychiatrists in the West, according to their detractors, have imposed their own value judgments and have overlooked the ways in which these cultures fashion and sanction discrete phenomena such as possession and bewitchment, the symptology of which differs substantially from one society to the next.[9]

So effective have been the anthropologists' arguments against universal psychiatric diagnostic systems and for recognition of non-Western cultures' distinctiveness that psychiatrists and psychologists have begun to accept cultural and social explanations of illnesses. For example, in a 1992 report to the Social Sciences Research Council, psychologist Frank Kessel pointed out that "health phenomena that have long been regarded as natural manifestations of universal biological processes are now understood to be—to a significant degree—*locally variable, culturally mediated, socially situated, historically contingent, politically conditioned, and differentiated by gender and age.*"[10] The latest American Psychiatric Association's diagnostic manual, the fourth *Diagnostic and Statistical Manual* (1994) (DSM-IV), has become more sensitized to cultural manifestations that appear bizarre to members of highly industrialized and urbanized Western societies. By recognizing the existence of "culture-bound syndromes," but not the less value-laden "idioms of distress," the manual reflects a compromise between Western diagnostic traditions and anthropological thinking emphasizing cultural relativism. Accordingly, such a syndrome refers to "recurrent, locality-specific patterns of aberrant behavior and troubling experience that may or may not be linked to a particular DSM-IV diagnostic category."[11] The adjective "aberrant," however, suggests that psychiatrists are not yet ready to dispense entirely with "contemporary Western culture-bound empiricist notions of normality and illness," that is, with making value judgments about behavior.[12] Nonetheless, the DSM-IV, in a discussion of possession beliefs among North African and Middle Eastern societies, acknowledges that the behaviors associated with spirit possession—"shouting, laughing, hitting the head against a wall, singing, or weeping"—are "not considered pathological locally."[13] Similarly, neither Russian peasants nor the monks and clerics who specialized in exorcism thought *klikushi* were suffering from a mental illness. They sought not medical but spiritual help for the demoniacs.

If one can depart from psychiatric labels and pursue an argument that *klikushestvo* arose from specific cultural and religious contexts, one must still test purely biological explanations. Given the age and gender profiles of an overwhelming number of shriekers, as well as the tendency of possession to take on a collective dimension, can *klikushestvo* be explained biologically, an approach that is viewed by many historians and anthropologists as reductionist because it favors unitary over multicausal explanations? The hallucinatory capacities of some foods in the Russian and Ukrainian peasant diet (particularly rye, which is subject to spoilage under certain conditions, as well as the ubiquitous wild mushroom), the composition of the witches' salve, and the similarity of the possession symptoms from region to region suggest that biological causes have relevance and plausibility.

Historians have contemplated biological causation with regard to demon possession in early modern Europe and the American colonies. Reflecting on the effects of spoiled grain and grain adulterated "with toxic and narcotic vegetables and cereals" in early modern Europe, historian Piero Camporesi, for example, has noted:

> It is in this social panorama, traversed by profound anxieties and fears, alienating frustrations, devouring and uncontrollable infirmities and dietary chaos that adulterated and stupefying grains contributed to delirious hypnotic states and crises, which could explode into episodes of collective possession or sudden furies of dancing [a reference to St. Vitus's dance]. . . . The horrible dances of the sick inside churches, where the troubled presence of the contaminated and the impure was united with the consecrated and the supernatural, resulted in spectacular, bewildering performances.[14]

While not ruling out social stressors, Camporesi suggests that collective instances of possession in the past could partly be attributed to the effects of food poisoning. Given the high dependence of early modern European societies on grain, ergot—a fungus that develops on rye under cold and wet conditions—may have been responsible for making that grain "stupefying" and for producing the "delirious states" that erupted into an epidemic of possession or wild dancing. Historians and scientists investigating witchcraft episodes in Western Europe and the American colonies have long debated, inconclusively, the possibility that ergotism may have fueled the frenzied witchcraft episodes of the seventeenth century.[15]

Because rye constituted the dominant grain in the Russian and Ukrainian peasant diet and the Claviceps strains that produce ergot, according to Mary Matossian, were relatively harmless in areas of Ukraine,[16] ergotism could conceivably provide an explanation not only for possession in Russian villages but also for its geographical specificity. Such an explanation would be a counterweight to the cultural and economic interpretations already provided; that is, that the Russian Orthodox Church had less influence upon its Ukrainian-speaking than Russian-speaking rural parishioners and that nonagricultural migratory labor for men was more prevalent in central and northern Russia than in the Ukrainian provinces. Affecting more women than men, ergot poisoning might also account for the gender imbalance in *klikushestvo*. While dancing did not characterize the Russian variant of possession, epidemics of possession and the tight links between the sacred and supernatural did.

The connection between ergotism and possession, however, fails on a number of grounds. First of all, nineteenth-century reports of ergotism epidemics suggest that significant areas of Ukraine experienced these crises, but not epidemics of *klikushestvo,* multiple times (see Table 5.1). There also appears to be little overlap between epidemics of ergotism and those of possession in the Russian provinces. Given that Moscow, Vologda, Smolensk, and Tomsk provinces appear frequently as locations of both epidemics and individual cases of possession (see Table 5.2), their relative absence from the list of areas prone to ergot poisoning is notable.

Second, the symptoms of ergot poisoning do not correspond to the behavioral manifestations of demon possession in the Russian context. Of the two strains of ergotism, the rarer, dry gangrenous form attacks the body's extremities—fingers, toes, and limbs—resulting in "the falling away of the affected portions."[17] The more common type, "convulsive ergotism, is characterized by epileptiform convulsions; spasms of the fingers, toes, face, vocal chords, oesophagus and diaphragm; violent retching and diarrhea; ravenous hunger; crawling and tingling sensations underneath the skin; pronounced anaesthesia of the skin; paralysis of the lower limbs; delirium; imbecility and loss of speech."[18] Although convulsions and spasms, anaesthesia of the skin, and the loss of consciousness figured in *klikushestvo,* the possessed did not manifest signs of imbecility or the physical symptoms of vomiting and diarrhea, ravenous hunger, and paralysis of the lower limbs.

The particular vulnerability of pregnant women, children, and adolescents to the convulsive variety of ergotism also suggests that demon possession with its dissimilar age profile constituted a different phenomenon.[19] While women of childbearing age predominated among *klikushi,* few of them were identified as being pregnant. Women over 40 also figured prominently among demoniacs in epidemics. Most important, children did not succumb to possession, and adolescents did only rarely.[20] Finally, *klikushestvo* was not fatal, as ergotism could be.

A connection between ergot poisoning and *klikushestvo* also becomes less plausible in light of the late-nineteenth-century Russian medical profession's reluctance to make such a linkage, in spite of its familiarity with and concern about both phenomena. None of the physicians or psychiatrists who reported epidemics of *klikushestvo* referred to ergot poisoning. The fact that Russian medical specialists were interested in the mental disorders associated with ergotism renders this omission striking.[21]

Table 5.1 Incidence of Epidemics of Ergotism in Nineteenth-Century Russian, Belarusian, and Ukrainian Provinces, 1804–1889

Date	*Location*
1804	Minsk, Podolia, Volynia, other areas of Ukraine, and Ekaterinoslav
1819	Viatka
1821	several provinces
1832	Kazan, Nizhnii Novgorod, Viatka, Grodno, Kostroma
1834	Viatka, the Don region
1835–36	Novgorod
1837	Tver, Tula, St. Petersburg, Volynia, Moscow
1838	Kazan
1840	Vladimir
1843–55	Vladimir, Volynia, Viatka, Ekaterinoslav, Kaluga, Kiev, Kostroma, Minsk, Novgorod, St. Petersburg, Smolensk, Tver, Taurida, Tomsk, Khar'kov, Chernigov, Iaroslavl'
1844	Novgorod
1850	Kiev
1853	Mogilev, Kiev, and Chernigov
1854	Crimea
1858	Smolensk, Ekaterinoslav, Iaroslavl'
1863	Kostroma, Kazan, Simbirsk
1864	Simbirsk, Kazan, Viatka, Novgorod, Kostroma, Volynia
1865	Nizhnii Novgorod
1872	Kherson, Tomsk
1879	Novgorod, Viatka
1880	Kiev
1881	Poltava
1887	Chernigov
1888–89	Kostroma
1889	Viatka

Source: N. N. Reformatskii, *Dushevnoe razstroistvo pri otravlenii sporyn'ei (Bolezn' "zlaia korcha")* (Moscow: Tipo-litografiia Vysoch. Utverzhd. T-va I. N. Kushnerev i Ko., 1893), 40–49. In updating Reformatskii's chart, Mary Matossian notes that 1909 and 1926 witnessed numerous epidemics of ergot, while 1905–1907 and 1915–1919 were climatically suited to ergot formation. See her *Poisons of the Past: Molds, Epidemics, and History* (New Haven: Yale University Press, 1989), 24.

Table 5.2 Epidemics of *Klikushestvo* in the Countryside, 1820–1926

Dates	*Location*
1820	village of Khaniatino, Kolomna district, Moscow province; village of Sibirtsevo, Kainsk okrug, Tomsk province
1820s–30s	village of Cheksara, Vologda province
1824	village Aksenovka, Sol'vychegodsk district, Vologda province
1825	village of Men'shikovo, Kainsk okrug, Tomsk province
1829	village of Murashino, Kainsk okrug, Tomsk province
1833	village of Berezovo, Tomsk province
1837	village of Brodino, Vologda province
1860s	village of Aleksandrovskoe, Iaroslavl' province
1861	Bukreevskii khutor, Pavlograd district, Ekaterinoslav province
1868	Iaroslavl'; villages of Biakontovo and Syrovo, Podol'sk district, Moscow province
1879	village of Vrachevo, Novgorod province
1895	villages of Novgorodovo and Bol'shoe Petrovskoe, Podol'sk district, Moscow province
1898	village of Romantsevo, Podol'sk district, Moscow province
1899	villages of Ashchepkovo and Ivanika, Gzhatsk district, Smolensk province
1900	villages of Bol'shoi Dvor and Zabolotna, Tikhvin district, Novgorod province
1909	villages of Khomutovo & Roshchino, Moscow province
1922	village of Novoslobodka, Nizhnii Novgorod province
1926	villages of Bykovo and Vereia, Bronnitsy district, Moscow province

Sources: N. P. Brukhanskii, "K voprosu o psikhicheskoi zarazitel'nosti. (Sluchai psikhicheskoi epidemii v Moskovskoi gub. v 1926 g.)," *Obozrenie psikhiatrii, nevrologii i refleksologii,* nos. 4–5 (1926): 279–90; "Delo o klikushakh," *Zhurnal Ministerstvo iustitsii,* no. 9 (September 1862): 617–26; E. A. Genik, "Vtoraia epidemiia istericheskikh sudorog v Podol'skom uezda, Moskovskoi gubernii," *Nevrologicheskii vestnik* 6, no. 4 (1898): 146–59; I. Iakovenko, "Epidemiia istericheskikh sudorog v Podol'skom uezda, Moskovskoi gub.," *Vestnik obshchestvennoi gigieny, sudebnoi i prakticheskoi meditsiny* 25, no. 3 (March 1895): 93–109; N. P. Karabchevskii, *Okolo pravosudiia: Stat'i, soobshcheniia i sudebnye ocherki* (St. Petersburg: Trud, 1902), 228–32; N. Kostrov, "Koldovstvo i porcha mezhdu krest'ianami Tomskoi gubernii," *Zapiski zapadno-sibirskago otdela Imperatorskago russkago geograficheskago obshchestva* 1 (1879), pt. 2:5, 6, 11–12; N. V. Krainskii, *Porcha, klikushi i besnovatye, kak iavleniia russkoi narodnoi zhizni* (Novgorod: Gubernskaia tipografiia, 1900); M. Lakhtin, *Besooderzhimost' v sovremennoi derevne: Istoriko-psikhologicheskoe izsledovanie* (Moscow: Tipo-litografiia T-va I. N. Kushnerev, 1910); N. A. Nikitina, "K voprosu o russkikh koldunakh," *Sbornik Muzeia antropologii i etnografii* 7 (1928): 301; RGIAgM, f. 91, op. 2, d. 559; S. Shteinberg, "Klikushestvo i ego sudebno-meditsinskoe znachenie," *Arkhiv sudebnoi meditsiny i obshchestvennoi gigieny* 6, no. 2 (1870): 78; *Sudebnyi vestnik* 3, no. 170, 8 August 1868; and L. Vesin, "Narodnyi samosud nad koldunami. (K istorii narodnykh obychaev)," *Severnyi vestnik* 7, no. 9 (September 1892), pt. 2:64–66.

Finally, Russian peasants generally distinguished between symptoms of possession and those of ergotism. The popular term for a characteristic symptom of ergotism—*zlaia korcha* (the evil writhing)—does not appear in popular descriptions of possession or bewitchment, which peasants preferred to describe as *porcha* (bewitchment or hexing).[22] Of the 49 hospital cases that the Russian physician N. N. Reformatskii examined from the 1889 epidemic of ergotism in Nolin district, Viatka province, only one of the victims initially attributed his ailment to "an unclean spirit." According to thirty-seven-year-old Mikhail Kurakin, after having neglected his Christian duties, he had finally gone to confession and taken communion during Lent of that year. When the communion wine and bread aggravated the demon sitting in his stomach, he reasoned, the demon began making life miserable for him. Kurakin's symptoms—an unsteady walk as if he were drunk; pains in his arms, legs, and stomach; dizziness; blurred vision; fear for his life; and insomnia—did not correspond to those of *klikushestvo,* with the exception of insomnia and stomach pain. Thus, in spite of believing that a demon was responsible for his ailment, Kurakin did not display the behavioral and physical symptoms of possession.[23] His was a completely different illness.

The connection between ergotism and demon possession appears most credible in the intersection of both phenomena with women's reproduction. Ergot poisoning produces "irregular menstrual flows, spontaneous abortions, and miscarriages."[24] Fears of infertility among candidates for *klikushestvo* became heightened during wedding celebrations when the community and family placed high expectations on the consummation of a marriage for the purposes of procreation. Beyond this, anecdotal evidence exists regarding female *klikushi* who experienced miscarriages or who were infertile, but that evidence does not amount to statistical significance as so few sources provide this type of information. References to patterns of irregular menstruation in the psychiatric reports of *klikushi*'s health profiles are attributable to the continuing medical belief that menses and other features of women's reproduction controlled their mental state. In these cases the women began to menstruate outside their regular menses during religious holidays or before church services, which because of Orthodox taboos against menstruating women, rendered them unable to attend the divine liturgy. Thus, for example, N. V. Krainskii noted that the twenty-eight-year-old shrieker Vasilisa of Ashchepkovo complained that she inevitably began to menstruate during major religious holidays or when she traveled to monasteries, making it impossible for her to seek the kind of religious help she needed. Another victim of possession in Ashchepkovo, thirty-three-year-old Mar'ia Fedorova, complained that she began to menstruate whenever she was about to attend a church service, even if she had just completed her cycle. Krainskii also examined thirty-five-year-old Matrena

Vasil'eva from the village Potapova (located 40 versts from Ashchepkovo), who reported menstruating on all the high holidays, adding, "When I have sin with my husband, often the blood flows then as well." Although hoping to avoid sexual intercourse, Vasil'eva explained that she conceded to her husband's requests for sex as a way of assuring that he would not seek other women. "You see," she explained, "he will not spare me if I am ill or not ill."[25] These instances of menstrual flow at specific times, connected to either religious holidays or sexual intercourse, suggest a correlation between menstruation and emotional anxiety, not one between ergot and menses.

Before looking more closely at the impact of stress on demoniacs, the relationship between diet and possession needs to be taken one step further to consider the effects of famine. Particularly noteworthy is the lack of coincidence between epidemics of *klikushestvo* and famine conditions, especially during the widespread 1891–1892 famine in European Russia or its immediate aftermath. The single concrete example in the Russian sources connecting possession and famine dates back to the early eighteenth century. According to the eyewitness account of Ivan Filipov, who in 1714 settled in the Old Believer Vyg community in Karelia, an early frost some time after his arrival killed all the grain before it could be harvested. In order to stretch food supplies until the male leaders could return from the Volga area with grain provisions, community members began to forgo meals and to adulterate their remaining flour with straw. According to Filipov, the devil subsequently began to torment those mothers who stole bread from the rationed communal supplies and "secretly fed their children without having the food blessed." Those attacks occurred during church services, leading "the possessed" to fall to the ground and scream. Anxiously awaiting food supplies to stem the panic seizing the inhabitants, male elders admonished the food thieves and ordered special prayer services for the demoniacs and the reading of the Gospels over them. Through their solicitous acts, these religious elders subscribed to the possibility of demon possession and validated the victims' actions. In the end, according to the eyewitness report, a miracle saved the community from the terrifying epidemic of possession: one of the possessed women experienced a vision in which a flame and thunder attacked and chased away the demons that swarmed the outside of the Vyg community chapel. That miraculous sign represented a divine exorcism and redemption of all the demoniacs.[26]

The anxieties that precipitated the epidemic of possession in the Vyg community may provide a key to understanding *klikushestvo*. While coincident with food shortages, possession among the eighteenth-century Old Believers resulted not from the famine itself, but from the guilt and heightened stress on the part of the women who, in order to fulfill their responsibility to feed their children, broke God's commandment by stealing food. A possessed woman's miraculous vision, resulting in the expulsion of all the demons and foreshadowing the arrival of food, aborted the epidemic of possession, suggesting the sociocultural underpinnings of the phenomenon. The removal of the stressors that had precipitated the possession-like symptoms produced a rapid recovery among the victims. The fact that the behavioral and gender-specific manifestations of *klikushestvo* in the Vyg case are similar to all the other instances described in this book also supports sociocultural explanations of the phenomenon.

Cross-cultural anthropological studies of societies that subscribe to various possession beliefs suggest that women, as in the case of the *klikushi,* tend to predominate among victims of possession. Offering differing explanations for this gender imbalance, anthropologists have pointed to such factors as women's limited authority in the public realm, the impact of psychological disturbance and stress, and the effects of diet and calcium levels on women. Douglas Raybeck, Judy Shoobe, and James Grauberger point out that, "as in most interpretive disputes within anthropology, there has been a tendency for proponents of each position to deemphasize or even denigrate the utility of alternative explanations."[27] These medical anthropologists propose instead a multicausal explanation combining sociocultural reasons with physiological effects that has applicability to *klikushestvo.* The crux of their argument rests on the premise that a connection exists "between stress, its physiologic effects on the body (particularly a reduction in the body's ability to retain calcium), and behavioral manifestations that may be associated with trance states" or possession cults. Instances of prolonged stress among both sexes, they argue, cause a gradual decrease in "the body's reserve of calcium, even if there is an adequate intake of calcium. . . . [W]omen, owing to their lower levels of calcitonin, are more susceptible than men to this phenomenon. Among individuals already deficient in calcium, a sudden stressor or an abrupt increase in the magnitude of an existing stressor could elevate epinephrine levels so that hypocalcemia and associated behavior—such as tremors, convulsions, cognitive disorientation, and anxiety—would occur because of the epinephrine-induced production of lactate . . . Finally, hyperventilation from physical exertion or emotional stress may also contribute to the onset of these behaviors." These anthropologists also point out that symptoms demonstrating "elevated levels of autonomic reactivity associated with stress" include "gastrointestinal complaints, sleeping disorders, arthritic or rheumatic conditions, nasal irritation and congestion, and a flushed, feverish appearance."[28]

Klikushi experienced many of the traits Raybeck and his associates identify with stressors. These included tremors, convulsions, cognitive disorientation, anxiety, and gastrointestinal complaints such as distended stomachs. Some of the Russian shriekers complained of insomnia, while others did not. If they were suffering from stress, are there sociocultural conditions that can explain heightened stress levels?

With such a question in mind for different possession cults among contemporary societies, Raybeck, Shoobe, and Grauberger differentiate possession victims by age and the sociocultural experiences of individual age groups. They hypothesize that the physiology of post-menopausal women with "low estrogen levels and less calcitonin and vitamin D" renders them "more susceptible to the calcium-depleting effects of stressors." At the same time, by reducing stressful situations, more advantageous social situations for older women can counteract that susceptibility. In reviewing the anthropological literature regarding possession cults, Raybeck and colleagues demonstrate a high incidence of both older and younger married women among the victims, including those who have been recently married and have experienced marital tensions with spouses and in-laws in extended households, married women whose marital stability appears to be threatened, and post-menopausal women whose social status has declined. Curing ceremonies or exorcisms, in these anthropologists' opinion, are able to effect rapid recoveries among demoniacs because their participation in these rituals, for which they have the highest regard, "often eliminates or reduces the original stress."[29]

In applying Raybeck, Shoobe, and Grauberger's argument to Russian *klikushestvo,* age differentials and experiences appear relevant. Of the 72 *klikushi* from the peasantry (including recent migrants to cities) for whom information about age is available, more than two-thirds first experienced seizures of demon possession in their childbearing ages (between 18 and 40), with 20.8 percent of those falling in the early years of marriage (between the ages of 18 and 24), 34.7 percent in marriages of several years' duration (between the ages of 25 and 34), and the remaining 13.8 percent in the late childbearing years (35 to 40). Post-menopausal women had a higher visibility in epidemics (25.5%) than in solitary cases (4.8%). Few of them showed signs of possession prior to the epidemics. Also appearing with greater regularity in epidemics are women between the ages of 25 and 34, accounting for 35.3 percent of victims of epidemics. Among the individual cases, while just over three-quarters of peasant women had their first experiences of shrieking in the childbearing years, 47.6 percent were between the ages of 16.5 and 24 (19% falling in the pre-18 age category and 28.6% between 18 and 24, the years usually associated with marriage). What, if anything, do these frequencies tell us?

First, as the above profiles suggest, it is essential to differentiate between those who were victims of possession epidemics and those who were not. In the epidemics, anxieties about the possibility of bewitchment through tainted food or other means and about threats to fertility and virility were heightened by the collective nature of possession. More likely to be involved in these collective experiences of possession than in solitary cases, women over 40 tended to be individuals whose possession was limited to a single episode. Likewise, men had far greater representation in these epidemics.

As founts of cultural knowledge and political players within households, elder Russian women enjoyed respect within the village. Within extended households they served in authority roles as *bol'shukhi,* that is, heads of the female members of the family and household. Ordering women under their authority to carry out their responsibilities, they had charge over all domestic functions. Widowed *bol'shukhi* with underage sons might also serve in the public arena as household heads and accordingly have a voice in male-dominated village assemblies. Firmly ensconced in positions of authority, these women were not likely candidates for demon possession.

Marginalized older women, however, present another story. A woman's poverty and dependence on the commune for charitable handouts of grain diminished her status as household head. That position could be challenged in the postemancipation period by male communal members who coveted their land allotments, a problem that became acute as property values increased from the 1880s onward.[30] Within the household not all elderly women necessarily received respect from daughters-in-law, as evidenced by the examples of witchcraft charges provided earlier and by instances of familial tensions that came before village and cantonal courts. Marginalized older women were prime candidates for demon possession, especially in epidemics where the security of numbers prevented the spotlight from being focused solely on them. A single elderly woman's attracting attention on the public stage might backfire if neighbors thought that she was up to mischief. The fears that these elderly *klikushi* expressed about tensions within the village, as well as acts of unneighborliness or improper actions on the part of family members were heightened at times of greatest susceptibility to harm, when epidemics of possession were well under way and malevolent actions on the part of a witch or sorcerer were indiscriminately targeting community members. Catharsis for these women came through the identification and expulsion of evil by way of countermagic, exorcism, reconciliation, or violence.

With so little information on possessed men, one can only speculate that collective incidents of possession provided these men with a public setting in which it was acceptable for them to express their emotions. Fears of emasculation arose during weddings when sorcerers were believed to strike their enemies. In the case of middle-aged men, such anxieties may have accompanied demotions in status or some other kind of marginalization within the family and community. Here was an opportunity to receive sympathy rather than censure and undoubtedly some power through the identification of the malevolent witch or sorcerer within the community.

As for women of childbearing age, it is important to remember that a woman's status in Russian society was predicated upon a variety of factors. The number of children (especially sons) she bore; her abilities as worker and provider; her submissiveness to male authority; and, until age conferred upon her the status of *bol'shukha,* her subordination to older women within the household—all contributed to her social reputation. When women could not meet expectations, their "self-image, social position, and ultimately general health . . . [were] threatened."[31] While the vast majority of Russian peasant women coped with all these demands, those who did not might have become susceptible to demon possession. In a society in which marriage was almost universal, single women no doubt felt anxious about not fulfilling their responsibilities when their options became limited to leaving the village altogether, adopting a religious vocation, or remaining in the village to experience the malicious gossip of neighbors and relatives.

Likewise, newly married women felt especially vulnerable to family and community censure. The insecurity of the transition from maiden to wife manifested itself in anxieties over intercourse and fertility expressed during wedding celebrations. Even after the consummation of marriages, family and community kept close watch on the frequency and outcomes of pregnancies. At the same time, the unrelenting demands of mothers- and sisters-in-law marked a drastic change from the more solicitous attitudes of natural mothers and the greater freedoms accorded girls of marriageable age as they indulged in courting rituals, with the spotlight of attention and admiration upon them. The older these wives became, the more they may have resented the authority of mothers-in-law. This was especially true if husbands were abusive or had abandoned them to their in-laws and greater labor responsibilities while they pursued work outside the village for significant portions of the year. Migrant work for a spouse might have been a blessing for an abused woman; on the other hand, it might also have increased her burdens to an intolerable level, leaving her with no ally against in-laws who cast aspersions on her family loyalty, work habits, and marital fidelity.[32] Given the low life expectancy of the nineteenth century despite some improvement by the turn of the century, the years between 24 and 40 for women were also times when they lost husbands and society pressured them to remarry, starting the cycle of anxiety and uncertainty all over again.

Women of childbearing age who were unable to cope with life's burdens may have succumbed to demon possession, which offered a temporary relief from those burdens, solicitude rather than rancor from others, and some alteration in personal circumstances upon having been healed. In other words, *klikushestvo* may have empowered some of its victims. While those who experienced miraculous cures became the subject of community memory and pride, others achieved greater respect and social status as a result of routing out evil from the community. Still others remained content to be shriekers for several years. Having played out their emotional anxieties through possession, they found their new elevated role as sufferer preferable to returning to their everyday positions.

While these generalities about women's positions in Russian society reveal aspects of women's subordination and burdens, they obscure the shriekers' individuality. Reading their biographies, documented best in psychiatric reports (the miracle stories generally being too truncated and focused on the illness and cure rather than the victims' personal histories), the observer is struck by the tragedies experienced by some of these women. For example, one cannot help being sympathetic with the seventeen-year-old *klikusha* who prior to her possession had been raped and had undergone a botched abortion, or with the woman who could not initially cope with losing an infant when she was thirty-seven and who then experienced a difficult delivery of her eleventh child. A woman who dragged her cousin's son out of the ice also found expression for her emotional anxieties in demon possession. Another did likewise after defending her husband from the attack of seven men. So, too, did women who suffered humiliation because of their philandering husbands. These personal stories suggest strongly that *klikushestvo* was a spiritual and cultural outlet for women whose emotional burdens needed release.

By allowing these women's suffering to be publicly expressed, Russian peasant society participated in their social healing. The "mimetic" nature of possession, Edward Schieffelin points out, "is never merely the product of the actor alone. Because it is an articulation made on the basis of other previous articulations, it implies a history shared with others, and because it requires others to constitute it through participation and recognition, it is a social product. As such mimesis is fundamental to the process whereby inner experience and purpose become manifested in the world and constituted in culturally intelligible ways."[33] The similar behavioral patterns of *klikushi* were part of a script understood by and played out in front of family, neighbors, and clerics.

It is the solitary women whose possession symptoms lasted years on end who do not fit the model proposed by medical anthropologists Raybeck, Shoobe, and Grauberger. In their cases the possession experience itself, no matter how sorrowful it might appear to educated observers, may have served as the stress alleviator. Neither held responsible for their actions by church or community nor having to wrestle "with their internal conflicts and anxieties," these women through their possession found themselves in "a preferable state."[34] Instances in which threats of incarceration—made by psychiatrists, clergy, and others—reportedly halted *klikushi's* demonic behavior occurred not because the stressors had been removed and the demons expelled. They transpired this way because the threats came from individuals who did not subscribe to the possession myth, which promised release rather than punishment. It should not be surprising that psychiatrists at the turn of the twentieth century enjoyed only fleeting luck with hypnosis on *klikushi,* who did not see any redemptive value from such treatment. The psychiatrists' attempt to impose their own meanings upon the behaviors failed to alter the drama's essential script.

Understandably, *klikushestvo* represented an enigma to individuals who subscribed to universal rationalist scientific principles and who hoped to reshape their society according to such precepts. By interfering in the possession drama and rewriting the script, rationalists wished to exorcise possession by secular rather than spiritual means. Teaching peasants to disavow their superstitions and isolating recalcitrant shriekers in mental asylums, the rationalists believed, would purge peasant society of such traumatic and reputedly unhealthy behavior. In editing the script of possession, the enlightened crusaders were redefining the phenomenon as an aberrant behavior that belonged in the private realm away from the prying eyes of the community. It is only through an examination of the spiritual drama of *klikushestvo* that it becomes clear that Russian peasants subscribed to a broader definition of acceptable behaviors and had effective strategies for coping with stress among women. Russian *klikushi* will not have cried out in vain if they have been rendered more intelligible through the humanistic exploration of that drama.

APPENDIX I

DATABASE OF *KLIKUSHI/KLIKUNY*

Table I.1 1820–1926

Identified by estate ("soslovie")	%	*base Ns*
Peasants	77.7	(202)
Rural Factory	3.8	(10)
Urban	2.7	(7)
Meshchane	2.3	(6)
Noble	1.5	(4)
Other	2.9	(7)
Unknown	9.2	(24)
TOTAL	**99.9**	**(260)**

Identified by sex	%	*base Ns*
Women	88.1	(229)
Men	11.9	(31)
TOTAL	**100.0**	**(260)**

Table I.2 1861–1926

Identified by estate ("soslovie")	%	*base Ns*
Peasants	74.5	(111)
Rural Factory	2.0	(3)
Urban	4.0	(6)
Meshchane	2.7	(4)
Noble	2.7	(4)
Other	2.7	(4)
Unknown	11.4	(17)
TOTAL	**100.0**	**(149)**

Identified by sex	%	*base Ns*
Women	86.6	(129)
Men	13.4	(20)
TOTAL	**100.0**	**(149)**

Sources: V. Appellesov, "Strannyi sposob izlecheniia bol'noi," *Iaroslavskiia eparkhial'nyia vedomosti,* unofficial section, no. 48, 29 November 1872, 389–90; D. I. Azbukin, "O perepisi dushevno-bol'nykh v Vasil'skom uezde, Nizhegorodskoi gubernii," *Nevrologicheskii vestnik* 20, no. 2 (1913): 204; "Barynia kol'dunia," *Moskovskiia vedomosti,* 30 June 1859, 1152; Sergei A. Belokurov, ed., "Dela sviat. Nikona patriarkha pache zhe reshchi chudesa vrachebnaia," *Chteniia v Imperatorskom obshchestve istorii i drevnostei rossiiskikh pri Moskovskom universiteta,* bk. 1 (1886), pt. 5:110–11; "Blagodatnaia pomoshch' po molitvam k Sviatiteliu Feodosiiu, Arkhiepiskopu Chernigovskomu, Chudotvortsu," *Chernigovskiia eparkhial'nyiia iavestiia,* supplement and unofficial section, 36, no. 24, 15 December 1896, 869–70; N. P. Brukhanskii, "K voprosu o psikhicheskoi zarazitel'nosti. (Sluchai psikhicheskoi epidemii v Moskovskoi gub. v 1926 g.)," *Obozrenie psikhiatrii, nevrologii i refleksologii,* nos. 4–5 (1926): 279–81; Jeffrey Burds, "A Culture of Denunciation: Peasant Labor Migration and Religious Anathematization in Rural Russia, 1860–1905," *Journal of Modern History* 68, no. 4 (December 1996): 786–818; Serafim Chichagov, comp., *Letopis' Serafimo-Diveevskago monastyria Nizhegorodskoi gub. Ardatovskago uezda s zhizneopisaniem osnovatelei eia: prepodobnago Serafima i skhimonakhini Aleksandry, urozhd. A. S. Mel'gunovoi,* 2d ed. (St. Petersburg: Serafimo-Diveevskii monastyr', 1903), 400, 514–15, 518, 526–27, 739; *Chudesa pri otkrytii moshchei prepodobnago Serafima Sarovskago* (Moscow: Otd. tip. Tovarestva I. D. Sytina, 1903), 8; "Chudesnaia pomoshch' po molitvam k sviatiteliu Feodosiiu Uglitskomu, Arkhiepiskopu Chernigovskomu Chudotvortsu," *Chernigovskiia eparkhial'nyia izvestiia,* supplement and unofficial section, 36, no. 21, 1 November 1896, 725; "Chudesnyia istseleniia pri moshchakh Sviatitelia Feodosiia Uglitskago v dni otkrytiia i proslavleniia ikh," *Chernigovskiia eparkhial'nyia izvestiia,* supplement and unofficial section, 36, no. 18, 15 September 1896, 621, 622; no. 20, 15 October 1896, 663–66, 667; "Chudesnyia istseleniia u moshchei sviatitelia Feodosiia, Arkhiepiskopa Chernigovskago, Chudotvortsa," *Chernigovskiia eparkhial'nyia izvestiia,* supplement and unofficial section, 36, no. 22, 15 November 1896, supplement, 743, 745–46; "Delo o klikushakh," *Zhurnal Ministerstva iustitsii,* no. 9 (September 1862): 617–26; Valentina Iovovna Dmitrieva, *Klikushi ili porchennye i kak ikh lechit',* 2d ed. (Moscow: Gosudarstvennoe izdatel'stvo, 1926), 12–14, 16–21; *The Englishwoman in Russia: Impressions of the Society and Manners of the Russians at Home* (New York: Charles Scribner, 1855), 156–57; V. M. Eremin, *Gefsimansko-Chernigovskii skit pri Sviato-Troitskoi Sergievoi Lavre (kratkii ocherk istorii 1844–1990)* (Moscow: Izd. Sviato-Troitskoi Sergievoi Lavry, Sergiev Posad, 1992), 39–41; V. N. Ergol'skii, "Prestuplenie pod vliianiem demonomanicheskikh galliutsinatsii. (Sudebno-psikhiatricheskii sluchai)," *Arkhiv psikhiatrii, neirologii i sudebnoi psikhopatologii* 24, no. 2 (1894): 61–72; Gregory L. Freeze, "Institutionalizing Piety: The Church and Popular Religion, 1750–1850," in *Imperial Russia: New Histories for the Empire,* ed. Jane Burbank and David L. Ransel (Bloomington: Indiana University Press, 1998), 233–34; E. A. Genik, "Tret'ia epidemiia isterii v Moskovskoi gubernii," *Sovremennaia psikhiatriia* 6 (August 1912): 589, 592–93; Genik, "Vtoraia epidemiia istericheskikh sudorog v Podol'skom uezda, Moskovskoi gubernii," *Nevrologicheskii vestnik* 6, no. 4 (1898): 146–54; G. B. Grossman, "K voprosu o klikushestve," *Prakticheskii vrach* 5, no. 19 (13 May 1906): 317; I. Iakovenko, "Epidemiia istericheskikh sudorog v

Podol'skom uezda, Moskovskoi gub.," *Vestnik obshchestvennoi gigieny, sudebnoi i prakticheskoi meditsiny* 25, no. 3 (March 1895): 95–108; "Istselenie oderzhimoi. Razskaz sviashcheniia. (Zhurnal *Voskresenie* no. 16)," *Rebus* 12, no. 45 (7 November 1893): 429–31; N. P. Karabchevskii, *Okolo pravosudiia: Stat'i, soobshcheniia i sudebnye ocherki* (St. Petersburg: Trud, 1902), 228–32; N. P. Kazachenko-Trirodov, "Psikhoterapiia pri klikushestve," *Obozrenie psikhiatrii, nevrologii i refleksologii* 1, nos. 4–5 (1926): 293; A. Klementovskii, *Klikushi: Ocherk* (Moscow: V. tip. Katkova i komp., 1860), 34; N. Kostrov, "Koldovstvo i porcha mezhdu krest'ianami Tomskoi gubernii," *Zapiski zapadno-sibirskago otdela Imperatorskago russkago geograficheskago obshchestva* 1 (1879), pt. 2:5, 6, 8, 11–12; N. V. Krainskii, *Porcha, klikushi i besnovatye, kak iavleniia russkoi narodnoi zhizni* (Novgorod: Gubernskaia tipografiia, 1900), 50, 52–53, 59, 69, 81, 86, 121–59, 183–87, 192–206; M. Lakhtin, *Besooderzhimost' v sovremennoi derevne: Istoriko-psikhologicheskoe izsledovanie* (Moscow: Tipo-lit. Tovarestva I. N. Kushnerev, 1910), 13–29; A. Lebedev, *Sviatitel' Tikhon Zadonskii i vseia Rossii chudotvorets. (Ego zhizn', pisaniia i proslavlenie)*, 3d ed. (St. Petersburg: Tipografiia V. Smirnova, 1896), 196–97; "Letopis' Obshchestva nevropatologov i psikhiatrov pri Imperatorskom Kazanskom universitete," *Protokol VIII zasedaniia Obshchestva nevropatologov i psikhiatrov 18 dekabria 1913 goda*, in *Nevrologicheskii vestnik* 21, no. 1 (1914): 318; A. L. Liubushin, "Organicheskoe slaboumie u isterichnoi zhenshchiny," *Obozrenie psikhiatrii, nevrologii i eksperimental'noi psikhologii*, no. 9 (September 1899): 695–705; V. A. Muratov, "K voprosu ob ostrykh isterichеskikh psikhozakh," *Nevrologicheskii vestnik* 10, no. 1 (1902): 149–53; M. P. Nikitin, "K voprosu o russkikh koldunakh," *Obozrenie psikhiatrii, nevrologii i eksperimental'noi psikhologii*, nos. 9–10 (September–October 1903): 661–68, 746–52; Nikitin, "Religioznoe chuvstvo, kak istseliaiushchii faktor," *Obozrenie psikhiatrii, nevrologii i eksperimental'noi psikhologii*, nos. 1–2 (January–February 1904): 101–8; N. A. Nikitina, "K voprosu o russkikh koldunakh," *Sbornik Muzeia antropologii i etnografii* 7 (1928): 301; E. Poselianin, ed., *Bogomater': Polnoe illiustrirovannoe opisanie eia zemnoi zhizni i posviashchennykh eia imeni chudotvornykh ikon* (St. Petersburg: Knigoizdatel'stvo P. P. Soikina, [n.d.]; rpt., 1980), 270, 387, 399–400, 484, 485, 552, 553, 554, 551; REM, f. 7, op. 1, d. 493, ll. 1–16; RGIA, f. 796, op. 195, d. 1449, ll. 124 ob.–127 ob.; RGIAgM, f. 91. op. 2, d. 559, ll. 7–7 ob., 13, 23–23 ob.; idem, f. 217, op. 1, d. 2883, ll. 95–96, 34–35 ob., 201–2, 225–26 ob.; N. Sergievskii, *Sviatitel' Tikhon, Episkop Voronezhskii i Zadonskii i vseia Rossii chudotvorets: Ego zhizn' i podvigi, chudesa, proslavlenie po smerti i tvoreniia* (1898; rpt., Jordanville, N.Y.: Holy Trinity Monastery, 1965), 132–43, 177–79, 181–84; K. V. Shalabutov, "Sluchai besooderzhimosti," *Nevrologicheskii vestnik* 19, no. 3 (1912): 525–28; Vera Shevzov, "Popular Orthodoxy in Late Imperial Rural Russia," 2 vols. (Ph.D. diss., Yale University, 1994), 430, 614–15; S. Shteinberg, "Klikushestvo i ego sudebno-meditsinskoe znachenie," *Arkhiv sudebnoi meditsiny i obshchestvennoi gigieny* 6, no. 2 (1870): 78; *Skazanie o zhizni, podvigakh i chudesakh sviatitelia i chudotvortsa Ioasafa, Episkopa Belogradskago i Oboianskago, Predlagaemoe blagochestivomu vnimaniiu Kurskoi pastvy Soborom kurskikh episkopov*, in *Kurskiia eparkhial'nyia vedomosti*, no. 31, 5 August 1911, 84–86; N. I. Skliar, "O simptomokomplekse trevogi i strakha s dvigatel'nym bezpokoistvom pri psikhogennykh psikhozakh," *Sovremennaia psikhiatriia*, nos. 1–2 (January–February 1917): 22–23; P. Skubachevskii, "Belgorodskiia torzhestva: Vpechatleniia ochevidtsa," *Vera i razum*, no. 19 (October 1911): 126–27; *Smolenskii vestnik*, 12 October 1890; *Sudebnyi vestnik*, 8 August 1868; *Sudebnyi vestnik*, 10 March 1870; I. K. Surskii, *Otets Ioann Kronshtadtskii* (rpt., Forestville, Calif.: St. Elias Publications, 1980), 62, 63–64, 131, 186–87, 262, 263–64, 264–66, 267–68, 269–70, 293–94; I. Veriuzhskii, *Istoricheskie skazaniia o zhizni sviatykh, podvizavshikhsia v Vologodskoi eparkhii proslavliaemykh v seiu tserkov'ia i mestno chtimykh* (Vologda: Pechatano v tipografii V. A. Gudkova-Beliakova, 1880), 537–38; L. Vesin, "Narodnyi samosud nad koldunami. (K istorii narodnykh obychaev)," *Severnyi vestnik* 7, no. 9 (September 1892), pt. 2:64–66, 73, 77–78; and *Zhitie, chudesa i istseleniia prep. Serafima, Sarovskago Chudotvortsa* (Odessa: Tip. E. I. Fesenko, 1907), 134.

APPENDIX II

Table II.1 Database of Witchcraft Cases, 1861–1917

Date	*Number*
1860s	5
1870s	14
1880s	22
1890s	28
1900s	7
1910s	3
Unknown	1
TOTAL	**80**

Sources: E. A. Alferova, "Sl. Krygskaia," *Khar'kovskii sbornik* 12 (1898), pt. 2:24; V. Appellesov, "Strannyi sposob izlecheniia bol'noi," *Iaroslavskiia eparkhial'nyia vedomosti,* unofficial section, no. 48, 29 November 1872, 389–90; V. Beliaev, "Sluchai iz narodnoi zhizni. (Iz nabliudenii sel'skago sviashchennika)," *Rukovodstvo dlia sel'skikh pastyrei,* no. 23 (10 June 1862): 197–200; "Delo o klikushakh," *Zhurnal Ministerstva iustitsii,* no. 9 (September 1862): 617–18; P. Ef., "Popytka okoldovat' volostnoi sud," *Kievskaia starina,* no. 3 (1884): 509; Stephen P. Frank, *Crime, Cultural Conflict, and Justice in Rural Russia, 1856–1914* (Berkeley: University of California Press, 1999), 193–94, 199, 271, 272–73; A. Genik, "Vtoraia epidemiia istericheskikh sudorog v Podol'skom uezde, Moskovskoi gubernii," *Nevrologicheskii vestnik* 6, no. 4 (1898): 146–59; B. D. Grinchenko, *Etnograficheskie materialy, sobrannye v Chernigovskoi i sosednikh s nei guberniiakh,* vol. 2, *Razskazy, skazki, predaniia, poslovitsy, zagadki i pr.* (Chernigov: Tip. gubernskago zemstva, 1897), 137–38; G. B. Grossman, "K voprosu o klikushestve," *Prakticheskii vrach* 5, no. 19 (13 May 1906): 317; I. Iakovenko, "Epidemiia istericheskikh sudorog v Podol'skom uezde, Moskovskoi gub.," *Vestnik obshchestvennoi gigieny, sudebnoi i prakticheskoi meditsiny* 25, no. 3 (March 1895): 93–109; A. I. Kirpichnikov, "Ocherki po mifologii XIX veka," *Etnograficheskoe obozrenie* 6, no. 4 (1894): 3–5, 10; E. I. Kobelev, "Sl. Popovka," *Khar'kovskii sbornik* 12 (1898), pt. 2:103, 120–21; N. V. Krainskii, *Porcha, klikushi i besnovatye, kak iavleniia russkoi narodnoi zhizni* (Novgorod: Gubernskaia tipografiia, 1900); S. A. Krasnokutskii, "So slov sel'skoi babki," *Kievskiia eparkhial'nyia vedomosti,* no. 26, 25 June 1880, 5; M. Lakhtin, *Besooderzhimost' v sovremennoi derevne: Istoriko-psikhologicheskoe izsledovanie* (Moscow: Tipo-litografiia T-va I. N. Kushnerev, 1910), 26–27; A. A. Levenstim, "Sueverie i ugolovnoe pravo: Izsledovanie po istorii russkago prava i kul'tury," *Vestnik prava* 36, no. 2 (1906): 181–87, 204–5; S. V. Maksimov, *Nechistaia, nevedomaia i krestnaia sila* (St. Petersburg: Tov. R. Golike i A. Vil'borg, 1903), 152–55; M. P. Nikitin, "K voprosu o klikushestve," *Obozrenie psikhiatrii, nevrologii i eksperimental'noi psikhologii,* nos. 9–10 (September–October 1903): 661–62, 746, 748–49, 750–51, 753; N. A. Nikitina, "K voprosu o russkikh koldunakh," *Sbornik Muzeia antropologii i etnografii* 7 (1928): 299, 305, 306; RGIAgM, f. 217, op. 1, d. 413, l. 86, d. 2886, ll. 78–78 ob.; S. Shteinberg, "Klikushestvo i ego sudebno-meditsinskoe znachenie," *Arkhiv sudebnoi meditsiny i obshchestvennoi gigieny* 6, no. 2 (June 1870): 64–81; N. I. Skliar, "O simptomokomplekse trevogi i strakha sdvigatel'nym bezpokoistvom pri psikhogennykh psikhozakh," *Sovremennaia psikhiatriia,* nos. 1–2 (January–February 1917): 22–23; *Smolenskii vestnik,* 12 October 1890; *Smolenskii vestnik,* 11 October 1892; *Sudebnyi vestnik,* 8 August 1868; *Sudebnyi vestnik,* 10 March 1870; P. A. Tulub, "Sueverie i prestuplenie. (Iz vospominanii mirovogo sud'i)," *Istoricheskii vestnik,* no. 3 (March 1901): 1086–90; L. Vesin, "Narodnyi samosud nad koldunami. (K istorii narodnykh obychaev)," *Severnyi vestnik* 7, no. 9 (September 1892), pt. 2:57–79; and Russell Zguta, "The Ordeal by Water (Swimming of Witches) in the East Slavic World," *Slavic Review* 36, no. 2 (June 1977): 228–29.

NOTES

CONFRONTING *KLIKUSHESTVO*

1. The story of Ashchepkovo is based on N. V. Krainskii, *Porcha, klikushi i besnovatye, kak iavleniia russkoi narodnoi zhizni* (Novgorod: Gubernskaia tipografiia, 1900), 93, 99–109, 114. In the 1890s a Smolensk newspaper, *Smolenskii vestnik,* regularly reported incidents of fire in villages, damage costs, and often the causes of the fires, among which cigarette smoking and carelessness with matches and fire figured prominently. An 1894 report from the Gzhatsk district blamed a fire in the village Kuznetsovskaia on the fact that all the dependable adults were laboring out in the fields, leaving only the weak, elderly, and small children behind in the village (17 July 1894). A wave of fires visited three villages in Mokrin canton (the same canton to which Ashchepkovo belonged) in July 1894 (28 July 1894). Ashchepkovo itself was hit by fire some time in the first half of September 1898, a few months after the epidemic of possession. The fire destroyed nine peasant huts and outbuildings (out of a total of 46 households), incurring a loss of 8,200 rubles (15 October 1898).

2. In January 1895 a Smolensk newspaper reporter commented on the significant increase in horse thefts in the province, which in turn prompted special police attention (*Smolenskii vestnik,* 15 January 1895).

3. Beginning in 1890 rural cantonal courts acquired the authority to fine peasants for being careless with fire and smoking in public, among other infractions. See N. P. Druzhinin, "Krest'ianskii sud v ego poslednem fazise," *Nabliudatel',* no. 3 [1893]: 243–57; and Druzhinin, "Preobrazovannyi volostnoi sud," in N. P. Druzhinin, ed., *Iuridicheskoe polozhenie krest'ian* (St. Petersburg, 1897), 332. I thank Professor Stephen Frank for pointing this fact out to me and providing the relevant citations.

4. While declaring *samosud* (mob violence) illegal, the government was fairly lax in punishing the offense. The law focused on regulating relations between

landlords and peasants rather than relations among peasants. Conflicts among peasants were not viewed as a threat to the status quo until the entire society was on the verge of collapse in the early twentieth century. While the courts normally sentenced convicted murderers to hard labor in Siberia, they were reluctant to deplete a village's labor supply by sentencing participants in mob violence to lengthy stays in prison. They only tried to deter peasants from extralegal activities with light prison sentences. Naturally, peasants took advantage of this situation (Christine D. Worobec, "Horse Thieves and Peasant Justice in Post-Emancipation Imperial Russia," *Journal of Social History* 21, no. 2 [Winter 1987]: 285–86, 288).

5. According to a meteorological report, a severe drought from July through August enveloped the southeastern provinces, stretching from Smolensk, Riazan, Kaluga, and Tambov down to Kherson and Taurida (B. Srevnevskii, "Obzor pogody za avgust 1897 g. (nov. stil')," *Meteorologicheskii vestnik,* no. 9 [September 1897]: 407–24).

6. Krainskii, *Porcha,* 100.

7. Ibid., 101–2.

8. For a description of Easter icon processions in Voronezh province, see Fedor Nikonov, "O blagochestivykh obychaiakh i religioznykh uchrezhdeniiakh, sushchestvuiushchikh u zhitelei voronezhskoi eparkhii," *Voronezhskii literaturnyi sbornik* 1 (1861): 359–61.

9. Krainskii, *Porcha,* 103–4.

10. Peasants frequently appealed to the land captain or other authorities when they felt injustices had been committed. In this case, however, the pitting of the community against the outside official world to which a community member had defected understandably exacerbated internal tensions.

11. Krainskii, *Porcha,* 106–7.

12. Ibid., 108–9.

13. Ibid., 167.

14. For further information about hooliganism, see Joan Neuberger, *Hooliganism: Crime, Culture, and Power in St. Petersburg, 1900–1914* (Berkeley: University of California Press, 1993).

15. Michel Foucault, *The Order of Things: An Archaeology of the Human Sciences* (New York: Vintage Books, 1973); Foucault, *Power/Knowledge: Selected Interviews and Other Writings, 1972–1977* (New York: Pantheon, 1980).

16. Charles Stewart, *Demons and the Devil: Moral Imagination in Modern Greek Society* (Princeton: Princeton University Press, 1991), 146.

17. Stuart Clark, *Thinking with Demons: The Idea of Witchcraft in Early Modern Europe* (Oxford: Clarendon Press, 1997), 109.

18. Mark D. Steinberg, "Stories and Voices: History and Theory," *Russian Review* 55, no. 3 (July 1996): 348.

19. Ruth Harris, *Lourdes: Body and Spirit in the Secular Age* (New York: Viking, 1999), 289.

20. Gananath Obeyesekere, *Medusa's Hair: An Essay on Personal Symbols and Religious Experience* (Chicago: University of Chicago Press, 1981), 84, 101, 103, 197.

21. *Pamiatniki starinnoi russkoi literatury* (1860–1862; rpt., The Hague: Mouton, 1970), 168 (editorial comments).

22. F. M. Dostoevskii, *Brat'ia Karamazovy: Roman v chetyrekh chastiakh s*

epilogom (Paris: Bookking International, 1995), 48–49; A. V. Balov, "Ocherki Poshekhon'ia: Verovaniia," *Etnograficheskoe obozrenie,* no. 4 (1901): 114–16.

23. Pavel Iakobii, "Religiozno-psikhicheskiia epidemiia. Iz psikhiatricheskoi ekspertizy," *Vestnik Evropy* nos. 10–11 (October–November 1903): 751, 738.

24. While in Moscow in the summers of 1993 and 1994, I had numerous conversations with Russians who had recently seen *klikushi* at monasteries.

25. I had access to notes taken on two files from the Tenishev archive, thanks to the generosity of Professor Jeffrey Burds; the couple of shriekers described there are included in the database. Section 203 of the Tenishev ethnographic program that guided ethnographers in the field is devoted to *klikushestvo.* It asked field-workers to seek answers to a series of questions, most of which are far too leading for the comfort of modern ethnographers and anthropologists. By not seeking to shed light on the shriekers' biographies and everyday lives, larger responses on the part of the community, the drama of religious exorcisms, and the shriekers' tendencies to go on pilgrimages to monasteries renowned for their miracle cures, the following queries are also limited: "Do they [the people] recognize the shriekers as being demon possessed? What measures are taken to treat them [and] to exorcize the demons? Do they bathe the shriekers in an ice-hole in winter on the day of the Epiphany? Do they cover the shriekers' heads during their seizures? Do they put a pot [*gorshok*] on their heads? Do they hang a yoke around their necks? Do they suggest to the shriekers that they are possessed by the souls of those who have drowned or hanged themselves? Do they believe that the shriekers are distinguished by their ability to see the future? Do shriekers sense the approach of a priest ahead of time? Do they curse the priest, justifying their actions [by pointing to] the fact that the spirits inhabiting the shriekers abuse the priest? Do the shriekers feel particularly agitated during the singing of the Cherubikon hymn? What type of prayer is read over the shriekers? Do the shriekers explain their illness by [saying] that they swallowed the devil who was in a small pitcher or that they swallowed a water beetle? Does the spirit inside the *klikushi* shriek out, in the people's opinion, the [name of the] sorcerer who caused the injury to the ill person?" See B. M. Firsov and I. G. Kiseleva, comps., *Byt velikorusskikh krest'ian-zemlepashtsev: Opisanie materialov etnograficheskogo biuro kniazia V. N. Tenisheva (na primere Vladimirskoi gubernii)* (St. Petersburg: Izdatel'stvo Evropeiskogo Doma, 1993), 400.

26. Ann Goldberg, *Sex, Religion, and the Making of Modern Madness: The Eberbach Asylum and German Society, 1815–1849* (New York: Oxford University Press, 1999), 8.

27. A conclusion also reached by Stephen P. Frank, *Crime, Cultural Conflict, and Justice in Rural Russia, 1856–1914* (Berkeley: University of California Press, 1999), 15.

28. The exceptions include Bengt Ankarloo and Stuart Clark, eds., *Witchcraft and Magic in Europe: The Eighteenth and Nineteenth Centuries* (Philadelphia: University of Pennysluania Press, 1999); Bengt Ankarloo and G. Henningsen, eds., *Early Modern Witchcraft: Centres and Peripheries* (Oxford: Clarendon, 1989); Robin Briggs, *Witches and Neighbors: The Social and Cultural Context of European Witchcraft* (New York: Viking, 1996); and Nancy Caciola, "Discerning Spirits: Sanctity and Possession in the Later Middle Ages" (Ph.D. diss., University of Michigan, 1994). Although Clark *(Thinking with Demons)* looks at the intellectual

underpinnings of witchcraft beliefs, he devotes a chapter to possession in his monumental study. Joseph Klaits also devotes a chapter to the possessed in his book *Servants of Satan: The Age of the Witch Hunts* (Bloomington: Indiana University Press, 1985).

29. The notion originates with Caroline Walker Bynum, *Holy Feast and Holy Fast* (Berkeley: University of California Press, 1987), 23; and is developed by Caciola, "Discerning Spirits," 268, 371 ff.

30. Clark, *Thinking with Demons,* 441.

31. G. S. Rousseau and Roy Porter, "Introduction: The Destinies of Hysteria," in Sander L. Gilman et al., *Hysteria beyond Freud* (Berkeley: University of California Press, 1993), viii.

32. Porter, "The Body and the Mind, The Doctor and the Patient: Negotiating Hysteria," in Sander L. Gilman et al., *Hysteria beyond Freud,* 228.

33. Unfortunately, the American Psychiatric Association's concession to the cultural and social underpinnings of psychopathology in response to the recommendations of a task force of prominent anthropologists and cross-cultural psychiatrists is relegated to an appendix, much to the consternation of the task force members. Byron J. Good, "Culture and DSM-IV: Diagnosis, Knowledge and Power," *Culture, Medicine and Psychiatry* 20, no. 2 (June 1996): 127–32; Roberto Lewis-Fernández, "Cultural Formulation of Psychiatric Diagnosis," *Culture, Medicine and Psychiatry* 20, no. 2 (June 1996): 133–44.

34. For a similar point with regard to other religious behaviors, see Goldberg, *Sex,* 8.

35. Jerrold E. Levy, "Some Comments upon the Ritual of the *Sanni* Demons," *Comparative Studies in Society and History* 11, no. 2 (April 1969): 226.

1: STATE AND CHURCH PERCEPTIONS

1. Rossiiskii gosudarstvennyi arkhiv drevnykh aktov (henceforth cited as RGADA), f. 7, op. 1, d. 75 ("O klikushakh, prislannykh v Tainuiu kantseliariiu"), ll. 1–3 ob. Peter I created the Secret Chancery in 1718 to replace the Preobrazhenskii Prikaz (founded in 1697). The Secret Chancery was abolished in 1762 (John P. LeDonne, *Absolutism and Ruling Class: The Formation of the Russian Political Order, 1700–1825* [New York: Oxford University Press, 1991], 123, 124, 125).

2. RGADA, f. 7, op. 1, d. 75, 11. 1 ob.–3 ob.

3. RGADA, f. 7, op. 1, d. 75, 11. 5–5 ob. Historians of medicine have identified the "falling sickness" as epilepsy. The classical study of this subject is Owsei Temkin, *The Falling Sickness: A History of Epilepsy from the Greeks to the Beginnings of Modern Neurology,* 2d ed. (Baltimore: Johns Hopkins University Press, 1971). In the medieval and early imperial periods, Russians often spoke of demon possession and the falling sickness, sometimes merging the two. Possession and epilepsy shared the symptoms of convulsions, rolling of the eyes, and grinding of the teeth, followed by deep sleep (Temkin, *The Falling Sickness,* 85).

4. RGADA, f. 7, op. 1, d. 75, l. 5 ob.

5. The miracle story bore the signature of Venedikt, a monk at the Voskresenskii Monastery in New Jerusalem. S. A. Belokurov, ed., "Dela sviat. Nikona Patriarkha, pache zhe reshchi chudesa vrachebnaia," *Chteniia v Imperatorskom ob-*

shchestve istorii i drevnostei rossiiskikh pri Moskovskom universiteta, bk. 1, pt. 5 (1887): 110–11.

6. P. Skubachevskii, "Belgorodskiia torzhestva: Vpechatleniia ochevidtsa," *Vera i razum,* no. 19 (October 1911): 126. Tickets of admission were first issued for the canonization ceremonies of Serafim of Sarov in 1903 and, in this case, only to members of the upper classes and church officials because of the royal family's participation and corresponding security needs. As a result, thousands of pilgrims and parish priests huddled in the courtyard around the main cathedral, desperately hoping to hear some of the sounds of the liturgical services. While Nicholas II and his family did not attend the 1911 glorification ceremonies, the attending police issued tickets for purposes of maintaining crowd control (Gregory L. Freeze, "Subversive Piety: Religion and the Political Crisis in Late Imperial Russia," *Journal of Modern History* 68, no. 2 [June 1996]: 327).

7. Skubachevskii, "Belgorodskiia torzhestva," 126–27.

8. David Harley, in a discussion of contested understandings of witchcraft and demon possession during the Salem witch trials, identifies "fraud, disease and social conflict . . . [as] the main stays of modern explanations" of these phenomena ("Explaining Salem: Calvinist Psychology and the Diagnosis of Possession," *American Historical Review* 101 [1996]: 328).

9. Gregory L. Freeze, "Institutionalizing Piety: The Church and Popular Religion, 1750–1850," in *Imperial Russia: New Histories for the Empire,* ed. Jane Burbank and David L. Ransel (Bloomington: Indiana University Press, 1998), 220.

10. Valerie I. J. Flint makes this argument regarding the point at which Western European Christianity in the early Middle Ages felt comfortable incorporating non-Christian magic into its practices (*The Rise of Magic in Early Medieval Europe* [Princeton: Princeton University Press, 1991], 6).

11. The same had been true of the medieval Russian Orthodox Church (Eve Levin, "*Dvoeverie* and Popular Religion," in *Seeking God: The Recovery of Religious Identity in Orthodox Russia, Ukraine, and Georgia,* ed. Stephen K. Batalden [DeKalb: Northern Illinois University Press, 1993], 45).

12. Henry Maguire, "Magic and the Christian Image," in *Byzantine Magic,* ed. Henry Maguire (Washington, D.C.: Dumbarton Oaks Research Library and Collection, distributed by Harvard University Press, 1995), 51.

13. For a discussion of official and lay supplicatory prayers in pre-Petrine Russia, see Eve Levin, "Supplicatory Prayers as a Source for Popular Religious Culture in Muscovite Russia," in *Religion and Culture in Early Modern Russia and Ukraine,* ed. Samuel H. Baron and Nancy Shields Kollmann (DeKalb: Northern Illinois University Press, 1997), 96–114.

14. *Stoglav,* chap. 41, question 22, and *Akty istoricheskie,* vol. 1, no. 154, 252f., cited by Valerie Kivelson, "Identifying Witches and Sorcerers: Political Sorcery in Muscovy, 1467–1584" (paper presented at the NEH-sponsored conference on "Cultural Identity in a Multiethnic State: Muscovy 1362–1584," March 9–12, 1994), 16–17; See also Kivelson, "Through the Prism of Witchcraft: Gender and Social Change in Seventeenth-Century Muscovy," in *Russia's Women: Accommodation, Resistance, Transformation,* ed. Barbara Evans Clements, Barbara Alpern Engel, and Christine D. Worobec (Berkeley: University of California Press, 1991), 80; and Kivelson, "Patrolling the Boundaries: Witchcraft Accusations and Household Strife in Seventeenth-Century Muscovy," *Harvard Ukrainian*

Studies 19 (1995): 322. I thank Professor Kivelson for sharing her unpublished manuscript with me. The *Ulozhenie* of 1649 punished blasphemy with burning at the stake. (*Polnoe sobranie zakonov Rossiiskoi Imperii s 1649 goda* [hereafter cited as *PSZ*), 1st ser., vol. 1, chap. 1.1, cited in Elena Borisovna Smilianskaia, "Sledstviia po 'dukhovnym delam' kak istochnik po istorii obshchestvennogo soznaniia v Rossii pervoi polovine XVIII v." [Kandidatskaia diss., Moskovskii gosudarstvennyi universitet imeni M. V. Lomonosova, 1987], 107).

15. Kivelson, "Identifying Witches and Sorcerers"; Kivelson, "The Devil Stole His Mind: The Tsar and the Moscow Uprising of 1648," *American Historical Review* 98 (1993): 733–56. Reference to the Razriadnyi Prikaz is made by O. D. Zhuravel', *Siuzhet o dogovore cheloveka s d'iavolom v drevnerusskoi literature* (Novosibirsk: Sibirskii khronograf, 1996), 42.

16. Edward L. Keenan, "Afterword: Orthodoxy and Heterodoxy," in Baron and Kollmann, *Religion and Culture,* 204.

17. In the late seventeenth century there were instances in which *klikushi* were persecuted. In 1677, for example, a few were sentenced to death in Tiumen (Kenneth Steven Dix, "Madness in Russia, 1775–1864: Official Attitudes and Institutions for Its Care" [Ph.D. diss., University of California, Los Angeles, 1977], 217).

18. LeDonne, *Absolutism,* 124.

19. Tsar Aleksei and Nikon did not openly attack *iurodstvo,* no doubt because of the popularity of the phenomenon. Peter I, however, felt secure enough to deal the final blow in 1716 (D. S. Likhachev, A. M. Panchenko, and V. Popyrko, *Smekh v drevnei Rusi* [Leningrad: Nauka, 1984], 115, 132, 151–52).

20. LeDonne, *Absolutism,* 124, 202.

21. *PSZ,* scr 1, vol. 5, no. 2906; also quoted in James Cracraft, *The Church Reform of Peter the Great* (London: Macmillan, 1971), 290 n. My translation.

22. *PSZ,* vol. 5, no. 2985. The Military Statute of 30 March, attacking superstition, sorcery, apostasy, and blasphemy, does not mention *klikushestvo* or demon possession. This omission may have been the beginning of the identification of possession with women, as the statute was directed at soldiers. *PSZ,* vol. 5, no. 3006, articles 1–7.

23. Trans. in Alexander V. Muller, ed. and trans., *The Spiritual Regulation of Peter the Great* (Seattle: University of Washington Press, 1972), 15.

24. Noncertified corpses referred to those bodies that the laity and local clerics, and not the ecclesiastical hierarchy, deemed saintly because they were uncorrupted and because they became the sites of miraculous cures.

25. Muller, *The Spiritual Regulation,* 19–20, 29. Muller translates *klikushi* as "squallers" in deference to the term first used in the 1720s by the Englishman Thomas Consett. Consett appropriated the pejorative legal understanding of *klikushi* by defining them as "persons that feign themselves bewitch'd, screaming and shrieking with the utmost Distraction," whose purpose was to extract money from those who witnessed their distress. (*The Present State and Regulations of the Church of Russia* [London: J. Brotherton, 1729], 1:38), quoted in Muller, *The Spiritual Regulation,* 109 n.

26. *PSZ,* ser. 1, vol. 2, no. 532; also cited in *Polnoe sobranie postanovlenii i rasporiazhenii po vedomstvu pravoslavnago ispovedaniia Rossiiskoi Imperii,* ser. 1, vol. 8 (St. Petersburg, 1898), 101.

27. *PSZ,* ser. 1, vol. 7, art. 2451; also cited in *Polnoe sobranie postanovlenii,* 8:101.

28. *Polnoe sobranie postanovlenii,* 8:95–101.

29. Quoted in I. S. Beliaev, "Ikotniki i klikushki," *Russkaia starina* (April 1905): 163.

30. Beliaev, "Ikotniki," 163, 159, 161.

31. *PSZ,* ser. 1, vol. 10, art. 7450.

32. All the information about the Mezensk epidemic in this paragraph stems from Beliaev, "Ikotniki," 145–56.

33. The eighteenth-century spiritual elder Paisii Ivanovich Velichkovskii (1722–1794) recognized *ikota* as an ailment that resulted not from food but from the devil's machinations ("O razlichnykh skorbiakh i tiagotakh ot besov," in Sergei Tomchenko, comp., *Zhitiia i tvoreniia russkikh sviatykh: Zhizneopisaniia i dukhovnye nastavleniia velikikh podvizhnikov Khristianskogo blagochestiia, prosiiavshikh v zemle Russkoi. Narodnye pochitaniia i prazdniki Pravoslavnoi Tserkvi* [Moscow: Sovremennik, Donskoi monastyr', 1993], 279).

34. Beliaev, "Ikotniki," 156–57.

35. Ibid., 157.

36. Ibid., 157–58.

37. RGADA, f. 7, op. 1 ["Dela Preobrazhenskogo prikaza i Tainoi kantseliarii"], d. 553.

38. RGADA, f. 7, op. 1, dd. 1082, 1323, 1548, and 1572. The fifth case, d. 1970, involved a man who confessed to indecently handling the empress's portrait.

39. LeDonne, *Absolutism,* 165–66.

40. Elena Borisovna Smilianskaia, "Sledstvennye dela 'o sueveriiakh' v Rossii pervoi polovine XVIII v. v svete problem istorii obshchestvennogo soznaniia," *Rossica* (1996): 3–6.

41. RGADA, f. 1183, g. 1746, d. 407, l. 9 ob., cited in Freeze, "Institutionalizing Piety," 224.

42. *Opisanie dokumentov i del, khraniashchikhsia v arkhive Sviateishago Pravitel'stvuiushchago Sinoda* (1751; rpt., St. Petersburg: Sinodal'naia tipografiia, 1909), 31:13–14; Smilianskaia, "Sledstviia po 'dukhovnym delam,'" 51.

43. Rossiiskii gosudarstvennyi istoricheskii arkhiv (henceforth cited as RGIA), op. 35, d. 528, ll. 1–3, reproduced in full in E. B. Smilianskaia, "Donesenie 1754 g. v Sinod Suzdal'skogo episkopa Porfiriia 'iakoby vo grade Suzhdale koldovstvo i volshebstvo umnozhilos,'" in *Khristianstvo i tserkov' v Rossii feodal'nogo perioda (materialy),* ed. N. N. Pokrovskii (Novosibirsk: Nauka Sibirskoe otdelenie, 1989), 257–60.

44. *Trebnik* (Moscow, 1720), ll. 46, 47 ob., cited and quoted in Smilianskaia, "Sledstvennye dela 'o sueveriiakh,'" 8.

45. Archbishop Veniamin, *Novaia skrizhal' ili ob"iasnenie o tserkvi, o liturgii i o vsekh sluzhbakh i utvariakh tserkovnykh,* 16th ed. (1899; rpt., Moscow: Russkii dukhovnyi tsentr, 1992), 2:449–50, 457.

46. *Opisanie dokumentov i del* (1770; rpt., Petrograd: Sinodal'naia tipografiia, 1914), 50:373–74.

47. The physician noted that the women were suffering from an ailment caused by their female organs, rather than by possession. It is not clear whether

the churchmen accepted the medical diagnosis over the spiritual one of possession. Gosudarstvennyi arkhiv Iaroslavskoi Oblasti, f. 197 (Rostovskaia konsistoriia), op. 1, t. 1, d. 3973, ll. 48, 50, 58–59.

48. *Opisanie dokumentov i del,* 50:413–21.

49. *Polnoe sobranie postanovlenii,* ser. 3, vol. 1 (St. Petersburg, 1910), 546–47, 570–72, 657–58, 659, quotation on 658.

50. Ibid., 1:659.

51. Quoted in Maguire, "Magic and the Christian Image," in Maguire, *Byzantine Magic,* 61.

52. *Polnoe sobranie postanovlenii,* 1:659, 658.

53. Quoted in M. Lakhtin, *Besooderzhimost' v sovremennoi derevne: Istoriko-psikhologicheskoe izsledovanie* (Moscow: Tipo-litografiia Tovarestva I. N. Kushnerev, 1910), 12.

54. Frank, *Crime, Cultural Conflict,* 269–70.

55. The Senate's 1737 decision to call in a doctor to examine the victims of *ikota* in Mezensk district is the earliest case I have found involving a doctor as an expert witness. This does not seem to have been regular practice in the lesser courts until the early nineteenth century (Krainskii, *Porcha,* 50). A doctor's written evaluation of individuals claiming to suffer from *klikushestvo* appears in the judicial record on the Moscow court of conscience *(sovestnyi sud)* in 1820 (Rossiiskii gosudarstvennyi istoricheskii arkhiv goroda Moskvy [hereafter cited as RGIAgM], f. 91, op. 2 [Moskovskii sovestnyi sud: Obshchee deloproizvodstvo grazhdanskie dela ugolovnye dela, 1782–1861], d. 559, ll. 23–23 ob.).

56. Stewart, *Demons and the Devil,* 82.

57. Jaroslav Pelikan, *The Christian Tradition: A History of the Development of Doctrine,* vol. 2, *The Spirit of Eastern Christendom (600–1700)* (Chicago: University of Chicago Press, 1974), 220–22.

58. Included in Bishop Dimitrii, comp., *Domashnii molitvoslov dlia userdstvuiushchikh* (Kharbin: Bratstvo imeni sv. Ioanna Bogoslova pri Bogoslovskom fakul'tete Instituta sv. Vladimira, 1943), 306–8.

59. *Zakon Bozhii: Pervaia kniga o Pravoslavnoi vere* (Paris: YMCA Press, 1956), 167.

60. R. W. Blackmore, trans., *The Doctrine of the Russian Church Being the Primer or Spelling Book, the Shorter and Longer Catechisms, And a Treatise on the Duty of Parish Priests* (Aberdeen: A. Brown, 1845), 52, 42.

61. S. V. Bulgakov, *Pravoslavie: Prazdniki i posty; Bogosluzhenie; Treby; Raskoly, eresi, sekty; Protivnye khristianstvu i pravoslaviiu ucheniia; Zapadnye khristianskie veroispovedeniia; Sobory Vostochnoi, Russkoi i Zapadnoi Tserkvei (Iz "Nastol'noi knigi dlia sviashchenno-tserkovno-sluzhitilei")* (1917; rpt., Moscow: Sovremennik, 1994), 121.

62. Kallistos Ware and Mother Mary, trans., *The Lenten Triodion* (London: Faber and Faber, 1978), 179, 304, 351, 373.

63. Caciola, "Discerning Spirits," 281.

64. Michael S. Flier, "Till the End of Time: The Apocalypse in Russian Historical Experience before 1500," in *Orthodox Russia: Studies in Belief and Practice, 1492–1936,* ed. Valerie A. Kivelson and Robert H. Greene (forthcoming). I am grateful to Professor Flier for sending me a copy of the revised version and for allowing me to cite it.

65. M. V. Alpatov, *Drevnerusskaia ikonopis'. Early Russian Icon Painting* (Moscow: Iskusstvo, 1978), no. 113.

66. For commentary on Last Judgment icons, see G. Vzdornov, *Issledovanie o Kievskoi Psaltiri* (Moscow: Iskusstvo, 1978), 138; David Coomler, *The Icon Handbook: A Guide to Understanding Icons and the Liturgy, Symbols, and Practices of the Russian Orthodox Church* (Springfield, Ill.: Templegate, 1995), 83; and David M. Goldfrank, "Who Put the Snake on the Icon and the Tollbooths on the Snake? A Problem of Last Judgment Iconography," *Harvard Ukrainian Studies* 19 (1995): 180–99.

67. V. G. Briusova, *Russkaia zhivopis' 17 veka* (Moscow: Iskusstvo, 1984), no. 164.

68. See, for example, the 1640–1641 Iaroslavl' icon of "The Heavenly Ladder" from the Church Nikola-Nadein (Briusova, *Russkaia zhivopis',* 69); and the early-sixteenth-century "The Vision of St. John Climacus" (Alpatov, *Drevnerusskaia ikonopis',* no. 185).

69. This analysis of a thirteenth-century mosaic from the cupola of the Baptistery in Florence is applicable to the Russian examples (Caciola, "Discerning Spirits," 253).

70. Caciola, "Discerning Spirits," 123.

71. *Ikonen: Ein Kalender für 1988* (Colgne: Ikonen Gallerie Rotmann, 1987), depiction for September. The sexual image is repeated in an 1844 representation of "Nikita Beating the Demon" (*Pozdniaia russkaia ikona konets XVIII–XIX vek* [St. Petersburg: Limbus, 1994], 45, no. 23). For a medieval example of a face appearing in the devil's groin, see Eve Levin, *Sex and Society in the World of the Orthodox Slavs, 900–1700* (Ithaca: Cornell University Press, 1989), 278.

72. Coomler, *Icon Handbook,* 85.

73. Ibid., 140.

74. Alpatov, *Drevnerusskaia ikonopis',* no. 179.

75. Briusova, *Russkaia zhivopis',* 134, no. 181.

76. T. A. Novichkova, *Russkii demonologicheskii slovar'* (St. Petersburg: Peterburskii pisatel', 1995), 53.

77. Veniamin, *Novaia skrizhal',* 1:54.

78. Caciola, "Discerning Spirits," 72.

79. Michael Kantor, ed. and comp., *Medieval Slavic Lives of Saints and Princes* (Ann Arbor: University of Michigan, 1983), 207.

80. Muriel Heppell, trans., *The "Paterik" of the Kievan Caves Monastery,* Harvard Library of Early Ukrainian Literature, English Translations, vol. 1 (Cambridge, Mass.: Ukrainian Research Institute of Harvard University; distributed by Harvard University Press, 1989), 146–47.

81. Bushkovitch, *Religion and Society in Russia: The Sixteenth and Seventeenth Centuries* (New York: Oxford University Press, 1992), 101, 103.

82. For a critical discussion of miracle stories as a valuable historical source, see Isolde Thyrêt, "Ecclesiastical Perceptions of the Female and the Role of the Holy in the Religious Life of Women in Muscovite Russia" (Ph.D. diss., University of Washington, 1992), 20–23, 28.

83. Published in both Old Church Slavonic and modern Russian in G. M. Prokhorov, E. G. Vodolazkin, and E. E. Shevchenko, eds. and trans., *Prepodobnye Kirill, Ferapont i Martinian Belozerskie,* 2d rev. ed. (St. Petersburg: Glagol, 1994), 138–39.

84. Caciola, "Discerning Spirits," 76.

85. Prokhorov, Vodolazkin, and Shevchenko, *Prepodobnye Kirill, Ferapont i Martinian,* 144–47.

86. Thyrêt, "Ecclesiastical Perceptions of the Female," 50, 52, 54; Thyrêt, "Muscovite Miracle Stories as Sources for Gender-Specific Religious Experience," in Baron and Kollmann, *Religion and Culture,* 121.

87. Thyrêt, "Ecclesiastical Perceptions of the Female," 64, 69, 79–80; Thyrêt, "Muscovite Miracle Stories," 122–24.

88. Prokhorov, Vodolazkin, and Shevchenko, *Prepodobnye Kirill, Ferapont i Martinian,* 138–67, 286–307.

89. Ibid., 140–41.

90. Ibid., 290–97.

91. Ibid., 296–97.

92. Ibid., 294–95.

93. Ibid., 292–93.

94. Discussed and quoted in A. V. Pigin, *Iz istorii russkoi demonologii XVII veka: Povest' o besnovatoi zhene Solomonii: Issledovanie i teksty* (St. Petersburg: Bulanin, 1998), 109.

95. Ibid., 105.

96. The canonization of Dmitrii (1651–1709) was the first of a series of glorifications that honored the bishops who had been instrumental in reforming the Orthodox Church in the seventeenth and eighteenth centuries. A graduate of the Ukrainian Petro Mohyla Academy of Kiev, Dmitrii was best known for his new and up-to-date *Chetii Minei,* a chronicle of saints' lives, and educational material for the clergy. For his biography see Ieromonakh Ioann [Kologrivov], *Ocherki po istorii russkoi sviatosti* (Brussels: Izd. "Zhizn' s Bogom," 1961), 269–86.

97. "Prilozhenie XXIV: Kopiia s zapiski o chudesakh Preosviashchennago Dmitriia Mitropolita Rostovskago," in *Opisanie dokumentov i del* (1752; rpt., Petrograd: Sinodal'naia Tipografiia, 1915), 32:983–1150. Miracles attributed to St. Dmitrii prior to the 1750s as well as the condition of the saint's remains were apparently falsified. For further information, see Freeze, "Subversive Piety," 320n; and Freeze, "Institutionalizing Piety," 242 n. 64.

98. Belokurov, "Dela sviat. Nikona Patriarkha," 83–114. Having stripped Nikon of his authority as patriarch in 1666, the Russian Orthodox Church never recognized him as a saint.

99. Hilandar Research Library, Ohio State University, Saratov State University Collection 1255, "Iavlenie i chudesa tolgskoi ikony Bogoroditsy so slovom pokhval'nym i sluzhboi." The watermarks are from 1689 and 1711.

100. "Prilozhenie XXII: Reestr kto imiany ot Akhtyrskiia chudotvornyia Presviatyia Bogomatere ikony boleznovavshiia poluchili istselenii znachit' po semu," in *Opisanie dokumentov i del,* 32:931–62.

101. Pigin, *Iz istorii russkoi demonologii,* 112, 82, 114.

102. *Opisanie dokumentov i del,* 32:990.

103. Ibid., 32:994, 1140.

104. A. Lebedev, *Sviatitel' Tikhon Zadonskii i vseia Rossii chudotvorets. (Ego zhizn', pisaniia i proslavlenie),* 3d ed. (St. Petersburg: Tipografiia V. Smirnova, 1896), 193–216; N. Sergievskii, *Sviatitel' Tikhon, Episkop Voronezhskii i Zadonskii i*

vseia Rossii chudotvorets: Ego zhizn' i podvigi, chudesa, proslavlenie po smerti i tvoreniia (1898; rpt., Jordanville, N.Y.: Holy Trinity Monastery, 1965), 132–43, 158–85.

105. Like Dmitrii of Rostov, Feodosii had been part of the circle of Ukrainian church reformers that included Iov of Novgorod, Mitrofan of Voronezh, Lazar' Baranovich, and Stefan Iavorskii. By canonizing Feodosii Uglitskii, the Holy Synod sought to celebrate Muscovy's annexation of a significant portion of Ukraine and thus emphasize the spiritual and cultural heritage of Kievan Rus' (A. V., "Sviatitel' Feodosii Uglitskii, Arkhiepiskop Chernigovskii. [Po povodu 200-letiia so dnia blazhennoi konchiny Sviatitelia Feodosiia]," *Chernigovskiia eparkhial'nyia izvestiia,* supplement and unofficial section, 36, no. 3, 1 February 1896, 87, 86).

106. "Opredelenie Sviateishago Sinoda: ot 26 iiunia–5 iiulia 1896 g. za no. 1916, o proslavlenii i otkrytii moshchei sviatitelia Feodosiia Uglitskago, archiepiskopa Chernigovskago," *Vera i razum,* no. 15 (August 1896), pt. 3:380; "Izvestiia i zametki," *Vera i razum,* no. 17 (September 1896): 439–44.

107. *Chernigovskiia eparkhial'nyia izvestiia,* supplement and unofficial section, 36, no. 18, 15 September 1896, 580.

108. Ibid., nos. 18–24, 15 September–15 December 1896, 619–22, 641–49, 663–69, 721–26, 743–47, 803–7, 866–70.

109. "Kolduny i klikushi. (Po povodu sudebnykh protsessov ob ubiistvakh koldunov)," *Rukovodstvo dlia sel'skikh pastyrei* 35, no. 4 (23 January 1894): 81–88; no. 6 (6 February 1894): 145–51; no. 7 (13 February 1894): 172–74, esp. 148, 149, 82, 151.

110. A. Kh., "K voprosu o koldunakh," *Rukovodstvo dlia sel'skikh pastyrei,* no. 24 (12 June 1894): 149–54.

111. After living in the forest as a hermit for 15 years, in the tradition of the desert fathers, Serafim returned to Sarov in 1810 and began to minister to the faithful as a spiritual elder, receiving up to 2,000 visitors from various parts of Russia a day. For a fuller biographical account of Serafim of Sarov, see Robert Nichols, "The Orthodox Elders *(Startsy)* of Imperial Russia," *Modern Greek Studies Yearbook* 1 (1985): 10–11.

112. A few of the examples of cures of demon possession at the Sarovskaia Hermitage were published in Archimandrite Serafim Chichagov, comp., *Letopis' Serafimo-Diveevskago monastyria Nizhegorodskoi gub. Ardatovskago uezda s zhizneopisaniem osnovatelei eia: prepodobnago Serafima i skhimonakhini Aleksandry, urozhd. A. S. Mel'gunovoi,* 2d ed. (St. Petersburg: Serafimo-Diveevskii monastyr', 1903), 514–15, 518, 526–27, 739. For a report on the Holy Synod's decisions concerning the status of Father Serafim, see "Deianie Sviateishago Sinoda," *Vera i Razum,* no. 3 (February 1903), pt. 3:64–65.

113. "Deianie Sviateishago Sinoda," 65. Empress Alexandra was convinced that the canonization of Seraphim would help her produce a male heir.

114. *Chudesa pri otkrytii moshchei prepodobnago Serafima Sarovskago* (Moscow: Otd. Tip. T-va I. D. Sytina, 1903), 8–10.

115. M. P. Nikitin, "Religioznoe chuvstvo, kak istseliaiushchii faktor," *Obozrenie psikhiatrii, nevrologii i eksperimental'noi psikhologii,* nos. 1–2 (January–February 1904): 1–9, 100–8.

116. *Zhitie, chudesa i istseleniia Prepodobnago Serafima, Sarovskago Chudotvortsa* (Odessa: Tip. E. I. Fesenko, 1907), 131–34.

117. RGIA, f. 796, op. 195, d. 1449 [Kanonizatsiia Pitirima].

118. Ibid., ll. 124 ob.–125.

119. Ibid., ll. 125–125 ob., 126, 126 ob.

120. Ibid., ll. 126 ob.–127 ob.

121. Ibid., ll. 98 ob.–99 ob., ll. 131–37 ob.

122. Sergei Goloshchapov, "Vera v chudesa s tochki zreniia sovremennoi bogoslovskoi nauki," *Vera i razum,* nos. 5–6 (February–March 1912): 661, 663–64, 666, 668, 674–75, 752, 759, 765.

123. V. Vinogradov, "Chudesnyia istseleniia Iisusom Khristom bol'nykh," *Vera i razum,* nos. 1–2 (1913): 27–28, 29, 172, 174–78, 182–83, 184.

124. Archimandrite Evdokim, "O moshchei prepod. Serafima Sarovskago," *Bogoslovskii vestnik* (July–August 1903): 516, 525.

125. "Izvestiia i zametki," *Vera i razum,* no. 14 (July 1903): 441.

126. Sv. Porfirii Amfiteatrov, "Pervaia godovshchina otkrytia sv. moshchei Sviatitelia i Chudotvortsa Ioasafa, Episkopa Belgorodskago," *Kurskiia eparkhial'nyia vedomosti,* no. 7, 22 February 1912, 859.

127. "By the end of the [nineteenth] century, fully one-third of Russia's active monasteries had been founded during precisely this century, most of them during the reign of Alexander II." William Mills Todd III, "Dostoevsky's Russian Monk in Extra-Literary Dialogue: Implicit Polemics in *Russkii vestnik,* 1879–1881," in Robert P. Hughes and Irina Paperno, eds., *Christianity and the Eastern Slavs,* vol. 2, *Russian Culture in Modern Times* (Berkeley: University of California Press, 1994), 125 (*California Slavic Studies,* 17).

128. Krainskii, *Porcha,* 100, 176; M. P. Nikitin, "K voprosu o klikushestve," *Obozrenie psikhiatrii, nevrologii i eksperimental'noi psikhologii,* nos. 9–10 (September–October 1903): 662, 749; Vladimir Ivanovich Iakovenko, *Dushevno-bol'nye moskovskoi gubernii 1900 g.* (Moscow: Moskovskoe gubernskoe zemstvo, 1900), 54.

129. The nineteenth-century ethnographer Sergei Vasil'evich Maksimov recorded two examples of priests refusing to accept the veracity of *klikushestvo* (*Nechistaia sila. Nevedomaia sila,* in Maksimov, *Sobranie sochinenii,* vol. 18 [St. Petersburg: Tov. R. Golike i A. Vil'borg, 1903], 165–66).

130. Father Ioann's reputation became tainted in the revolutionary years 1905–1907 when he supported the reactionary and militant Black Hundreds. The Russian Orthodox Church abroad canonized him in 1964 and the Moscow Patriarchate in 1988. For a scholarly biography of this charismatic priest, see Nadieszda Kizenko, "The Making of a Modern Saint: Ioann of Kronstadt and the Russian People, 1855–1917" (Ph.D. diss., Columbia University, 1995); and Kizenko, "Ioann of Kronstadt and the Reception of Sanctity, 1850–1988," *Russian Review* 57, no. 3 (July 1998): 325–44.

131. For references to exorcising demons from women in the diaries of Ioann of Kronstadt, see Bishop Arsenii [Zhadanovskii], *Vospominaniia* (Moscow: Izd-vo Pravoslavnogo Sviato-Tikhonovskogo Bogoslovskogo Instituta, 1995), 174, 181. For eyewitness accounts, see I. K. Surskii, *Otets Ioann Kronshtadtskii* (rpt., Forestville, Calif.: St. Elias, 1980), 62–64, 131, 187, 191, 260–61, 262–70, 294.

132. Tsentral'nyi gosudarstvennyi arkhiv oktiabrskoi revoliutsii, f. 2219, op. 1, d. 72, l. 2, quoted in and trans. Kizenko "The Making of a Modern Saint," 158.

133. V. M., *Dva dnia v Kronshtadte, iz dnevnika studenta* ([Sergiev Posad]:

Sviato-Troitskaia Sergieva Lavra, 1902), 70, quoted in and trans. by Kizenko, "The Making of a Modern Saint," 171.

134. In his memoirs the atheist Aleksandr Serebrov commented on the pandemonium in the Kronstadt cathedral during one of Father Ioann's public confessions, noting that a *klikusha* appeared the next day when the confessed were taking communion. Aleksandr Serebrov [A. N. Tikhonov], *Vremia i liudi: Vospominaniia, 1898–1905* (Moscow: Moskovskii rabochii, 1960), 44–45.

135. W. Jardine Grisbrooke, ed. and trans., *Spiritual Counsels of Father John of Kronstadt* (London: James Clarke, 1967), 155.

2: PEASANT VIEWS

1. The analysis in the first two paragraphs owes much to the work of Ganath Obeyesekere in his study of possession among Sri Lankan and Sinhalese Buddhists of Ceylon, although I do not share his insistence on Freudian analysis. See Obeyesekere, *Medusa's Hair,* 102, 103; and Obeyesekere, "The Ritual Drama of the *Sanni* Demons: Collective Representations of Disease in Ceylon," *Comparative Studies in Society and History* 11, no. 2 (April 1969): 174–216. For a critique of Obeyesekere's interpretations, see Levy, "Some Comments," 217–26. The notion of redemption comes from the anthropologist Edward L. Schieffelin's analysis of evil spirit sickness among the Bosavic people of Papua New Guinea. Schieffelin also views possession as a ritual drama, choosing to define evil spirit sickness as part of "a traditional drama which had conventionally understood roles, behaviors, and significance as well as performance expectations" ("Evil Spirit Sickness, The Christian Disease: The Innovation of a New Syndrome of Mental Derangement and Redemption in Papua New Guinea," *Culture, Medicine and Psychiatry* 20, no. 1 [March 1996]: 1–39, esp. 6). I am indebted to Professor David Sabean of the University of California, Los Angeles, for suggesting that I explore both Obeyesekere's work and the idea of redemption.

2. Krainskii, *Porcha,* 162.

3. Alan Macfarlane, *Witchcraft in Tudor and Stuart England: A Regional and Comparative Study* (London: Routledge and Kegan Paul, 1970), 3, 103; Clifford Geertz, "Ethos, World View, and the Analysis of Sacred Symbols," in Geertz, *The Interpretation of Cultures: Selected Essays* (New York: Basic Books, 1973), 130–31; Keith Thomas, *Religion and the Decline of Magic* (New York: Charles Scribner's Sons, 1971), 543.

4. Robert Rowland, "'Fantasticall and Devilishe Persons': European Witch-beliefs in Comparative Perspective," in Ankarloo and Henningsen, *Early Modern European Witchcraft,* 165; David Warren Sabean, *Power in the Blood: Popular Culture and Village Discourse in Early Modern Germany* (Cambridge: Cambridge University Press, 1984), 109–10.

5. Out of my database of 260 shriekers for the period between 1820 and 1926, some 149 (129 women and 20 men) are identified with the postemancipation period through 1917. The more than 100 witches and sorcerers from both Russian and Ukrainian areas figure in 80 instances of sorcery described in ethnographic, psychiatric, juridical, and newspaper reports in the postemancipation period. It is impossible to pinpoint the exact number of witches and sorcerers because of the imprecise nature of some descriptions (in five cases) that stipulate

that peasants suspected either "all" the women or only "some" women in a particular village of witchcraft. See Appendixes I and II for the sources upon which these databases are based. All subsequent numerical references in this chapter refer to the postemancipation and pre-1917 data regarding shriekers, witches, and sorcerers.

6. The idea of reintegration into the Christian community comes from Schieffelin, "Evil Spirit Sickness," 30, 28.

7. Obeyesekere, *Medusa's Hair,* 80.

8. The ethnographer G. Popov noted that Russian peasants attributed hernias and abscesses on the face, throat, anus, sexual organs, arms, or legs to the work of sorcerers. The abscesses might very well have been syphilitic chancres (*Russkaia narodno-bytovaia meditsina: Po materialam etnograficheskago biuro kniazia V. N. Tenisheva* [St. Petersburg: Tip. A. S. Suvorina, 1903], 26).

9. Language problems also surfaced in the classroom. In 1905 teachers claimed that Ukrainian students had difficulty comprehending more than half of the materials presented in Russian in the schools of Poltava province (Bohdan Krawchenko, *Social Change and National Consciousness in Twentieth-Century Ukraine* [New York: St. Martin's Press, 1985], 264–65 n. 102; 264 n. 95).

10. Little is known about popular piety among Russian and Ukrainian peasants in general, but especially among those in the Ukrainian countryside. In the medieval period Ukrainians had cultural experiences with possession and shared with Great Russians the saints' lives from the Kievan Monastery of the Caves (Pecherskaia Lavra) of the Kievan Rus' period. Later, in the seventeenth century, the standard Ukrainian Orthodox prayer book, compiled by the theologian Petro Mohyla, contained a service of exorcism. In its late-seventeenth- and early-eighteenth-century phase of Ukrainization, the Russian Orthodox Church adopted that prayer book and continued to use the Mohyla prayers of exorcism in the nineteenth century. See note 49 for further information about these prayers.

11. For a critique of the paradigm of *dvoeverie* or dual faith, see Levin, "*Dvoeverie* and Popular Religion." See also the pioneering work on popular Orthodoxy of Vera Shevzov, "Chapels and the Ecclesial World of Prerevolutionary Russian Peasants," *Slavic Review* 55, no. 3 (Fall 1996): 585–613; Shevzov, "Miracle-Working Icons, Laity, and Authority in the Russian Orthodox Church, 1861–1917," *Russian Review* 58, no. 1 (January 1999): 26–48; Shevzov, "Popular Orthodoxy in Late Imperial Rural Russia," 2 vols. (Ph.D. diss., Yale University, 1994); Kizenko, "The Making of a Modern Saint"; Kizenko, "Ioann of Kronstadt," 325–44; and Christine D. Worobec, "Death Ritual among Russian and Ukrainian Peasants: Linkages between the Living and the Dead," in Stephen P. Frank and Mark D. Steinberg, eds., *Cultures in Flux: Lower-Class Values, Practices, and Resistance in Late Imperial Russia* (Princeton: Princeton University Press, 1994), 11–33.

12. Freeze, "Institutionalizing Piety," 210–49; Freeze, "The Rechristianization of Russia: The Church and Popular Religion, 1750–1850," *Studia Slavica Finlandensia* 7 (1990): 101–36; Freeze, "Subversive Piety," 308–50; Shevzov, "Chapels and the Ecclesial World"; Shevzov, "Miracle-Working Icons"; Shevzov, "Popular Orthodoxy."

13. Mary R. O'Neill, "From 'Popular' to 'Local' Religion: Issues in Early Modern European Religious History," *Religious Studies Review* 12, nos. 3–4 (July–October 1986): 222–23.

14. Veniamin, *Novaia skrizhal'*, 1:54.

15. "The Tale of Savva Grudtsyn," in Serge A. Zenkovsky, ed. and trans., *Medieval Russia's Epics, Chronicles, and Tales*, rev. ed. (New York: E. P. Dutton, 1974), 460.

16. Firsov and Kiseleva, *Byt velikorusskikh krest'ian-zemlepashtsev*, 149.

17. RGIAgM, f. 217, op. 1, d. 94, l. 6 ob.

18. Firsov and Kiseleva, *Byt velikorusskikh krest'ian-zemlepashtsev*, 126.

19. Provincial newspapers regularly reported on unnatural and accidental deaths, including drownings. For example, in Smolensk province, with a rural population of around 1,400,000, there were 15 drownings in October and November 1890 and 41 in July 1894 (*Smolenskii vestnik*, 14 November 1890, 19 December 1890, and 14 August 1894). For the 1897 population figure for Smolensk province, see "Smolenskaia guberniia," in F. A. Brokgaus and I. A. Efron, eds., *Entsiklopedicheskii slovar'* (St. Petersburg, 1907), 60:548.

20. "Derevenskie znakhari v Smolenskoi gubernii," *Smolenskii vestnik*, 30 September 1892.

21. Peasants were made aware of miraculous healings at holy springs by church publications. The Tikhonova Hermitage near Kaluga, for example, sold books devoted to the subject. Lakhtin, *Besooderzhimost'*, 21. Listings of miraculous cures were also regular features of diocesan newspapers and religious periodicals for the laity such as *Russkii palomnik*.

22. D. N. Ushakov, "Materialy po narodnym verovaniiam velikorusov," *Etnograficheskoe obozrenie* 8, nos. 2–3 (1896); reprinted in V. I. Dal', *O poveriiakh, sueveriiakh i predrassudkakh russkogo naroda; Materialy po russkoi demonologii (Iz etnograficheskikh rabot); Russkie bylichki, byval'shchiny i skazki o mifologicheskikh personazhakh (iz fol'klornykh sbornikov)* (Moscow: Terra, Knizhnaia lavka, 1997), 152–53.

23. "Istselenie oderzhimoi: Razskaz sviashcheniia. (Zhurnal *Voskresenie*, no. 16)," *Rebus* 12, no. 45 (7 November 1893): 429–30.

24. Novichkova, *Russkii demonologicheskii slovar'*, 47, 195; E. I. Itkina, comp., *Russkii risovannyi lubok kontsa XVIII–nachala XX veka: Iz sobraniia Gosudarstvennogo Istoricheskogo muzeia Moskva* (Moscow: Russkaia kniga, 1992), 84, plate 67.

25. Novichkova, *Russkii demonologicheskii slovar'*, 293.

26. L. Vesin, "Narodnyi samosud nad koldunami. (K istorii narodnykh obychaev)," *Severnyi vestnik* 7, no. 9 (September 1892), pt. 2:66.

27. Caciola, "Discerning Spirits," 91.

28. Krainskii, *Porcha*, 101–3; Lakhtin, *Besooderzhimost'*, 18.

29. Kallistos Ware and Mother Mary, trans., *The Festal Menaion* (London: Faber and Faber, 1969), 357. My emphasis.

30. Novichkova, *Russkii demonologicheskii slovar'*, 278, 281.

31. Novichkova, *Russkii demonologicheskii slovar'*, 281; S. S. Averintsev, A. N. Meshkov, and Iu. N. Popov, eds., *Khristianstvo: Entsiklopedicheskii slovar'* (Moscow: Nauchnoe izdatel'stvo "Bol'shaia Rossiiskaia entsiklopediia," 1993), 1:291.

32. M. Zabylin, *Russkii narod: Ego obychai, obriady, predaniia, sueveriia i poeziia* (Moscow: M. Berezin, 1880), 241.

33. This description of Lent comes from Likhachev, Panchenko, and Popyrko, *Smekh v drevnei Rusi*, 195.

34. Ware and Mother Mary, trans., *The Lenten Triodion,* 117, 119, 121, 142, 143, 144.

35. Aleksandr Evgenievich Burtsev, *Nechistaia i nevedomaia v skazkakh, razskazakh i legendakh russkago naroda* (Petrograd: Tipografiia S. Samoilova, 1915), 1:54.

36. *Smolenskii vestnik,* 12 October 1890, 3.

37. Timothy Ware, *The Orthodox Church* (Harmondsworth, Eng.: Penguin, 1963), 286–89.

38. Translated in H. Hamilton Maughan, *The Liturgy of the Eastern Orthodox Church* (London: Faith Press, 1916), 53.

39. Krainskii, *Porcha,* 178–79. In the early 1890s Elena Akimova Ivanova, a twenty-nine-year-old migrant peasant living in Moscow, sought spiritual help for her postpartum depression from the clerics at the Panteleimon Chapel. After several visits there, she became convinced that she was possessed. When she attempted to commit suicide, her husband took her to the Aleksandrovskaia Hospital on 26 September 1892. Ivanova was subsequently transferred to the Preobrazhenskaia Hospital for the Insane (RGIAgM, f. 217, op. 1, d. 1338, ll. 17–20). For another example of a woman seeking spiritual help at the Panteleimon Chapel, but who was later incarcerated in the Preobrazhenskaia Hospital, see d. 2883, ll. 26–27 ob.

40. *Smolenskii vestnik,* 12 October 1890, 3.

41. V. Sanin, *Na veselykh gorakh: Ocherki torzhestvennykh molebstvii staroobriadtsev, illiustrirovannye risunkami s natury khudozhnika Vl. A. Kuznetsova i otchety o podgotovitel'nykh trudakh k Vserossiiskomu s"ezdu staroobriadtsev chasovennago soglasiia* (Ekaterinburg: Tipografiia gazety *Ural'skii krai,* 1910), 28.

42. The anthropologist Lesley A. Sharp makes such an observation in reference to community reactions to individuals possessed by the evil spirits, *njarinintsy,* in Madagascar (*The Possessed and the Dispossessed: Spirits, Identity, and Power in a Madagascar Migrant Town* [Berkeley: University of California Press, 1993], 241).

43. The testimony constituted part of the Holy Synod's verification of the Tambov woman's miraculous cure at the grave of Tikhon of Zadonsk (Sergievskii, *Sviatitel' Tikhon,* 182–83).

44. A woman's amazing strength was also a characteristic of possession during the early modern Western European witchcraft era (Sarah Ferber, "Charcot's Demons: Retrospective Medicine and Historical Diagnosis in the Writings of the Salpêtrière School," in Marijke Gijswijt-Hofstra, Hilary Marland, and Hans de Waardt, eds., *Illness and Healing Alternatives in Western Europe,* [London: Routledge, 1997]: 131).

45. Schieffelin, "Evil Spirit Sickness," 22.

46. Quoted in Blackmore, *The Doctrine of the Russian Church,* 223 n; my emphasis. Feodosius Pecherskii, the eleventh-century founder of the Monastery of the Caves in Kiev, also characterized possessed individuals as suffering involuntarily in contrast to drunkards who bore responsibility for their actions (G. V. Morozov, D. R. Lumts, and N. I. Felinskaia, *Osnovnye etapy razvitiia otechestvennoi sudebnoi psikhiatrii* [Moscow, 1976], 6, cited in Julie Vail Brown, "The Professionalization of Russian Psychiatry: 1857–1911" [Ph.D. diss., University of Pennsylvania, 1981], 88 n).

47. Lakhtin, *Besooderzhimost',* 17.

48. Maksimov, *Nechistaia sila,* 161.

49. According to the medical ethnographer G. I. Popov, the reading of prayers occurred in such disparate places as Dorogobuzh district, Smolensk province; Melenki and Iur'ev districts, Vladimir province; Insar district, Penza province; Rostov district, Iaroslavl' province; Egor'evsk district, Riazan province; Makar'ev district, Kostroma province; and Cherepovets district, Novgorod province. Prayers of exorcisms came from the *Bolshoi Trebnik,* the Mohyla *Trebnik,* and various manuscripts. Popov even reproduces a few examples of prayers from the *Bolshoi Trebnik* and Mohyla *Trebnik* (*Russkaia narodno-bytovaia meditsina,* 268, 392–95). The nineteenth- and early-twentieth-century scholar A. I. Almazov notes that in the seventeenth-century Petro Mohyla *Trebnik,* the service of exorcism includes (in the following order) Psalms 142, 22, and 27; a series of prayers to God, the Mother of God, and saints; Psalm 91; and "*Kanon molebnyi k Gospodu nashemu Isusu Khristu . . . k vsem sviatym, o izbavlenii neduzhnago ot oburevaniia besovskago.*" The latter is followed by a reading from Mark 26:14–17, a prayer to Christ, Psalm 67, and a series of psalms, prayers, incantations, and readings from the Gospels (Almazov, *Chin nad besnovatym. [Pamiatnik grecheskoi pis'mennosti XVII v.]* [Odessa: Ekonomicheskaia tipografiia, 1901], 1, 35–40). The eighteenth-century monk Paisii Velichkovskii felt that the Jesus prayer was the best weapon with which to fight demons (Velichkovskii, "O tom, chtoby terpet' napraslinu i vsiakoe ukorenie i dosazhdenie" and "O tom, chego osobenno boiatsia besy," in Tomchenko, *Zhitiia i tvoreniia russkikh sviatykh,* 273, 281).

50. *Smolenskii vestnik,* 30 September 1892.

51. Lakhtin, *Besooderzhimost',* 18.

52. Popov, *Russkaia narodno-bytovaia meditsina,* 269.

53. Popov, *Russkaia narodno-bytovaia meditsina,* 387, 389; Maksimov, *Nechistaia sila,* 163. For descriptions of *opakhivanie* or *zapakhivanie,* see Maksimov, *Nechistaia sila,* 268–71; L. S. Belogrits-Kotliarevskii, "Mifologicheskoe znachenie nekotorykh prestuplenii, sovershaemykh po sueveriiu," *Istoricheskii vestnik* 33 (July 1888): 106–9; P. Ivanov, "Tolki naroda ob urozhae, voine i chume," *Etnograficheskoe obozrenie* 13, no. 3 (1901): 134; "K voprosu ob opakhivanii," *Etnograficheskoe obozrenie* 22, nos. 3–4 (1910): 175–78; and "Obriad opakhivan'ia," *Chernigovskiia eparkhial'nyia izvestiia,* no. 18, 1876, 515–18.

54. Maksimov, *Nechistaia sila,* 164, 163; Popov, *Russkaia narodno-bytovaia meditsina,* 391, 387.

55. Nikitin, "K voprosu o klikushestve," 750; Popov, *Russkaia narodno-bytovaia meditsina,* 387–88.

56. Ponomarev, "Ocherki narodnago prava. Koldovstvo," *Severnyi vestnik,* no. 5 (1895): 82, cited in Krainskii, *Porcha,* 86–87; Popov, *Russkaia narodno-bytovaia meditsina,* 384, 377. Other areas where peasants used horse collars to stop the fits of shriekers include Viazniki, Melenki, and Shuia districts, Vladimir province; Dorogobuzh, Iukhnov, and Gzhatsk districts, Smolensk province; Griazovets district, Vologda province; Vetluga district, Kostroma province; and Zaraisk district, Riazan province (Popov, *Russkaia narodno-bytovaia meditsina,* 388).

57. Ushakov, "Materialy," 154.

58. These words are from the Orthodox *Festal Menaion* and the 14 September celebration of "the Universal Exaltation of the Precious and Life-Giving

Cross." The special prayers contain numerous references to the cross as an "adversary of demons" (Ware and Mother Mary, trans., *The Festal Menaion,* 138, 139, 140, 147, 152).

59. In rare instances peasants also used horse collars to identify witches. For example, at the end of the nineteenth century in the Perm village of Ust'-Mullianka, male peasants, hoping to pinpoint the woman responsible for making a bull ill, forced all the women in the settlement to climb through such a collar (A. A. Levenstim, "Sueverie v ego otnoshenii k ugolovnomu pravu," *Zhurnal Ministerstva iustitsii,* no. 1 [January 1897]: 205). For references to peasants using harnesses to punish petty thieves and parents who had not protected their daughters' premarital chastity, see E. I. Iakushkin, *Obychnoe pravo: Materialy dlia bibliografii obychnago prava,* vol. 1 (Iaroslavl', 1875), xxvii, xxxviii; Christine D. Worobec, *Peasant Russia: Family and Community in Post-Emancipation Russia* (Princeton: Princeton University Press, 1991), 171; and Worobec, "Horse Thieves," 290.

60. Ponomarev, "Ocherki," 82, cited in Krainskii, *Porcha,* 87; Popov, *Russkaia narodno-bytovaia meditsina,* 384.

61. D. A. Rovinskii, *Russkie narodnye kartinki,* 5 vols. and 4 folios (St. Petersburg, 1881–1893), no. 721, cited in and trans. Dianne Ecklund Farrell, "Popular Prints in the Cultural History of Eighteenth-Century Russia" (Ph.D. diss., University of Wisconsin, 1980), 275.

62. Ponomarev, "Ocherki," 82, cited in Krainskii, *Porcha,* 85, 86; Maksimov, *Nechistaia sila,* 16; Popov, *Russkaia narodno-bytovaia meditsina,* 384; Lakhtin, *Besooderzhimost',* 20.

63. Krainski, *Porcha,* 114, 120.

64. Schieffelin, "Evil Spirit Sickness," 30.

65. Krainskii, *Porcha,* 101–3.

66. Ibid., 135, 149.

67. Nikitin, "K voprosu o klikushestve," 758–59.

68. RGIAgM, f. 203, op. 371, g. 1886–1887, d. 8, ll. 1–2, 5, quoted in and discussed by Jeffrey Burds, "A Culture of Denunciation: Peasant Labor Migration and Religious Anathematization in Rural Russia, 1860–1905," *Journal of Modern History* 68, no. 4 (December 1996): 786–818. The psychiatrist N. V. Krainskii noted that police officers in Moscow at the Panteleimon Chapel were obliged to take *klikushi* to a hospital, but that lower-ranked police were generally respectful of shriekers; indeed, he himself saw an elderly gendarme escort a shrieker through the crowds so she could get close to the icons. Krainskii, *Porcha,* 179.

69. Maksimov, *Nechistaia sila,* 165–66.

70. Krainskii, *Porcha,* 138, 163.

71. Quoted in Surskii, *Otets Ioann Kronshtadtskii,* 268–69.

72. For a general, if brief, discussion of pilgrimages in the life of Russian peasants, see M. M. Gromyko, *Mir russkoi derevni* (Moscow: Molodaia Gvardiia, 1991), 116–20.

73. Publication of saints' portraits in miniature also spread word of a holy person's miraculous powers. Even though Serafim of Sarov was not canonized until 1903, tens of thousands of copies of depictions of the deceased monk were distributed in the final decades of the nineteenth century, thereby announcing the church's recognition of his holiness. The Russian scholar B. V. Sapunov notes that images of saints in the second half of the nineteenth century were gentler

than those of the punishing saints of the medieval period. They were portrayed as protectors and helpers of "suffering humanity" ("Nekotorye siuzhety russkoi ikonopisi i ikh traktovka v poreformennoe vremia," in *Kul'tura i iskusstvo Rossii XIX veka: Novye materialy i issledovaniia: Sbornik statei,* ed. G. A. Printseva [Leningrad: Iskusstvo, 1985], 147).

74. Robert L. Nichols, "The Icon and the Machine in Russia's Religious Renaissance, 1900–1909," in William C. Brumfield and Milos M. Velimirovic, eds., *Christianity and the Arts in Russia* (Cambridge: Cambridge University Press, 1991), 136.

75. The reporter, writing under the pseudonym "Village Dweller," disapproved of the religious celebration. Reflecting upon the immorality of the practice of naked men and half-dressed women bathing in a lake in remembrance of St. Vladimir's christianization of Rus', he pointed to the women and men as "having lost all shame, or more correctly, being unable in their religious passion to feel shame, as well as the dangers of drinking unsanitary lake water and forcing children into the cold water" (*Smolenskii vestnik,* 12 June 1891).

76. V. Grachev, "Prazdnik vozneseniia Gospodnia v gorode Smolenske," *Smolenskie gubernskie vedomosti,* 26 May 1894.

77. Obeyesekere, *Medusa's Hair,* 2.

78. *Chernigovskiia eparkhial'nyia izvestiia,* supplement and unofficial section, 36, no. 20, 15 October 1896, 665.

79. *Zhitie, chudesa i istseleniia Prepodobnago Serafima,* 132.

80. Sergievskii, *Sviatitel' Tikhon,* 183.

81. Nikitin, "K voprosu o klikushestve," 662.

82. Krainskii, *Porcha,* 102.

83. Rossiiskii etnograficheskii muzei (hereafter cited as REM), Otdel pis'mennykh istochnikov, f.7, op. 1, d. 493, ll. 12–13.

84. Krainskii, *Porcha,* 109–10.

85. Ibid., 144.

86. Surskii, *Otets Ioann Kronshtadtskii,* 263.

87. *Sudebnyi vestnik* 5, no. 66 (10 March 1870): 1. The identification of crossroads with the devil is a Christian concept. The exorcism of John Chrysostom refers to the meeting of three roads as one of many locations where devils hid (Stewart, *Demons and the Devil,* 217).

88. Caciola, "Discerning Spirits," 295, 317.

89. Briggs, *Witches and Neighbors,* 76.

90. Rowland assesses European witchcraft as having the first two functions, subsuming individuals' use of cultural norms to define themselves as witches under the second. I have separated out this phenomenon as it reverses the normal pattern of the strong avenging themselves on the weak to a situation where the weak were sometimes able to get the better of their wealthier neighbors (Rowland, "'Fantasticall and Devilishe Persons,'" 169–70).

91. Briggs, *Witches and Neighbors,* 19, 5. For other discussions of witchcraft as the inversion of neighborliness, see Annabel Gregory, "Witchcraft, Politics and 'Good Neighbourhood' in Early Seventeenth-Century Rye," *Past and Present* 133 (November 1991): 31–66; and Anne Reiber DeWindt, "Witchcraft and Conflicting Visions of the Ideal Village Community," *Journal of British Studies* 34, no. 4 (October 1995): 427–63.

92. Rowland, "'Fantasticall and Devilishe Persons,'" 169.

93. Briggs, *Witches and Neighbors,* 408.

94. Obeyesekere, *Medusa's Hair,* 139.

95. Firsov and Kiseleva, *Byt velikorusskikh krest'ian-zemlepashtsev,* 131, 132.

96. Some of the more important works on the early modern European witchcraze that investigate the relationship between elite and popular culture and the elite's formulation of the demonic include Ankarloo and Henningsen, *Early Modern European Witchcraft;* Anne Llewellyn Barstow, *Witchcraze: A New History of the European Witch Hunts* (San Francisco: Pandora, 1994); Clark, *Thinking with Demons;* Richard Kieckhefer, *European Witch Trials: Their Foundations in Popular and Learned Culture* (Berkeley: University of California Press, 1976); Klaits, *Servants of Satan;* Christina Larner, *Enemies of God: The Witch-hunt in Scotland* (London: Chatoo and Windus, 1981); Macfarlane, *Witchcraft in Tudor and Stuart England;* and Thomas, *Religion.*

97. Alan Harwood, *Witchcraft, Sorcery, and Social Categories among the Safwa* (London: Published for the International African Institute by the Oxford University Press, 1980), xv; John Middleton and E. H. Winter, *Witchcraft and Sorcery in East Africa* (London: Routledge and Kegan Paul, 1963), 3; E. E. Evans-Pritchard, *Witchcraft, Oracles, and Magic among the Azande* (Oxford: Clarendon Press, 1937), 9–10.

98. Joseph L. Conrad, "Russian Ritual Incantations: Tradition, Diversity, and Continuity," *Slavic and East European Journal* 33, no. 3 (1989): 423.

99. P. V. Ivanov, "Narodnye razskazy o ved'makh i upyriakh. (Materialy dlia kharakteristiki mirosozertsaniia krest'ianskago naseleniia Kupianskago uezda)," *Sbornik Khar'kovskago istoriko-filologicheskago obshchestva* 3 (1891): 156–57. In Kupiansk district, Khar'kov province, both witches and healers dabbled in fortune-telling, for which the six of spades was an important card. Ivanov, "Narodnye razskazy," 160–61. Peasants in the village Popovka, Gorodishchensk district, Khar'kov province, identified two male sorcerers in their midst, claiming that they were also healers (E. I. Kobelev, "Sl. Popovka," *Khar'kovskii sbornik* 12 [1898], pt. 2:120).

100. V. Mansikka, "Predstaviteli zlogo nachala v russkikh zagovorakh," *Zhivaia starina* 18, no. 4 (1909): 3–7.

101. Vesin, "Narodnyi samosud," 69.

102. Ivanov, "Narodnye razskazy," 170.

103. M. N. Parunov, *Leshie, rusalki, kolduny, ved'my i oborotni: Narodnye predrazsudki i sueveriia* (St. Petersburg: Tip. K. Plotnikova, 1873), 22. In Western Europe magical ointments associated with witches could also contain herbs such as nightshade, aconite, and hemlock, in addition to blood, bones, and baby's fat (Robert D. Anderson, "The History of Witchcraft: A Review with Some Psychiatric Comments," *American Journal of Psychiatry* 126 [June 1970]: 1732–1733).

104. V. P. Makhlaiuk, *Lekarstvennye rasteniia v narodnoi meditsine* (Moscow: Niva Rossii, 1992), 36–37, 112, 372; Eve Levin, "Childbirth in Pre-Petrine Russia," in Clements, Engel, and Worobec, *Russia's Women,* 55. The narcotic and hallucinogenic properties of the plants associated with the witch's salve may also indicate that peasants occasionally took these substances for recreational purposes. A Belarusian tale from the late 1860s described witches snorting a substance that gave them the capacity to fly to Bald Mountain in Kiev (Iu. F. Krachkovskii, "Byt

zapadno-russkago selianina," *Chteniia v Imperatorskom obshchestve istorii i drevnostei rossiiskikh pri Moskovskom universitete,* bk. 4 [October–December 1873], pt. 5: 127–28).

105. Linda J. Ivanits, *Russian Folk Belief* (Armonk, N.Y.: M.E. Sharpe, 1989), 200–1; V. Miloradovich, "Ukrains'kaia ved'ma. (Ocherk)," *Kievskaia starina* (February 1901): 232; Iv. Ben'kovskii, "Smert', pogrebenie i zagrobnaia zhizn' po poniatiiam i verovaniiu naroda," *Kievskaia starina* (September 1896): 243; N. A. Nikitina, "K voprosu o russkikh koldunakh," *Sbornik Muzeia antropologii i etnografii* 7 (1928): 306–7.

106. For a discussion of medieval Russian beliefs in witchcraft that were distinctive from Western European beliefs, see Russell Zguta, "Was There a Witch Craze in Muscovite Russia?" *Southern Folklore Quarterly* 41 (1977): 119–28; Zguta, "Witchcraft Trials in Seventeenth Century Russia," *American Historical Review* 82 (1977): 1187–1207; and Kivelson, "Through the Prism of Witchcraft," 74–94.

107. Cited in S. V. Maksimov, *God na severe* (1864; rpt., Archangel: Severo-Zapadnoe knizhnoe izdatel'stvo, 1984), 481. Chukharev was sentenced to 35 lashes with the knout and ordered to make a public ecclesiastical penance. See also M. A. Orlov, *Istoriia snoshenii cheloveka s d'iavolom* (1904; rpt., Moscow: Respublika, 1992), 225–26; and Russell Zguta, "Witchcraft and Medicine in Pre-Petrine Russia," *Russian Review* 37, no. 4 (October 1978): 438–48.

108. Nikitina, "K voprosu o russkikh koldunakh," 307.

109. Ibid., 308.

110. Ivanov, "Narodnye razskazy," 168. See also ibid., 170, 172, for other stories of this type. The identification of a mill as a place for clandestine meetings because of its safe distance from settlements comes from Carlo Ginzburg, *The Cheese and the Worms: The Cosmos of a Sixteenth-Century Miller,* trans. John and Anne Tedeschi (Baltimore: Johns Hopkins University Press, 1992), 120.

111. Jeffrey Brooks, *When Russia Learned to Read: Literacy and Popular Literature, 1861–1917* (Princeton: Princeton University Press, 1985), 246–59; Patrick B. Mullen, "Modern Legend and Rumor Theory," *Journal of the Folklore Institute* 9, nos. 2–3 (1972): 100–1, cited in Anthony J. Amato, an early draft of "In the Wild Mountains: Idiom, Economy, and Ideology among the Hutsuls, 1849 to 1939" (Ph.D. diss., Indiana University, 1998), chap. 7.

112. Recorded in V. N. Dobrovol'skii, *Smolenskii etnograficheskii sbornik,* vol. 1 (St. Petersburg: Tipografiia E. Evdokimova, 1891), in *Zapiski Imperatorskago russkago geograficheskago obshchestva po otdeleniiu etnografii,* 20:133. Other stories normally identified the place of the witches' sabbath as Bald Mountain in Kiev. A. N. Afanas'ev, *Poeticheskiia vozzreniia slavian na prirodu: Opyt sravnitel'nago izucheniia slavianskikh predanii i verovanii, v sviazi s mificheskimi skazaniiami drugikh rodstvennykh narodov* (1865–1869; rpt., The Hague: Mouton, 1970), 1:471; Dobrovol'skii, *Smolenskii etnograficheskii sbornik,* 133–35; Ivanov, "Narodnye razskazy," 169, 175; Krachkovskii, "Byt zapadno-russkago selianina," 126, 127–28; Zabylin, *Russkii narod,* 239. Ukrainian peasants in the Kupiansk district village of Tarasovka were less specific in their geographical placement of the witches' sabbath, noting that it took place in "some kind of witches' church" in Kiev. Ivanov, "Narodnye razskazy," 215. Like their Russian and Ukrainian counterparts, Hungarian peasants believed that witches gathered on specific mountains or hills such as the Gellert Hill in Buda, or the Tokaj (Tekla Dömötör, *Hungarian Folk Beliefs* [Bloomington: Indiana University Press, 1982], 67).

113. Ivanov, "Narodnye razskazy," 170; I. Trusevich, "Znakhari, ved'my i rusalki. (Predaniia, poveriia, poslovitsy i pesni zhitelei Poles'ia)," *Kievlianin,* no. 71, 19 June 1865.

114. Miloradovich, "Ukrains'kaia ved'ma," 222.

115. Volodymyr Hnatiuk, comp., *Znadoby do ukrains'koi demonol'ohii,* vol. 2, no. 2, in *Etnohrafichnyi zbirnyk* 34 (1912): xviii. For examples and discussion of these tales, see V. Miloradovich, "Zametki o malorusskoi demonologii," *Kievskaia starina* (September 1899): 380–400; P. M. Shinkarev, "Sl. Belo-Kurakino," *Khar'kovskii sbornik* 9 (1895), pt. 2:272–73; and P. Marusov, "Sl. Kaban'e," *Khar'kovskii sbornik* 7 (1893): 434.

116. For a similar belief among contemporary Sri Lankans, see Obeyesekere, *Medusa's Hair,* 139.

117. Maksimov, *Nechistaia sila,* 24.

118. For an in-depth discussion of religious anathematization of migrant workers within the Moscow dioceses, see Burds, "Culture of Denunciation," 786–818, esp. 787 for the quote.

119. The gender ratios for witches identified in both the Russian and Ukrainian provinces for the postemancipation period are imprecise because of the lack of information for five cases in which "several" women, sometimes all the women of a village, were suspected of being witches. The data for sixteenth- and seventeenth-century Europe and Muscovy are derived from Kivelson, "Through the Prism of Witchcraft," in Clements, Engel, and Worobec, *Russia's Women,* 74–75. Robin Briggs notes that men constituted between 20 and 25 percent of those charged with witchcraft in early Modern Europe, with the exception of significant regions in France where they constituted a majority (*Witches and Neighbors,* 22).

120. I borrowed the designation "genealogical freaks" from Thomas, *Religion,* 200.

121. Ushakov, "Materialy," 166.

122. A. Kolchin, "Verovaniia krest'ian Tul'skoi gubernii," *Etnograficheskoe obozrenie* 11, no. 3 (1899): 35.

123. Hnatiuk, *Znadoby do ukrains'koi demonol'ohii,* xiv; Natalie Kononenko, review of *The Bathhouse at Midnight: An Historical Survey of Magic and Divination in Russia,* by W. F. Ryan, *Russian Review* 59, no. 3 (July 2000): 455. By contrast, in seventeenth-century England, seventh sons, seventh sons of seventh sons, and sometimes seventh daughters enjoyed the reputation of being healers by touch (Thomas, *Religion,* 200–2).

124. Klaits, *Servants of Satan,* 21.

125. Hnatiuk, *Znadoby do ukrains'koi demonol'ohii,* xiv; Ivanov, "Narodnye razskazy," 164; Kolchin, "Verovaniia krest'ian," 35. The image of witches with tails was also recorded in Vladimir district, Vladimir province (Firsov and Kiseleva, *Byt velikorusskikh krest'ian-zemlepashtsev,* 129). Ukrainian peasants in Khar'kov province stressed the animal-like nature of female witches, distinguishing them from humans because of the black strip of hair on their backs that stretched from the neck to the waist. See Ivanov, "Narodnye razskazy," 64; and Miloradovich, "Ukrains'kaia ved'ma," 218.

126. Maksimov, *Nechistaia sila,* 152–53.

127. A point that Keith Thomas makes in regard to witchcraft cases in sixteenth- and seventeenth-century England in *Religion,* 551.

128. P. A. Tulub, "Sueverie i prestuplenie. (Iz vospominanii mirovogo sud'i)," *Istoricheskii vestnik,* no. 3 (March 1901): 1086–90.

129. This information came from a parish priest (Bernard Pares, *Russia and Reform* [London, 1907], 116). I thank Professor Stephen Frank for this reference.

130. Joanna Hubbs, *Mother Russia: The Feminine Myth in Russian Culture* (Bloomington: Indiana University Press, 1988), 39; Andreas Johns, "Baba Iaga and the Russian Mother," *Slavic and East European Journal* 42, no. 1 (1998): 29.

131. For an example, see Novichkova, *Russkii demonologicheskii slovar',* 42.

132. The tale is translated in full in Ivanits, *Russian Folk Belief,* 194–95. For the original Russian version, see A. I. Ivanov, "Verovaniia krest'ian Orlovskoi gub.," *Etnograficheskoe obozrenie* 12, no. 4 (1901): 98.

133. Nikitina, "K voprosu o russkikh koldunakh," 309. In the village Gusinka in Kupiansk district, Khar'kov province, Ukrainian peasants at the end of the nineteenth century claimed that an individual could become a witch by climbing into the carcass of a dead horse or cow (Ivanov, "Narodnye razskazy," 170–71).

134. Ukrainian peasants identified a witch as having a milk pail and sometimes a strainer on her head. The word for milk pail, *doinka,* is close to the word *doinki,* for udder or teats, and thus has sexual connotations.

135. Vesin, "Narodnyi samosud," 118.

136. Ivanov, "Narodnye razskazy," 162–64; G. A. Kalashnikov and A. M. Kalashnikov, "Sl. Nikol'skoe," *Khar'kovskii sbornik* 8 (1894), pt. 2:288; Marusov, "Sl. Kaban'e," 449; Maksimov, *Nechistaia sila,* 147.

137. Translated in Ivanits, *Russian Folk Belief,* 200.

138. Thomas, *Religion,* 568.

139. Barstow, *Witchcraze,* 29.

140. Johns, "Baba Iaga," 30.

141. In a 1926 epidemic of demon possession at a wedding in industrial Bronnitsy uezd, Moscow province, suspicions of sorcery fell on a healer who was homosexual (N. P. Brukhanskii, "K voprosu o psikhicheskoi zarazitel'nosti. [Sluchai psikhicheskoi epidemii v Moskovskoi gub. v 1926 g.]," *Obozrenie psikhiatrii, nevrologii i refleksologii,* nos. 4–5 [1926]: 279, 281–82).

142. Vesin, "Narodnyi samosud," 62–63; the reference to ergot may be found in Novichkova, *Russkii demonologicheskii slovar',* 254. The knots that sorcerers and witches made in grain were also called *zakrutki* or *kukli.* According to Ukrainian peasants, witches made *zakruty* at dawn by twisting the top of grain stalks into a knot and pouring ashes, salt, earth from a grave, egg yolk, grain, and coal into it. Then they would break the stalks in half and knead them down through the roots, leaving them woven through the earth. Should peasants mistakenly harvest the *zakrutki,* they would begin to ache all over or die (Miloradovich, "Ukrainskaia ved'ma," 224). Russian and Ukrainian peasants often asked priests to say special prayers over grain that they believed had been tampered with in this way by sorcerers and witches. By 1892, however, villagers of Porech'e district, Smolensk province, had dispensed with the priest's services and were simply leaving the spoiled knotted grain uncut. See *Smolenskii vestnik,* 8 July 1892; and "Zakrutki," *Kievskiia eparkhial'nyia vedomosti,* no. 33, 15 August 1879, 9–10.

143. For examples of disinterment of deceased witches, see D. K. Zelenin, "K voprosu o rusalkakh. (Kult pokoinikov, umershikh neestvestvennoiu smert'iu,

u russkikh i u finnov)," *Kievskaia starina,* nos. 3–4 (1911): 383–86, 390–91; and Zelenin, *Ocherki russkoi mifologii,* vol. 1, *Umershie neestestvennoiu smert'iu i rusalki* (Petrograd: Tip. A. V. Orlova, 1916), 66–73, 81–82. The ethnographer P. V. Ivanov noted that by the end of the nineteenth century, peasants in Kupiansk district, Khar'kov province, less frequently attributed drought to the actions of witches ("Narodnye razskazy," 214). During an 1893 drought peasants of the village Novovladimirovka, Kherson province, dunked Aleksandra Loposhchenkova—whom they suspected of being a witch—into a pond three times, threw her in a hole, and poured water on her (*Smolenskii vestnik,* 23 September 1893, also cited in A. I. Kirpichnikov, "Ocherki po mifologii XIX veka," *Etnograficheskoe obozrenie* 6, no. 4 [1894]: 3–4). For other examples of the swimming of witches in nineteenth-century Ukraine, see Russell Zguta, "The Ordeal by Water (Swimming of Witches) in the East Slavic World," *Slavic Review* 36, no. 2 (June 1977): 228–29.

144. Vesin, "Narodnyi samosud," 76–77.

145. REM, f. 7, op. 1, d. 493, l. 16; S. N. Isaevich, "Eshche raskazets o vovkulakakh i charovnikakh," *Kievskaia starina* 12 (1883): 700.

146. Nikitin, "K voprosu o klikushestve," 750–52.

147. Vesin, "Narodnyi samosud," 66; Brukhanskii, "K voprosu," 280.

148. Nikitin, "K voprosu o klikushestve," 750–52.

149. I. Iakovenko, "Epidemiia istericheskikh sudorog v Podol'skom uezde, Moskovskoi gub.," *Vestnik obshchestvennoi gigieny, sudebnoi i prakticheskoi meditsiny* 25, no. 3 (March 1895): 95, 98, 99–106.

150. E. A. Genik, "Vtoraia epidemiia istericheskikh sudorog v Podol'skom uezde, Moskovskoi gubernii," *Nevrologicheskii vestnik* 6, no. 4 (1898): 146–49, 152–54.

151. Kirpichnikov, "Ocherki," 10.

152. For an overview of the debate, see Stephen L. Hoch, "On Good Numbers and Bad: Malthus, Population Trends and Peasant Standard of Living in Late Imperial Russia," *Slavic Review* 53, no. 1 (Spring 1994): 42–75.

153. Cited in Joseph Bradley, *Muzhik and Muscovite: Urbanization in Late Imperial Russia* (Berkeley: University of California Press, 1985), 301. For a discussion of government and philanthropists' programs to deal with unemployment and underemployment, see Adele Lindenmeyr, "Charity and the Problem of Unemployment: Industrial Homes in Late Imperial Russia," *Russian Review* 45, no. 1 (January 1986): 1–22; and Lindenmeyr, *Poverty Is Not a Vice: Charity, Society, and the State in Imperial Russia* (Princeton: Princeton University Press, 1996), esp. chaps. 8 and 9.

154. Gromyko, *Mir russkoi derevni,* 88.

155. Macfarlane, *Witchcraft in Tudor and Stuart England,* 196. For other discussions of the interplay between guilt feelings and witchcraft accusations in Tudor and Stuart England and nineteenth-century France, see Thomas, *Religion,* 557–58; and Judith Devlin, *The Superstitious Mind: French Peasants and the Supernatural in the Nineteenth Century* (New Haven: Yale University Press, 1987), 108, 124.

156. For a discussion of forms of mutual aid among Russian peasants, see Gromyko, *Mir russkoi derevni,* 73–85.

157. Krainskii, *Porcha,* 77–78; Vesin, "Narodnyi samosud," 64–66; Stephen P. Frank, "Popular Justice, Community, and Culture among the Russian Peasantry, 1870–1900," in *The World of the Russian Peasant: Post-Emancipation*

Culture and Society, ed. Ben Eklof and Stephen P. Frank (Boston: Unwin Hyman, 1990), 133–34.

158. The Moscow circuit court sentenced six peasants to four years' hard labor and three (including two women) to two months in jail for murdering Dar'ia Vasil'eva. The court subsequently appealed to Nicholas II to commute the hard labor sentences to one year in jail (*Smolenskii vestnik,* 11 October 1892).

159. Vesin, "Narodnyi samosud," 69–72.

160. Krainskii, *Porcha,* 101–3, 124, 131, 135, 137–38, 148–50, 155–56.

161. Based on biographical descriptions of the persons who suffered from possession in the Ashchepkovo epidemic in Krainskii, *Porcha,* 121–57, 213.

162. Ibid., 213.

163. Iakobii, "Religiozno-psikhicheskiia epidemiia," 738.

164. Jeffrey Burds, *Peasant Dreams and Market Politics: Labor, Migration, and the Russian Village, 1861–1905* (Pittsburgh: University of Pittsburgh Press, 1998), 23.

165. Accusations of witchcraft involving household strife date back to the medieval period (Kivelson, "Patrolling the Boundaries," 302–23).

166. Krainskii, *Porcha,* 87–89.

167. Burtsev, *Nechistaia i nevedomaia sila,* 15; Ivanov, "Narodnye razskazy," 165–67.

168. In 1881 Riazan peasants of Ranenburg district attacked the alleged witch Arina only after she refused to give them a bit of her blood to reverse the spell she had placed on the village elder's possessed wife. They cut her fingers to extract blood but left her alive. Vesin, "Narodnyi samosud," 77–78.

169. Kivelson, "Patrolling the Boundaries," 304–5.

3: LITERARY AND ETHNOGRAPHIC PORTRAYALS

1. Paraphrase of Dostoevsky's comments, quoted in Cathy Frierson, *Peasant Icons: Representations of Rural People in Late Nineteenth-Century Russia* (New York: Oxford University Press, 1993), 49.

2. "V oblasti sueverii i predrassudkov (Ocherk iz byta sovremennoi derevni)," *Iuridicheskii vestnik,* no. 11 (1890): 362, 368–69, quoted in Frank, *Crime, Cultural Conflict,* 180.

3. Donald Fanger, "The Peasant in Literature," in *The Peasant in Nineteenth-Century Russia,* ed. Wayne S. Vucinich (Stanford: Stanford University Press, 1968), 238.

4. Barbara Heldt, *Terrible Perfection: Women and Russian Literature* (Bloomington: Indiana University Press, 1987), 2, 13.

5. Frierson, *Peasant Icons,* 46.

6. Richard F. Taruskin, "Christian Themes in Russian Opera," in Brumfield and Velimirovic, *Christianity and the Arts in Russia,* 97–98.

7. John Bowlt, "Orthodoxy and the Avant-Garde," in Brumfield and Velimirovic, *Christianity and the Arts,* 148–49.

8. Donald Fanger, *The Creation of Nikolai Gogol* (Cambridge, Mass.: Belknap Press of Harvard University Press, 1979), 87.

9. Hubbs, *Mother Russia,* 210, 212.

10. Roman Szporluk, "Ukraine from an Imperial Periphery to a Sovereign State," *Daedalus* 126, no. 3 (Summer 1997): 95.

11. Vasilii Gippius, *Gogol'* (Leningrad, 1924), 26, quoted in Fanger, *Creation,* 87.

12. A. S. Pushkin, *Sochineniia,* vol. 1, *Stikhotvoreniia, skazki* (Moscow: Gosudarstvennoe izdatel'stvo khudozhestvennoi literatury, 1962), 332.

13. John Mersereau, introduction to Orest Somov, *Selected Prose in Russia,* ed. John Mersereau and George Harjan (Ann Arbor: University of Michigan, 1974), vi.

14. Somov, "Kievskie ved'my," in Somov, *Selected Prose,* 127–28.

15. Ibid., 133–34. The cossack Bliskavka "found a small chest containing human bones and hair, dried bats and toads, remnants of snakeskin, wolves' teeth, demons' toes; aspen coal, bones of a black cat, a lot of . . . wondrous shells, dried herbs and roots."

16. Ibid., 135.

17. Ibid., 140.

18. For a discussion of the ethnographic materials at Gogol's disposal, see Paul A. Karpuk, "Gogol's Research on Ukrainian Customs for the *Dikanka* Tales," *Russian Review* 56, no. 2 (April 1997): 209–32.

19. Quoted in Fanger, *Creation,* 88.

20. William Edward Brown, *A History of Russian Literature of the Romantic Period,* vol. 4 (Ann Arbor, Mich.: Ardis, 1986), 270.

21. Nikolai Gogol, *Sobranie sochinenii,* vol. 2, 154 n, trans. and quoted in Brown, *A History of Russian Literature of the Romantic Period,* 238.

22. Karpuk, "Gogol's Research," 232.

23. Malcolm V. Jones, introduction to Jones and Robin Feuer Miller, eds., *The Cambridge Companion to the Classic Russian Novel* (Cambridge: Cambridge University Press, 1998), 8.

24. Richard Hoops, "Musorgsky and the Populist Age," in Malcolm Hamrick Brown, ed., *Musorgsky: In Memoriam, 1881–1981* (Ann Arbor, Mich.: UMI Research Press, 1982), 291.

25. Musorgsky to Mili Alexeivich Balakirev, 26 September 1860, excerpted in Alexandra Orlova, *Musorgsky's Days and Works: A Biography in Documents,* trans. and ed. Roy J. Guenther (Ann Arbor, Mich.: UMI Research Press, 1983), 83.

26. Edward R. Reilly, "The First Extant Version of *Night on Bare Mountain,"* in Brown, *Musorgsky,* 138. Khotinskii's *Charodeistvo i tainstvennyia iavleniia v noveishee vremia* (St. Petersburg: Izd. E. N. Akhmatovoi, 1866) also explored animal magnetism and somnambulism.

27. Musorgsky to Nikolskii, 12 July 1867, excerpted and trans. in Orlova, *Musorgsky's Days,* 146, 147.

28. Solomon Volkov, *St. Petersburg: A Cultural History,* trans. Antonina W. Bouis (New York: Free Press, 1995), 86–87.

29. J. Leyda and S. Bertensson, eds. and trans., *The Musorgsky Reader: A Life of Modeste Petrovich Musorgsky in Letters and Documents* (New York: W. W. Norton, 1947), 90, quoted in Reilly, "First Extant Version," 141, 148.

30. Musorgsky to Nikolai Rimsky-Korsakov, 5 July 1867, excerpted and trans. in Orlova, *Musorgsky's Days,* 143–44.

31. Letter to Nikolskii, 12 July 1867, excerpted and trans. in Orlova, *Musorgsky's Days,* 146, 147.

32. Thomas Hodge, program notes on *St. John's Night on Bald Mountain,*

Modest Mussorgsky (1839–1881), http://www.laphil.org/library/notes/MussorgskyStJohnsNightonBaldMountain.html.

33. According to the ethnographer and historian Ivan Pryzhov, in the 1840s and 1850s the journal *Maiak* collected information about witchcraft and demon possession in medieval Europe as well as in contemporary Russia, while in the 1850s the new periodical *Domashnaia beseda* paid informants generously for reports about shriekers and possession ("Russkie klikushi," in Pryzhov, *26 Moskovskikh prorokov, iurodivykh, dur i durakov i drugie trudy po Russkoi istorii i etnografii,* ed. L. Ia. Lur'e [St. Petersburg: EZRO, 1996], 99). Pryzhov's article first appeared in *Vestnik Evropy* 10 (1868): 641–72. All subsequent references are to the reprint in Pryzhov, *26 Moskovskikh prorokov.*

34. Victor Terras, *A History of Russian Literature* (New Haven: Yale University Press, 1991), 361, 362.

35. Quoted in Terras, *History of Russian Literature,* 343.

36. Leskov [M. Stebnitskii, pseud.], "Russkoe obshchestvo v Parizhe," *Biblioteka dlia chteniia* 177, no. 5 (May 1863): 18, also quoted in Hugh McLean, *Nikolai Leskov: The Man and His Art* (Cambridge, Mass.: Harvard University Press, 1977), 115. My translation.

37. McLean, *Nikolai Leskov,* 115.

38. A. F. Pisemskii, *Sobranie sochinenii v deviati tomakh* (Moscow: Biblioteka Ogonek, 1959), 2:244–86; 557–59. I first became acquainted with this story in Vladimir Semenov's analysis of Leskov's short story "Zhitie odnoi baby" (Semenov, *Nikolai Leskov: Vremia i knigi* [Moscow: Sovremennik, 1981], 62). By 1857 *Sovremennik* had more than double the circulation of any other journal (W. Bruce Lincoln, *Between Heaven and Hell: The Story of a Thousand Years of Artistic Life in Russia* [New York: Viking, 1998], 225).

39. Maksimov, *Nechistaia sila,* 161.

40. Pisemskii, *Sobranie sochinenii v deviati tomakh,* 2:258.

41. See the entry on Klementovskii in Brokgaus and Efron, eds., *Entsiklopedicheskii slovar',* 29:355.

42. A. Klementovskii, *Klikushi: Ocherk* (Moscow: V tip. Katkova i komp., 1860), 36.

43. Pisemskii, *Sobranie sochinenii v deviati tomakh,* 2:255.

44. *Tul'skie gubernskie vedomosti,* nos. 41–42, 1841, quoted in Pryzhov, "Russkie klikushi," in Pryzhov, *26 Moskovskikh prorokov,* 99.

45. Pisemskii, *Sobranie sochinenii v deviati tomakh,* 1:287–341. The story was first published in *Otechestvennye zapiski,* no. 9 (1855).

46. Leskov, *Sobranie sochinenii,* ed. B. G. Bazanov et al. (Moscow: Gos. izd. Khudozhestvennoi literatury, 1956), 1:263–385, 501–5. The story first appeared in *Biblioteka dlia chteniia,* which boasted 5,000 subscribers when it was founded in 1834. Donald Fanger, "Gogol and His Reader," in William Mills Todd III, ed., *Literature and Society in Imperial Russia, 1800–1914* (Stanford: Stanford University Press, 1978): 69. "Zhitie" was not reprinted in Leskov's lifetime. The writer had reworked the story but decided not to publish it because of censorship restrictions. The rewritten version appeared in print only in 1924 under the modified title "The Amur in Bast Shoes" (Leskov, *Sobranie sochinenii,* 1:501–2).

47. Quoted in Fanger, "The Peasant in Literature," 245.

48. Leskov, *Sobranie sochinenii,* 1:285.

49. For negative portrayals of shriekers in manorial correspondence, see *Sbornik starinnykh bumag, khraniashchikhsia v muzee P. I. Shchukina,* vol. 9 (Moscow, 1901), 142–44. I am grateful to Professor John Bushnell for this reference. The association between feigned possession and women's disdain for work may have stemmed back to the sixteenth-century Stoglav, which "singled out women among the false prophets for abandoning their housework" (Harriet Murav, *Holy Foolishness: Dostoevsky's Novels and the Poetics of Cultural Critique* [Stanford: Stanford University Press, 1992], 44).

50. Leskov, *Sobranie sochinenii,* 1:271, 298.

51. Ibid., 1:317.

52. Ibid., 1:319.

53. When Leskov repudiated Orthodoxy, he became highly critical of religious healers as superstitious charlatans. McLean, *Nikolai Leskov,* 358. In the short story "Night Owls," Leskov savagely portrays Father Ioann of Kronstadt as a false healer and a hypocrite, whose feeble arguments cannot stand up to the more sophisticated and humane Tolstoyan religious philosophy espoused by the tale's heroine. He also satirizes the domicile, the "Expectension," or private home where travelers rented rooms, hoping to receive the blessing of a renowned religious figure such as Father Ioann. In such manner, Leskov repudiated his earlier favorable description of Krylushkin's home in "The Vita of One Woman" as a refuge for the physically and spiritually ill (*Satirical Stories of Nikolai Leskov,* trans. and ed. William B. Edgerton [New York: Pegasus, 1969], 242–326).

54. Leskov, *Sobranie sochinenii,* 1:324.

55. Ibid., 1:370.

56. Ibid., 1:377.

57. The ovarian theory of hysterical disease was popular from the 1840s onward among European medical practitioners, who sometimes performed unnecessary, brutal clitoridectomies (Edward Shorter, *From Paralysis to Fatigue: A History of Psychosomatic Illness in the Modern Era* [New York: Free Press, 1992], 82–86).

58. Klementovskii, *Klikushi,* 62.

59. Pryzhov, "Russkie klikushi," in Pryzhov, *26 Moskovskikh prorokov.*

60. After the Napoleonic Wars, Pryzhov's father became a porter and clerk at the Moscow Mariinskaia Hospital where Feodor Dostoevsky's father Mikhail Andreevich worked as a physician (Pryzhov, "Ispoved'," in Pryzhov, *26 Moskovskikh prorokov,* 13; L. Ia. Lur'e, "Zhizn' i sochineniia Ivana Pryzhova," in Pryzhov, *26 Moskovskikh prorokov,* 4).

61. Dostoevsky modeled his character Tolkachenko after Pryzhov in his novel *The Devils.* Lur'e, "Zhizn' i sochineniia," in Pryzhov, *26 Moskovskikh prorokov,* 5, 6, 7. See also Murav, *Holy Foolishness,* 4.

62. For further details on Pryzhov's life and association with Nechaev, see Abbott Gleason, *Young Russia: The Genesis of Russian Radicalism in the 1860s* (New York: Viking Press, 1980), 364–72.

63. Pryzhov, "Ispoved'," in Pryzhov, *26 Moskovskikh prorokov,* 14, 16, 19.

64. Pryzhov is referring here to Feodosii Pecherskii's *Slovo o tropariakh* ("Russkie klikushi," in Pryzhov, *26 Moskovskikh prorokov,* 79, 82).

65. Pryzhov, "Russkie klikushi," in Pryzhov, *26 Moskovskikh prorokov,* 82, 83.

66. Ibid., 87–88, 89.

67. Leskov ended his "Vita of One Woman" with the narrator's observation that upon his return to Gostomlia five years after Nast'ia's death, "demon-possessed women are far less noticeable than before" (*Sobranie sochinenii,* 1:383).

68. Pryzhov, "Russkie klikushi," in Pryzhov, *26 Moskovskikh prorokov,* 95, 96.

69. Ibid., 97.

70. See, for example, Krainskii, *Porcha,* 213; and A. N. Minkh, "Klikushi," *Etnograficheskoe obozrenie* 13, no. 1 (1901): 166–67.

71. Pryzhov, "Russkie klikushi," in Pryzhov, *26 Moskovskikh prorokov,* 97, 99, 104.

72. Pryzhov, *26 Moskovskikh prorokov.*

73. Pryzhov, "Ispoved'," in Pryzhov, *26 Moskovskikh prorokov,* 19.

74. Murav, *Holy Foolishness,* 5.

75. Pryzhov, *26 Moskovskikh prorokov,* 60–62. On the basis of the Spiritual Regulation of 1721 that warned against fraudulent claims with regard to icons, Orthodox church authorities in the nineteenth century seized for investigative purposes icons that were reported suddenly to work miracles. An excellent discussion of the church's attempt to control veneration of icons, sometimes to the consternation of local populations who believed that the icons rightfully belonged to them, may be found in Shevzov, "Popular Orthodoxy," 2:chap. 4; and Shevzov, "Miracle-Working Icons."

76. The hospital even charged admission of 20 kopecks for a consultation with its famous patient. For further information about Koreish, see Pryzhov, *26 Moskovskikh prorokov,* 33–43; N. N. Bazhenov, *Istoriia Moskovskogo dollgauza nyne moskovskoi gorodskoi Preobrazhenskoi bol'nitsy dlia dushevno-bol'nykh. (Glava iz istorii russkoi meditsiny i kul'turno-bytovoi istorii Moskve* (Moscow: Izd. Moskovskago gorodskago obshchestvennago upravleniia, 1909), 71–76; and Murav, *Holy Foolishness,* 45–48.

77. Fyodor Dostoyevsky, *The Village of Stepanchikovo and Its Inhabitants: From the Notes of an Unknown,* trans. Ignat Avsey, rev. ed. (London: Penguin, 1995), 6.

78. Lincoln, *Between Heaven and Hell,* 170, 175.

79. Vissarion G. Belinskii and P. V. Annenkov were extremely critical of "The Landlady." Belinskii decried Dostoevsky's departure from the "natural" school in favor of the fantastic and melodramatic. Consequently, the story fell into oblivion until the last two decades of the nineteenth century when educated society embraced it as a precursor to Dostoevsky's sociopsychological inquiries in his later novels. Editorial commentary can be found in F. M. Dostoevskii, *Polnoe sobranie sochinenii,* (Leningrad: Izd. Nauka, 1972), 1:510–11; and Joe Andrew, *Russian Writers and Society in the Second Half of the Nineteenth Century* (Atlantic Highlands, N.J.: Humanities Press, 1982), 74.

80. Terras, *History of Russian Literature,* 271–72.

81. R. Neuhauser, "*The Landlady:* A New Interpretation," *Canadian Slavonic Papers* 10, no. 1 (Spring 1968): 44, 45.

82. Dostoevskii, *Polnoe sobranie sochinenii,* 1:268, 270.

83. Ibid., 1:292, 293.

84. Neuhauser, "*The Landlady,*" 57.

85. Belinskii referred to "The Landlady" as "a mixture of Hoffmann and [Aleksandr] Marlinskii [pen name for the Decembrist Aleksandr Bestuzhev], with

some Russian folklore thrown in for good measure." Terras, *History of Russian Literature,* 271.

86. Zhuravel acknowledges the influences of the work of A. Ia. Gurevich, N. N. Pokrovskii, and E. B. Smilianskaia on her ideas (*Siuzhet o dogovore cheloveka,* 3, 113, 142).

87. Quoted in Malcolm V. Jones, *Dostoyevsky after Bakhtin: Readings in Dostoyevsky's Fantastic Realism* (Cambridge: Cambridge University Press, 1990), 171–72.

88. Dostoevskii, *Brat'ia Karamazovy,* 17, 22.

89. Nina Perlina, *Varieties of Poetic Utterance: Quotation in "The Brothers Karamazov"* (Lanham, Md.: University Press of America, 1985), 20.

90. Dostoevskii, *Brat'ia Karamazovy,* 25, 29, 129–30.

91. Perlina, *Varieties of Poetic Utterance,* 84.

92. Dostoevskii, *Brat'ia Karamazovy,* 48. When Dostoevsky was a child, his family went on annual pilgrimages to the Trinity–St. Sergii Monastery in Sergiev Posad to celebrate Sergius's saint day (A. Boyce Gibson, *The Religion of Dostoevsky* [London: SCM Press, 1973], 8–9). It would not have been unusual for Dostoevsky to have seen shriekers on those occasions.

93. Dostoevskii, *Brat'ia Karamazovy,* 49.

94. Ibid.

95. For a discussion of the concept of *umilenie,* see G. P. Fedotov, *The Russian Religious Mind: Kievan Christianity, The Tenth to the Thirteenth Centuries* (New York: Harper Torchbooks, 1960), 393.

96. Sergei Hackel, "The Religious Dimension: Vision or Evasion? Zosima's Discourse in Malcolm V. Jones and Garth M. Terry, eds., *The Brothers Karamazov,"* in *New Essays on Dostoyevsky* (Cambridge: Cambridge University Press, 1983), 144. Hackel cites Book 6, chapter 3.

97. Coomler, *Icon Handbook,* 238.

98. Dostoevsky, *Diary of a Writer,* trans. Boris Brasol (New York: Charles Scribner's Sons, 1949), 1:286, 2:983.

99. For a discussion of the influences of the monks at the Optina Hermitage upon Dostoevsky, see Leonard J. Stanton, "Zedergol'm's *Life of Elder Leonid of Optina* as a Source of Dostoevsky's *The Brothers Karamazov," Russian Review* 49, no. 4 (1990): 443–55; and Hackel, "The Religious Dimension," 142–45. Dostoevsky's vita of the Elder Zosima in *The Brothers Karamazov* also had a major impact on Archimandrite Agapit's *Life of the Optin Elder and Hieromonk Amvrosy* not only in terms of style but also biographical detail (Perlina, *Varieties of Poetic Utterance,* 162–64).

100. I have changed the translation of *"Veruiushchie baby"* from "Women of Faith" to "Devout Women." Anna Dostoevsky, *Dostoevsky: Reminiscences,* trans. and ed. Beatrice Stillman (New York: Liveright, 1975), 293.

101. Mark S. Micale argues that the rural French found greater psychological comfort at Lourdes than they did in medical clinics (*Approaching Hysteria: Disease and Its Interpretations* [Princeton: Princeton University Press, 1995], 268).

102. Tolstoy believed in the sincerity of peasants' beliefs, but dismissed Orthodox ritual as superstition. In March 1890 he wrote to his old friend Nikolai Petrovich Wagner—a professor of zoology at the University of Petersburg and a writer who used the pen name Kot-Murlyka—that "superstitions are the spoonful

of tar which ruins the barrel of honey, and it's impossible not to hate them or at least not to make fun of them. I recently visited the Optina Monastery and saw people there burning with true love for God and mankind, and at the same time considering it necessary to stand for several hours a day in church, take communion, and give and receive blessings, thereby paralyzing the active power of life in themselves. I can't help hating these superstitions." Tolstoy to N. P. Wagner, 25 March 1890, in R. F. Christian, ed. and trans., *Tolstoy's Letters* (New York: Charles Scribner's Sons, 1978), 2:454–55.

103. Tolstoy's meaningful reply apparently helped to save Liubochinskaia's life. Tolstoy to Z. M. Liubochinskaia, 25 August 1899, in *Tolstoy's Letters,* 581–82.

104. Leo Tolstoy, "The Kreutzer Sonata," in *Great Short Works of Leo Tolstoy,* introduction by John Bayley and trans. Louise and Aylmer Maude (New York: Harper and Row, 1967), 382–83.

105. Maria Carlson, *"No Religion Higher than Truth": A History of the Theosophical Movement in Russia, 1875–1922* (Princeton: Princeton University Press, 1993), 7.

106. For a discussion of the Silver Age's fascination with the demonic, see Kristi A. Groberg "'The Shade of Lucifer's Dark Wing': Satanism in Silver Age Russia," in Bernice Glatzer Rosenthal, ed., *The Occult in Russian and Soviet Culture* (Ithaca: Cornell University Press, 1997), 99–133.

107. Linda J. Ivanits, "Three Instances of the Peasant Occult in Russian Literature," in Rosenthal, *The Occult in Russian and Soviet Culture,* 65.

108. Carl R. Proffer, ed., *The Unpublished Dostoevsky: Diaries and Notebooks (1860–1881),* vol. 2, trans. Arline Boyer and Carl Proffer (Ann Arbor, Mich.: Ardis, 1975), 120.

109. Groberg, "'The Shade of Lucifer's Dark Wing,'" 125.

110. Frank, *Crime, Cultural Conflict, and Justice,* 174.

111. N. P. Karabchevskii, *Okolo pravosudiia: Stat'i, soobshcheniia i sudebnye ocherki* (St. Petersburg: Trud, 1902), 218–35, esp. 218–19.

112. Levenstim, "Sueverie i ugolovnoe pravo: Izsledovanie po istorii russkago prava i kul'tury," *Vestnik prava* 36, nos. 1–2 (1906): 291–343, 181–251; Levenstim, "Sueverie," nos. 1–2 (January–February 1897): 157–219, 62–127; Tulub, "Sueverie i prestuplenie," 1082–1101; Vesin, "Narodnyi samosud," 57–79.

113. Frank, *Crime, Cultural Conflict, and Justice* 174; Karabchevskii, *Okolo pravosudiia,* 235.

114. Frank, *Crime, Cultural Conflict, and Justice,* 175.

115. A. Kushnerev, "Matushka Avdot'ia. (Iz Iukhnovskago u.)," *Smolenskii vestnik,* 18 December 1892.

116. Nikolai Rudinskii, "Znakharstvo v Skopinskom i Dankovskom uezdakh Riazanskoi gubernii," *Zhivaia starina* 6, no. 2 (1896): 193, 195.

117. Popov, *Russkaia narodno-bytovaia meditsina,* [iii], v, viii, vii, 47.

118. Ibid., 33, 39, 40, 41, 49, 50, 63, 87, 272.

119. Ibid., 363, 399.

4: PSYCHIATRIC DIAGNOSES

1. In the nineteenth and early twentieth centuries, European scientists studying the brain and mind did not make rigid distinctions between the new fields of neurology and psychiatry or between mental and nervous illnesses

(Janet Oppenheim, *"Shattered Nerves": Doctors, Patients, and Depression in Victorian England* [New York: Oxford University Press, 1991], 7; David Joravsky, *Russian Psychology: A Critical History* [Oxford: Basil Blackwell, 1989], 88). For the sake of simplicity, I shall use "psychiatrists" to refer collectively to psychiatrists and neurologists, unless otherwise stated.

2. Russian psychiatrists and neurologists frequented the lectures and laboratories of such renowned Europeans as psychiatrist Jean Martin Charcot at the Salpêtrière Hospital in Paris; biologist Theodore M. Meynert at the University of Vienna; and experimental psychologist Wilhelm Wundt, psychiatrist Paul Emil Flechsig, and neurophysiologist Karl Ludwig at the University of Leipzig (Brown, "Professionalization," 202; Joravsky, *Russian Psychology,* 83).

3. Porter, "The Body and the Mind," in Gilman et al., *Hysteria beyond Freud,* 229.

4. Rita Felski, *The Gender of Modernity* (Cambridge, Mass.: Harvard University Press, 1995), 182.

5. *Dictionnaire des sciences médicales* (1821), quoted in Tony James, *Dream, Creativity, and Madness in Nineteenth-Century France* (Oxford: Clarendon Press, 1995), 7. While its definition remained constant throughout the nineteenth century, somnambulism as a diagnostic category was more popular at the beginning and end of that period; by the turn of the century it resurfaced "under the guise of hypnotism and studies of 'doubling of personality'" (*Dictionnaire des sciences médicales,* quoted in James, *Dream, Creativity, and Madness,* 8).

6. Andrew Scull's assessment of eighteenth-century British medical thinking is also valid for nineteenth-century thought (*The Most Solitary of Afflictions: Madness and Society in Britain, 1700–1900* [New Haven: Yale University Press, 1993], 80).

7. Ann Goldberg makes a similar argument with regard to the mission of German alienists and psychiatrists in the first half of the nineteenth century (*Sex,* 12).

8. For further information about proposals to decentralize care of the mentally ill in Imperial Russia, see Julie Vail Brown, "Social Influences on Psychiatric Theory and Practice in Late Imperial Russia," in Susan Gross Solomon and John F. Hutchinson, eds., *Health and Society in Revolutionary Russia* (Bloomington: Indiana University Press, 1990), 34–38.

9. Scull, *The Most Solitary of Afflictions,* 392.

10. See T. I. Iudin, *Ocherki istorii otechestvennoi psikhiatrii* (Moscow: Gosudarstvennoe izdatel'stvo meditsinskoi literature MEDGIZ, 1951), 109, 128, 321; Brown, "Professionalization," 74, 101, 105, 198, 201; and Joravsky, *Russian Psychology,* 86.

11. Brown, "Professionalization," 163.

12. Brown, "Social Influences," in Solomon and Hutchinson, *Health and Society,* 29–30.

13. In Orel's asylums men accounted for 65.44 percent of the patients and in Voronezh asylums 69.26 percent. A similar pattern emerged at Moscow's Preobrazhenskaia Hospital, for the Insane which between 1868 and 1 November 1886 admitted 2,255 men (60.85%) and 1,450 women (39.14%). At Moscow's Alekseev Psychiatric Hospital between 1898 and 1913 the percentage of male patients was somewhat lower at 58.78, reflecting the increased migration of women into the

city. The sources for the statistics are Brown, "Professionalization," 260; P. A. Arkhangel'skii, *Otchet po osmotru russkikh psikhiatricheskikh zavedenii proizvedennomu po porucheniiu moskovskago gubernskago zemskago sanitarnago soveta* (Moscow: Tip. V. V. Islen'eva, 1887), 268; and RGIAgM, f. 2384, [Moskovskaia gorodskaia Psikhiatricheskaia bol'nitsa im. N. A. Alekseeva (Kanatchikovye dachi) Moskovskoi gorodskoi Dumy (1895–1914 gg.)], op. 1, d. 3, 444; d. 4, 480–81; d. 5, 476–77; d. 7, 528–29; d. 8, 58–59; d. 9, 104–5; d. 10, 96–97; d. 12, 98–99; d. 13, 76–77; d. 14, 14–15; d. 15, ll. 43 ob.–44. These *dela* or files contain published materials; thus page numbers rather than *listy* (with the exception of *delo* 15) are cited.

Pavel Iakobii argued that the incarceration of dangerous elements in society in madhouses deterred families from sending mentally disturbed female relatives to such institutions. Another psychiatrist, Vladimir Iakovenko, believed that the large number of men in the asylums reflected a reality that men were more prone to insanity than women (Brown, "Professionalization," 259–60, 267).

14. Today an organic cause must be ruled out before an epidemic is qualified as an example of mass hysteria (Gary W. Small and Armand M. Nicholi, Jr., "Mass Hysteria Among Schoolchildren," *Archives of General Psychiatry* 39 [June 1982]: 721–24). Other articles on modern-day cases of mass hysteria include Abubakar Ali-Gombe, Elspeth Guthrie, and Niall McDermott, "Mass Hysteria: One Syndrome or Two?" *British Journal of Psychiatry* 168 (1996): 633–35; Raymond L. M. Lee and S. E. Ackerman, "The Sociocultural Dynamics of Mass Hysteria: A Case Study of Social Conflict in West Malaysia," *Psychiatry* 43 (February 1980): 78–88; François Sirois, "Epidemic Hysteria," in Alec Roy, ed., *Hysteria* (Chichester: John Wiley and Sons, 1982), 101–15; and Sirois, *Epidemic Hysteria* (Copenhagen, 1974).

15. Krainskii, *Porcha,* 187.

16. P. I. Kovalevskii, a Khar'kov psychiatrist who organized the 1887 congress of Russian psychiatrists, articulated his fear of growing and uncontrollable madness at that meeting. Quoted in Martin A. Miller, *Freud and the Bolsheviks: Psychoanalysis in Imperial Russia and the Soviet Union* (New Haven: Yale University Press, 1998), 13.

17. Iakovenko, *Dushevno-bol'nye,* 18–19, appendix, 5.

18. Ibid., 150.

19. Ibid., 61.

20. F. A. Shcherbina, comp., *Svodnyi sbornik po 12 uezdam Voronezhskoi gubernii: Statisticheskie materialy podvornoi perepisi po gubernii i obzor materialov, sposobov po sobiraniiu ikh i priemov po razrabotke* (Voronezh: Tip. Isaeva, 1897), 133, quoted in Chris J. Chulos, "Myths of the Pious or Pagan Peasant in Post-Emancipation Central Russia (Voronezh Province)," *Russian History* 22, no. 2 (Summer 1995): 186.

21. A total of eight districts, including 187 cantons and 783 villages, were surveyed. P. P. Kashchenko, *Statisticheskii ocherk polozheniia dushevno-bol'nykh v Nizhegorodskoi gubernii* (Nizhnii Novgorod: Izd. Nizhegorodskago gubernskago zemstva, 1895), v, vii.

22. L. I. Aikenval'd noted the fear of families in Ufa province that mentally disturbed individuals would be incarcerated in hospitals (*Itogi perepisi dushevnobol'nykh Ufimskoi gubernii [1913 g.]* [Ufa: Ufimskoe gubernskoe zemstvo, 1914], 498).

23. N. L. Ostapovich, "Opyt perepisi nervno- i dushevnobol'nykh v sele Nizhnii Mamon Verkhne-Mamonskogo raiona TsChO," *Zhurnal nevropatologii i psikhiatrii,* no. 3 (1931): 22–23.

24. I. Strel'chuk and Rumshevich, "Zhizn' i byt dushevno bol'nykh na sele. (Organizatsiia vnebol'nichnoi pomoshchi dushevnobol'nym selianam)," *Zhurnal nevropatologii i psikhiatrii,* no. 5 (1930): 127.

25. The notion of peasants being opaque or illegible to state authorities until governments could undertake accurate enumerations of the rural population and map its resources comes from James C. Scott, *Seeing like a State: How Certain Schemes to Improve the Human Condition Have Failed* (New Haven: Yale University Press, 1998), 77–78.

26. Krainskii, *Porcha,* 213; G. B. Grossman, "K voprosu o klikushestve," *Prakticheskii vrach* 5, no. 19 (13 May 1906): 316–18; Iakobii, "Religiozno-psikhicheskiia epidemiia," 738.

27. Kashchenko, *Statisticheskii ocherk,* 12.

28. Iakobii, "Religiozno-psikhicheskiia epidemiia," 737–38.

29. V. I. Iakovenko, comp., *Mediko-khoziastvennyi otchet po Pokrovskoi psikhiatricheskoi bol'nitse moskovskago gubernskago zemstva za 1899 god—1902 god,* vols. 7–10 (Moscow: Moskovskoe gubernskoe zemskoe sobranie, 1900–1903), 7:68, 8:63, 9:68, 10:62.

30. Jann Matlock, *Scenes of Seduction: Prostitution, Hysteria, and Reading Difference in Nineteenth-Century France* (New York: Columbia University Press, 1994), 151.

31. P. I. Kovalevskii (1849–1923), the founder of the first Russian psychiatric journal *Arkhiv psikhiatrii, neirologii i sudebnoi psikhopatologii* and author of the initial psychiatric textbook in Russia, warned of the degenerative nature of insanity (*Rukovodstvo k pravil'nomu ukhodu za dushevnymi bol'nymi–dlia rodstvennikov i okruzhaiushchikh* [Khar'kov, 1880], cited in Brown, "Professionalization," 241).

32. Krainskii, *Porcha;* Nikitin, "K voprosu o klikushestve," 656–68, 746–56; Nikitin, "Religioznoe chuvstvo," 1–9, 100–8. In 1915 Krainskii became a professor of psychiatry at Warsaw University (Iudin, *Ocherki,* 139).

33. Brown, "Professionalization," 255, 256–57.

34. P. A. Kovalevskii, "Polozhenie nashikh dushevnykh bol'nykh," *Arkhiv psikhiatrii, neirologii i sudebnoi psikhopatologii* 5 (1890): 83–84, quoted in Julie Vail Brown, "Societal Responses to Mental Disorders in Prerevolutionary Russia," in William O. McCagg and Lewis Siegelbaum, eds., *The Disabled in the Soviet Union: Past and Present, Theory and Practice* (Pittsburgh: University of Pittsburgh Press, 1989), 25.

35. Commonly used in late-nineteenth- and early-twentieth-century European asylums, these drugs possessed "either stimulant or narcotic effects" and threatened the nervous system. See Oppenheim, *"Shattered Nerves,"* 115; and Scull, *The Most Solitary of Afflictions,* 290–91.

36. Iakovenko, *Dushevno-bol'nye,* 38, 39.

37. Miller, *Freud and the Bolsheviks,* 14.

38. Iakovenko, *Dushevno-bol'nye,* 49; see 43–52 for other graphic examples.

39. Ibid., 57–58.

40. K. P. Sulima, "Koe-chto o polozhenii dushevno-bol'nykh v iugo-zapadnom krae," *Arkhiv psikhiatrii, neirologii i sudebnoi psikhopatologii* 6 (1885): 51; also

quoted in Brown, "Professionalization," 243–44; my translation.

41. Kashchenko, *Statisticheskii ocherk,* 51, 99.

42. The chronicling of abuses against the mentally ill continued into the early Soviet period (Strel'chuk and Rumshevich, "Zhizn' i byt dushevnobol'nykh," 125–26).

43. P. P. Kashchenko, *Kratkii otchet po perepisi dushevno-bol'nykh v S-Petersburgskoi gubernii* (St. Petersburg, 1910), 15, cited in Brown, "Societal Responses," in McCagg and Siegelbaum, *The Disabled,* 28.

44. V. N. Bekhterev's preface to Krainskii, *Porcha,* v.

45. Krainskii, *Porcha,* 174, 187, 215, 217. For similar criticisms of monks who ministered to demoniacs, see Grossman, "K voprosu o klikushestve," 316–18; and V. M. Bekhterev, *Vnushenie i ego rol' v obshchestvennoi zhizni,* 3d rev. ed. (St. Petersburg: Izdanie K. L. Rikker, 1908), 87.

46. Lakhtin, *Besooderzhimost',* 45–46.

47. "Khronika," *Sovremennaia psikhiatriia,* no. 12 (December 1911): 709.

48. Kotsovskii, "O tak nazyvaemom 'Baltskom dvizhenii' v Bessarabii," *Trudy Bessarabskago obshchestva estestvoispytatelei i liubitelei estestvoznaniia* 3 (1911–1912): 147–80, esp. 148, 150, 153. See also V. S. Iakovenko, "Psikhicheskaia epidemiia na religioznoi pochve v Anan'evskom i Tiraspol'skom uezdakh Khersonskoi gub.," *Sovremennaia psikhiatriia* 5 (March–April 1911): 191–98, 229–45; and "Khronika," 705–11.

49. "Khronika," 709.

50. Nikitin was a rare example of a Russian psychiatrist who was fascinated rather than repulsed by the successful healings at religious shrines and the psychological dynamics involved. See "K voprosu o klikushestve," 656–68, 746–56; and "Religioznoe chuvstvo," 1–9, 100–8.

51. Micale has characterized the Catholic cult of Lourdes in the 1880s and 1890s as well as Jean Martin Charcot's famous psychiatric clinic at the Salpêtrière Hospital and Hippolyte Bernheim's school at Nancy "as alternative psychotherapeutic cultures" (*Approaching Hysteria,* 263).

52. Porter, "The Body and the Mind," in Gilman et al., *Hysteria beyond Freud,* 229, 241.

53. Ibid., 255.

54. A. Klementovskii and S. Shteinberg were the earliest physicians to write about demon possession in the Russian village. See Klementovskii, *Klikushi;* and Shteinberg, "Klikushestvo i ego sudebno-meditsinskoe znachenie," *Arkhiv sudebnoi meditsiny i obshchestvennoi gigieny* 6, no. 2 (June 1870): 64–81.

55. Elaine Showalter, "Hysteria, Feminism, and Gender," in Gilman et al., *Hysteria beyond Freud,* 309.

56. Iakovenko, "Epidemiia istericheskikh sudorog," 93–109.

57. Genik, "Vtoraia epidemiia istericheskikh sudorog," 146–59, esp. 146. My calculation of 1.5 liters per person is based on half a bucket of vodka being equivalent to 6 liters. According to 1895 official statistics for the Russian Empire, the per capita consumption of vodka averaged 0.53 buckets. David Christian notes that in 1859 one to five buckets constituted the norm for peasant weddings that lasted several days (*Living Water: Vodka and Russian Society on the Eve of Emancipation* [Oxford: Clarendon Press, 1990], 87, 71).

58. Genik, "Vtoraia epidemiia istericheskikh sudorog," 146–59.

59. Krainskii, *Porcha.*

60. Porter, "The Body and the Mind," in Gilman et al., *Hysteria beyond Freud,* 231.

61. See the discussion of Pryzhov's writing in Chapter 3; for a discussion of French writings, see Temkin, *The Falling Sickness,* 320. Paul Regnard's *Les Maladies épidémiques de l'esprit: Sorcellerie, magnétisme, délire des grandeurs* (Paris: Plon, Nourrit, 1887) was translated into Russian in 1889. The work is cited in the bibliography of a Soviet textbook on mental illness, V. P. Osipov, *Kurs obshchego ucheniia o dushevnykh bolezniakh* (Berlin: RSFSR gosudarstvennoe izdatel'stvo, 1923).

62. Krainskii, *Porcha,* 93, 94, 95.

63. Ibid., 98–99, 123.

64. Ibid., 149, 155, 156, 139.

65. For a discussion of Charcot's theories, see Micale, *Approaching Hysteria,* 24, 164; and Shorter, *From Paralysis to Fatigue,* 175, 179–80.

66. Krainskii, *Porcha,* 121–22.

67. Ibid., 132, 140, 146.

68. Ibid., 153.

69. See, for example, D. I. Azbukin, "O perepisi dushevno-bol'nykh v Vasil'skom uezde, Nizhegorodskoi gubernii," *Nevrologicheskii vestnik* 20, no. 2 (1913): 203–4; and Lakhtin, *Besooderzhimost',* 35–45.

70. Krainskii, *Porcha,* 218–19.

71. Krainskii, *Porcha,* 239, 237, 242. See also M. P. Nikitin's discussion of Krainskii's findings in his "K voprosu o klikushestve," 659.

72. Micale, *Approaching Hysteria,* 24.

73. Krainskii, *Porcha,* 229, 209.

74. Grossman, "K voprosu o klikushestve," 317.

75. Bekhterev, preface to Krainskii, *Porcha,* iii; my emphasis.

76. Bekhterev, preface to Krainskii, *Porcha,* ii, v. Krainskii also subscribed to the notions of autosuggestion and imitation (*Porcha,* 210, 240). Bekhterev and Krainskii were not the first Russian psychiatrists to see these factors as key to *klikushestvo.* In 1895 during an epidemic of bewitchment at a wedding in Podol'sk district, Moscow province, I. Iakovenko made these same observations ("Epidemiia istericheskikh sudorog," 108).

77. Nikitin, "K voprosu o klikushestve," 659–60.

78. In 1906 V. P. Osipov became a professor of psychiatry at the University of Kazan in 1906; he established a psychiatric clinic there in 1914 (Iudin, *Ocherki,* 130).

79. V. P. Osipov, "Oderzhimost' gadami i eia mesto v klassifikatsii psikhozov," *Obozrenie psikhiatrii, nevrologii i eksperimental'noi psikhologii,* nos. 2–3 (February–March 1905): 125.

80. Ibid., 128, 135, 136–37, 187–88, 190.

81. In nineteenth-century Central Europe, popular thought equated the uterus with a live animal; that belief shifted in the course of the century to the possibility that an animal could inhabit the abdomen. While doctors treated women with such complaints as hysterics, they dismissed similar complaints on the part of men (Shorter, *From Paralysis to Fatigue,* 52–54).

82. Regina Schulte looks at the clash between peasant and elite cultures in Bavaria (*The Village in Court: Arson, Infanticide, and Poaching in the Court Records of*

Upper Bavaria, 1848–1910, trans. Barrie Selman [Cambridge: Cambridge University Press, 1994], esp. 73–74).

83. Goldberg, *Sex,* 62.

84. N. P. Kazachenko-Trirodov, "Psikhoterapiia pri klikushestve," *Obozrenie psikhiatrii, nevrologii i refleksologii* 1, nos. 4–5 (1926): 292, 293.

85. Kazachenko-Trirodov, "Psikhoterapiia," 293. For a discussion of Freud's reception in pre- and postrevolutionary Russia, see James L. Rice, *Freud's Russia: National Identity in the Evolution of Psychoanalysis* (New Brunswick, N.J.: Transaction, 1993).

86. Kazachenko-Trirodov, "Psikhoterapiia," 292.

87. V. N. Ergol'skii, "Prestuplenie pod vliianiem demonomanicheskikh galliutsinatsii (Sudebno-psikhiatricheskii sluchai)," *Arkhiv psikhiatrii, neirologii i sudebnoi psikhopatologii* 24, no. 2 (1894): 61, 75.

88. Ergol'skii, "Prestuplenie," 71–72, 74, 75–76. Vladimir Iakovenko and E. A. Genik complained that compared to European psychiatric literature, its Russian counterpart hardly broached the causation of induced insanity among two persons as described in Ergol'skii's example. Attempting to remedy the situation, they wrote about individual cases in Tver and Moscow provinces. Genik's example involved a wealthy peasant family where lead poisoning played a role in causing the contagious mental illness. See Iakovenko, *Indutsirovannoe pomeshatel'stvo ("folie à deux"), kak odin iz vidov patologicheskago podrazhaniia* (St. Petersburg: Tip. M. M. Stasiulevicha, 1887); and Genik, "Sluchai *folie à deux,*" *Nevrologicheskii vestnik* 5, no. 4 (1897): 59–72.

89. Goldberg, *Sex,* 46.

90. Iakobii, "Religiozno-psikhicheskiia epidemiia," 732–58, 117–66; Iakobii, "'Antikhrist': Sudebno-psikhiatricheskii ocherk," *Sovremennaia psikhiatriia* 3 (June–July, August 1909): 288–301; 337–55.

91. Miller, *Freud and the Bolsheviks,* 13.

92. For further discussion of Iakobii's ideas regarding "police psychiatry," see Brown, "Professionalization," 257–63, 268.

93. Iakobii, "Religiozno-psikhicheskiia epidemiia," 125, 732–34, 751, 155.

94. Ibid., 125, 737, 738, 739, 154.

95. Ibid., 739–40.

96. See in particular P. Tarnovskaia, "Zhenskaia prestupnost' v sviazi s rannimi brakami," *Severnyi vestnik,* no. 5 (May 1898): 133–49; and the discussion of Tarnovskaia's ideas in Laura Engelstein, *The Keys to Happiness: Sex and the Search for Modernity in Fin-de-Siècle Russia* (Ithaca: Cornell University Press, 1992), 137–39; and Sander L. Gilman, *Difference and Pathology: Stereotypes of Sexuality, Race, and Madness* (Ithaca: Cornell University Press, 1985), 95. For a discussion of German notions of sexual degeneracy, see Gilman, 194ff.

97. Iakobii, "'Antikhrist,'" 347, 353.

98. Iakobii, "Religiozno-psikhicheskiia epidemiia," 740, 125, 165; Iakobii, "'Antikhrist,'" 344, 346.

99. Iakobii, "Religiozno-psikhicheskiia epidemiia," 154.

100. Gilman, *Difference and Pathology,* 196.

101. Iakobii, "Religiozno-psikhicheskiia epidemiia," 166, 154; Iakobii, "'Antikhrist,'" 354.

102. Bekhterev, *Vnushenie,* 91–92.

103. Bekhterev, *Vnushenie,* 92–93, 95–117, 119–32, esp. 97, 132. The definition of psychopathy comes from Elizabeth Lunbeck. Lunbeck further notes that "as a category it [psychopathy] was far more malleable than feeblemindedness . . . Feeblemindedness connoted precision and, as measured by the tests, referred to a discrete deficiency of intellectual capacity concerning the parameters of which there was little controversy. Psychopathy was, by contrast, usefully but dangerously indeterminate, a rubric that comfortably encompassed incarcerated criminals and dissipated high-lives, promiscuous girls and lazy men, deficiencies so various, so numerous, and in the end, so elusive that some wondered whether it referred to anything at all." Turn-of-the-century psychiatrists could not agree whether psychopathy was "'constitutional' (inborn) or acquired or even temporary, and . . . whether it was at bottom a weakness of the brain or simply bad behavior" (Lunbeck, *The Psychiatric Persuasion: Knowledge, Gender, and Power in Modern America* [Princeton: Princeton University Press, 1994], 65, 66).

104. Bekhterev, *Vnushenie,* 132, 139.

105. Ibid., 152–53, 165, 173.

106. Quoted in Joravsky, *Russian Psychology,* 91.

107. In 1913 Bekhterev himself lost his job at the St. Petersburg Military-Medical Academy because he served as an expert witness on the side of the defense against the government in the infamous Beilis case. Beilis was falsely charged with having committed a Jewish ritual murder of a Christian child. Brown, "Professionalization," 387–88, 397 n. 6, 371–72, 398 n. 7.

108. V. P. Osipov, "O politicheskikh ili revoliutsionnykh psikhozakh," *Nevrologicheskii vestnik* 17, no. 3 (1910): 437–38.

109. N. I. Skliar, "O vliianiia tekushchikh politicheskikh sobytii na dushevnyia zabolevaniia," *Russkii vrach,* no. 8 (1906), cited in Osipov, "O politicheskikh ili revoliutsionnykh psikhozakh," 443. A. N. Bernshtein credited Skliar with being an objective clinical observer of the psychological effects of the 1905 Revolution. Watching events from Burashevo, Skliar was a significant distance away from the strikes, political meetings, barricades, shootings, and pogroms (Bernshtein, "Psikhicheskiia zabolevaniia zimoi 1905–1906 g. v Moskve," *Sovremennaia psikhiatriia,* no. 4 [1907]: 50).

110. I. S. German, "O psikhicheskom razstroistve depressivnago kharaktera, razvivshemsia u bol'nykh na pochve perezhivaemykh politicheskikh sobytiia," *Zhurnal nevropatologii i psikhiatrii imeni S. S. Korsakova* 3 (1907): 313–24; F. Kh. Gadziatskii, "Dushevnyia razstroistva v sviazi s politicheskimi sobytiiami v Rossii," *Voenno-meditsinskii zhurnal* (September 1908): 89–99; Bernshtein, "Psikhicheskiia zabolevaniia."

111. V. I. Iakovenko, "Zdorovyia i boleznennyia proiavleniia v psikhike sovremennago russkago obshchestva," *Zhurnal obshchestva russkikh vrachei v pamiat' N. I. Pirogova,* no. 4 (1907): 282, 285, cited in Osipov, "O politicheskikh ili revoliutsionnykh psikhozakh," 460.

112. V. F. Chizh, "Znachenie politicheskoi zhizni v etiologii dushevnykh boleznei," *Obozrenie psikhiatrii* nos. 1, 3 (1908): 1–12, 149–62, quoted and cited in Osipov, "O politicheskikh ili revoliutsionnykh psikhozakh," 460.

113. S. Iaroshevskii, "Materialy k voprosu o massovykh nervnopsikhicheskikh zabolevaniiakh," *Obozrenie psikhiatrii, nevrologii i eksperimental'noi*

psikhologii, no. 1 (January 1906): 1, 8.

114. Bernshtein, "Psikhicheskiia zabolevaniia," 54, 55–56.

5: SORTING THROUGH MULTIPLE REALITIES

1. Rosenthal, "Political Implications of the Occult Revival," in Rosenthal, *The Occult in Russian and Soviet Culture,* 398–99; Laura Engelstein, "Paradigms, Pathologies, and Other Clues to Russian Spiritual Culture: Some Post-Soviet Thoughts," *Slavic Review* 57, no. 4 (Winter 1998): 875.

2. Boris Mironov, "Peasant Popular Culture and the Origins of Soviet Authoritarianism," in Frank and Steinberg, *Cultures in Flux,* 54–73.

3. An issue of the *Journal of Modern History,* devoted to the study of various types of denunciation in modern Russian/Soviet, German, and French history, makes a strong argument in favor of such an approach. According to the issue's editors, Sheila Fitzpatrick and Robert Gellately, denunciations of individuals to the state or other institutional agencies characterize not only authoritarian, but also democratic political systems. Ideological proclivities determine whether such denunciations are viewed as demonstrative of either negative collusion with repressive regimes or positive civic duty toward a benign government (*Practices of Denunciation in Modern European History, 1789–1989,* in *Journal of Modern History* 68, no. 4 [December 1996]).

4. There has been a resurgence of demon possession in the parish of Medjugorje in Bosnia in the last 15 years. Predating ethnic tensions and violence, it appears to be the product of the parish's becoming a highly visible pilgrimage site, which in turn has increased the burdens of women parishioners and resulted in the demotion of their status. See the fascinating article by Mart Bax, "Ruža's Problems: Gender Relations and Violence Control in a Bosnian Rural Community," in *Gender Politics in the Western Balkans: Women and Society in Yugoslav Successor States,* ed. Sabrina P. Ramet (University Park: Pennsylvania State University Press, 1999), 259–73.

5. In the summer of 1993, Dr. Elena Borisovna Smilianskaia of the Moscow State University Library's Manuscript Division and I took the train to Sergiev Posad with the intention of interviewing *klikushi* at the monastery. Having previously witnessed demoniacs at the monastery, Lena was surprised by their absence. Discrete inquiries revealed that the patriarch had banned the shriekers from the services in the monastery's main church.

6. *Zhenshchina* denotes a married woman, while *devushka* or *devochka* refers to a girl or an unmarried woman of more advanced years. Sometimes the noun *deva* is used for a spinster. Even the common reference to a peasant woman, *krest'ianka,* carries the implication that she is married.

7. Robert L. Spitzer, Miriam Gibbon, Andrew E. Skodol, Janet B. W. Williams, and Michael B. First, *DSM-III R Casebook: A Learning Companion to the Diagnostic and Statistical Manual of Mental Disorders (Third Edition, Revised)* (Washington, D.C.: American Psychiatric Press, 1989), 232.

8. Robert E. Bartholomew, "Ethnocentricity and the Social Construction of 'Mass Hysteria,'" *Culture, Medicine, and Psychiatry* 14 (1990): 454.

9. Bartholomew, "Ethnocentricity," 474, 454, 458, 475. For other arguments in favor of cultural relativism in place of rigid psychiatric labels, see L.

Hinton and A. Kleinman, "Cultural Issues and International Psychiatric Diagnosis," *International Revue of Psychiatry* 1 (1993): 111–29. Lee and Ackerman, "The Sociocultural Dynamics of Mass Hysteria," 78–88.

10. Frank Kessel, "On Culture, Health, and Human Development: Emerging Perspectives," *Items* 46, no. 4 (December 1992): 65; Kessel's emphasis.

11. Quoted and discussed in Nimrod Grisaru, Danny Budowski, and Eliezer Witztum, "Possession by the 'Zar' among Ethiopian Emigrants to Israel: Psychopathology or Culture-Bound Syndrome?" *Psychopathology* 30 (1997): 231. For a discussion of the omission of the anthropological category "idioms of distress," see Lewis-Fernández, "Cultural Formulation," 138.

12. Bartholomew, "Ethnocentricity," 478.

13. Quoted in Grisaru, Budowski, and Witztum, "Possession," 231.

14. Piero Camporesi, *Bread of Dreams: Food and Fantasy in Early Modern Europe,* trans. David Gentilcore (Cambridge: Polity Press, 1989), 17, 83–84.

15. See, for example, Camporesi, *Bread of Dreams;* Linnda R. Caporael, "A Biologist Diagnoses Disease," in Marc Mappen, ed., *Witches and Historians: Interpretations of Salem* (Malabar, Fla.: Krieger, 1980), 63–71; Kristy Duncan, "Was Ergotism Responsible for the Scottish Witch-Hunts?" *Area* 25, no. 1 (1993): 30–36; Mary Kilbourne Matossian, *Poisons of the Past: Molds, Epidemics, and History* (New Haven: Yale University Press, 1989); and Nicholas P. Spanos and Jack Gottlieb, "The Disease Diagnosis Disputed," in Mappen, *Witches and Historians,* 72–82.

16. Matossian, *Poisons of the Past,* 157. Matossian cites the central, non–black-soil provinces of Orel, Kursk, Voronezh, Tambov, Penza, Tula, and Kaluga as having climatic conditions that produced the highest alkaloid yields of claviceps strains, the deadliest form of ergot (39).

17. Caporael, "A Biologist," in Mappen, *Witches and Historians,* 64; Matossian, *Poisons of the Past,* 9.

18. Duncan, "Was Ergotism Responsible?" 30–31.

19. In an epidemic of ergotism in Nolin district, Viatka province, in 1889–1890, the physician N. N. Reformatskii found that while children accounted for 28.1 percent of the victims, they made up 40.9 percent of the fatal cases (*Obshchii obzor epidemii "zloi korchi" v Nolinskom uezde Viatskoi gubernii v 1889–1890 godu* [Kazan: Tipografiia Imperatorskago universiteta, 1890], 10, 11).

20. Of the 152 individuals in my database who became possessed during epidemics, 57 percent were not identified by age. Of the remaining 66 victims, 6 (or 9.1%) were adolescents between the ages of 12 and 18. One of them had been possessed since age nine. Only one other person in the database of 260 shriekers, an adult woman who claimed that she had been a shrieker since age two (no doubt an exaggeration), had become possessed as a child. I am not counting four nineteen-year-olds (three women and one man) among the adolescents as they were of marriageable age. Although the ages of a significant number of victims of *klikushestvo* is unknown, the number of adolescents and children was probably not that much higher as the reporters and eyewitnesses discriminated in their use of language between children and adults.

21. Among the works devoted specifically to ergotism in the Russian Empire and Soviet Union, see M. I. Gurevich, "O psikhicheskom zabolevanii na pochve otravleniia sporyn'ei," *Sovremennaia psikhiatriia* (March 1911): 179–191; 245–55; Maevskii i Nikol'skaia, "'Zlaia korcha' (Rafaniia)," *Zhurnal nevropatologii i*

psikhiatrii, no. 4 (1931): 29–33; N. N. Reformatskii, *Dushevnoe razstroistvo pri otravelnii sporyn'ei (Bolezn' "zlaia korcha")* (Moscow: Tipo-litografiia Vysoch. Utverzhd. T-va I. N. Kushnerev i Ko., 1893); Reformatskii, *Obshchaia klinicheskaia kartina "zloi korchi" po nabliudeniiam v Nolinskom uezde* (Kazan: V tipografii Imperatorskago universiteta, 1892); Reformatskii, *Obshchii obzor;* and R. Stolin, "Sluchai ergotin-psikhosa," *Zhurnal nevropatologii i psikhiatrii,* no. 1 (1931): 108–11.

22. Matossian unpersuasively equates ergotism with *porcha* or bewitchment (*Poisons of the Past,* 22).

23. Reformatskii, *Obshchii obzor,* 12–13; Reformatskii, *Dushevnoe razstroistvo,* 287–88, 290.

24. Matossian, *Poisons of the Past,* 101–2.

25. Krainskii, *Porcha,* 122, 146, 159.

26. Ivan Filipov, *Istoriia Vygovskoi staroobriadcheskoi pustyni* (St. Petersburg: Izdanie D. E. Kozhanchikova, 1862), i, 109–12; Robert O. Crummey, *The Old Believers and the World of Antichrist: The Vyg Community and the Russian State, 1694–1855* (Madison: University of Wisconsin Press, 1970), 65–66.

27. Douglas Raybeck, Judy Shoobe, and James Grauberger, "Women, Stress, and Participation in Possession Cults: A Reexamination of the Calcium Deficiency Hypothesis," *Medical Anthropology Quarterly* 3, no. 2 (1989): 139. For a concise delineation of the various anthropological models at variance with one another, see Sharp, *The Possessed,* 14.

28. Raybeck, Shoobe, and Grauberger, "Women, Stress," 143, 145, 146–47.

29. Ibid., 144, 152, 153, 154.

30. For a discussion of the further marginalization of women household heads during the Stolypin reforms, see Corinne Gaudin, "'No Place to Lay My Head': Marginalization and the Right to Land during the Stolypin Reforms," *Slavic Review* 57, no. 4 (Winter 1998): 764–72.

31. An apt observation that Janice Boddy makes with regard to the importance of fertility for women in Northern Sudan in her *Wombs and Alien Spirits: Women, Men, and "Zar" Cult in Northern Sudan* (Madison: University of Wisconsin Press, 1989), 186.

32. For a discussion of the positive consequences of male migrant work on female spouses, see Barbara Alpern Engel, "The Woman's Side: Male Outmigration and the Family Economy in Kostroma Province," *Slavic Review* 45 (1986): 257–71.

33. Schieffelin, "Evil Spirit Sickness," 7.

34. Ibid., 27.

BIBLIOGRAPHY

ARCHIVAL SOURCES

Gosudarstvennyi arkhiv Iaroslavskoi Oblasti, fond 197. Rostovskaia konsistoriia, op. 1, t. 1, d. 3973.

Hilandar Research Library, Ohio State University, Saratov State University Collection, 1255; Iavlenie i chudesa tolgskoi ikony Bogoroditsy so slovom pokhval'nym i sluzhboi.

Rossiiskii etnograficheskii muzei (REM). Otdel pis'mennykh istochnikov, fond 7. Materialy Etnograficheskogo Biuro V. N. Tenisheva, 1897–1901, op. 1, d. 493.

Rossiiskii gosudarstvennyi arkhiv drevnykh aktov (RGADA), fond 7, op. 1. Dela Preobrazhenskogo prikaza i Tainoi kantseliarii.

Rossiiskii gosudarstvennyi istoricheskii arkhiv (RGIA), fond 796. Kantseliariia Sinoda, op. 195, d. 1449. Kanonizatsiia Pitirima.

Rossiiskii gosudarstvennyi istoricheskii arkhiv goroda Moskvy (RGIAgM), fond 91, op. 2. Moskovskii sovestnyi sud: Obshchee deloproizvodstvo–grazhdanskie dela ugolovnye dela, 1782–1861. dela 559, 575, 659.

Fond 217. Dom umalishennykh v g. Moskve 1779–1838 gg.; Preobrazhenskaia bol'nitsa dlia dushevno-bol'nykh v g. Moskve 1839–1917 gg., op. 1.

Fond 2384. Moskovskaia gorodskaia Psikhiatricheskaia bol'nitsa im. N. A. Alekseeva (Kanatchikovye dachi) Moskovskoi gorodskoi Dumy (1895–1914 gg.), op. 1. Dokumental'nye materialy postaennogo khraneniia za 1895–1914 gg.

NEWSPAPERS AND JOURNALS

Chernigovskiia eparkhial'nyia izvestiia

Etnograficheskoe obozrenie

Iaroslavskiia eparkhial'nyia vedomosti

Khar'kovskii sbornik
Kievlianin
Kievskiia eparkhial'nyia vedomosti
Kievskiia gubernskiia vedomosti
Kurskiia eparkhial'nyia vedomosti
Moskovskiia tserkovnyia vedomosti
Moskovskiia vedomosti
Nevrologicheskii vestnik
Novgorodskiia eparkhial'nyia vedomosti
Obozrenie psikhiatrii, nevrologii i eksperimental'noi psikhologii
Obozrenie psikhiatrii, nevrologii i refleksologii
Russkiia vedomosti
Russkii palomnik
Saratovskiia eparkhial'nyia vedomosti
Smolenskie gubernskie vedomosti
Smolenskii vestnik
Sovremennaia psikhiatriia
Strannik
Sudebnyi vestnik
Tambovskiia eparkhial'nyia vedomosti
Tserkovnye vedomosti
Vera i razum
Vladimirskiia eparkhial'nyia vedomosti
Vladimirskiia gubernskiia vedomosti
Vologodskiia eparkhial'nyia vedomosti
Zhurnal nevropatologii i psikhiatrii imeni S. S. Korsakova

REFERENCE WORKS

American Psychiatric Association. *Diagnostic and Statistical Manual of Mental Disorders*. 3d ed. Washington, D.C.: American Psychiatric Association, 1980.

———. *Diagnostic and Statistical Manual of Mental Disorders*. 3d ed., revised. Washington, D.C.: American Psychiatric Association, 1987.

———. *Diagnostic and Statistical Manual of Mental Disorders*. 4th ed. Washington, D.C.: American Psychiatric Association, 1994.

Averintsev, S. S., A. N. Meshkov, and Iu. N. Popov, eds. *Khristianstvo: Entsiklopedicheskii slovar'*. 3 vols. Moscow: Nauchnoe izdatel'stvo "Bol'shaia Rossiiskaia entsiklopediia," 1993.

Brokgaus, F. A., and I. A. Efron, eds. *Entsiklopedicheskii slovar'*. 86 vols. St. Petersburg: Tipografiia Akts. Obshch. Brokgaus-Efron, 1890–1907.

Soikin, P. P., comp. *Pravoslavnyia russkiia obiteli: Polnoe illiustrirovannoe opisanie vsekh pravoslavnykh russkikh monastyrei v Rossiiskoi Imperii i na Afone*. 1910. Reprint, St. Petersburg: Izdatel'stvo Voskresenie, 1994.

PUBLISHED PRIMARY SOURCES

Afanas'ev, A. N. *Poeticheskiia vozzreniia slavian na prirodu: Opyt sravnitel'nago izucheniia slavianskikh predanii i verovanii, v sviazi s mificheskimi skazaniiami drugikh rodstvennykh narodov*. 3 vols. 1865–69. Reprint, The Hague: Mouton, 1970.

Aikhenval'd, L. I., ed. *Itogi perepisi dushevno-bol'nykh Ufimskoi gubernii (1913 g.)*. Ufa: Ufimskoe gubernskoe zemstvo, 1914.

Alferova, E. A. "Sl. Krygskaia." *Khar'kovskii sbornik* 12, pt. 2 (1898): 3–29.

Almazov, Aleksandr Ivanovich. *Chin nad besnovatym (Pamiatnik grecheskoi pis'mennosti XVII v.)*. Odessa: Ekonomicheskaia tipografiia, 1901.

Alpatov, M. V. *Drevnerusskaia ikonopis'. Early Russian Icon Painting*. Moscow: Iskusstvo, 1978.

Amfiteatrov, Porfirii, "Pervaia godovshchina otkrytia sv. moshchei Sviatitelia i Chudotvortsa Ioasafa, Episkopa Belgorodskago." *Kurskiia eparkhial'nyia vedomosti,* no. 7, 22 February 1912, 856–60.

Antonovich, V. B. "Koldovstvo (dokumenty, protsessy, issledovanie V. B. Antonovicha)." In *Trudy etnograficheskо-statisticheskoi ekspeditsii v zapadnorusskii krai* 1, pt. 2. Ed. P. P. Chubinskii, 319–60. St. Petersburg, 1872.

Appellesov, V. "Strannyi sposob izlecheniia bol'noi." *Iaroslavskiia eparkhial'nyia vedomosti,* unofficial section, no. 48, 29 November 1872, 389–90.

Arkhangel'skii, P. A. *Otchet po osmotru russkikh psikhiatricheskikh zavedenii proizvedennomu po porucheniiu moskovskago gubernskago zemskago sanitarnago soveta*. Moscow: Tipografiia V. V. Islen'eva, 1887.

Artsikhovskaia, E. *O koldovstve, porche i klikushestve*. St. Petersburg: sklad izdanii v redaktsii zhurnala *Narodnoe Obrazovanie,* 1905.

Azbukin, D. I. "O perepisi dushevno-bol'nykh v Vasil'skom uezde, Nizhegorodskoi gubernii." *Nevrologicheskii vestnik* 20, no. 2 (1913): 193–208.

Balov, A. V. "Ocherki Poshekhon'ia: Verovaniia." *Etnograficheskoe obozrenie,* no. 4 (1901): 81–134.

Bazhenov, N. N. *Istoriia moskovskago dollgauza nyne moskovskoi gorodskoi Preobrazhenskoi bol'nitsy dlia dushevno-bol'nykh (Glava iz istorii russkoi meditsiny i kul'turno-bytovoi istorii Moskve)*. Moscow: Izd. Moskovskago gorodskago obshchestvennago upravleniia, 1909.

Bekhterev, V. M. *Vnushenie i ego rol' v obshchestvennoi zhizni*. 3d ed. St. Petersburg: Izd. K. L. Rikkera, 1908.

Beliaev, I. S. "Ikotniki i klikushki." *Russkaia starina* (April 1905): 144–63.

Beliaev, V. "Sluchai iz narodnoi zhizni (Iz nabliudenii sel'skago sviashchennika)." *Rukovodstvo dlia sel'skikh pastyrei,* no. 23 (10 June 1862): 197–200.

Belliustin, I. S. *Description of the Clergy in Rural Russia: The Memoir of a Nineteenth-Century Parish Priest*. Trans. Gregory L. Freeze. Ithaca: Cornell University Press, 1985.

Belogrits-Kotliarevskii, L. S. "Mifologicheskoe znachenie nekotorykh prestuplenii, sovershaemykh po sueveriiu." *Istoricheskii vestnik* 33 (July 1888): 105–15.

Belokurov, Sergei A., ed. "Dela sviat. Nikona patriarkha pache zhe reshchi chudesa vrachebnaia." *Chteniia v Imperatorskom obshchestve istorii i drevnostei rossiiskikh pri Moskovskom universiteta,* bk. 1, pt. 5 (1887): 83–114.

Ben'kovskii, Iv. "Smert', pogrebenie i zagrobnaia zhizn' po poniatiiam i verovaniiu naroda." *Kievskaia starina* (September 1896): 229–61.

Bernshtein, A. N. "Psikhicheskiia zabolevaniia zimoi 1905–6 g. v Moskve." *Sovremennaia psikhiatriia,* no. 4 (1907): 49–67.

Blackmore, R. W., trans. *The Doctrine of the Russian Church Being the Primer or Spelling Book, the Shorter and Longer Catechisms, and A Treatise on the Duty of Parish Priests*. Aberdeen: A. Brown, 1845.

"Blagodatnaia pomoshch' po molitvam k Sviatiteliu Feodosiiu, Arkhiepiskopu Chernigovskomu, Chudotvortsu." *Chernigovskiia eparkhial'nyia izvestiia*, supplement and unofficial section, 36, no. 24, 15 December 1896, 866–70.

Briussov, Valeri. *The Fiery Angel: A Sixteenth Century Romance*. Trans. Ivor Montagu and Sergei Nalbandov. 1930. Reprint, Westport, Conn.: Hyperion, 1977.

Brukhanskii, N. P. "K voprosu o psikhicheskoi zarazitel'nosti (Sluchai psikhicheskoi epidemii v Moskovskoi gub. v 1926 g.)." *Obozrenie psikhiatrii, nevrologii i refleksologii*, nos. 4–5 (1926): 279–90.

Bulgakov, S. V. *Pravoslavie: Prazdniki i posty; Bogosluzhenie; Treby; Raskoly, eresi, sekty; Protivnye khristianstvu i pravoslaviiu ucheniia; Zapadnye khristianskie veroispovedeniia; Sobory Vostochnoi, Russkoi i Zapadnoi Tserkvei (Iz "Nastol'noi knigi dlia sviashchenno-tserkovno-sluzhitilei")*. 1917. Reprint, Moscow: Sovremennik, 1994.

Burtsev, Aleksandr Evgenievich. *Nechistaia i nevedomaia v skazkakh, razskazakh i legendakh russkago naroda*. 2 vols. Petrograd: Tipografiia S. Samoilova, 1915.

Chichagov, Serafim, archimandrite, comp. *Letopis' Serafimo-Diveevskago monastyria Nizhegorodskoi gub. Ardatovskago uezda s zhizneopisaniem osnovatelei eia: prepodobnago Serafima i skhimonakhini Aleksandry, urozhd. A. S. Mel'gunovoi*. 2d ed. St. Petersburg: Serafimo-Diveevskii monastyr', 1903.

Christian, R. F., ed. and trans. *Tolstoy's Letters*. 2 vols. New York: Charles Scribner's Sons, 1978.

Chudesa pri otkrytii moshchei prepodobnago Serafima Sarovskago. Moscow: Otd. tip. Tovarestva I. D. Sytina, 1903.

"Chudesnaia pomoshch' po molitvam k sviatiteliu Feodosiiu Uglitskomu, Arkhiepiskopu Chernigovskomu Chudotvortsu." *Chernigovskiia eparkhial'nyia izvestiia*, supplement and unofficial section, 36, no. 21, 1 November 1896, 743–47.

"Chudesnyia istseleniia pri moshchakh Sviatitelia Feodosiia Uglitskago v dni otkrytiia i proslavleniia ikh." *Chernigovskiia eparkial'nyia izvestiia*, supplement and unofficial section, 36, no. 18, 15 September 1896, 619–22; no. 20, 15 October 1896, 663–69.

"Chudesnyia istseleniia u moshchei sviatitelia Feodosiia, Arkhiepiskopa Chernigovskago, Chudotvortsa." *Chernigovskiia eparkhial'nyia izvestiia*, supplement and unofficial section, 36, no. 22, 15 November–1 December 1896, 743–47, 803–7.

Dal', Vladimir. *O poveriiakh, sueveriiakh i predrassudkakh russkogo naroda; Materialy po russkoi demonologii (Iz etnograficheskikh rabot); Russkie bylichki, byval'shchiny i skazki o mifologicheskikh personazhakh (iz fol'klornykh sbornikov)*. Moscow: Terra, Knizhnaia lavka, 1997.

Davidov, Ia. A. "Demonomaniia." *Arkhiv psikhiatrii, neirologii i sudebnoi psikhopatologii* 7, no. 1 (1886): 85–102.

"Delo o klikushakh." *Zhurnal Ministerstvo iustitsii*, no. 9 (September 1862): 617–26.

Dimitrii, Bishop. *Domashnii molitvoslov dlia userdstvuiushchikh*. Kharbin: Bratstvo imeni sv. Ioanna Bogoslova pri Bogoslovskom fakul'tete Instituta sv. Vladimira, 1943.

Dmitrieva, Valentina Iovovna. *Klikushi ili porchennye i kak ikh lechit'*. 2d ed. Moscow: Gosudarstvennoe izdatel'stvo, 1926.

Dobrovol'skii, V. N. *Smolenskii etnograficheskii sbornik*. Vol. 1. St. Petersburg: Tipografiia E. Evdokimova, 1891. *Zapiski Imperatorskago russkago geograficheskago obshchestva po otdeleniiu etnografii,* vol. 20.

Dostoevskii, Fedor M. *Brat'ia Karamazovy: Roman v chetyrekh chastiakh s epilogom.* Paris: Bookking International, 1995.

———. *Diary of a Writer.* 2 vols. Trans. Boris Brasol. New York: Charles Scribner's Sons, 1949.

———. *Polnoe sobranie sochinenii.* 30 vols. Leningrad: Izd. Nauka, 1972.

———. *The Village of Stepanchikovo and Its Inhabitants: From the Notes of an Unknown.* Trans. Ignat Avsey. Rev. ed. London: Penguin, 1995.

Dostoevsky, Anna. *Dostoevsky: Reminiscences.* Trans. and ed. Beatrice Stillman. New York: Liveright, 1975.

Druzhinin, N. P., ed. *Iuridicheskoe polozhenie krest'ian.* St. Petersburg, 1897.

———. "Krest'ianskii sud v ego poslednem fazise." *Nabliudatel',* no. 3 (1893): 243–57.

Ef., P. "Popytka okoldovat' volostnoi sud." *Kievskaia starina,* no. 3 (1884): 508–9.

Efimenko, P. *Sbornik malorossiiskikh zaklinanii.* Moscow: Izd. Imperatorskago obshchestva istorii i drevnostei rossiiskikh pri Moskovskom universitete, 1874.

———. "Sud nad ved'mami." *Kievskaia starina* (November 1883): 374–401.

Eleonskaia, Elena Nikolaevna. *K izucheniiu zagovora i koldovstva v Rossii.* Vol. 1. Moscow: Izd. Kommissii po Narodnoi slovesnosti pri etnograficheskom otdele I.O.L.E.A.I.E., 1917.

The Englishwoman in Russia: Impressions of the Society and Manners of the Russians at Home. New York: Charles Scribner, 1855.

Ergol'skii, V. N. "O sudebno-psikhiatricheskoi ekspertize v sektantskikh delakh." *Vestnik obshchestvennoi gigieny, sudebnoi i prakticheskoi meditsiny* 30, no. 2 (May 1896), pt. 3: 1–42.

———. "Prestuplenie pod vliianiem demonomanicheskikh galliutsinatsii. (Sudebno-psikhiatricheskii sluchai)." *Arkhiv psikhiatrii, neirologii i sudebnoi psikhopatologii* 24, no. 2 (1894): 61–76.

Esipov, G. V. "Koldovstvo v XVII i XVIII stoletiiakh iz arkhivnykh del." *Drevnaia i novaia Rossiia* 3 (1878): 64–70, 156–64, 234–44.

Evdokim, Arkhimandrite. "O moshchei prepod. Serafima Sarovskago." *Bogoslovskii vestnik* (July–August 1903): 513–63.

Filipov, Ivan. *Istoriia Vygovskoi staroobriadcheskoi pustyni.* St Petersburg: Izd. D. E. Kozhanchikova, 1862.

Firsov, B. M., and I. G. Kiseleva, comps. *Byt velikorusskikh krest'ian-zemlepashtsev: Opisanie materialov etnograficheskogo biuro kniazia V. N. Tenisheva (na primere Vladimirskoi gubernii).* St. Petersburg: Izdatel'stvo Evropeiskogo Doma, 1993.

Freud, Sigmund. "A Neurosis of Demoniacal Possession in the Seventeenth Century." In *Freud: Studies in Parapsychology.* Ed. P. Rieff. New York: Collier Books, 1963.

Gadziatskii, F. Kh. "Dushevnyia razstroistva v sviazi s politicheskimi sobytiiami v Rossii." *Voenno-meditsinskii zhurnal* (September 1908): 89–99.

Genik, E. A. "Sluchai *folie à deux.*" *Nevrologicheskii vestnik* 5, no. 4 (1897): 59–72.

———. "Tret'ia epidemiia isterii v Moskovskoi gubernii." *Sovremennaia psikhiatriia*

6 (August 1912): 588–604.

———. "Vtoraia epidemiia istericheskikh sudorog v Podol'skom uezde, Moskovskoi gubernii." *Nevrologicheskii vestnik* 6, no. 4 (1898): 146–59.

German, I. S. "O psikhicheskom razstroistve depressivnago kharaktera, razvivshemsia u bol'nykh na pochve perezhivaemykh politicheskikh sobytiia." *Zhurnal nevropatologii i psikhiatrii imeni S. S. Korsakova* 3 (1907): 313–24.

Goloshchapov, Sergei. "Vera v chudesa s tochki zreniia sovremennoi bogoslovskoi nauki." *Vera i razum,* nos. 5–6, 8 (1912): 658–76, 749–71, 206–23.

Grinchenko, B. D. *Etnograficheskie materialy, sobrannyia v Chernigovskoi i sosednikh s nei guberniiakh.* Vol. 2. Chernigov: Tip. Gubernskago zemstva, 1897.

Grisbrooke, W. Jardine, ed. and trans. *Spiritual Counsels of Father John of Kronstadt.* London: James Clarke, 1967.

Grossman, G. B. "K voprosu o klikushestve." *Prakticheskii vrach,* 13 May 1906, 316–18.

Grushetskii, N. *Kolduny i ved'my, domovye, leshie, rusalki, chary i nagovory, primety i pover'ia: Ocherki narodnykh sueverii.* Moscow: M. E. Konusov, 1898.

Heppell, Muriel, trans. *The "Paterik" of the Kievan Caves Monastery.* Harvard Library of Early Ukrainian Literature, English Translations. Vol. 1. Cambridge, Mass.: Ukrainian Research Institute of Harvard University; distributed by Harvard University Press, 1989.

Hnatiuk, Volodymyr, comp. *Znadoby do ukrains'koi demonol'ohii.* 2 vols. L'viv: Nakladom Naukovoho Tovarystva imeni Shevchenka, 1912. In *Etnohrafichnyi zbirnik,* 33, 34.

Iakobii, P. I. "'Antikhrist': Sudebno-psikhiatricheskii ocherk." *Sovremennaia psikhiatriia* 3 (June–July, August 1909): 288–301, 337–55.

———. "Religiozno-psikhicheskiia epidemiia: Iz psikhiatricheskoi ekspertizy." *Vestnik Evropy,* nos. 10–11 (October–November 1903): 732–58, 117–66.

Iakovenko, I. "Epidemiia istericheskikh sudorog v Podol'skom uezda, Moskovskoi gub." *Vestnik obshchestvennoi gigieny, sudebnoi i prakticheskoi meditsiny* 25, no. 3 (March 1895): 93–109.

Iakovenko, Vladimir Ivanovich. *Dushevno-bol'nye Moskovskoi gubernii 1900 g.* Moscow: Moskovskoe gubernskoe zemstvo, 1900.

———. *Indutsirovannoe pomeshatel'stvo ("folie à deux") kak odin iz vidov patologicheskago podrazhaniia.* St. Petersburg: Tip. M. M. Stasiulevicha, 1887.

———, comp. *Mediko-khoziaistvennyi otchet po Pokrovskoi psikhiatricheskoi bol'nitse Moskovskago gubernskago zemstva za 1899 god–1902 god.* Vols. 7–10. Moscow: Moskovskoe gubernskoe zemskoe sobranie, 1890–1903.

Iakovenko, V. S. "Psikhicheskaia epidemiia na religioznoi pochve v Anan'evskom i Tiraspol'skom uezdakh Khersonskoi gub." *Sovremennaia psikhiatriia* 5 (March–April 1911): 191–98, 229–45.

Iakushkin, E. I. *Obychnoe pravo: Materialy dlia bibliografii obychnago prava.* Vols. 1–2. Iaroslavl', 1875, 1896.

Iaroshevskii, S. "Materialy k voprosu o massovykh nervnopsikhicheskikh zabolevaniiakh." *Obozrenie psikhiatrii, nevrologii i eksperimental'noi psikhologii,* no. 1 (January 1906): 1–9.

Ikonen: Ein Kalender für 1988. Cologne: Ikonen Gallerie Rotmann, 1987.

Isaevich, S. N. "Eshche raskazets o vovkulakakh i charovnikakh." *Kievskaia starina* 12 (1883): 700.

"Istselenie oderzhimoi. Razskaz sviashchennia (Zhurnal *Voskresenie,* no. 16)." *Rebus* 12, no. 45 (7 November 1893): 429–31.

Itkina, E. I., comp. *Russkii risovannyi lubok kontsa XVIII–nachala XX veka: Iz sobraniia Gosudarstvennogo Istoricheskogo muzeia Moskva.* Moscow: Russkaia kniga, 1992.

Ivanov, A. I. "Verovaniia krest'ian Orlovskoi gub." *Etnograficheskoe obozrenie* 12, no. 4 (1901): 68–118.

Ivanov, I. "Znakharstvo, sheptaniia i zagovory (V Starobel'skom i Kupianskom uezdakh Khar'kovskoi gubernii)." *Kievskaia starina* 13 (1885): 730–44.

Ivanov, P. "Tolki naroda ob urozhae, voine i chume." *Etnograficheskoe obozrenie* 13, no. 3 (1901): 134.

Ivanov, P. V. "Narodnye razskazy o ved'makh i upyriakh. (Materialy dlia kharakteristiki mirosozertsaniia krest'ianskago naseleniia Kupianskago uezda)." *Sbornik Khar'kovskago istoriko-filologicheskago obshchestva* 3 (1891): 156–228.

"K voprosu ob opakhivanii." *Etnograficheskoe obozrenie* 22, nos. 3–4 (1910): 175–78.

Kalashnikov, G. A., and A. M. Kalashnikov. "Sl. Nikol'skoe." *Khar'kovskii sbornik* 8, pt. 2 (1894): 173–342.

Kantor, Marvin, ed. and comp. *Medieval Slavic Lives of Saints and Princes.* Ann Arbor: University of Michigan, 1983.

Kantorovich, Ia. *Srednevekovye protsessy o ved'makh.* 1899. Reprint, Moscow: Kniga, 1990.

Karabchevskii, N. P. *Okolo pravosudiia: Stat'i, soobshcheniia i sudebnye ocherki.* St. Petersburg: Trud, 1902.

Kashchenko, P. P. *Kratkii otchet po perepisi dushevno-bol'nykh v S.-Peterburgskoi gubernii.* St. Petersburg: Tipo-lit. Energiia, [1911].

———. *Statisticheskii ocherk polozheniia dushevno-bol'nykh v Nizhegorodskoi gubernii.* Nizhnii Novgorod: Nizhegorodskoe gubernskoe zemstvo, 1895.

Kazachenko-Trirodov, N. P. "Psikhoterapiia pri klikushestve." *Obozrenie psikhiatrii, nevrologii i refleksologii* 1, nos. 4–5 (1926): 292–94.

Kh., A. "K voprosu o koldunakh." *Rukovodstvo dlia sel'skikh pastyrei,* no. 24 (12 June 1894): 149–54.

Khotinskii, Matvei. *Charodeistvo i tainstvennyia iavleniia v noveishee vremia.* St. Petersburg: Izd. E. N. Akhmatovoi, 1866.

"Khronika." *Sovremennaia psikhiatriia,* no. 12 (December 1911): 705–11.

Kirpichnikov, A. I. "Ocherki po mifologii XIX veka." *Etnograficheskoe obozrenie* 6, no. 4 (1894): 1–42.

Klementovskii, A. *Klikushi: Ocherk.* Moscow: V tip. Katkova i komp., 1860.

Kobelev, E. I. "Sl. Popovka." *Khar'kovskii sbornik* 12, pt. 2 (1898): 103–34.

Kolchin, A. "Verovaniia krest'ian Tul'skoi gubernii." *Etnograficheskoe obozrenie* 11, no. 3 (1899): 1–60.

"Kolduny i klikushi (Po povodu sudebnykh protsessov ob ubiistvakh koldunov)." *Rukovodstvo dlia sel'skikh pastyrei,* no. 4 (23 January 1894): 81–88; no. 6 (6 February 1894): 145–51; no. 7 (13 February 1894): 172–74.

[Koposov, V.]. *Mediko-khoziaistvennyi otchet Saratovskoi gubernskoi zemskoi psikhiatricheskoi lechebnitsy za 1887 god.* Saratov: Tipografiia gubernskago zemstva, 1888.

Kostrov, N. N. "Koldovstvo i porcha u krest'ian Tomskoi gub." *Zapiski Zapadnago sibirskago otdela Imperatorskago russkago geograficheskago obshchestva* 1, pt. 2 (1879): 1–16.

Kotsovskii, A. D. "O tak nazyvaemom 'Baltskom dvizhenii' v Bessarabii." *Trudy Bessarabskago obshchestva estestvoispytatelei i liubitelei estestvoznaniia* 3 (1911–1912): 142–80.

Krachkovskii, Iu. F. "Byt zapadno-russkago selianina." *Chteniia v Imperatorskom obshchestve istorii i drevnostei rossiiskikh pri Moskovskom universitete,* bk. 4, pt. 5 (October–December 1873): 1–212.

Krainskii, N. V. *Porcha, klikushi i besnovatye, kak iavleniia russkoi narodnoi zhizni.* Novgorod: Gubernskaia tipografiia, 1900.

Krasnokutskii, S. A. "So slov sel'skoi babki." *Kievskiia eparkhial'nyia vedomosti,* no. 31, 1 August 1879, 11–16; no. 44, 31 October 1879, 3–5; no. 26, 25 June 1880, 3–7; no. 30, 23 July 1880, 9–13; no. 37, 10 September 1880, 4–7; no. 38, 17 September 1880, 5–10.

Lakhtin, M. *Besooderzhimost' v sovremennoi derevne: Istoriko-psikhologicheskoe izsledovanie.* Moscow: Tipo-litografiia T-va I. N. Kushnerev, 1910.

Lebedev, A. *Sviatitel' Tikhon Zadonskii i vseia Rossii chudotvorets (Ego zhizn', pisaniia i proslavlenie).* 3d ed. St. Petersburg: Tipografiia V. Smirnova, 1896.

Leskov, Nikolai S. *Satirical Stories of Nikolai Leskov.* Trans. and ed. William B. Edgerton. New York: Pegasus, 1969.

———. *Sobranie sochinenii.* 11 vols. Moscow: Gos. izd. Khudozhestvennoi literatury, 1956.

———. [M. Stebnitskii, pseud.]. "Russkoe obshchestvo v Parizhe," *Biblioteka dlia chteniia* 177, no. 5 (May 1863): 1–31.

"Letopis' Obshchestva nevropatologov i psikhiatrov pri Imperatorskom Kazanskom universitete." *Protokol VIII zasedaniia Obshchestva nevropatologov i psikhiatrov 18 dekabria 1913 godu,* in *Nevrologicheskii vestnik* 21, no. 1 (1914): 318.

Levenstim, A. A. "Sueverie i ugolovnoe pravo: Izsledovanie po istorii russkago prava i kul'tury." *Vestnik prava* 36, nos. 1–2 (1906): 291–343, 181–251.

———. "Sueverie v ego otnoshenii k ugolovnomu pravu." *Zhurnal Ministerstva iustitsii,* nos. 1–2 (January–February 1897): 157–219, 62–127.

Liubushin, A. L. "Organicheskoe slaboumie u isterichnoi zhenshchiny." *Obozrenie psikhiatrii, nevrologii i eksperimental'noi psikhologii,* no. 9 (September 1899): 694–706.

Maksimov, S. V. *God na severe.* Arkhangel'sk: Severo-zapadnoe knizhnoe izdatel'stvo, 1884.

———. *Nechistaia sila. Nevedomaia sila.* Vol. 18 of *Sobranie sochinenii.* St. Petersburg: Tipo-lit. Aktsionernago O-va "Samoobrazovanie," 1896.

Mansikka, V. "Predstaviteli zlogo nachala v russkikh zagovorakh." *Zhivaia starina* 18, no. 4 (1909): 3–30.

Markov, Evgenii. "Derevenskii koldun." *Istoricheskii vestnik* 28, no. 4 (April 1887): 1–24.

Marusov, P. "Sl. Kaban'e." *Khar'kovskii sbornik* 7 (1893): 413–60.

Maughan, H. Hamilton. *The Liturgy of the Eastern Orthodox Church.* London: Faith Press, 1916.

Mikhailov, N. I. "Narodnye predrazsudki: Vera v porchu i vrachevanie." *Biblioteka dlia chteniia* 156 (1859): 1–44.

Miloradovich, V. P. "Ukrains'kaia ved'ma." *Kievskaia starina* 72 (February 1901): 217–33.

———. "Zametki o malorusskoi demonologii." *Kievskaia starina* (August–September 1899): 196–209, 379–400.

Minkh, A. N. "Klikushi." *Etnograficheskoe obozrenie* 13, no. 1 (1901): 166–67.

Mitskevich, S. I. *Menerik i emiriachen'e: Formy isterii v kolymskom krae*. In *Materialy Komissii po izucheniiu iakutskoi avtonomnoi sovetskoi sotsialisticheskoi respubliki* 15 (1929): i-53.

Muller, Alexander V., ed. and trans. *The Spiritual Regulation of Peter the Great*. Seattle: University of Washington Press, 1972.

Muratov, V. A. "K voprosu ob ostrykh istericheskikh psikhozakh." *Nevrologicheskii vestnik* 10, no. 1 (1902): 147–79.

Nikitin, M. P. "K voprosu o klikushestve." *Obozrenie psikhiatrii, nevrologii i eksperimental'noi psikhologii,* nos. 9–10 (September–October 1903): 656–68, 746–56.

———. "Religioznoe chuvstvo, kak istseliaiushchii faktor." *Obozrenie psikhiatrii, nevrologii i eksperimental'noi psikhologii,* nos. 1–2 (January–February 1904): 1–9, 100–8.

Nikitina, N. A. "K voprosu o russkikh koldunakh." *Sbornik Muzeia antropologii i etnografii* 7 (1928): 229–325.

Nikonov, Fedor. "O blagochestivykh obychaiakh i religioznykh uchrezhdeniiakh, sushchestvuiushchikh u zhitelei Voronezhskoi eparkhii." *Voronezhskii literaturnyi sbornik* 1 (1861): 323–72.

Obninskii, Petr Narkizovich. "V oblasti sueverii i predrazsudkov (Ocherk iz byta sovremennoi derevni)." *Iuridicheskii vestnik,* no. 11 (1890): 359–81.

"Obriad opakhivan'ia." *Chernigovskiia eparkhial'nyia izvestiia,* no. 18 (1876): 515–18.

Opisanie dokumentov i del, khraniashchikhsia v arkhive Sviateishego Sinoda. 31 vols. St. Petersburg, 1869–1916.

"Opredelenie Sviateishago Sinoda: ot 26 iiunia–5 iiulia 1896 g. za, no. 1916, o proslavlenii i otkrytii moshchei sviatitelia Feodosiia Uglitskago, arkhiepiskopa Chernigovskago." *Vera i razum,* no. 15, pt. 3 (August 1896): 378–81.

Orlov, M. A. *Istoriia snoshenii cheloveka s d'iavolom*. 1904. Reprint, Moscow: Respublika, 1992.

Orlova, Alexandra. *Musorgsky's Days and Works: A Biography in Documents*. Trans. and ed. Roy J. Guenther. Ann Arbor, Mich.: UMI Research Press, 1983.

Osipov, V. P. *Kurs obshchego ucheniia o dushevnykh bolezniakh*. Berlin: RSFSR gosudarstvennoe izdatel'stvo, 1923.

———. "O politicheskikh ili revoliutsionnykh psikhozakh." *Nevrologicheskii vestnik* 17, no. 3 (1910): 437–92.

———. "Oderzhimost' gadami i eia mesto v klassifikatsii psikhozov." *Obozrenie psikhiatrii, nevrologii i eksperimental'noi psikhologii,* nos. 2–3 (February–March 1905): 122–39, 185–90.

Ostapovich, N. L. "Opyt perepisi nervno- i dushevnobol'nykh v sele Nizhnii Mamon Verkhne-Mamonskogo raiona TsChO." *Zhurnal nevropatologii i psikhiatrii,* no. 3 (1931): 22–30.

Pamiatniki starinnoi russkoi literatury. 4 vols. 1860–1862. Reprint, The Hague: Mouton, 1970.

Pares, Bernard. *Russia and Reform*. London, 1907.
Parunov, M. N. *Leshie, rusalki, kolduny, ved'my i oborotni: Narodnye predrazsudki i sueveriia*. St. Petersburg: Tip. K. Plotnikova, 1873.
Pisemskii, A. F. *Sobranie sochinenii v deviati tomakh*. 9 vols. Moscow: Biblioteka Ogonek, 1959.
Polnoe sobranie postanovlenii i rasporiazhenii po vedomstvu pravoslavnago ispovedaniia Rossiiskoi Imperii. 19 vols. St. Petersburg: V Sinodalnoi tip., 1915.
Polnoe sobranie zakonov Rossiiskoi Imperii s 1649 goda. 1st Series, 1649–1825. 45 vols. St. Petersburg, 1830.
Popov, G. I. "'Meriachen'e.' (Nabroski o psikho-neirozakh sredi iakutov)." *Sibirskii vrach*, no. 26 (29 June 1914): 463–65.
———. *Russkaia narodno-bytovaia meditsina: Po materialam etnograficheskago biuro kniazia V. N. Tenisheva*. St. Petersburg: Tip. A. S. Suvorina, 1903.
Popov, P. "Porchel'niki v Meshchovskom uezde." *Rukovodstvo dlia sel'skikh pastyrei* (21 October 1862): 263–66.
Poselianin, E., ed. *Bogomater': Polnoe illiustrirovannoe opisanie eia zemnoi zhizni i posviashchennykh eia imeni chudotovornykh ikon*. St. Petersburg: Knigoizdatel'stvo P. P. Soikina, [n.d.]; rpt. 1980.
———. "Chudesa Prepodobnago Serafima." *Pastyrskii sobesednik*, nos. 48–49 (1903), supplement: 191–93.
Pozdniaia russkaia ikona konets XVIII-XIX vek. St. Petersburg: Limbus Press, 1994.
Proffer, Carl R., ed. *The Unpublished Dostoevsky: Diaries and Notebooks (1860–81)*. Vol. 2. Trans. Arline Boyer and Carl Proffer. Ann Arbor, Mich.: Ardis, 1975.
Prokhorov, G. M., E. G. Vodolazkin, and E. E. Shevchenko, eds. and trans. *Prepodobnye Kirill, Ferapont i Martinian Belozerskie*. 2d ed. St. Petersburg: Glagol, 1994.
Prorozov, L. "Vtoroe Vserossiiskoe Soveshchanie po voprosam psikhiatrii i nevrologii (Moskva 12–17 noiabria 1923 g.)." *Zhurnal psikhologii, nevrologii i psikhiatrii* 4 (1924): 168–70.
Prugavin, A. S. *Golodaiushchee krest'ianstvo: Ocherki golodovki 1898–99 goda*. Moscow: Izd. Posrednika, 1906.
Pryzhov, Ivan G. *26 moskovskikh prorokov, iurodivykh, dur i durakov i drugie trudy po russkoi istorii i etnografii*. Ed. L. Ia. Lur'e. St. Petersburg: EZRO, 1996.
Pushkin, A. S. *Sochineniia*. Vol. 1, *Stikhotvoreniia, skazki*. Moscow: Gosudarstvennoe izdatel'stvo khudozhestvennoi literatury, 1962.
Reformatskii, N. N. *Dushevnoe razstroistvo pri otravlenii sporyn'ei (Bolezn' "zlaia korcha")*. Moscow: Tipo-litografiia Vysoch. utverzhd. T-va I. N. Kushnerev i Ko., 1893.
———. *Obshchaia klinicheskaia kartina "zloi korchi" po nabliudeniiam v Nolinskom uezde*. Kazan: V tipografii Imperatorskago universiteta, 1892.
———. *Obshchii obzor epidemii "zloi korchi" v Nolinskom uezde Viatskoi gubernii v 1889–1890 godu*. Kazan: Tipografiia Imperatorskago universiteta, 1890.
Rovinskii, D. *Russkiia narodnyia kartinki*. 5 vols. In *Sbornik otdeleniia russkago iazyka i slovesnosti Imperatorskii akademii nauk*. Vols. 23–27. St. Petersburg, 1881.
Rudinskii, Nikolai. "Znakharstvo v Skopinskom i Dankovskom uezdakh Riazanskoi gubernii." *Zhivaia starina* 6, no. 2 (1896): 169–201.
Sanin, V. *Na veselykh gorakh: Ocherki torzhestvennykh molebstvii staroobriadtsev, illiustrirovannye risunkami s natury khudozhnika Vl. A. Kuznetsova i otchety o*

podgotovitel'nykh trudakh k Vserossiiskomu s"ezdu staroobriadtsev chasovennago soglasiia. Ekaterinburg: Tipografiia gazety *Ural'skii Krai,* 1910.

Sbornik starinnykh bumag, khraniashchikhsia v muzeie P. I. Shchukina. 10 vols. Moscow: Tov. Tip. Mamontova, 1896–1902.

Serebrov, Aleksandr [Tikhonov, A. N.]. *Vremia i liudi: Vospominaniia 1898–1905.* Moscow: Moskovskii rabochii, 1960.

Sergievskii, N. *Sviatitel' Tikhon, Episkop Voronezhskii i Zadonskii i vseia Rossii chudotvorets: Ego zhizn' i podvigi, chudesa, proslavlenie po smerti i tvoreniia.* 1898. Reprint, Jordanville, N.Y.: Holy Trinity Monastery, 1965.

Shalabutov, K. V. "Sluchai besooderzhimosti." *Nevrologicheskii vestnik* 19, no. 3 (1912): 521–31.

Shinkarev, P. M. "Sl. Belo-Kurakino." *Khar'kovskii sbornik* 9, pt. 2 (1895): 239–342.

Shteinberg, S. "Klikushestvo i ego sudebno-meditsinskoe znachenie." *Arkhiv sudebnoi meditsiny i obshchestvennoi gigieny* 6, no. 2 (1870): 64–81.

Sikorskii, I. A. "Epidemicheskiia vol'nyia smerti i smerto-ubiistva v Ternovskikh khutorakh (bliz Tiraspolia)." *Voprosy nervno-psikhicheskoi meditsiny* 2, no. 3 (July–September 1897): 453–511.

———. "Psikhopaticheskaia epidemiia 1892 goda v Kievskoi gubernii." *Universitetskiia izvestiia [Universiteta sv. Vladimira, Kiev],* no. 4, pt. 2 (April 1893): 1–46.

Skavronskii, N. *Ocherki Moskvy.* 1862. Reprint, Moscow: Moskovskii rabochii, 1993.

Skazanie o zhizni, podvigakh i chudesakh sviatitelia i chudotvortsa Ioasafa, Episkopa Belogradskago i Oboianskago, Predlagaemoe blagochestivomu vnimaniiu Kurskoi pastvy Soborom kurskikh episkopov. In *Kurskiia eparkhial'nyia vedomosti,* no. 31, 5 August 1911.

Skliar, N. I. "O simptomokomplekse trevogi i strakha s dvigatel'nym bezpokoistvom pri psikhogennykh psikhozakh." *Sovremennaia psikhiatriia,* nos. 1–2 (January–February 1917): 12–32.

Skubachevskii, P. "Belgorodskiia torzhestva: Vpechatleniia ochevidtsa," *Vera i razum,* no. 19 (October 1911): 118–28.

Somov, Orest. *Selected Prose in Russian.* Ed. John Mersereau, Jr., and George Harjan. Ann Arbor: University of Michigan, 1974.

Sreznevskii, B. "Obzor pogody za avgust 1897 g. (nov. stil')." *Meteorologicheskii vestnik,* no. 9 (September 1897): 407–24.

Strel'chuk, I., and Rumshevich. "Zhizn' i byt dushevno bol'nykh na sele (Organizatsiia vnebol'nichnoi pomoshchi dushevnobol'nym selianam)." *Zhurnal nevropatologii i psikhiatrii,* no. 5 (1930): 123–30.

Sulima, K. P. "Epidemiia ikoty (Singultus) v selenii Ketrosy, Iampol'skago uezda, Podol'skoi gubernii." *Vestnik obshchestvennoi gigieny, sudebnoi i prakticheskoi meditsiny* 4 (October–December 1889): 36–40.

———. "Koe-chto o polozhenii dushevno-bol'nykh v iugo-zapadnom krae." *Arkhiv psikhiatrii, neirologii i sudebnoi psikhopatologii* 6, no. 1 (1885): 47–52.

Sumtsov, N. F. "Kolduny, ved'my i upyri." *Sbornik Khar'kovskago istoriko-filologicheskago obshchestva* 3 (1891): 229–78.

Tarnovskaia, P. "Zhenskaia prestupnost' v sviazi s rannimi brakami." *Severnyi vestnik,* no. 5 (May 1898): 133–49.

Tokarskii, A. A. *Meriachenie i bolezn' sudorozhnykh nodergivanii.* 2d ed. Moscow, 1893.

———. *Psikhicheskiia epidemii.* Moscow: I. N. Kushnerev, 1893.

Tolstoy, Leo. *Great Short Works of Leo Tolstoy*. Trans. Louise and Aylmer Maude. New York: Harper and Row, 1967.

Tomchenko, Sergei, comp. *Zhitiia i tvoreniia russkikh sviatykh: Zhizneopisaniia i dukhovnye nastavleniia velikikh podvizhnikov Khristianskogo blagochestiia, prosiiavshikh v zemle Russkoi. Narodnye pochitaniia i prazdniki Pravoslavnoi Tserkvi*. Moscow: Sovremennik, Donskoi monastyr', 1993.

Tulub, P. A. "Sueverie i prestuplenie. (Iz vospominanii mirovogo sud'i)." *Istoricheskii vestnik,* no. 3 (March 1901): 1,082–1,101.

V., A. "Sviatitel' Feodosii Uglitskii, Arkhiepiskop Chernigovskii (Po povodu 200–letiia so dnia blazhennoi konchiny Sviatitelia Feodosiia)." *Chernigovskiia eparkhial'nyia izvestiia,* supplement and unofficial section, 36, no. 3, 1 February 1896, 85–91.

Veniamin, archbishop. *Novaia skrizhal' ili ob"iasnenie o tserkvi, o liturgii i o vsekh sluzhbakh i utvariakh tserkovnykh*. 2 vols. 16th ed. 1899. Reprint, Moscow: Russkii dukhovnyi tsentr, 1992.

Veriuzhskii, I. *Istoricheskie skazaniia o zhizni sviatykh, podvizavshikhsia v Vologodskoi eparkhii proslavliaemykh v seiu tserkov'ia i mestno chtimykh*. Vologda: Pechatano v tipografii V. A. Gudkova-Beliakova, 1880.

Vesin, L. "Narodnyi samosud nad koldunami. (K istorii narodnykh obychaev)." *Severnyi vestnik* 7, no. 9, pt. 2 (September 1892): 57–79.

Vinogradov, V. "Chudesnyia istseleniia Iisusom Khristom bol'nykh," *Vera i razum,* nos. 1–2 (1913): 8–30, 171–95.

Ware, Kallistos, and Mother Mary, trans. *The Festal Menaion*. London: Faber and Faber, 1969.

———. *The Lenten Triodion*. London: Faber and Faber, 1978.

Zabylin, M. *Russkii narod: Ego obychai, obriady, predaniia, sueveriia i poeziia*. Moscow: M. Berezin, 1880.

Zakon Bozhii: Pervaia kniga o Pravoslavnoi vere. Paris: YMCA Press, 1956.

"Zakrutki." *Kievskiia eparkhial'nyia vedomosti,* no. 33, 15 August 1879, 9–10.

Zelenin, D. K. "K voprosu o rusalkakh (Kult pokoinikov, umershikh neestvestvennoi smert'iu, u russkikh i u finnov)." *Kievskaia starina,* nos. 3–4 (1911): 354–424.

———. *Ocherki russkoi mifologii*. Vol. 1, *Umershie neestestvennoiu smert'iu i rusalki*. Petrograd: Tip. A. V. Orlova, 1916.

Zenkovsky, Serge A., ed. and trans. *Medieval Russia's Epics, Chronicles and Tales*. Rev. ed. New York: E. P. Dutton, 1974.

[Zhadanovskii], Arsenii. *Vospominaniia*. Moscow: Izd-vo Pravoslavnogo Sviato-Tikhonovskago Bogoslovskogo Instituta, 1995.

Zhitie, chudesa i istseleniia Prepodobnago Serafima, Sarovskago Chudotvortsa. Odessa: Tip. E. I. Fesenko, 1907.

Zhizn', podvigi i chudesa prepodobnago Serafima Sarovskago, s prilozheniem opisaniia Sarovskoi pustyni. Moscow: Otdel. tip. I. D. Sytina, 1903.

Zotov, V. R. "Dokumental'naia istoriia chorta." *Istoricheskii vestnik* 15, no. 1 (January 1884): 158–74.

SELECTED SECONDARY SOURCES

Ali-Gombe, Abubakar, Elspeth Guthrie, and Niall McDermott. "Mass Hysteria: One Syndrome or Two?" *British Journal of Psychiatry* 168 (1996): 633–35.

Amato, Anthony J. "In the Wild Mountains, Idiom, Economy, and Ideology among the Hutsuls, 1849 to 1939." Ph.D. diss., Indiana University, 1998.

Anderson, R. D. "The History of Witchcraft: A Review with Some Psychiatric Comments." *American Journal of Psychiatry* 126 (1970): 1727–35.

Andrew, Joe. *Russian Writers and Society in the Second Half of the Nineteenth Century*. Atlantic Highlands, N.J.: Humanities Press, 1982.

Ankarloo, Bengt, and Stuart Clark, eds. *Witchcraft and Magic in Europe: The Eighteenth and Nineteenth Centuries*. Philadelphia: University of Pennsylvania Press, 1999.

Ankarloo, Bengt, and G. Henningsen, eds. *Early Modern Witchcraft: Centres and Peripheries*. Oxford: Clarendon, 1989.

Baron, Samuel H., and Nancy Shields Kollmann, eds. *Religion and Culture in Early Modern Russia and Ukraine*. DeKalb: Northern Illinois University Press, 1997.

Barstow, Anne Llewellyn. *Witchcraze: A New History of the European Witch Hunts*. San Francisco: Pandora, 1994.

Bartholomew, Robert E. "Ethnocentricity and the Social Construction of 'Mass Hysteria.'" *Culture, Medicine, and Psychiatry* 14 (1990): 455–94.

Batalden, Stephen K., ed. *Seeking God: The Recovery of Religious Identity in Orthodox Russia, Ukraine, and Georgia*. DeKalb: Northern Illinois University Press, 1993.

Bax, Mart. "Ruža's Problems: Gender Relations and Violence Control in a Bosnian Rural Community." In *Gender Politics in the Western Balkans: Women and Society in Yugoslav Successor States*. Ed. Sabrina P. Ramet, 259–73. University Park: Pennsylvania State University Press, 1999.

Boddy, Janice. *Wombs and Alien Spirits: Women, Men, and the "Zar" Cult in Northern Sudan*. Madison: University of Wisconsin Press, 1989.

Boyer, Paul, and Stephen Nissenbaum. *Salem Possessed: The Social Origins of Witchcraft*. Cambridge, Mass.: Harvard University Press, 1974.

Bradley, Joseph. *Muzhik and Muscovite: Urbanization in Late Imperial Russia*. Berkeley: University of California Press, 1985.

Briggs, Robin. *Witches and Neighbors: The Social and Cultural Context of European Witchcraft*. New York: Viking, 1996.

Briusova, V. G. *Russkaia zhivopis' 17 veka*. Moscow: Iskusstvo, 1984.

Brooks, Jeffrey. *When Russia Learned to Read: Literacy and Popular Literature, 1861–1917*. Princeton: Princeton University Press, 1985.

Brown, Julie Vail. "Female Sexuality and Madness in Russian Culture: Traditional Values and Psychiatric Theory." *Social Research* 53, no. 2 (Summer 1986): 369–85.

———. "The Professionalization of Russian Psychiatry: 1857–1911." Ph.D. diss., University of Pennsylvania, 1981.

———. "Psychiatrists and the State in Late Imperial Russia." In *Social Control and the State*. Ed. Stanley Cohen and Andrew Scull, 267–87. New York: St. Martin's Press, 1983.

———. "Revolution and Psychosis: The Mixing of Science and Politics in Russian Psychiatric Medicine, 1905–13." *Russian Review* 46, no. 3 (July 1987): 283–302.

Brown, Malcolm Hamrick, ed. *Musorgsky: In Memoriam, 1881–1981*. Ann Arbor, Mich.: UMI Research Press, 1982.

Brown, William Edward. *A History of Russian Literature of the Romantic Period*. Vol. 4. Ann Arbor: Ardis, 1986.

Brumfield, Willam C., and Milos M. Velimirovic, eds. *Christianity and the Arts in Russia*. Cambridge: Cambridge University Press, 1991.

Burds, Jeffrey. "A Culture of Denunciation: Peasant Labor Migration and Religious Anathematization in Rural Russia, 1860–1905." *Journal of Modern History* 68, no. 4 (December 1996): 786–818.

———. *Peasant Dreams and Market Politics: Labor, Migration, and the Russian Village, 1861–1905*. Pittsburgh: University of Pittsburgh Press, 1998.

Bushkovitch, Paul. *Religion and Society in Russia: The Sixteenth and Seventeenth Centuries*. New York: Oxford University Press, 1992.

Bynum, Caroline Walker. *Holy Feast and Holy Fast*. Berkeley: University of California Press, 1987.

Caciola, Nancy. "Discerning Spirits: Sanctity and Possession in the Later Middle Ages." 2 vols. Ph.D. diss., University of Michigan, 1994.

Camporesi, Piero. *Bread of Dreams: Food and Fantasy in Early Modern Europe*. Trans. David Gentilcore. Cambridge: Polity Press, 1989.

Carlson, Maria. *"No Religion Higher than Truth": A History of the Theosophical Movement in Russia, 1875–1922*. Princeton: Princeton University Press, 1993.

Castillo, Richard J. "Spirit Possession in South Asia, Dissociation or Hysteria." *Culture, Medicine and Psychiatry* 18, nos. 1–2 (March–June 1994): 1–22, 141–62.

Christian, David. *Living Water: Vodka and Russian Society on the Eve of Emancipation*. Oxford: Clarendon Press, 1990.

Chulos, Chris J. "Myths of the Pious or Pagan Peasant in Post-Emancipation Central Russia (Voronezh Province)." *Russian History* 22, no. 2 (Summer 1995): 181–216.

Clark, Stuart. *Thinking with Demons: The Idea of Witchcraft in Early Modern Europe*. Oxford: Clarendon Press, 1997.

Clements, Barbara Evans, Barbara Alpern Engel, and Christine D. Worobec, eds. *Russia's Women: Accommodation, Resistance, Transformation*. Berkeley: University of California Press, 1991.

Conrad, Joseph L. "Russian Ritual Incantations: Tradition, Diversity, and Continuity." *Slavic and East European Journal* 33, no. 3 (1989): 422–44.

Coomler, David. *The Icon Handbook: A Guide to Understanding Icons and the Liturgy, Symbols, and Practices of the Russian Orthodox Church*. Springfield, Ill.: Templegate, 1995.

Cracraft, James. *The Church Reform of Peter the Great*. London: Macmillan, 1971.

Crapanzano, Vincent, and Vivian Garrison, eds. *Case Studies in Spirit Possession*. New York: John Wiley and Sons, 1977.

Crummey, Robert O. *The Old Believers and the World of Antichrist: The Vyg Community and the Russian State, 1694–1855*. Madison: University of Wisconsin Press, 1970.

Demos, John Putnam. *Entertaining Satan: Witchcraft and the Culture of New England*. Oxford: Oxford University Press, 1982.

Devlin, Judith. *The Superstitious Mind: French Peasants and the Supernatural in the Nineteenth Century*. New Haven: Yale University Press, 1987.

DeWindt, Anne Reiber. "Witchcraft and Conflicting Visions of the Ideal Village Community." *Journal of British Studies* 34, no. 4 (October 1995): 427–63.

Dix, Kenneth Steven. "Madness in Russia, 1775–1864: Official Attitudes and Institutions for Its Care." Ph.D. diss., University of California, Los Angeles, 1977.

Dömötör, Tekla. *Hungarian Folk Beliefs*. Bloomington: Indiana University Press, 1982.

Duncan, Kristy. "Was Ergotism Responsible for the Scottish Witch-Hunts?" *Area* 25, no. 1 (1993): 30–36.

Engel, Barbara Alpern. "The Woman's Side: Male Outmigration and the Family Economy in Kostroma Province." *Slavic Review* 45 (1986): 257–71.

Engelstein, Laura. *The Keys to Happiness: Sex and the Search for Modernity in Fin-de-Siècle Russia*. Ithaca: Cornell University Press, 1992.

———. "Paradigms, Pathologies, and Other Clues to Russian Spiritual Culture: Some Post-Soviet Thoughts." *Slavic Review* 57, no. 4 (Winter 1998): 864–77.

Eremin, V. M. *Gefsimansko-Chernigovskii skit pri Sviato-Troitskoi Sergievoi Lavre (kratkii ocherk istorii 1844–1990)*. Moscow: Izd. Sviato-Troitskoi Sergievoi Lavry, Sergiev Posad, 1992.

Evans-Pritchard, E. E. *Witchcraft, Oracles, and Magic among the Azande*. Oxford: Clarendon Press, 1937.

Fanger, Donald. *The Creation of Nikolai Gogol*. Cambridge, Mass.: Belknap Press of Harvard University Press, 1979.

———. "The Peasant in Literature." In *The Peasant in Nineteenth-Century Russia*. Ed. Wayne S. Vucinich, 231–62. Stanford: Stanford University Press, 1968.

Farrell, Dianne Ecklund. "Popular Prints in the Cultural History of Eighteenth-Century Russia." Ph.D. diss., University of Wisconsin, 1980.

Favret-Saada, Jeanne. *Deadly Words: Witchcraft in the Bocage*. Trans. Catherine Cullen. Cambridge: Cambridge University Press, 1980.

Fedotov, G. P. *The Russian Religious Mind: Kievan Christianity, the Tenth to the Thirteenth Centuries*. New York: Harper Torchbooks, 1960.

Felski, Rita. *The Gender of Modernity*. Cambridge, Mass.: Harvard University Press, 1995.

Fitzpatrick, Sheila, and Robert Gellately, eds. *Practices of Denunciation in Modern European History, 1789–1989*. In *Journal of Modern History* 68, no. 4 (December 1996).

Flier, Michael S. "Till the End of Time: The Apocalypse in Russian Historical Experience before 1500." In *Orthodox Russia: Studies in Belief and Practice, 1492–1936*. Ed. Valerie A. Kivelson and Robert H. Greene. Forthcoming.

Foucault, Michel. *Madness and Civilization: A History of Insanity in the Age of Reason*. New York: Vintage Books, 1973.

———. *The Order of Things: An Archaeology of the Human Sciences*. New York: Vintage Books, 1973.

———. *Power/Knowledge: Selected Interviews and Other Writings, 1972–1977*. New York: Pantheon, 1980.

Frank, Stephen P. *Crime, Cultural Conflict, and Justice in Rural Russia, 1856–1917*. Berkeley: University of California Press, 1999.

———. "Narratives within Numbers: Women, Crime and Judicial Statistics in Imperial Russia, 1834–1913." *Russian Review* 55, no. 4 (October 1996): 541–66.

———. "Popular Justice, Community, and Culture among the Russian Peasantry, 1870–1900." In *The World of the Russian Peasant: Post-Emancipation Culture and Society*. Ed. Ben Eklof and Stephen P. Frank, 133–53. Boston: Unwin Hyman, 1990.

Frank, Stephen P., and Mark D. Steinberg, eds. *Cultures in Flux: Lower-Class Values, Practices, and Resistance in Late Imperial Russia*. Princeton: Princeton University Press, 1994.

Freeze, Gregory L. "Institutionalizing Piety: The Church and Popular Religion, 1750–1850." In *Imperial Russia: New Histories for the Empire*. Ed. Jane Burbank and David L. Ransel, 210–49. Bloomington: Indiana University Press, 1998.

———. "The Rechristianization of Russia: The Church and Popular Religion, 1750–1850." *Studia Slavica Finlandensia* 7 (1990): 101–36.

———. "Subversive Piety: Religion and the Political Crisis in Late Imperial Russia." *Journal of Modern History* 68, no. 2 (June 1996): 308–50.

Frierson, Cathy. *Peasant Icons: Representations of Rural People in Late Nineteenth-Century Russia*. New York: Oxford University Press, 1993.

Gaudin, Corinne. "'No Place to Lay My Head': Marginalization and the Right to Land during the Stolypin Reforms." *Slavic Review* 57, no. 4 (Winter 1998): 747–73.

Geertz, Clifford. *The Interpretation of Culture*. New York, 1973.

Gibson, A. Boyce. *The Religion of Dostoevsky*. London: SCM Press, 1973.

Gijswijt-Hofstra, Marijke, Hilary Marland, and Hans de Waardt, eds. *Illness and Healing Alternatives in Western Europe*. London: Routledge, 1997.

Gilman, Sander L. *Difference and Pathology: Stereotypes of Sexuality, Race, and Madness*. Ithaca: Cornell University Press, 1985.

Gilman, Sander L., Helen King, Roy Porter, G. S. Rousseau, and Elaine Showalter. *Hysteria beyond Freud*. Berkeley: University of California Press, 1993.

Ginzburg, Carlo. *The Cheese and the Worms: The Cosmos of a Sixteenth-Century Miller*. Trans. John and Anne Tedeschi. Baltimore: Johns Hopkins University Press, 1992.

———. *Ecstasies: Deciphering the Witches' Sabbath*. Trans. Raymond Rosenthal. New York: Pantheon Books, 1991.

Gleason, Abbot. *Young Russia: The Genesis of Russian Radicalism in the 1860s*. New York: Viking Press, 1980.

Goldberg, Ann. *Sex, Religion, and the Making of Modern Madness: The Eberbach Asylum and German Society, 1815–1849*. New York: Oxford University Press, 1999.

Goldfrank, David M. "Who Put the Snake on the Icon and the Tollbooths on the Snake?—A Problem of Last Judgment Iconography." *Harvard Ukrainian Studies* 19 (1995): 180–99.

Good, Byron J. "Culture and DSM-IV: Diagnosis, Knowledge and Power." *Culture, Medicine and Psychiatry* 20, no. 2 (June 1996): 127–32.

Gregory, Annabel. "Witchcraft, Politics and 'Good Neighbourhood' in Early Seventeenth-Century Rye." *Past and Present* 133 (November 1991): 31–66.

Grisaru, Nimrod, Danny Budowski, and Eliezer Witztum. "Possession by the 'Zar' among Ethiopian Emigrants to Israel: Psychopathology or Culture-Bound Syndrome?" *Psychopathology* 30 (1997): 223–33.

Gromyko, M. M. *Mir russkoi derevni*. Moscow: Molodaia Gvardiia, 1991.

Hahn, Robert A. "Culture-Bound Syndromes Unbound." *Social Science and Medicine* 21, no. 2 (1985): 165–71.

Harley, David. "Explaining Salem: Calvinist Psychology and the Diagnosis of Possession." *American Historical Review* 101, no. 2 (April 1996): 307–30.

Harner, Michael J. "The Role of Hallucinogenic Plants in European Witchcraft."

In *Hallucinogens and Shamanism,* ed. Michael J. Harner. New York: Oxford University Press, 1973.

Harris, Ruth. *Lourdes: Body and Spirit in the Secular Age*. New York: Viking, 1999.

Harwood, Alan. *Witchcraft, Sorcery and Social Categories among the Safwa*. London: Oxford University Press, 1970.

Heldt, Barbara. *Terrible Perfection: Women and Russian Literature*. Bloomington: Indiana University Press, 1987.

Hinton, L., and A. Kleinman. "Cultural Issues and International Psychiatric Diagnosis." *International Revue of Psychiatry* 1 (1993): 111–29.

Hoch, Stephen L. "On Good Numbers and Bad: Malthus, Population Trends and Peasant Standard of Living in Late Imperial Russia." *Slavic Review* 53, no. 1 (Spring 1994): 42–75.

Hodge, Thomas. Program notes on *St. John's Night on Bald Mountain,* by Modest Mussorgsky (1839–1881). http://www.laphil.org/library/notes/MussorgskyStJohnsNightonBaldMountain.html.

Hubbs, Joanna. *Mother Russia: The Feminine Myth in Russian Culture*. Bloomington: Indiana University Press, 1988.

Hughes, Robert P., and Irina Paperno, eds. *Christianity and the Eastern Slavs*. Vol. 2, *Russian Culture in Modern Times*. Berkeley: University of California Press, 1994. *California Slavic Studies,* 17.

Iudin, T. I. *Ocherki istorii otechestvennoi psikhiatrii*. Moscow: Gosudarstvennoe izdatel'stvo meditsinskoi literatury MEDGIZ, 1951.

Ivanits, Linda. *Russian Folk Belief*. Armonk, N.Y.: M.E. Sharpe, 1989.

James, Tony. *Dream, Creativity, and Madness in Nineteenth-Century France*. Oxford: Clarendon Press, 1995.

Johns, Andreas. "Baba Iaga and the Russian Mother." *Slavic and East European Journal* 42, no. 1 (1998): 21–36.

Jones, Malcolm V. *Dostoyevsky after Bakhtin: Readings in Dostoyevsky's Fantastic Realism*. Cambridge: Cambridge University Press, 1990.

Jones, Malcolm V., and Garth M. Terry, eds. *New Essays on Dostoyevsky*. Cambridge: Cambridge University Press, 1983.

Jones, Malcolm V., and Robin Feuer Miller, eds. *The Cambridge Companion to the Classic Russian Novel*. Cambridge: Cambridge University Press, 1998.

Joravsky, David. *Russian Psychology: A Critical History*. Cambridge, Mass.: Basil Blackwell, 1989.

Karpuk, Paul A. "Gogol's Research on Ukrainian Customs for the *Dikan'ka* Tales." *Russian Review* 56, no. 2 (April 1997): 209–32.

Kehoe, Alice B., and Dody H. Giletti. "Women's Preponderance in Possession Cults: The Calcium Deficiency Hypothesis Extended." *American Anthropologist* 83, no. 3 (1981): 549–61.

Kessel, Frank. "On Culture, Health, and Human Development: Emerging Perspectives." *Items* 46, no. 4 (December 1992): 65–72.

Kieckhefer, Richard. *European Witch Trials: Their Foundations in Popular and Learned Culture, 1300–1500*. Berkeley: University of California Press, 1976.

Kivelson, Valerie. "The Devil Stole His Mind: The Tsar and the Moscow Uprising of 1648." *American Historical Review* 98, no. 3 (June 1993): 733–56.

———. "Identifying Witches and Sorcerers: Political Sorcery in Muscovy, 1467–1484." Paper presented at the NEH-sponsored Conference on "Cultural

Identity in a Multiethnic State: Muscovy 1362–1584," March 9–12, 1994.

———. "Patrolling the Boundaries: Witchcraft Accusations and Household Strife in Seventeenth-Century Muscovy." *Harvard Ukrainian Studies* 19 (1995): 302–23.

Kizenko, Nadieszda. "Ioann of Kronstadt and the Reception of Sanctity, 1850–1988." *Russian Review* 57, no. 3 (July 1998): 325–44.

———. "The Making of a Modern Saint: Ioann of Kronstadt and the Russian People, 1855–1917." Ph.D. diss., Columbia University, 1995.

Klaits, Joseph. *Servants of Satan: The Age of the Witch Hunts*. Bloomington: Indiana University Press, 1985.

[Kologrivov], Ioann. *Ocherki po istorii russkoi sviatosti*. Brussels: Izd. "Zhizn' s Bogom," 1961.

Kononenko, Natalie. Review of *The Bathhouse at Midnight: An Historical Survey of Magic and Divination in Russia,* by W. F. Ryan. *Russian Review* 59, no. 3 (July 2000): 454–55.

Krawchenko, Bohdan. *Social Change and National Consciousness in Twentieth-Century Ukraine*. New York: St. Martin's Press, 1985.

Larner, Christina. *Enemies of God: The Witch-hunt in Scotland.* London: Chatoo & Windus, 1981.

LeDonne, John P. *Absolutism and Ruling Class: The Formation of the Russian Political Order, 1700–1825*. New York: Oxford University Press, 1991.

Lee, Raymond L. M., and S. E. Ackerman. "The Sociocultural Dynamics of Mass Hysteria: A Case Study of Social Conflict in West Malaysia." *Psychiatry* 43 (February 1980): 78–88.

Levin, Eve. *Sex and Society in the World of the Orthodox Slavs, 900–1700*. Ithaca: Cornell University Press, 1989.

Levy, Jerrold E. "Some Comments upon the Ritual of the *Sanni* Demons." *Comparative Studies in Society and History* 11, no. 2 (April 1969): 217–26.

Lewis, I. M. *Ecstatic Religion: An Anthropological Study of Spirit Possession and Shamanism*. London: Penguin, 1971.

Lewis-Fernández, Roberto. "Cultural Formulation of Psychiatric Diagnosis." *Culture, Medicine and Psychiatry* 20, no. 2 (June 1996): 133–44.

Likhachev, D. S., A. M. Panchenko, and V. Popyrko. *Smekh v drevnei Rusi*. Leningrad: Nauka, 1984.

Lincoln, W. Bruce. *Between Heaven and Hell: The Story of a Thousand Years of Artistic Life in Russia*. New York: Viking, 1998.

Lindenmeyr, Adele. "Charity and the Problem of Unemployment: Industrial Homes in Late Imperial Russia." *Russian Review* 45, no. 1 (January 1986): 1–22.

———. *Poverty is Not a Vice: Charity, Society, and the State in Imperial Russia*. Princeton: Princeton University Press, 1996.

Lunbeck, Elizabeth. *The Psychiatric Persuasion: Knowledge, Gender, and Power in Modern America*. Princeton: Princeton University Press, 1994.

McCagg, William O., and Lewis Siegelbaum, eds. *The Disabled in the Soviet Union: Past and Present, Theory and Practice*. Pittsburgh: University of Pittsburgh Press, 1989.

Macfarlane, Alan. *Witchcraft in Tudor and Stuart England: A Regional and Comparative Study*. London: Routledge & Kegan Paul, 1970.

McLean, Hugh. *Nikolai Leskov: The Man and His Art*. Cambridge, Mass.: Harvard University Press, 1977.

Maguire, Henry, ed. *Byzantine Magic*. Washington, D.C.: Dumbarton Oaks Research Library and Collection, distributed by Harvard University Press, 1995.

Makhlaiuk, V. P. *Lekarstvennye rasteniia v narodnoi meditsine*. Moscow: Niva Rossii, 1992.

Mappen, Marc, ed. *Witches and Historians: Interpretations of Salem*. Malabar, Fla.: Krieger, 1980.

Matlock, Jann. *Scenes of Seduction: Prostitution, Hysteria, and Reading Difference in Nineteenth-Century France*. New York: Columbia University Press, 1994.

Matossian, Mary Kilbourne. *Poisons of the Past: Molds, Epidemics, and History*. New Haven: Yale University Press, 1989.

Micale, Mark. *Approaching Hysteria: Disease and Its Interpretations*. Princeton: Princeton University Press, 1995.

Middleton, John, and E. H. Winter. *Witchcraft and Sorcery in East Africa*. London: Routledge & Kegan Paul, 1963.

Miller, Martin A. *Freud and the Bolsheviks: Psychoanalysis in Imperial Russia and the Soviet Union*. New Haven: Yale University Press, 1998.

Murav, Harriet. *Holy Foolishness: Dostoevsky's Novels and the Poetics of Cultural Critique*. Stanford: Stanford University Press, 1992.

Neuberger, Joan. *Hooliganism: Crime, Culture, and Power in St. Petersburg, 1900–1914*. Berkeley: University of California Press, 1993.

Neuhauser, R. "*The Landlady:* A New Interpretation." *Canadian Slavonic Papers* 10, no. 1 (Spring 1968): 42–67.

Nichols, Robert L. "The Orthodox Elders *(Startsy)* of Imperial Russia." *Modern Greek Studies Yearbook* 1 (1985): 1–30.

Novichkova, T. A. *Russkii demonologicheskii slovar'*. St. Petersburg: Peterburgskii pisatel', 1995.

Obeyesekere, Gananath. "The Idiom of Possession." *Social Science and Medicine* 4 (1970): 97–111.

———. *Medusa's Hair: An Essay on Personal Symbols and Religious Experience*. Chicago: University of Chicago Press, 1981.

———. "The Ritual Drama of the Sanni Demons: Collective Representations of Disease in Ceylon." *Comparative Studies in Society and History* 11, no. 2 (April 1969): 174–216.

O'Neill, Mary R. "From 'Popular' to 'Local' Religion: Issues in Early Modern European Religious History." *Religious Studies Review* 12, nos. 3–4 (July–October 1986): 222–26.

Oppenheim, Janet. *"Shattered Nerves": Doctors, Patients, and Depression in Victorian England*. New York: Oxford University Press, 1991.

Pelikan, Jaroslav. *The Christian Tradition: A History of the Development of Doctrine*. Vol. 2, *The Spirit of Eastern Christendom (600–1700)*. Chicago: University of Chicago Press, 1974.

Perlina, Nina. *Varieties of Poetic Utterance: Quotation in "The Brothers Karamazov"*. Lanham, Md.: University Press of America, 1985.

Pigin, A. V. *Iz istorii russkoi demonologii XVII veka: Povest' o besnovatoi zhene Solomonii: Issledovanie i teksty*. St. Petersburg: Izd. Dmitrii Bulanian, 1998.

Raybeck, Douglas, Judy Shoobe, and James Grauberger. "Women, Stress, and Participation in Possession Cults: A Reexamination of the Calcium Deficiency

Hypothesis." *Medical Anthropology Quarterly* 3, no. 2 (1989): 139–61.

Rice, James L. *Freud's Russia: National Identity in the Evolution of Psychoanalysis*. New Brunswick, N.J.: Transaction Publishers, 1993.

Rosenthal, Bernice Glatzer, ed. *The Occult in Russian and Soviet Culture*. Ithaca: Cornell University Press, 1997.

Roy, Alec, ed. *Hysteria*. Chichester: John Wiley & Sons, 1982.

Ryan, W. F. "The Witchcraft Hysteria in Early Modern Europe: Was Russia an Exception?" *Slavonic and East European Review* 76, no. 1 (January 1998): 49–84.

Sabean, David Warren. *Power in the Blood: Popular Culture and Village Discourse in Early Modern Germany*. Cambridge: Cambridge University Press, 1984.

Sapunov, B. V. "Nekotorye siuzhety russkoi ikonopisi i ikh traktovka v poreformennoe vremia." In *Kul'tura i iskusstvo Rossii XIX veka: Novye materialy i issledovaniia: Sbornik statei*. Ed. G. A. Printseva, 141–49. Leningrad: Iskusstvo, 1985.

Schieffelin, Edward L. "Evil Spirit Sickness, the Christian Disease: The Innovation of a New Syndrome of Mental Derangement and Redemption in Papua New Guinea." *Culture, Medicine and Psychiatry* 20, no. 1 (March 1996): 1–39.

Schulte, Regina. *The Village in Court: Arson, Infanticide, and Poaching in the Court Records of Upper Bavaria, 1848–1910*. Trans. Barrie Selman. Cambridge: Cambridge University Press, 1994.

Scott, James C. *Seeing like a State: How Certain Schemes to Improve the Human Condition Have Failed*. New Haven: Yale University Press, 1998.

Scull, Andrew. *The Most Solitary of Afflictions: Madness and Society in Britain, 1700–1900*. New Haven: Yale University Press, 1993.

Semenov, Vladimir. *Nikolai Leskov: Vremia i knigi*. Moscow: Sovremennik, 1981.

Sharp, Lesley A. *The Possessed and the Dispossessed: Spirits, Identity, and Power in a Madagascar Migrant Town*. Berkeley: University of California Press, 1993.

Shevzov, Vera. "Chapels and the Ecclesial World of Prerevolutionary Russian Peasants." *Slavic Review* 55, no. 3 (Fall 1996): 585–613.

———. "Miracle-Working Icons, Laity, and Authority in the Russian Orthodox Church, 1861–1917." *Russian Review* 58, no. 1 (January 1999): 26–48.

———. "Popular Orthodoxy in Late Imperial Rural Russia." 2 vols. Ph.D. diss., Yale University, 1994.

Shorter, Edward. *From Paralysis to Fatigue: A History of Psychosomatic Illness in the Modern Era*. New York: Free Press, 1992.

Sirois, F. *Epidemic Hysteria*. Copenhagen: Munksgaard, 1974.

Small, Gary W., and Armand M. Nicholl, Jr. "Mass Hysteria Among Schoolchildren: Early Loss as a Predisposing Factor." *Archive of General Psychiatry* 39 (June 1982): 721–24.

Smilianskaia, Elena Borisovna. "Donesenie 1765 g. v Sinod Suzdal'skogo episkopa Porfiriia 'iakoby vo grade Suzhdale koldovstvo i volshebstvo umnozhilos.'" In *Khristianstvo i tserkov' v Rossii feodal'nogo perioda (materialy)*. Ed. N. N. Pokrovskii, 254–60. Novosibirsk: Nauka Sibirskoe otdelenie, 1989.

———. "Sledstvennye dela 'o sueveriiakh' v Rossii pervoi poloviny XVIII v. v svete problem istorii obshchestvennogo soznaniia." *Rossica* (Prague, 1996): 3–20.

———. "Sledstviia po 'dukhovnym delam' kak istochnik po istorii obshchestvennogo soznaniia v Rossii pervoi polovine XVIII v." Kandidatskaia diss., Moskovskii gosudarstvennyi universitet imeni M. V. Lomonosova, 1987.

Solomon, Susan Gross, and John F. Hutchinson, eds. *Health and Society in Revolutionary Russia*. Bloomington: Indiana University Press, 1990.

Spanos, Nicholas P., and Jack Gottlieb. "Demonic Possession, Mesmerism, and Hysteria: Social Psychological Perspective on Their Historical Interrelationships." *Journal of Abnormal Psychology* 88 (1979): 527–46.

Spitzer, Robert L., Miriam Gibbon, Andrew E. Skodol, Janet B. W. Williams, and Michael B. First. *DSM-III-R Casebook: A Learning Companion to the Diagnostic and Statistical Manual of Mental Disorders (Third Edition, Revised)*. Washington, D.C.: American Psychiatric Press, 1989.

Stanton, Leonard J. "Zedergol'm's *Life of Elder Leonid of Optina* as a Source of Dostoevsky's *The Brothers Karamazov*." *Russian Review* 49, no. 4 (1990): 443–55.

Steinberg, Mark D. "Stories and Voices: History and Theory." *Russian Review* 55, no. 3 (July 1996): 347–54.

Stewart, Charles. *Demons and the Devil: Moral Imagination in Modern Greek Society*. Princeton: Princeton University Press, 1991.

Surskii, I. K. *Otets Ioann Kronshtadtskii*. Reprint, Forestville, Calif.: St. Elias, 1980.

Szporluk, Roman. "Ukraine from an Imperial Periphery to a Sovereign State," *Daedalus* 126, no. 3 (Summer 1997): 85–119.

Temkin, Owsei. *The Falling Sickness: A History of Epilepsy from the Greeks to the Beginnings of Modern Neurology*. 2d ed. Baltimore: Johns Hopkins University Press, 1971.

Terras, Victor. *A History of Russian Literature*. New Haven: Yale University Press, 1991.

Thomas, Keith. *Religion and the Decline of Magic*. New York: Charles Scribner's Sons, 1971.

Thompson, Ewa M. *Understanding Russia: The Holy Fool in Russian Culture*. Lanham, Md.: University Press of America, 1987.

Thyrêt, Isolde. "Ecclesiastical Perceptions of the Female and the Role of the Holy in the Religious Life of Women in Muscovite Russia." Ph.D. diss., University of Washington, 1992.

Todd, William Mills, III, ed. *Literature and Society in Imperial Russia, 1800–1914*. Stanford: Stanford University Press, 1978.

Turner, Victor. *Process, Performance, and Pilgrimage: A Study in Comparative Symbology*. New Delhi: Concert, 1979.

Volkov, Solomon. *St. Petersburg: A Cultural History*. Trans. Antonina W. Bouis. New York: Free Press, 1995.

Vzdornov, G. *Issledovanie o Kievskoi Psaltiri*. Moscow: Iskusstvo, 1978.

Ware, Timothy. *The Orthodox Church*. Harmondsworth, Eng.: Penguin, 1963.

Worobec, Christine D. "Horse Thieves and Peasant Justice in Post-Emancipation Imperial Russia." *Journal of Social History* 21, no. 2 (Winter 1987): 281–93.

———. *Peasant Russia: Family and Community in the Post-Emancipation Period*. Princeton: Princeton University Press, 1991.

———. "Temptress or Virgin? The Precarious Sexual Position of Women in Post-Emancipation Ukrainian Peasant Society." *Slavic Review* 42, no. 2 (Summer 1990): 227–38.

Zguta, Russell. "The Ordeal by Water (Swimming of Witches) in the East Slavic World." *Slavic Review* 36, no. 2 (June 1977): 220–30.

———. "Was There a Witch Craze in Muscovite Russia?" *Southern Folklore Quarterly* 41 (1977): 119–28.

———. "Witchcraft and Medicine in Pre-Petrine Russia." *Russian Review* 37, no. 4 (October 1978): 438–48.

———. "Witchcraft Trials in Seventeenth Century Russia." *American Historical Review* 82, no. 5 (December 1977): 1187–1207.

Zhuravel', O. D. *Siuzhet o dogovore cheloveka s d'iavolom v drevnerusskoi literature.* Novosibirsk: Sibirskii khronograf, 1996.

INDEX